D0938296

The Aging Individual

 **Susan Krauss Whitbourne, PhD,** is the author of 7 books and 80 articles, book chapters, and reviews, including a recent abnormal psychology textbook (coauthored with Richard Halgin), *Abnormal Psychology: The Human Experience of Psychological Disorders,* and is currently preparing a casebook (also coauthored with Halgin) for Oxford University Press. She is Professor of Psychology at the University of Massachusetts at Amherst, and in 1995 was awarded the College of Arts and Sciences Outstanding Teacher award. She currently serves as President of Division 20 of APA, and is a Fellow of Divisions 2 and 20 as well as the Gerontological Society of America. Her research focuses on identity development in adulthood and old age and the relationship between identity and physical functioning. A longitudinal study of development from college to midlife, published in 1992, generated considerable interest in psychology and the news media, with findings linking personality changes in middle adulthood to changes in the historical and social context. Dr. Whitbourne teaches in the clinical psychology program, in which she has developed a gerontological focus in clinical training and research activities.

The Aging Individual

Physical and Psychological Perspectives

Susan Krauss Whitbourne, PhD

SPRINGER PUBLISHING COMPANY

Springer Publishing Company, Inc.
536 Broadway
New York, NY 10012-3955

Cover design by Tom Yabut
Production Editor: Pamela Ritzer

96 97 98 99 00 / 5 4 3 2 1

Library of Congress Cataloging-in-Publication Data

Whitbourne, Susan Krauss
    The aging individual : physical and psychological perspectives /
Susan Krauss Whitbourne.
        p.   cm.
    Includes bibliographical references and index.
    ISBN 0-8261-9360-9
    1. Aging—Psychological aspects.   2. Aged—Psychology.   I. Title.
BF724.55.A35W55   1996
155.67—dc20   96-19417
                                                                                    CIP

Printed in the United States of America

To

Lisa Krauss Rock, my mother, and eminently "successful ager"

Contents

Preface

In the early 1980s, I decided to undertake a thorough and comprehensive revision of my *Adult Development* textbook. Following the tradition of a good developmental psychologist, the natural place to start was with expanded coverage of the physical aspects of adult development and aging. As I attempted to cross the interdisciplinary Mississippi between biology and psychology, my reading of biological handbooks and texts on the topic of aging soon led me to confront my total lack of ability to understand anything but the simplest level of discourse. It was evident that I would have to learn an entire new language, if not discipline, if I was going to be able to do a decent job covering the topic for my psychology-oriented readers. It then occurred to me that I could perform a real service to the field by translating the biological and physiological studies on aging into terms that not only I but my social science colleagues could comprehend. This decision is what led, some 5 years or so later, to the publication of my book *The Aging Body*. The positive response to that book, both critically and from my professional colleagues, in part inspired *The Aging Individual,* which incorporates and updates much of the research on which it was based.

I originally intended to give this book the simple, if not grandiose, title of "The Psychology of Aging." It became clear, however, that if I were going to be able to incorporate detailed material on physiology as well as all aspects of the field of psychological gerontology, the book would take on unwieldy proportions. Furthermore, many of my colleagues in the field of the psychology of aging have written excellent broad-based texts with which I have no desire to compete. The contributions that I can provide to teaching and scholarship, I believe, focus on a continued pursuit of the psychological implications of the physiological changes involved in the aging process (now a current area of research for me), along with a more complete integration of my work on identity and personality. *The Aging Individual* incorporates a cross-disciplinary approach linking these areas, bringing into the discussion relevant research within the traditional psychology of aging on cognition and personality.

This book represents, then, an integration of my somewhat varied theoretical interests along with material that I have found useful in my own teaching of an undergraduate course on the psychology of aging. The broad framework provided in Chapter 1 orients the reader to the territory of identity, laying down a model that is addressed in each of the subsequent chapters. As was true for *The Aging Body,* there is far greater specificity in each of the physical development chapters, based on my assumption that social scientists reading the book will have far less knowledge of these areas than they do of the more traditional psychological and social gerontological topics. Although this may give the book some unevenness in terms of levels of depth, I am hoping that the benefits of my somewhat unique perspective will allow the reader to gain a new understanding of how biology and psychology interact within the individual over the course of the aging process.

Acknowledgments

Although this book does not cover the topic of "social support," I would like to attest to its role in my life through the help of my family, colleagues, and students. The writing of this book, at a time when my children, Stacey Whitbourne and Jenny O'Brien, are actively developing through the preteen and teen years (and I with them!) has required many hours of sacrifice when I could not be there to watch them and cheer them on in their various activities. Their understanding and patience with me have allowed me to complete this project with only a minimum of parental guilt. I am infinitely grateful for the faith and support of my husband, Richard O'Brien, who is not only sympathetic and helpful in an emotional sense, but has also helped me wade through some of the thornier biological sections of the book with confidence. I would also like to thank Margaret Matlin, at SUNY Geneseo, for her continued interest in my work and generous inclusion of my ideas in her writing, and to Irene Hulicka, at SUNY Buffalo, for her years of incredibly supportive mentorship. The help of my research assistant Chantel Fox, in the final preparation of the manuscript, is also deeply appreciated. Finally, to my students, including the many undergraduates who have offered suggestions and feedback throughout my teaching of the Psychology of Aging course, I would like to express my gratitude. It is, ultimately, the students whom I hope will benefit from this book, and to you I offer my hopes that you will carry on where the rest of us leave off in this fascinating and exciting field.

Models of Identity and the Aging Process

LIFESPAN THEMES AND ISSUES

The most useful starting point for the psychological study of aging is to consider the aging process in the context of psychological issues throughout the lifespan. The changes that occur in later life take place against a backdrop of a long adaptational history, in which the individual has confronted numerous physiological, psychological, and contextual challenges. From the individual's perspective, this continuity is particularly salient, as a sense of the self as continuous over time is a central feature of lifespan psychological development. Although many changes occur in the later years of life, these changes must be seen in the context of both successful and unsuccessful adaptations to previous gains and losses throughout the earlier years of adulthood. This issue of continuity versus change is a major theme in lifespan developmental psychology as applied to the adult years and beyond.

Psychologists who focus on aging regard as a second central theme the need to distinguish between normal aging and disease. There is a natural tendency to assume that as individuals age, they develop chronic health problems such as arthritis, cardiovascular disease, and diabetes, but as prevalent as these problems may be, they are not considered inherent in the normal aging process. At the same time, psychologists who treat elderly individuals must be familiar with the more common diseases so that they can provide more effective services. What appear to be psychological difficulties such as, for example, depression, may be caused by physiological dysfunctions that have psychological side effects.

A third consideration in the psychological study of normal aging is the importance of individual differences. Gerontologists have been working for decades to refute the erroneous notion that all older people are alike. Instead, it is now a well-established principle that as people grow older they become more different. The many and varied experiences that older people have over their lifetimes cause them to become increasingly diverse. Although elders who share the same ethnic or cultural background may share certain life experiences, their reactions to these experiences are likely to reflect their own unique psychological and physical capacity to cope with the events in their lives.

A fourth point to consider is the extent to which an age-related change can be slowed down, is preventable, or can be compensated. Although the ultimate result of the aging process is a progressive loss of function, there are many steps that individuals can take to slow down the aging process, or to prevent deleterious effects of aging before they become apparent. Some of these behaviors fall into the category of "use it or lose it" (what I shall abbreviate as UIOLI); in other words, exercise and activity can keep the system in question better maintained than inactivity. Another group of behaviors fall into the category of "bad habits," or behaviors that the individual interested in maintaining positive functioning will avoid. Throughout this book, I will point out the ways in which individuals can take advantage of UIOLI, on the one hand, or suffer unnecessarily due to bad habits.

Finally, in examining the normal psychology of aging, it is essential to keep in mind the resilience that many elders show when faced with the potential stresses associated with the aging process. The study of coping has assumed an increasingly large role in the psychology of normal aging, as new evidence continues to be gained about the coping capacities of elders. Not only are older adults seen as able to navigate the sometimes difficult waters of later life, but are seen as creating new challenges, goals, and opportunities for themselves. The concept of control has also emerged as a major research focus, based on the belief that individuals can, to a certain extent, control their own destinies with regard to the aging process, and through personal effort, creativity, and determination, manage their own aging, if not actually "beat" it.

In examining the psychological aspects of aging, it will become apparent that there are many spontaneous coping strategies used successfully by many elders to compensate for and adapt to the changes they experience.

APPLICATION OF AN IDENTITY
MODEL TO THE PSYCHOLOGY OF AGING

A starting point for studying the development of the self in adulthood is a model based upon the conceptualization of identity as the source of self-definition within personality. In this model (Whitbourne, 1986a; Whitbourne, 1986b), identity is theorized to form an organizing schema through which the individual's experiences are interpreted. This model will be briefly described here and elaborated upon further in Chapter 10.

Content Domains and Processes of Identity

The content domains of identity involve the individual's self-appraisal of a variety of attributes along the dimensions of biological, psychological, and social functioning. The affective content of identity, for psychologically healthy adults, takes the positive self-referential form encapsulated in the expression "I am a competent, loving, and good person," competent at work, loving in family life, and morally righteous. This positive bias serves as an important motivator for the identity processes, as described below.

A schematic diagram of the identity illustrating the relationship among the content domains is presented in Figure 1.1. The "central core" contains those aspects of identity that are most salient to the individual and that represent combinations of qualities from the separate domains. At the central core it is assumed that fundamental self-conceptions derived from early interactions with parents and significant others form the underlying unconscious elements of the self (Whitbourne, 1989).

Identity content domains. The six identity content domains each have support within the literature as a separate area or focus within the self. The identity model integrates these separate domains and makes it possible to understand their interrelationships within one overarching umbrella. Brief descriptions of these areas are provided here, but each will be elaborated upon in subsequent chapters.

The content of the body, or physical identity, is a central feature of the self-concept (Bocknek & Perna, 1994), and incorporates three components (Fox & Corbin, 1989; Hennessy, 1989): the perception of (1) the appearance of one's own body; (2) competence, or the body's ability to perform tasks needed in daily

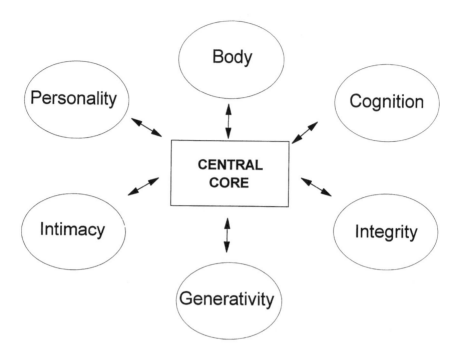

FIGURE 1.1 Identity content domains.

activities; and (3) one's own health. The area of appearance is regarded as central to the identity of older individuals for both men and women (Harris, 1994; Heidrich & Ryff, 1993a; Heidrich & Ryff, 1993b). Related to this concept is social physique anxiety, or the extent to which the individual feels that others are negatively evaluating one's bodily appearance (Hart, Leary, & Rejeski, 1989). The domain of competence has received less attention, but may show up as mobility level (the ability to move in the environment), which is a concern for older adults, or as concerns about being able to maintain one's independence (Dittman-Kohli, 1990). Interestingly, the desire to have a fit and strong body appears less often among older adults (Hooker & Kaus, 1994) as a personal goal or "possible self" (Markus & Nurius, 1986) than might be expected on the basis of social attitudes toward fitness, strength, and exercise.

Health is perhaps one of the strongest components of physical identity, particularly for older adults who describe concerns about their own health in numerous and varied ways across studies. The implications of good health for everyday functioning and the quality of daily life cannot, of course, be overemphasized. However, it is also likely that identity in terms of health has an additional meaning relevant to the role of health and illness in determining the length of one's life. Health, in this regard, may be seen as an index of the integrity of the body and an indicator of one's approaching mortality.

Compared to middle-aged adults, older adults regard health as a major contributor to overall psychological well-being (Ryff, 1989). Comparisons of the self to others are often made on the basis of health (Heidrich & Ryff, 1993b). Most impressively, when asked to describe spontaneously the "possible" self (Markus & Nurius, 1986) they "hope for" or "fear" the most that they will become, the vast majority of older people describe one related to health (Hooker, 1992), suggesting that "health is not simply a vague global concern for most older adults, but rather a concern that is intimately tied to self-conceptions in a way that is very concrete for individuals" (p. P91). There is also evidence that views about one's health begin to become incorporated into identity in middle age, and like the possible selves in old age, tend to focus on negative aspects (Hooker & Kaus, 1994).

In the domain of cognition, there is a growing body of evidence to support the notion that adults are aware of their intellectual skills and incorporate these into their identities. As will be shown in Chapter 9, views of intellectual and memory "self-efficacy," or the ability to succeed at a task, are areas of increasing research interest (Lachman, Bandura, Weaver, & Elliott, 1995; Lachman & Leff, 1989). Another area of cognitive identity is the self-attribution of oneself as having intellectual ability (Grover & Hertzog, 1991) or as being "wise" (Staudinger, Smith, & Baltes, 1993). Fear of the loss of intellectual ability is also a significant component of the possible selves of middle-aged and older adults (Hooker & Kaus, 1994). In terms of contributors to feelings of personal well-being, the ability to learn new information appears to play a significant role, particularly as individuals compare themselves to others whom they perceive as less advantaged or suffering from age-related losses (Heidrich & Ryff, 1993b).

The personality domain includes self-attributions of various characteristics relevant to the individual's enduring dispositions. These include emotions (Carstensen & Turk-Charles, 1994), coping and defense styles (Labouvie-Vief, Hakim-Larson, & Hobart, 1987), traits (McCrae & Costa, 1990), values (Ryff, 1989), and interests, hobbies, and beliefs (McCrae & Costa, 1988).

The next three domains are derived from Erikson's theory (Erikson, 1963) and the assumption, described as follows, is that identity is an overarching theme of development in the years of adulthood and old age. The domain of "intimacy" refers to the context of close relationships, both with sexual partners and with friends. The domain of "generativity" includes the extension of the self into the care and well-being of future generations, both through mentoring experiences at work and through parenting or parenting-like roles. The accomplishments of children, in particular, reflect on the individual's identity, although the effects are not unqualifiedly positive. Parents may experience vicarious enjoyment as well as pride regarding their children, but they may also feel some envy and a sense of having missed out on the benefits available to the younger generation (Ryff, Lee, Essex, & Schmutte, 1994). Finally, the domain of "ego integrity" involves the "existential" self and the view of oneself as belonging to a certain time and place in history (Erikson, Erikson, & Kivnick, 1986).

Identity processes. The individual's experiences, both past and present, are postulated to relate to identity through Piagetian-like processes of assimilation and accommodation. The process of identity assimilation is defined as the interpretation of life events relevant to the self in terms of the cognitive and affective schemas that make up identity. The events and experiences to which the assimilation function applies can include new aspects of physical or cognitive functioning, major life events, cumulative interactions with the environment over time, or minor incidents that can have a potential impact on identity. Thus, the experiences interpreted through identity assimilation can include physical changes associated with the aging process or involvement in a gratifying social role, such as community volunteer. Each type of experience can have different meaning across individuals depending on the nature of their current self-conceptualizations in identity. (See Figure 1.2.) The process of identity accommodation, by contrast, involves changing one's identity in response to these identity-relevant experiences. Bodily identity might change in content in response to one of these events when, for example, an illness or accident causes the individual to acknowledge new health limitations.

As in Piaget's (Piaget, 1975/1977) discussion of the equilibration process in the development of intelligence, it is assumed that the most desirable state is for the individual's identity to be in a state of dynamic balance with the environment so that alternation takes place between assimilation and accommodation. In this state, the individual's identity is flexible enough to change when warranted but not so unstructured that every new experience causes the person to question fundamental assumptions about the self's integrity and unity. Thus, equilibrium is not a static mode, but involves movement back and forth between assimilation and accommodation. However, it is also assumed that the directionality of processes is, as in Piaget's theory (1975/1977, p. 189) from assimilation to accommodation, with assimilation being the preferred mode for psychologically healthy adults who prefer and strive to see themselves in relation to events in a positive light. Accommodation is assumed to be prompted when assimilation can no longer fit new events into the individual's existing iden-

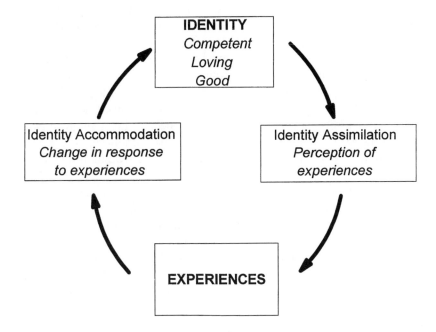

FIGURE 1.2 Model of identity processes.

tity (Kiecolt, 1994). Gradually, throughout the later years of adulthood, it is assumed that the identity of oneself as "old" replaces former age-related identities due to the continued use of accommodation to the normal aging process. More sudden changes in identity are presumed to result from diseases or accidents that cannot be accommodated over a period of time.

Erikson's Psychosocial Theory

In Erikson's (Erikson, 1963) eight-stage psychosocial model of the life cycle, it is assumed that change occurs systematically throughout the years of adulthood. Erikson proposed that after adolescence, with its often tumultuous search for identity, adults pass through three psychosocial crisis stages. The stages corresponding to the early and middle adult years focus on the establishment of close interpersonal relationships (intimacy vs. isolation), and the passing on to the future of one's creative products (generativity vs. stagnation). In the final stage (ego integrity vs. despair), the individual must resolve conflicted feelings about the past, adapt to the changes associated with the aging process, and come to grips with the inevitability of death. Erikson's ideas, although difficult to operationalize, have provided a major intellectual inspiration to workers in the field of adult personality development. The writings of Gould (1978), Levinson and associates (1978), and Vaillant (1977) are based on the fundamental ideas of Erikson's theory that changing circumstances and values in work and family relationships are the major preoccupations of adults, and that resolution of feelings about aging and mortality become increasingly important in the middle to later adult years. The work of these authors supports Erikson's fundamental proposal that personality continues to develop in important ways throughout life.

In Erikson's model, each psychosocial crisis is theorized to offer an opportunity for the development of a new function or facet of the ego. However, the crisis involving identity has special significance as it establishes the most important functions of the ego: self-definition and self-awareness. According to Erikson, adolescence is a time in which the ego becomes fully articulated within personality as the center of the "self"; the answer to the question "Who am I?" In this stage, as in the prior stages, parents, peers, and society serve as important influences on the resolution of psychosocial issues. The crises that follow this crucial period in development involving the issues of intimacy, generativity, and ego integrity, though conceived by Erikson as involving further differentiation of the ego, may be better conceived of as three of the main developmental tasks of adulthood. It has long been an assumption of lifespan theories that certain demands present themselves at particular choice points in adulthood (Havighurst, 1972). Adults must find intimate partners, find a way to leave something of themselves behind for future generations, and resolve ambivalent feelings toward mortality. Other developmental tasks involve more specific challenges in the work setting, the family, and the larger community. For example, retirement is a central developmental task of later adulthood, and is only tangentially related at a conceptual level to generativity and/or ego integrity.

Apart from the specific content of life tasks, the theories that take the developmental task approach are considered to be useful but limited in that they remain at a descriptive rather than explanatory level. Erikson's theory of adult development may be more reasonably viewed as a particularly compelling (if not comprehensive) version of developmental task theory. The epigenetic principle is not an explanatory mechanism and it does not involve the proposal of a structure unique to the personality other than the ego. We are left, then, with the ego as the main focus of Erikson's theory throughout the adult stages. It is the ego, translated into the individual's self or identity, that forms the central theme of Erikson's developmental scenario of adulthood and old age.

By placing identity squarely at the center of adult psychosocial development, it is possible to link conceptualizations of adult development to the theoretically rich literature on the self. Adult developmental processes, rather than being seen as a separate breed from the functioning of the self or identity, can then be understood within the broader context of psychology's attempts to understand the nature and function of self-conceptualizations. The processes of assimilation and accommodation theorized to be responsible for consistency and change in the self can then be seen as central to an analysis of development over the course of adulthood in the individual's sense of identity.

Identity in Relation to the Aging Process

The aging process involves a number of inherent changes that can have separate as well as cumulative effects on the individual's identity. Oddly enough, there is very little research in this area. A major purpose of this book is to bring together divergent perspectives within the psychology of aging to forge a new understanding of how older people's views of themselves interact with the physical and cognitive changes they experience as a result of the aging process. This approach will highlight the available research where it exists on the intersection between identity and the aging process, and point out areas where more work is needed. Throughout this book, then, as changes in physical and cognitive functioning are examined, the implications for identity will be discussed in terms of the identity model and available data.

The implications for identity of physical and cognitive changes associated with the aging process may be seen as both objective and subjective. The objective effects of an age-related change on the individual's adaptation involve the real alterations that occur in the individual's everyday life in direct response to a physical or cognitive change. For example, loss of mobility due to changes in the body's joints directly reduces the individual's ability to get to desired locations, both within the home and in travelling outside the home. The individual's adaptation to the environment is reduced in direct proportion to the extent to which a reduction in mobility has occurred. Secondly, age-related changes influence the individual's adaptation through the subjective or indirect effect of these changes on the individual's identity. Many of these changes have their potential impact through a perceived reduction in feelings of competence. Returning to the example of mobility, reductions in the ability to get around independently reduce the individual's sense of competence—personal power, strength, and effectiveness. To the extent that the individual's identity is altered through this secondary or indirect process, positive adaptation in the sense of well-being and satisfaction is likely to be reduced as well.

An additional factor to consider in this equation is the extent to which an age-related change can be prevented, compensated, or in other ways coped with successfully. In this sense, the relationship between age-related changes and identity may be conceived of as dynamic, reciprocal, and transactional in that individuals may alter the course of their development on the basis of their self-conceptions and ideas about change. Relevant concepts for this analysis are the principles of UIOLIs and bad habits, which play important roles in these dynamic processes. If UIOLI is available to the individual, that is if the age-related change can be offset or slowed through behavioral methods, then it is possible for the older person to experience less of a sense of despondency regarding an age-related change, and more of a sense of personal control. Positive adaptation, it would seem, in this case would depend on the individual's willingness to confront the age-related change, look for ways to implement the UIOLI principle, and work to prevent the deleterious effects of this process. On the other hand, a negative outcome will develop if the individual erroneously adopts a fatalistic attitude toward a preventable age-related deficit and lets bad habits take their toll in an unabated fashion. What about age-related changes that cannot be ameliorated? In these cases, the individual may experience frustration associated with unsuccessful efforts to adopt the UIOLI principle, and give up in despair. The individual who either does nothing or engages in what may be pleasurable bad habits may actually be adapting in a more positive manner because he or she has avoided frustration and at least is engaging in some pleasurable, albeit unhealthy, activities.

These are only some of the factors that mitigate the relationship between aging, identity, and adaptation in later adulthood. A central factor to consider, moreover, is the extent to which the individual is aware of or concerned about specific age-related changes in physical and psychological functioning. As will be explained in the next section, identity may extend into the individual's awareness of and sensitivity to the effect of aging on the self.

A MULTIPLE THRESHOLD MODEL
OF AGING AND IDENTITY

In extending the identity model to the normal aging process, a number of relevant factors have emerged. These include the nature of the age-related change in terms of whether its onset is sudden or gradual and whether it is amenable to modification through behavioral control, the direct effect of the change on adaptation, and the effect of the change on the individual's sense of competence and personal control. Also relevant is the extent to which the individual has suffered deleterious changes due to physical diseases or disorders that occur apart from the normal aging process. Although it is important to consider the effects of normal aging independently of disease, the two sets of processes often co-occur in the same individual. To the extent that normal age changes occur in the context of previously existing cardiovascular disease, stroke, arthritis, or cancer, these changes will serve to challenge identity in different ways. Relevant to this point, the extent to which an individual's parents or relatives have suffered from age-related disease or loss may serve as a further influence on how the individual approaches the aging process.

Definition and Concepts

Integrating these factors into a comprehensive framework is a model that I call the "multiple threshold model" of aging, a model that is an attempt to relate age changes to psychological adaptation in a way that integrates the concepts of the specific nature of aging changes, identity, coping processes, outcome, and age-related control behaviors. The term "threshold" in this model refers to the individual's point at which an age-related change is recognized. Before this threshold is reached, the individual does not think of the self as "aging" or "old," or even perhaps as having the real potential to be "aging" or "old." After the threshold is crossed, the individual becomes aware of having moved from the world of the middle-aged and young to the world of the elders. At this point, the individual recognizes the possibility that functions may be lost through aging (or disease), and begins to accommodate to this possibility by changing identity accordingly (see Figure 1.3).

The term "multiple" in this model refers to the fact that the aging process involves potentially every system in the body, so that there is in actuality no single threshold leading into the view of the self as aging. The individual may feel "old" in one domain of functioning, such as in the area of mobility, but feel "not old," "middle-aged," or possibly "young" in other domains, such as in the area of sensory acuity or intellectual functioning. Whether a threshold is crossed, I propose, depends in part then on the actual nature of the aging process and whether it has affected a particular area of functioning. However, it is also the case that individuals vary widely in the areas of functioning that they value. Mobility may not be as important to an individual whose major source of pleasure is derived from sedentary activities such as reading, solving crossword puzzles, writing, or in other ways working from a single location. Changes in the area of mobility will not have as much relevance to the individual's direct adaptation to the environment or to identity as would be the case for losses in

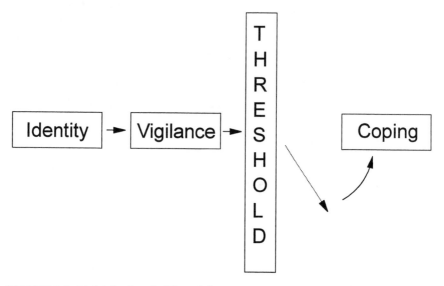

FIGURE 1.3 Multiple threshold model.

vision or memory. In the multiple threshold model, it is assumed that changes in areas important to the individual's adaptation and sense of competence will have greater potential for affecting identity than changes in relatively unimportant areas (although it is certainly true that changes in life-sustaining functions may supercede changes in nonvital functions, a point to be explored in later chapters).

Not only are changes in important functions likely to have a greater impact on adaptation and identity, but it is possible to assume further that the functions that are most central to identity will be watched for most carefully by the individual. Heightened vigilance to age-related changes in these central aspects of identity can be predicted, then, resulting in the individual's greater sensitivity to noticing early signs of age-related changes in some areas but not others. For example, the individual who takes great pride in a full and vibrant head of hair will be on the lookout for gray hairs and thinning, and the individual who values intellectual skills will scrutinize performance on activities involving memory for any signs of deterioration. As a result of the increased vigilance for areas of functioning central to identity, the impact of changes in these areas can be predicted to be even higher than they might otherwise be.

On the other hand, with increased vigilance may come increased motivation to take advantage of the UIOLI principle and to avoid bad habits. The adult who values being in peak physical shape will work devotedly for hours each day to avoid loss of muscle strength and aerobic capacity. Having valued these qualities, he or she will be more likely to hold onto them into old age, but at the same time, will be more sensitive to detecting any early signs of loss. This situation presents a double-edged sword, in which heightened vigilance leads to behavior that offsets the aging process, thus reducing the dreaded outcomes of loss, but also leads the individual to become acutely sensitive to signs that loss has occurred. It may be in this situation, then, that identity accommodation becomes important. The individual who recognizes that he or she is aging through accommodation is less likely to become discouraged and frustrated at evidence that certain age-related changes cannot be completely reversed. The individual who is assimilating and desperately attempts to hang on to a youthful identity has the potential to be demolished when an event occurs that makes it abundantly clear that the aging process has taken its inevitable toll.

The multiple threshold concept is most easily viewed as a set of linear processes, with the outcome of passing through threshold an alteration in the individual's level of well-being in response to the quality of the individual's coping strategies. The process is not entirely linear, however. Each time a threshold is passed, there is the potential for the individual's identity to be altered through identity accommodation. When this happens, the crossing of the threshold serves as an event relevant to the self that becomes integrated into identity. The resulting change in identity then alters the individual's subsequent vigilance regarding future age-related changes in other areas of functioning and the behaviors relevant to the threshold just crossed.

Throughout the subsequent chapters of this book, the concept of multiple thresholds will serve as an organizing theme. The many physical and psychological functions examined with regard to aging will serve as the potential thresholds, not all of which will be relevant to all individuals. As each function is examined, its relevance to the threshold model will be explored in terms of available research and, where research is unavailable, theoretical extrapolation.

Relation to Control Processes and Coping

The propositions regarding the multiple threshold involving specific areas of physical functioning and their relationship to identity come largely from theoretical analysis and clinical observation, although research in this area is beginning to proceed (Whitbourne & Primus, 1995). However, to be consistent with current research directions as well as to elaborate further on the behavioral correlates of assimilation and accommodation, it is necessary to take into account related concepts that pertain to the ways that individuals conceive of and address their own personal aging. One of these concepts is locus of control, which, with regard to the aging process, refers to the individual's intrinsic theories of aging, and whether aging can be controlled (an internal orientation) or whether there is nothing that can be done to alter the inevitable course of age-related decline (external orientation).

An internal locus of control orientation with regard to aging is regarded as highly adaptive in relation to abilities that can be modified through the UIOLI principle. For example, the view that memory is a "muscle" that can be exercised contributes to more positive memory functioning among older adults (Cavanaugh & Green, 1990). Conversely, the belief that memory deficits are inevitable and uncontrollable leads to a self-fulfilling prophecy in which negative memory beliefs lead to lowered levels of effort and hence performance (Elliott & Lachman, 1989). Over time, such beliefs can generalize across situations that reinforce feelings of helplessness and ultimately contribute to further deterioration over time (Lachman, 1990). In the area of physical functioning, beliefs about one's abilities can also serve as predictors of activity. For example, women with low levels of "balance confidence" may avoid participating in activities that could promote their functioning, even if they have no objective basis for fearing negative consequences (Myers, Powell, Maki, Holliday, Brawley, & Sherk, 1996).

A second related concept is that of coping with stress. This concept can be extremely useful for understanding the individual's approach to the aging process, if aging is considered a "stressor" that serves to mobilize coping strategies. Two major categories of coping mechanisms have been identified in the stress literature: emotion-focused and problem-focused coping (Lazarus & Folkman, 1984). In emotion-focused coping, the individual attempts to change the way he or she thinks about or appraises a stressful situation rather than changing the situation itself. Problem-focused coping involves attempts to reduce stress by changing the stressful situation.

Although locus of control can be distinguished at a conceptual level from coping, in practical terms the two concepts often serve as co-determinants of adaptational outcomes for the individual. For example, in one large investigation of coping and locus of control, it was found that individuals who believe that they can control their own aging were more likely to use problem-focused coping and those who believed that they were not in control of their aging were more likely to use emotion-focused coping (Krause, 1986). It has also been found that older adults with an internal locus of control are less likely to engage in the emotion-focused coping strategies of escape–avoidance, self-blame, and hostile reaction (Blanchard-Fields & Irion, 1988).

In the framework presented here, coping rather than control serves as a major focus. In addition to the overlap of the concepts of locus of control and coping, there are methodological difficulties involved in assessing locus of control in the elderly (Lachman, 1986), and there is evidence that control beliefs are poor predictors of relevant behaviors such as exercise adherence (Williams & Lord, 1995). Conceptually, coping strategies are closer to behavior than are locus of control beliefs, which may serve as an implicit backdrop but not as direct predictors of behavior. Furthermore, greater specificity exists in the measurement of coping, due to the development of instruments that are tailored to particular age-related stressful situations rather than to general beliefs in the causes of the aging process.

Relation Between Coping and Adaptation

As a general statement, it appears that individuals who use problem-focused coping strategies are more likely to maintain higher activity levels (Preston & Mansfield, 1984; Speake, 1987) and therefore maximize their physical functioning. These individuals view aging as a challenge to which they apply the coping strategies found to be effective in other life domains (Die, Seelbach, & Sherman, 1987). They are better able to meet their perceived physical needs and tailor their expectations and behavior to fit the changes in their physical identity (Hennessy, 1989). Active involvement in sports or exercise, for some elders, not only promotes physical functioning but can serve as an important coping mechanism (O'Brien & Conger, 1991). Coping style also seems to be related to reactions to a variety of physical health problems (Clark, Becker, Janz, & Lorig, 1991). For example, improved levels of coping and the use of social supports (in part, a problem-focused coping measure), were found to be predictive of reduced hospital readmissions for a sample of elderly cardiac patients (Berkman, Millar, Holmes, & Bonander, 1991). Training in problem-focused coping methods proved helpful in facilitating pain management and reducing anxiety among older individuals with chronic knee pain (Fry & Wong, 1991). In another investigation (Folkman, Bernstein, & Lazarus, 1987), the subjective experience of stress, particularly on a daily basis, was related to prescription drug misuse among a sample of elderly individuals. Similarly, in a study on women's recovery from hip fracture, a condition related to changes in bone strength due to aging or osteoporosis, the use of problem-focused coping was found to enable individuals to take advantage of rehabilitative methods that assisted in their recovery. As a consequence of more adaptive coping strategies, hip fracture patients were less likely to experience depressive symptoms that would have further lowered their perceived functional recovery (Roberto, 1992).

As the case of rehabilitation from hip fracture illustrates, the relationship between coping and health can be seen as cyclical. Individuals who successfully use coping strategies to manage stress may actually experience improved physical functioning. In one investigation, individuals reporting high levels of stress were found to have lower ratios of critical immune system markers (McNaughton, Smith, Patterson, & Grant, 1990). Active efforts to reduce stress through seeking social support or physical exercise can have physiological advantages in terms of improved immune system functioning (Fiatarone, et al., 1989; Thomas, Goodwin, & Goodwin, 1985). The aging immune system has been linked to increased vulnerability to influenza, infections, cancer, and certain age-associated autoimmune disorders such as diabetes and possibly atherosclerosis and Alzheimer's disease. Although there are other factors that affect the development of each of these conditions, particularly cancer (Ershler, 1993), a more competent immune system can lower the elderly individual's risk at least to certain forms of cancer and influenza (Ershler, 1990; Miller, 1993).

In contrast to the positive effects of problem-focused coping is evidence of the deleterious effects of emotion-focused coping on many psychological and physical health outcomes. Individuals who use avoidance as a coping strategy are likely to report higher levels of physical and psychological symptoms, depression, and psychosocial difficulties (Aldwin & Revenson, 1987; Billings & Moos, 1981; Bombardier, D'Amico, & Jordan, 1990; Felton, Revenson, & Hinrichsen, 1984) even continuing for months after the stressful situation has subsided (Smith, Patterson, & Grant, 1990). However, emotion-focused coping can have positive adaptive value if the situation is completely out of one's control, or if excessive rumination is harmful to improvement. As long as the individual follows prescribed treatment, the outcome may still be positive. As Lazarus (1981) points out, when faced with an uncontrollable stressor, direct confrontation is not always necessary for successful coping. In fact, in some cases denial may actually be adaptive (Pearlin & Schooler, 1978). The use of denial as a coping mechanism becomes maladaptive, however, if it prevents the individual from taking action that is beneficial to recovery. In diseases or other health problems that require vigilant attention to bodily signs, such as cancer, kidney failure or diabetes, coping by denial can lead to the development of life-threatening conditions.

Interaction of Identity and Coping

Although the identity and coping models provide insight into the ways that individuals adapt to the aging process, neither model alone seems sufficient to account for the individual variations in behavioral and emotional reactions to the changes in physical functioning and health associated with aging. In existing research on coping, the amount of variance accounted for leaves considerable room for the input of variables related to identity and the self. As a way of gaining a more comprehensive prediction of variations in response to challenges to physical identity associated with the aging process, it is necessary to combine the dimension of problem- vs. emotion-focused coping with the dimension of identity assimilation and accommodation. Such an approach produces a fourfold matrix to account for adaptation to the physical aging process. Specific behavioral and adaptive predictions can be made for individuals within each of the four cells created by this matrix (see Figure 1.4). For the purposes of this discussion, it is assumed that individuals can be classified on the basis of the predominant identity processes they use in relation to age-related experiences (Whitbourne, 1987) and that they can be classified in terms of predominant coping style. However, it is unlikely that "pure" forms exist and it is more reasonable to assume that these dimensions are continuous within individuals.

Moving through the matrix, specific behavioral predictions can be made for each of the four pure types. Individuals who use identity assimilation and emotion-focused coping are likely to deny the relevance of aging to their identities and, at the same time, engage in few behaviors intended to offset or compensate for aging changes (Felton & Revensen, 1987). Adverse consequences are more likely to occur for aging individuals who take an assimilative approach to age- or disease-related bodily changes and use emotion-focused coping. They may find it more comfortable not to think about the diagnosis or problem and instead go on with life as usual, not changing their identities in response to the knowledge that they are suffering a major change in health or functioning or even have a potentially terminal illness. Consequently, they will not take active efforts to protect and promote their body's ability to fight the condition or disease. They may manage to avoid confronting their problems by severely restricting their lifestyles (Aldwin, 1991), and in the process exacerbate processes of decline in functions that would otherwise respond to the UIOLI principle. On the other hand, these individuals may be protected from the "depressive realism" that can reduce the strivings of accommodative persons who confront and recognize their limitations (Hooker, 1992). They may use ego-enhancing strategies of making optimistic attributions (Heckhausen & Baltes, 1991) to compare themselves favorably with others and maintain a self that is invulnerable to the effects of aging (Baltes & Baltes, 1990).

The next square in the matrix, including individuals who use identity assimilation and problem-focused coping, has not been identified in previous research yet appears to be an important possibility to consider. Older adults with these characteristics would be predicted to become actively involved in

	Identity Assimilation	Identity Accommodation
Emotion-focused coping	Deny aging changes	Overreact to changes
Problem-focused coping	Change behavior	Become preoccupied

FIGURE 1.4 Interaction of coping and identity processes.

behavioral controls that could serve a preventative or compensatory function with regard to aging. However, they would not integrate into their identities the knowledge that their body has changed in fundamental ways or faces severe health threats. Thus, at the behavioral level, the individual is engaging in appropriate health maintenance and rehabilitative strategies, and is able to take advantage of these strategies in terms of improvements in physical health. However, the individual has chosen not to give particular thought or emphasis to the implications for identity of the problem or disorder. Such a group would correspond to the "foreclosed" categorization of Marcia's identity status (Marcia, 1966) framework for adolescents in which the individual arrives at a set of identity commitments without engaging in a process of exploration or the traditional "identity crisis." Indeed, this style of approaching psychosocial issues related to ego integrity was observed in a study of community elders (Walaskay, Whitbourne, & Nehrke, 1983–84), in which a group of "foreclosed" older persons were identified who had not struggled with existential questions regarding their mortality but had nevertheless gone ahead and made funeral arrangements, planning the event as if it were a social occasion. Behaviorally, these individuals appeared to have achieved ego integrity, or resolution of their feelings about death, but they had not processed these feelings at a deeper psychological level.

Identity accommodation may occur in conjunction with either problem- or emotion-focused coping. Individuals who tend to use accommodation to the point that they overreact to a diagnosis or physical disorder may suffer the same adverse consequences as those who deny through assimilation the significance of physical changes or illness. Such individuals believe that what they do in reaction to these changes or diseases will make no difference, and through the emotion-focused strategies of distancing, denial, or avoidance, fail to take the necessary steps to maximize their functioning (Lachman et al., 1995; Lohr, Essex, & Klein, 1988; Roberto, 1992; Woodward & Wallston, 1987). Their emotions are likely to be highly dysphoric (Rapkin & Fischer, 1992), and they feel a loss of the ability to control or predict the future course of their physical development or changes in health condition (Baum & Boxley, 1983).

Individuals who use accommodation but also take steps to confront the changes in physical status or health through problem-focused coping may be likely to take extremely active steps to help reduce their symptoms or the progress of the disease. It is probable that such individuals feel that they are able to control the events in their lives, leading them to be less likely to use palliative coping strategies in favor of ones that address the situation (Blanchard-Fields & Irion, 1989). These individuals would react to disease or physical changes by harnessing their available resources, and they would actively seek further medical treatment as well as less proven alternate treatments. They might be preoccupied with their bodies, but at the same time they would use every opportunity to talk to others and get help, using coping strategies such as confrontation, seeking social support, planful problem solving, and positive reappraisal. If they have a particular disease, they may "become" the disease, which then becomes a major focus of their lives. The risk of this type of coping in combination with identity accommodation is that although the individual adjusts well to the physical identity stressor by taking active steps, he or she may ruminate excessively about the disease.

Research currently underway using a newly developed Identity and Experiences Scale (IES) to measure the identity processes and the Ways of Coping scale to measure coping strategies will test this model, using health-related behaviors as the dependent variable. It is predicted that healthy adaptation within this model involves the balance between assimilation and accommodation in terms of the impact of age changes or disease on identity (Baltes & Staudinger, 1993; Ryff, 1989; Ryff, 1991). Flexibility of coping style would further promote positive adaptation. When problems arise, such individuals can focus on the physical identity stressor and are open to seeking help from others, but they avoid being preoccupied with the illness when necessary in order to focus on other concerns, such as family or work involvements. This ability to adapt to the challenges of aging reflects what Clark and Anderson (Clark & Anderson, 1967) described several decades ago as characteristic of "successful" aging and, more recently, has been identified as a protective factor against depression in later adulthood (Brandtstadter & Rothermund, 1994).

In this discussion of identity and coping, it is important to emphasize that the individual's use of these processes is not fixed across the span of the aging years. Individuals may use a variety of coping strategies that complement or off-set their identity style. Furthermore, assuming that there is a relationship between identity processes and coping, and given the emphasis in the coping literature on the variable nature of coping processes (Folkman & Lazarus, 1980; Folkman, Lazarus, Gruen, & DeLongis, 1986) it may be more reasonable to pro-pose that the identity processes are used within the same individual on differ-ent occasions, or even within the same individual on the same occasion (Brandtstadter & Renner, 1990). As is true for coping strategies, individuals may use one, then another, of the identity processes in their attempts to adapt to changes in the body's appearance, functioning, and health.

Role of Cultural Stereotypes

A final consideration in understanding the interaction between identity and age-related changes in physical and cognitive functioning is the role of cultural stereotypes and myths about the aging process. Age-related norms and expec-tations emphasize the uncontrollable losses that accumulate in the later adult years (Heckhausen & Baltes, 1991; Krueger & Heckhausen, 1993). The degree to which individuals ascribe to negative stereotypes about the aging process can have a detrimental impact on the motivation to cope actively with age-related changes (Ryff, 1991). To the extent that individuals come to hold these beliefs, they will be more likely to adopt the passive approaches involved in emotion-focused coping strategies. Further reinforcing this passivity are interactions with younger adults in which the older person is treated in a patronizing, infantiliz-ing manner. Such treatment can lower the individual's feelings of personal con-trol and self-efficacy (Whitbourne & Wills, 1993).

In this regard, it is also important to consider identity in relation to the "isms" of racism, sexism, and ageism. The individual's racial or ethnic identity and gender may be seen as influencing health behaviors to the extent that what is considered appropriate for one's age, sex, and cultural group may determine whether or not the individual maintains a sufficiently high activity level. For example, elderly women of Asian origin are unlikely to see themselves as active or athletic given their culture's expectations that women are traditionally fem-inine and dependent. Culture can also influence the individual's diet in that different cultures emphasize different types of food and food preparation mea-sures. In Asian culture, low-fat foods and a diet high in vegetables are a plus in helping older individuals avoid diseases related to high intake of cholesterol and low intake of natural fiber. Other cultures emphasize less healthy foods, such as the matzo balls, cream cheese, fatty cold cuts, and sour cream of traditional Jewish food. Many traditional ethnic foods, ranging from Mexican to French to southern Italian also involve reliance on cheeses or other rich dairy products, fatty meats, eggs, and chocolate. To the extent that the individual has been raised on these foods, and continues to eat and prepare them, dietary problems may be expected to ensue in later adulthood.

Health-seeking behaviors may also be expected to be influenced by the individual's gender, socialization, and cultural or ethnic background. Men who believe in a traditionally stoic approach to physical or psychological problems will resist seeking help as it may seem to be a sign of weakness. In various ethnic cultures, the need for professional help, in particular, may be regarded as non-normative, and rather than use the services of a mental health clinician, the individual feels it is more appropriate to rely on the family for support. Beyond the level of attitudes is the individual's ability to pay for health services. With changes in managed care, Medicaire, and Medicaid looming on the horizon, it becomes even more likely that individuals with limited economic resources will be unable to pay for help, even when the need is acknowledged.

Moving beyond the sphere of health are stressors within the environment whose presence influences the course of psychological development in later adulthood. Again, these stressors may be seen as linked to class, race, and ethnicity. First and foremost, poverty forces the older person to live in urban areas such as ghettos or public housing. Living within these environments poses a direct threat to the individual's physical well-being, as such environments create the risk of victimization. Not only are there subjective effects in terms of the older individual becoming limited in what he or she can do to compensate for age-related changes, but there are real effects of the environment that can create severe challenges to adjustment in old age.

CONCLUSIONS

The psychology of aging is at a turning point in its history, corresponding perhaps to the maturing of a field into its own "midlife," having reached the 50-year mark in its development as a professional specialty. Within the past decade alone, there has been a fantastic growth of studies in psychology relevant not only to the topic of this volume, but based on the assumption that aging is not just something that has to "happen" to a person. These authors challenge much of the accepted wisdom that aging involves inevitable decline in all major functions and are looking for ways that individuals can control their aging destiny. The proverbial half-full or half-empty glass of water provides an apt metaphor for this change in thinking. Two gerontologists can look at the same data curve and interpret them in very different ways. The gerontological pessimist who sees aging as inevitable decline will read a data curve as showing "loss" and the optimist will look in the same curve and read "stability" or will view the entire curve as methodologically unsound and disregard it altogether! Increasingly, the optimists are beginning to make their presence felt, and providing substantial bodies of data to back their claims.

The theme of this book will involve a natural moving back and forth between the documentation of decline and the presentation of alternate ways that individuals can age and can think about their own aging. Relevant research on personality and social processes will be integrated into these discussions where it can elaborate on the model of identity processes and multiple thresholds. By no means is this discussion definitive, as in many cases neither the data nor the theory are available. It is my hope that this book will stimulate thinking and new research in you, the reader, so that in your own work with aging individuals or in your own research, you will be able to develop and apply these concepts in a useful way.

REFERENCES

Aldwin, C. M. (1991). Does age affect the stress and coping process? Implications of age differences in perceived control. *Journal of Gerontology: Psychological Sciences, 46,* P174–180.

Aldwin, C. M., & Revenson, T. A. (1987). Does coping help? A reexamination of the relation between coping and mental health. *Journal of Personality and Social Psychology, 53,* 337–348.

Baltes, P. B., & Baltes, M. M. (1990). Psychological perspectives on successful aging: A model of selective optimization with compensation. In P. B. Baltes & M. M. Baltes (Ed.), *Successful aging: Perspectives from the behavioral sciences* (pp. 1–34). New York: Cambridge University Press.

Baltes, P. B., & Staudinger, U. M. (1993). The search for a psychology of wisdom. *Current Directions in Psychological Science, 2,* 75–80.

Baum, S. K., & Boxley, R. L. (1983). Age identification in the elderly. *Gerontologist, 23,* 532–537.

Berkman, B., Millar, S., Holmes, W., & Bonander, E. (1991). Predicting elderly cardiac patients at risk for readmission. Special Issue: Applied social work research in health and social work. *Social Work in Health Care, 16,* 21–38.

Billings, A. G., & Moos, R. H. (1981). The role of coping responses in attenuating the stress of life events. *Journal of Behavioral Medicine, 4,* 139–157.

Blanchard-Fields, F., & Irion, J. (1989). Coping strategies from the perspective of two developmental markers: Age and social reasoning. *Journal of Genetic Psychology, 149,* 141–151.

Blanchard-Fields, F., & Irion, J. C. (1988). The relation between locus of control and coping in two contexts: Age as a moderator variable. *Psychology and Aging, 3,* 197–203.

Bocknek, G., & Perna, F. (1994). Studies in self-representation beyond childhood. In J. M. Masling & R. F. Bornstein (Eds.), *Empirical perspectives on object relations theory* (pp. 29–58). Washington, DC: American Psychological Association.

Bombardier, C., D'Amico, C., & Jordan, J. (1990). The relationship of appraisal and coping to chronic illness adjustment. *Behavior Research and Therapy, 28,* 297–304.

Brandtstadter, J., & Renner, G. (1990). Tenacious goal pursuit and flexible goal adjustment: Explication and age-related analysis of assimilative and accommodative strategies in coping. *Psychology and Aging, 5,* 58–67.

Brandtstadter, J., & Rothermund, K. (1994). Self-percepts of control in middle and later adulthood: Buffering losses by rescaling goals. *Psychology and Aging, 9,* 265–273.

Carstensen, L. L., & Turk-Charles, S. (1994). The salience of emotion across the adult life span. *Psychology and Aging, 9,* 259–264.

Cavanaugh, J. C., & Green, E. E. (1990). I believe, therefore I can: Self-efficacy beliefs in memory aging. In E. A. Lovelace (Ed.), *Aging and cognition: Mental processes, self-awareness and interventions* (pp. 189–230). Amsterdam: North Holland.

Clark, M., & Anderson, B. (1967). *Culture and aging: An anthropological study of older Americans.* Springfield, IL: Charles C. Thomas.

Clark, N. M., Becker, M. H., Janz, N. K., & Lorig, K. (1991). Self-management of chronic disease by older adults: A review and questions for research. *Journal of Aging and Health, 3,* 3–27.

Die, A. H., Seelbach, W. C., & Sherman, G. D. (1987). Achievement motivation, achieving styles, and morale in the elderly. *Psychology and Aging, 2,* 407–408.

Dittman-Kohli, F. (1990). Possibilities and constraints for the construction of meaning in old age. *Ageing and Society, 10,* 279–294.

Elliott, E., & Lachman, M. E. (1989). Enhancing memory by modifying control beliefs, attributions, and performance goals in the elderly. In P. S. Fry (Ed.), *Psychology of helplessness and control and attributions of helplessness and control in the aged* (pp. 339–367). Amsterdam: North Holland.

Erikson, E. H. (1963). *Childhood and society* (2nd ed.). New York: Norton.

Erikson, E. H., Erikson, J., & Kivnick, H. Q. (1986). *Vital involvement in old age.* New York: W. W. Norton.

Ershler, W. B. (1990). Influenza and aging. In A. L. Goldstein (Ed.), *Biomedical advances in aging* (pp. 513–521). New York: Plenum.

Ershler, W. B. (1993). The influence of an aging immune system on cancer incidence and progression. *Journal of Gerontology, 48,* B3–7.

Felton, B., Revenson, T., & Hinrichsen, G. (1984). Stress and coping in the explanation of psychological adjustment among chronically ill adults. *Social Science and Medicine, 18,* 889–898.

Felton, B. J., & Revensen, T. A. (1987). Age differences in coping with chronic illness. *Psychology and Aging, 2,* 164–170.

Fiatarone, M. A., Morley, J. E., Bloom, E. T., Benton, D., Solomon, G. F., & Makinodan, T. (1989). The effect of exercise on natural killer cell activity in young and old subjects. *Journal of Gerontology: Medical Sciences, 44,* M37–45.

Folkman, S., Bernstein, L., & Lazarus, R. S. (1987). Stress processes and the misuse of drugs in older adults. *Psychology and Aging, 2,* 366–374.

Folkman, S., & Lazarus, R. S. (1980). An analysis of coping in a middle-aged community sample. *Journal of Health and Social Behavior, 21,* 219–239.

Folkman, S., Lazarus, R. S., Gruen, R., & DeLongis, A. (1986). Appraisal, coping, health status, and psychological symptoms. *Journal of Personality and Social Psychology, 50,* 571–579.

Fox, K. R., & Corbin, C. B. (1989). The physical self-perception profile: Development and preliminary validation. *Journal of Sport and Exercise Psychology, 11,* 408–430.

Fry, P. S., & Wong, P. T. (1991). Pain management training in the elderly: Matching interventions with subjects' coping styles. *Stress Medicine, 7,* 93–98.

Gould, R. L. (1978). *Transformations: Growth and change in adult life.* New York: Simon & Schuster.

Grover, D. R., & Hertzog, C. (1991). Relationships between intellectual control beliefs and psychometric intelligence in adulthood. *Journal of Gerontology: Psychological Sciences, 46,* P109–115.

Harris, M. B. (1994). Growing old gracefully: Age concealment and gender. *Journal of Gerontology: Psychological Sciences, 49,* P149–158.

Hart, E. A., Leary, M. R., & Rejeski, W. J. (1989). The measurement of social physique anxiety. *Journal of Sport and Exercise Psychology, 11,* 94–104.

Havighurst, R. J. (1972). *Developmental tasks and education* (3rd ed.). New York: McKay.

Heckhausen, J., & Baltes, P. B. (1991). Perceived controllability of expected psychological change across adulthood and old age. *Journal of Gerontology: Psychological Sciences, 46,* 165–173.

Heidrich, S. M., & Ryff, C. D. (1993a). Physical and mental health in later life: The self-system as mediator. *Psychology and Aging, 8,* 327–338.

Heidrich, S. M., & Ryff, C. D. (1993b). The role of social comparison processes in the psychological adaptation of elderly adults. *Journal of Gerontology: Psychological Sciences, 48,* P127–137.

Hennessy, C. H. (1989). Culture in the use, care, and control of the aging body. *Journal of Aging Studies, 3,* 39–54.

Hooker, K. (1992). Possible selves and perceived health in older adults and college students. *Journal of Gerontology: Psychological Sciences, 47,* P85–95.

Hooker, K., & Kaus, C. R. (1994). Health-related possible selves in young and middle adulthood. *Psychology and Aging, 9,* 126–133.

Kiecolt, K. J. (1994). Stress and the decision to change oneself: A theoretical model. *Social Psychology Quarterly, 57,* 49–63.

Krause, N. (1986). Stress and coping: Reconceptualizing the role of locus of control beliefs. *Journal of Gerontology, 41,* 617–622.

Krueger, J., & Heckhausen, J. (1993). Personality development across the adult life span: Subjective conceptions vs cross-sectional contrasts. *Journal of Gerontology: Psychological Sciences, 48,* P100–108.

Labouvie-Vief, G., Hakim-Larson, J., & Hobart, C. J. (1987). Age, ego level, and the life-span development of coping and defense processes. *Psychology and Aging, 2,* 286–293.

Lachman, M., Bandura, M., Weaver, S., & Elliott, E. (1995). Assessing memory control beliefs: The Memory Controllability Inventory. *Aging and Cognition, 2,* 67–84.

Lachman, M. E. (1986). Locus of control in aging research. *Psychology and Aging, 1,* 34–40.

Lachman, M. E. (1990). When bad things happen to older people: Age differences in attributional style. *Psychology and Aging, 5,* 607–609.

Lachman, M. E., & Leff, R. (1989). Perceived control and intellectual functioning in the elderly: A 5-year longitudinal study. *Developmental Psychology, 25,* 722–728.

Lazarus, R. (1981). The stress and coping paradigm. In C. Eisdorfer (Ed.), *Models for clinical psychopathology* (pp. 177–214). New York: Spectrum.

Lazarus, R. S., & Folkman, S. (1984). *Stress, appraisal, and coping.* New York: Springer.

Levinson, D. J., Darrow, C. N., Klein, E. B., Levinson, M. H., & McKee, B. (1978). *The seasons of a man's life.* New York: Alfred A. Knopf.

Lohr, M. J., Essex, M. J., & Klein, M. H. (1988). The relationships of coping responses to physical health status and life satisfaction among older women. *Journal of Gerontology: Psychological Sciences, 43,* P54–60.

Marcia, J. E. (1966). Development and validation of ego-identity status. *Journal of Personality and Social Psychology, 3,* 551–558.

Markus, H., & Nurius, P. (1986). Possible selves. *American Psychologist, 41,* 954–969.

McCrae, R. R., & Costa, P. T., Jr. (1988). Age, personality, and the spontaneous self-concept. *Journal of Gerontology: Social Sciences, 43,* S177–185.

McCrae, R. R., & Costa, P. T. Jr. (1990). *Personality in adulthood.* New York: Guilford.

McNaughton, M. E., Smith, L. W., Patterson, T. L., & Grant, I. (1990). Stress, social support, coping resources, and immune status in elderly women. *Journal of Nervous and Mental Disease, 178,* 460–461.

Miller, R. A. (1993). Aging and cancer— Another perspective. *Journal of Gerontology: Biological Sciences, 48,* B8–9.

Myers, A. M., Powell, L. E., Maki, B. E., Holliday, P. J., Brawley, L. R., & Sherk, W. (1996). Psychological indicators of balance confidence: Relationship to actual and perceived abilities. *Journal of Gerontology: Medical Sciences, 51A,* M37–43.

O'Brien, S. J., & Conger, P. R. (1991). No time to look back: Approaching the finish line of life's course. *International Journal of Aging and Human Development, 33,* 75–87.

Pearlin, L., & Schooler, C. (1978). The structure of coping. *Journal of Health and Social Behavior, 19,* 2–21.

Piaget, J. (1975/1977). *The development of thought* (A. Rosin, Trans.). Oxford: Basil Blackwell.

Preston, D. B., & Mansfield, P. K. (1984). An exploration of stressful life events, illness, and coping among the rural elderly. *Gerontologist, 24,* 490–494.

Rapkin, B. D., & Fischer, K. (1992). Framing the construct of life satisfaction in terms of older adults' personal goals. *Psychology and Aging, 7,* 138–149.

Roberto, K. (1992). Coping strategies of older women with hip fractures: Resources and outcomes. *Journal of Gerontology: Psychological Sciences, 47,* P21–26.

Ryff, C. D. (1989). In the eye of the beholder: Views of psychological well-being among middle-aged and older adults. *Psychology and Aging, 4,* 195–210.

Ryff, C. D. (1991). Possible selves in adulthood and old age: A tale of shifting horizons. *Psychology and Aging, 6,* 286–295.

Ryff, C. D., Lee, Y. H., Essex, M. J., & Schmutte, P. S. (1994). My children and me: Midlife evaluations of grown children and self. *Psychology and Aging, 9,* 195–205.

Smith, L. W., Patterson, T. L., & Grant, I. (1990). Avoidant coping predicts psychological disturbance in the elderly. *Journal of Nervous and Mental Disease, 178,* 525–530.

Speake, D. L. (1987). Health promotion activities and the well elderly. *Health Values: Achieving High Level Wellness, 11,* 25–30.

Staudinger, U. M., Smith, J., & Baltes, P. B. (1993). Wisdom-related knowledge in a life review task: age differences and role of professional specialization. *Psychology and Aging, 7,* 271–281.

Thomas, P. D., Goodwin, J. M., & Goodwin, J. W. (1985). Effect of social support on stress-related changes in cholesterol, uric acid level, and immune function in an elderly sample. *American Journal of Psychiatry, 142,* 735–737.

Vaillant, G. (1977). *Adaptation to life.* Boston: Little, Brown.

Walaskay, M., Whitbourne, S. K., & Nehrke, M. F. (1983-84). Construction and validation of an ego-integrity status interview. *International Journal of Aging and Human Development, 18,* 61–72.

Whitbourne, S. K. (1986a). *Adult development.* New York: Praeger.

Whitbourne, S. K. (1986b). *The me I know: A study of adult identity.* New York: Springer Verlag.

Whitbourne, S. K. (1987). Personality development in adulthood and old age: Relationships among identity style, health, and well-being. In K. W. Schaie (Ed.), *Annual Review of Gerontology and Geriatrics* (Vol. 7, pp. 189–216). New York: Springer.

Whitbourne, S. K. (1989). Comments on Lachman's "Personality and aging at the crossroads: Beyond stability versus change." In K. W. Schaie & C. Schooler (Ed.), *Social structure and aging: Psychological processes* (pp. 191–198). Hillsdale, NJ: Erlbaum.

Whitbourne, S. K. & Primus, L. (in press). Physical identity and the aging process. In J. E. Birren (Ed.), *Encyclopedia of aging*. San Diego, CA: Academic Press.

Whitbourne, S. K., & Wills, K.-J. (1993). Psychological issues in institutional care of the aged. In S. B. Goldsmith (Ed.), *Long-term care administration handbook* (pp. 19–32). Gaithersburg, MD: Aspen.

Woodward, N. J., & Wallston, B. S. (1987). Age and health care beliefs: Self-efficacy as a mediator of low desire for control. *Psychology and Aging, 2,* 3–8.

Williams, P., & Lord, S. R. (1995). Predictors of adherence to a structured exercise program for older women. *Psychology and Aging, 10,* 617–624.

2

How Aging is Studied

The study of aging is, by necessity, an enterprise in correlational or, at best, quasi-experimental designs. Age is not a legitimate "independent variable," as its levels cannot be experimentally manipulated. The status of age as a variable is, in this sense, similar to the status of gender, ethnicity, place of birth, occupation, and other subject-assigned variables. What makes age an even more difficult independent variable to approach, however, is its uncertain meaning in terms of the "dependent" variables of interest, namely the phenomena that are presumed to change in some systematic way in relation to this variable we call "age." Aging is, after all, intrinsically wrapped up in the passage of time. Time is an index of a physical process thought to have some connection with events in the universe (Fraser, 1987). The older a person is, the more times that person has experienced the rotation of the earth on its axis, and the rotation of the earth around the sun. What is the connection between these physical events and the changes in the body thought to be due to aging? The answer is that there is no direct connection. Age provides a convenient shorthand in units of time for indexing the number of physical events that occured in the universe while the organism is living. Age is an index of time, and time does not "cause" the aging of the body.

It is also the case that age as a variable is not necessarily a good index of an individual's physical, psychological, or social status. Gerontologists speak of the various "clocks" that measure the life of the individual, and these clocks may tick at a different pace, even within the same individual. For example, it is not unusual for athletes to retire in their twenties or even their teenage years. Individuals who are old enough to be grandparents may give birth to their first child. A precocious young person may have the wisdom of an elder, and an older adult may have the emotional maturity of a teenager. Although the physical changes of aging are more legitimately linked to time, it is known that the sedentary young adult may be less functional on a variety of physiological indicators than is the active elder.

The fact that age is a function of the passage of time, the difference between the present time and the date of the individual's birth, creates another dilemma for people who study the aging process. As people age, they also are passing through a certain period of history during which events external to the changes within the body influence their behavior. Periods of war, extreme poverty, and political repression are likely to take a heavy emotional toll on people living through these periods, who might change over the years in ways different from people living through more peaceful and prosperous times (Aldwin, Levenson, & Spiro, 1994; Elder, Shanahan, & Clipp, 1994). The aging of the body is also affected by the changes that occur in the environment that influence physical functioning. People who live in highly industrialized areas in which there are high levels of pollutants may experience a faster rate of physical aging than people who breathe nothing but "clean" air throughout their lives. Similarly, contemporary adults may be healthier than adults living in previous generations before it was discovered that high cholesterol foods can cause cardiovascular disease. It would be difficult, then, for a researcher to disentangle the effects of changes in the environment on the aging of the body and psychological qualities from the effects of internal changes taking place in the body's various physiological systems.

Researchers who study the human aging process have gone to great lengths to separate, at a conceptual level, the effects of changes within the individual, or "personal aging" from the effects of changes external to the individual, or "social time." The development of psychology's current schemes for making this separation followed years of experimentation with various kinds of strategies.

TRADITIONAL RESEARCH DESIGNS IN THE PSYCHOLOGY OF AGING

All of the early findings in psychology on the relationship between aging and human behavior were based on two types of research designs: longitudinal and cross-sectional. These two designs still form the basis for the majority of research on psychological gerontology.

Longitudinal designs

The most logical strategy for designing a study on aging would seem to involve selecting a sample of adults and following them over a period of years or decades. To study changes in old age, then, a researcher might start with a group of 50-year-olds and follow them for perhaps 30 years or more. At the end of that time, the researcher would be able to describe changes in the latter portion of the lifespan on a set of particular variables. This "longitudinal" study seems to be ideal, as what better way is there to study the aging process than to observe it directly? Since the researcher is following the same people over time, it would seem that any changes observed in them should be due to intrinsic properties of the aging process. However, as might be apparent from the above discussion, the longitudinal design is not without its disadvantages.

The first set of problems with the longitudinal design that might appear immediately upon further consideration are the practical ones. To embark on a longitudinal study is a major commitment of time and resources on the part of the researcher. For those who work in a setting where results are expected to be produced more than once every 30 years (obviously true in most universities and research labs!), the time frame involved in longitudinal research might very well be unacceptable. It would also be difficult to find researchers willing to delay gratification for that long of a period as well. Of course, most researchers who begin a longitudinal study find ways around this problem. They usually test people on several occasions between the beginning and end of the study, and these tests produce results that can be reported on intermittently. The most pertinent findings may not be revealed until the study is over, but there are often enough worthwhile data to merit publication of several shorter-term follow-ups.

Relevant to the point regarding time investment is the fact that a longitudinal study is very likely to outlive its originator. Investigators change jobs, locales, and research interests. If the study is initiated when the researcher is a middle-aged adult, it is possible that the researcher will retire or might not survive until the study's completion. Again, researchers have found ways around this problem. Other people can continue the study after the original researcher leaves. Alternatively, the researcher may be fortunate enough to find an existing data set from previous years which can be followed up after gaining access to the data. In my own research (Whitbourne & Waterman, 1979), I decided in 1975 to retest a sample of adults who had been tested 10 years before and whose data were made available by the original researcher. This essentially "added" 10 years to the life of the follow-up researchers, who did not have to start fresh with a new data collection.

Another related problem also characterizes longitudinal research. The long time frame involved in a longitudinal research project takes its toll on the participants as well as the researchers. Inevitable "attrition" or loss of participants from the original sample creates a number of practical and theoretical difficulties. First, in practical terms, the longer the study continues, the more likely it is that subjects will drop out of the sample. Some die, others lose interest, still others move away. The net result is that the size of the sample can dwindle over time to the point where it is nearly impossible to conduct adequate statistical tests of the data. Several strategies can be used to minimize the attrition problem, although none are without flaw. If the research is being conducted through an established institute or agency, it is possible for the researcher or the researcher's assistants to maintain continuous contact with study members in between test occasions. The researchers may send holiday greeting cards, birthday cards, occasional notes, or make telephone calls from time to time to check on study participants. These expressions of interest increase the likelihood that study members will feel involved enough in the project to want to continue their participation. Limitations in funding and staff, of course, may make such a continued enterprise unfeasible. Furthermore, if the study requires face-to-face contact, and study participants move to distant locations, the research team may not be able to afford the costs of travel and the data will be lost.

The theoretical difficulties caused by attrition are even more of a challenge to handle successfully. In study after study, it has been quite convincingly demonstrated that the "survivors" of a longitudinal investigation, those who remain in the sample over repeated testing occasions, are not fully representative of the entire sample who began the study. Compared to the drop-outs at initial testing, the survivors tend to have better health, a fact which is quite self-explanatory, and also to perform better on a number of psychological indices. These factors can complicate the interpretations that the researcher is likely to make on the basis of the data at follow-up. If the entire sample is included in the analyses at Time 1 and Time 2, it will appear as though the scores have increased when in fact, all that has happened is that the less able ones have disappeared from the sample at Time 2.

Although separating the drop-outs from the surviving participants is an important step in solving the attrition problem, it is not the total answer. The surviving group, over the period of testing, comes to represent an increasingly select group of individuals who are probably more hardy, healthy, and cooperative than was the original sample. Furthermore, the survivors have the advantage of having had more than one exposure to the test measures. The survivors may improve their scores, particularly on tests of ability, due solely to their greater familiarity with the instruments. Concerns about attrition along with the problem of practice effects, then, are present in most types of longitudinal research. As shall be discussed later, selection effects are also a nagging logical problem in cross-sectional studies.

As if these problems were not enough to discourage anyone from conducting longitudinal research, consider the final snag. Imagine that you are a researcher working in the 1930s on a study concerning the development of personality from childhood to adulthood. How do you measure personality? Obviously, you use the tools available to you, and these tools are going to be ones that fit with the prevailing theoretical atmosphere of the day. Freud's theory has gained quite a bit of interest and excitement, and you think it would provide a useful model for studying development. It is now 1950, psychoanalytic theory is being severely criticized, and trait theory has grown into ascendancy. Your measures based on psychodynamic theory are now hopelessly outdated. Do you throw out your earlier measures entirely and start with new ones that reflect contemporary thinking, or do you stay with what you have, even though it is limited? These problems are exacerbated still further when, in the 1980s, the next researcher working on the project wishes to test the sample using the increasingly popular concepts developed in stress and coping research. The trait theory measures are clearly inadequate, as would be ones derived from psychoanalytic theory.

The constant outdating of assessment measures occurs in every area of psychological functioning, not just personality. Longitudinal researchers must continually agonize over whether to update their test data and lose continuity with the past, or whether to maintain consistency over time and try to get as much information out of the old measures as possible. One solution to this dilemma is to form new ratings from the available data, as is possible to do when the original data are in the form of observations, interviews, and other open-ended material. This strategy was arrived at by workers at the Institute of Human Development in Berkeley, for example. Even though their data on child development were collected in the 1920s under one set of assumptions about human behavior, the measurement instruments were wide-ranging and comprehensive enough to allow later researchers following the sample throughout adulthood to conduct ratings along indices of current theoretical interest (Field & Millsap, 1991).

Even if all these problems can be overcome, the researcher conducting a longitudinal study would still be faced with one final difficulty in interpreting the study's findings. Earlier, it was observed that it is impossible to separate the effects of social time from the effects of personal aging. This is the heart of the difficulty in longitudinal research when one group of people is followed through one historical time period. The researcher cannot determine whether the changes shown by the sample are due to age per se or to the effects of the environment. Longitudinal studies, then, at best can only provide information on changes over time within a group of people.

Whether these changes over time are due to personal aging or to the effects of social time cannot be determined with any certainty. Fortunately, the problems of single-sample longitudinal designs can be corrected by altering the design so that another sample is studied, over a different period of history. With two or more longitudinal samples followed over two or more time periods, the inferential problems just described can be reduced if not eliminated. This strategy will be explained in more detail shortly.

Cross-Sectional Designs

As a perhaps more efficient alternative to a longitudinal study on aging, a researcher may select groups of people varying in age, test them, and compare their performance. The term used to describe this kind of research design is "cross-sectional," because the researcher is studying a "cross-section," by age, of the population. In this design, all testing is done at approximately one time (realistically, over a period extending up to several months), allowing for results to be published as soon as the last subject has left the laboratory and the last analysis has been rolled off the computer. The only time delays that occur are attributable to lack of energy on the part of the investigator in completing the manuscript and to delays in the process of peer review.

All other things being equal, and in contrast to the longitudinal study, the cross-sectional study can be completed within a reasonably short time span. There are none of the practical nightmares that plague the researcher doing a longitudinal study. However, the cross-sectional study is not without its disadvantages. To begin with, consider the issue of experimental control. In the cross-sectional study, respondents of different age groups are compared on a variable of interest. Differences between the groups are presumed to reflect their difference in age, rather than differences on other, extraneous, factors. The researcher must ensure that the older and younger groups are comparable on factors thought to be related to the variable under study.

Although the need to control for factors other than age seems obvious, there are a number of examples in the gerontological literature of cross-sectional research that did not involve this elementary precaution. A desire to conduct the research in as efficient a manner as possible has led many researchers to make serious errors in their selection of samples. Consider the example of a researcher who is attempting to establish whether there are age differences in memory for telephone numbers. To simplify data collection, the researcher decides to recruit older adult subjects from a long-term care residence. These people live under one roof and so can be tested without having to travel from test site to test site. For similar reasons, the researcher selects a group of college students as a comparison. These students will participate in the study for experimental credit, and can be tested in a laboratory setting near the researcher's office. When the researcher then finds that the older group has a poorer memory for telephone numbers than the younger group, the "natural" conclusion is that the older persons have suffered cognitive losses that impair their ability to remember sequences of seven digits. The researcher's mistake, of course, is to neglect or minimize differences between the samples in health status, educational background, living situation, and the demands placed on memory in daily life.

The flaws in the memory study may seem fairly evident, so it may be surprising to learn that much of the research on aging conducted in the 1960s and even into the more enlightened 1970s involved design flaws of similar magnitude. Samples of "captive" older adults served as the main source of data on age differences. These older samples were different in many important ways from the "captive" young persons (undergraduates in psychology courses) to whom they were compared. One important clue to the problems involved in the cross-sectional method came from investigations of intelligence. Longitudinal studies showed no decreases, and even increases in some intellectual abilities. By contrast, cross-sectional studies showed consistent differences between age groups in a negative direction beginning in mid-adulthood. It was clear that differences among age groups in education, health, and other important factors were leading cross-sectional studies to provide an inaccurately pessimistic view of the effects of aging on cognitive skills. Researchers are now more sensitive to the need to control for factors other than age when comparing groups of older and younger adults, but it is nevertheless important to look out for what the researcher might have missed when you draw conclusions from the results of cross-sectional research.

Many other problems remain, however, even after a researcher has controlled for as many factors as possible when comparing age groups of adults. One of these is the representativeness of each sample. Suppose that a researcher, to control for the effects of education, selects a group of college-educated older adults to compare to a group of state college students on a measure of intellectual functioning. The researcher can probably assume that the young adult sample represents a relatively broad spectrum of the population between the ages of 18 and 22 (this would not be as safe an assumption if the college students were attending an Ivy League university). What about the older adults? Considering that they grew up in the early part of the century, when most people did not attempt to gain a college education, it is likely that they represent a select proportion of the elderly population, particularly the women. Thus, having attained equality between age groups on education, the researcher now faces the prospect of sacrificing the ability to generalize the results to older adults as a whole. Furthermore, it is plausible that the older adults are a more select group than is the young adult sample, who are more typical of their age group. Some researchers are willing to sacrifice representativeness, on the grounds that it is better to err on the side of testing a more select older sample than a sample which is clearly handicapped compared to the younger group.

It is also important to recognize that the problem of attrition affects not only longitudinal studies, but also the cross-sectional design. The people who remain alive and are available to be tested in later adulthood are the sturdier ones who have survived the diseases and accidents that caused their peers to die at earlier ages. It is interesting to speculate, for example, when reading that older adults use fewer "hostile reaction" forms of coping than young adults, that the hostility-prone individuals have died through natural or unnatural causes before they could make it to old age (Irion & Blanchard-Fields, 1987). Similarly, the cross-sectional finding that older adults are better able to regulate their emotions (Labouvie-Vief, Hakim-Larson, DeVoe, & Schoeberlein, 1989) may reflect the fact that the ones who could not suffered life-shortening stress-related illnesses while in their middle adult years.

Another set of decisions concerning samples in cross-sectional research pertains to the number and age composition of the groups being compared. If a researcher is trying to estimate the magnitude of age differences between two groups, a sensible strategy would be to narrow the age gap within each group as much as possible. Conclusions can then be made about the average performance of, for example, 70-year-olds vs. the average performance of 20-year-olds. This seems to be a fairly straightforward matter. However, as with the issue of sampling in general, matters of convenience come into play. The researcher must cast a much wider net to find a group of 68- –72-year-olds, for instance, than would be needed to find people whose ages are in the broad range of from 60 to 80. It should come as no surprise, then, to find out that many researchers take the more practical course of action. Samples of "old" people in reports of some studies on aging have age ranges as wide as 30 or 35 years. The typical sample of older adults ranges over a 15-year span, compared to the 4- or 5-year span of the young adult (usually college) age groups. Why is the broad age range in older samples a problem? The main reason is that these samples include people with highly varied physical and psychological qualities. It is not clear what the average performance within this group represents. Just as the sample process involves casting a wide net, the conclusions will be equally imprecise.

Along similar lines, researchers are also faced with the question of deciding how many age groups of adults to include in the study. Should there be two groups, young and older adult, or three age groups, including a middle-aged sample? All other things being equal, it is preferable to have three (or more) age groups rather than two, giving the researcher the opportunity to "connect the dots" between their performance with greater confidence. When reading the results of cross-sectional research, then, it is necessary to look carefully not only at the age ranges of the samples, but at the number of samples being compared.

If you have been keeping a score card on the advantages vs. the disadvantages of conducting cross-sectional research compared to those associated with longitudinal research, you can see that one remaining advantage of cross-sectional research is that the measures of the variables under study do not have the problem of built-in obsolescence. A cross-sectional study carried out in the 1990s can take advantage of the latest thinking in psychology on whatever variable is being researched. However, cross-sectional research is faced with another and more subtle measurement limitation. The tests and instruments used to assess psychological functioning in the various age samples must have equivalent psychometric properties for each group. This means that before comparing younger and older adults on a measure of anxiety developed on a college student sample, the researcher must determine the reliability and validity of the measure for the older adult age groups. Similarly, researchers who study memory and other cognitive functions are faced with the problem of finding tests that will be neither too easy for the younger nor too difficult for the older groups of adults. College students may readily be able to memorize a list of 25 words, but the same list could be far too long for an older adult to remember. If the list is made shorter, all of the college students will remember every word, and the researcher will not be able to determine the precise nature of age differences in the memory function under study. The necessity of comparing age groups on the same measures, then, creates difficulties in cross-sectional research that are not present in longitudinal studies (Lachman, Weaver, Bandura, Elliott, & Lewkowicz, 1992).

The final consideration in evaluating cross-sectional studies is that the design does not permit the researcher to draw inferences about age "changes." The conclusions that many researchers draw to the effect that a particular function "increased" or "decreased" across adulthood are inappropriate when the data were collected following a cross-sectional design. The data allow the researcher to conclude only that one group was higher or lower than the other. Even sophisticated researchers state their conclusions in this kind of "age change" language; the reader should be on guard.

STRATEGIES TO SEPARATE PERSONAL AGING FROM SOCIAL TIME

By now you may be convinced that the "perfect" study on aging is virtually impossible to conduct. Age can never be a true independent variable because it cannot be manipulated. Furthermore, age is inherently linked with time and so personal aging can never be separated from social aging.

In speculating on ways to overcome these problems, researchers have suggested using a person's perceived age rather than chronological age as a way to classify the person developmentally. Kastenbaum and his co-workers experimented with this idea in their research on "subjective age": the age a person feels (Kastenbaum, Derbin, Sabatini, & Artt, 1972). It is intriguing to think about the use of subjective age as a substitute for chronological age, but as yet, the idea has not caught on in the field of gerontology. Instead, researchers turn to what are called "sequential" designs as a way of teasing apart the effects of personal aging from the effects of social time.

Basic Concepts: Age, Cohort, and Time of Measurement

To understand the sequential research design strategies, it is necessary to have a clear picture of the concepts of age, cohort, and time of measurement. These three factors are thought to influence jointly the individual's performance on any given psychological measure at any point in life.

If personal aging could be separated from social time, age would represent the inherent or intrinsic effects of the aging process alone on the individual's physical and psychological functioning (what some researchers call "ontogenetic" processes). A person of 60 years of age would attain a level of performance on a given measure due solely to the result of the aging process within the body, perhaps through the effects of aging on the nervous system. Age might also represent the sequence of predictable events that a person experiences through adulthood which, in turn, influence the individual's emotional adaptation and personality. So-called "stage" theories of personality development postulate just such a sequence of age-linked steps through adulthood. The validity of these theories rests on the assumption that people would go through these stages as a function of age, regardless of the environmental influences they are exposed to throughout their lives.

Cohort is determined by the year of an individual's birth. It is a concept similar to that of generation, although it can be measured in however long a time span as the researcher desires. A researcher may compare a cohort of people born in around 1910 with others born in about 1915 and 1920; cohorts can also be defined by 10- or 20-year intervals. The concept of cohort is similar to that of generation, in that it captures the sense of people who were born at around the same social time. The "1910 cohort" would have been exposed to influences in their early development that were perhaps different from the "1920 cohort." For instance, members of the 1910 cohort would have been small children during World War I, and as a result they would have experienced food deprivation due to rationing or emotional deprivation if their families were exposed to the war. The 1920 cohort would have spent their early childhood in a time of peace when the nation's economy was expanding and people were more carefree than a decade earlier. If cohort were the primary influence on personality development, members of the 1910 cohort would experience many difficulties in adjustment throughout adulthood, whereas the 1920 cohort would have a relatively even and positive course of personality growth throughout their adult years.

Finally, "time of measurement" is the index of social time at the point when the data are being collected. If time of measurement influences performance, people would receive similar scores, regardless of their age, on whatever variable is being measured. Everyone tested in the 1990s may have higher intelligence test scores than a comparable group of adults tested in the 1970s due to the "information explosion" that has accompanied the growth of high-technology industries and communciation. Similarly, if time of measurement were an effect, people tested in times of peace would probably receive more favorable personality test scores than people tested in times of war, regardless of their age at the time of testing. Of course, place of measurement is just as important as time of measurement, although it is generally not specified. One can only imagine the well-being scores of the survivors of atrocities in Bosnia tested in 1995 compared to the well-being of people living in the relatively placid environment of an affluent American suburb. Taking this analysis one step further, individual lives are affected by "time of measurement" in innumerable ways involving transient day-to-day alterations in general mood states. These short-term variations in factors affecting measured test scores are accounted for in part by a test's reliability (consistency), a piece of psychometric data that is not always readily available or obtainable.

Stepping back to look at three general sets of influences on data collected in studies on aging, you can easily see that age, cohort, and time of measurement are interdependent concepts. If you test a 70-year-old person who was born in 1920, the time of measurement must be 1990. If you are tested in 1980 and you were born in 1930, your age must, by definition, be 50. In other words, the concepts of age, cohort, and time of measurement are inextricably linked. Consequently, a researcher cannot draw unambiguous conclusions about any one variable without taking into account the effects of at least one other. This problem will become clearer as we discuss the sequential designs developed by Pennsylvania State psychologist K. Warner Schaie, the first researcher to tackle successfully the separation of personal from social aging.

Schaie's "Most Efficient Design"

The conceptualization of age, cohort, and time of measurement as separate indices can be credited to a landmark paper published by Schaie over 30 years ago (Schaie, 1965). In this paper, Schaie outlined the problems involved in traditional cross-sectional and longitudinal designs, and proposed a strategy for overcoming these problems by designing "sequential" studies that would allow for separation of the effects of age, cohort, and time of measurement. Schaie proposed three research designs, all of which involved applying the traditional developmental methodology over a sequence of years. Each design combines two of the three developmental concepts. When combined in a single investigation, these designs make up the "Most Efficient Design" that can simultaneously estimate the effects of age changes, cohort differences, and historical effects. A layout for a complete version of this design is shown in Table 2.1.

The "cohort-sequential" design compares the effects of age and cohort. As shown in Table 2.1, two cohorts are compared at two different ages necessitating that they are tested at different times of measurement. The two cohorts may be studied longitudinally, or there may be a new group of people (born the same year as the first group) introduced at the second time of testing. The "independent samples" method of introducing a new group at the second test occasion overcomes the problem of practice effects inherent in longitudinal designs. Alternatively, the researcher may use the "repeated measures" form of this design, if it is thought that practice effects would have little influence on test scores. In either case, if the cohort difference is significant, the researcher may conclude that early childhood influences, as reflected in birth cohort, have an effect on later adult performance. If all cohorts have similar scores, or show similar patterns of change or stability across the ages they are studied, the researcher can conclude that the results reflect the influence of personal aging. A third possibility is that members of the two cohorts show different patterns of performance at the ages tested. Perhaps one cohort increases its scores and another decreases over this age period. The researcher would then look for differential early life experiences between the cohorts that would make their appearance in later life. As an example, consider comparing two cohorts, one born before and the other born after the banning of leaded gasolines. The effect of these different experiences on the aging of the respiratory system may not become apparent until the groups reach middle age or beyond.

In the "time-sequential" research design, the researcher compares the effects of age with the effects of time of measurement. Two or more age groups are compared at two or more times of measurement necessitating that they represent different birth cohorts. The effects of time of measurement would be indicated if

TABLE 2.1 Layout of Developmental Research Designs

Years of testing (Time of measurement)	Year of birth (Cohort)			
	1930	1920	1910	1900
1970	**Cell A** 40 years old	**Cell B** 50 years old	**Cell C** 60 years old	**Cell D** 70 years old
1980	**Cell E** 50 years old	**Cell F** 60 years old	**Cell G** 70 years old	**Cell H** 80 years old
1990	**Cell I** 60 years old	**Cell J** 70 years old	**Cell K** 80 years old	**Cell L** 90 years old

Type of design	Factor(s) investigated	Specific effects studied	Cells compared
Longitudinal	Age changes	50 to 80 years	E–F–G–H
Cross-sectional	Age differences	50 to 70 years	C–G–K
Cohort-sequential	Age	60 vs. 70 years	F + C vs. J + G
	Cohort	1920 vs. 1910	F + J vs. C + G
Time-sequential	Age	60 vs. 70 years	F + C vs. G + D
	Time of measurement	1970 vs. 1980	C + D vs. F + G
Cross-sequential	Cohort	1920 vs. 1910	B + F vs. C +G
	Time of measurement	1970 vs. 1980	B + C vs. F + G
Cross-sectional sequences	Age differences across two cohorts and times of measurement	50 to 70 years in 1970 and 50 to 70 years in 1980	B–C–D vs. E–F–G
Longitudinal sequences	Age changes across two cohorts and times of measurement	60 to 70 years among the 1920 and 1910 cohorts	F–J vs. C–G

people in the sample, regardless of age, differed in their scores at one testing date compared to another testing date. Perhaps the variable being measured is "altruism." People in the 1980s may receive lower scores on this variable if, as it is sometimes thought, the 1980s was a time when materialistic values were emphasized in American society. In the 1990s, the "kinder and gentler" values of volunteerism may have the effect of increasing people's desire to help their fellow human beings. Age differences between the 60- and 70-year-olds would lead, instead, to the conclusion that people who are older are more altruistic, regardless of when they live. Finally, the combined effect of age and time of measurement may result in a reversal of age differences for the 1980 and 1990 testings. Perhaps the 60-year-olds were more altruistic in the 1980s and the 70-year-olds were more so in the 1990s due to differing sensitivities of the two age groups to society's prevailing values.

The third sequential design, called "cross-sequential," involves crossing the two factors of cohort and time of measurement. Two or more birth cohorts are compared at two or more times of measurement in this design, and as a result, age is not even a factor in the analysis. The purpose of this design is to compare these social time effects directly. On a measure of overall adjustment, for example, the two factors of cohort and time of measurement may show an interactive effect. People born in 1910 may experience the impact of contemporary society in different ways than people born in 1920. Perhaps the effect on the 1920 cohort of having been exposed in their teenage years to the economic depression of the 1930s caused them to become increasingly anxious about their economic situation as they faced the latter part of the century, with American society's growing reluctance to pay taxes for providing social services. The 1910 cohort may experience the opposite reaction, feeling increasingly happy over the last three decades of the century with its promise of an easing of cold war tensions. Apart from any changes due to age, then, performance on the measure of adjustment may reflect these different societal influences.

The kind of analyses of fictitious results described here represent the logic that would be used by a researcher in interpreting a set of real data collected through the sequential design strategies. The purpose of these analyses is to separate the effects of personal aging from social time, and more specifically, the influence of early vs. later life influences.

How successful can this type of analysis be? According to psychologist Paul Baltes, a colleague of Schaie who has developed his own theoretical approaches, the Most Efficient Design has serious limitations. These limitations stem from the interdependence of age, cohort, and time of measurement. As you read earlier, once you know two of these values, the third is automatically determined. Consequently, the three factors cannot vary independently, and this limits the designs from an experimental point of view. To understand this problem, consider the cohort-sequential design just described, in which birth cohorts differ in the years that they were tested. The effect that the researcher labels "age" or "cohort" could just as easily be labeled "time of measurement." Similarly, in order to set up the time-sequential design properly, the researcher must study at least two different cohorts in the two age groups at the two times of measurement. The results that may appear to be due to either "time of measurement" or "age" might instead be due to the fact that two different cohorts are being compared. Finally, the cross-sequential design is in effect no different from the cohort-sequential design. There are still two longitudinal studies being conducted with two different cohorts. Whether the data are arranged by age or time of measurement is really a matter of labelling.

All of these problems derive from the fundamental link between the three numerical indices of age, cohort, and time of measurement. There is no way to manipulate all three in a totally independent fashion (i.e., once two of these factors are defined, the value of the third is automatically determined). Consequently, interpretations derived from the sequential studies are always open to alternative explanations. The researcher may think that the cohort-sequential method shows age effects, but a critic may correctly attribute the findings to time of measurement differences.

Despite these difficulties, Schaie's exceptionally meticulous analyses of cohort and age contributions to psychological test data over the years of adulthood and old age have provided fascinating data with many "object lessons" for developmental psychologists. Perhaps one of the more interesting analyses to emerge from his recent publications pertains to the personality quality of "rigidity–flexibility." A common stereotype of aging is that it leads to greater inflexibility, and that older people are "set in their ways." Research by Schaie and his colleagues using sequential methods (Schaie & Willis, 1991) provided the first real demonstration of how cohort effects have clouded the findings from past studies, both longitudinal and cross-sectional. These analyses showed that over the past 70 years, within the Seattle Longitudinal Study (SLS) sample, successive generations have become increasingly more flexible in personality style, behaviors, and attitudes. This finding that might fit with many people's commonsense notions about changes in lifestyles and attitudes over the latter half of the 20th century. These generational shifts, concluded Schaie, "have led us to assume erroneously that most individuals become substantially more rigid as they age" (p. P283). Instead, there are modest declines in flexibility beginning in the decade of the 60s, but far more modest than would be predicted on the basis of social views of the elderly or past cross-sectional data (Chown, 1959).

The "Sequences" Designs of Baltes

In contrast to Schaie's research strategy which attempts to partition social time into cohort and time of measurement, Baltes focuses his efforts on making the basic distinction between personal aging and social time (Baltes, 1968). According to Baltes, it is not critical to ascertain whether a developmental finding reflects social time influences present at a person's birth or historical influences that are reflected in current test scores. What is of major interest is determining whether an apparent age effect is due to the aging of the body (and mind) or the result of exposure to social and historical events taking place during a person's lifetime. The strategies developed by Baltes directly pit personal aging against social time. These research designs are conceptually easy to understand and avert the interpretive problems involved in making sense of a huge set of developmental data.

For Baltes, then, the trick in developmental research is to evaluate the extent of "cohort" influences (which reflect social time) and compare these to "age" (the index of personal aging). There are two basic strategies for making these determinations. In the "longitudinal sequences" design, the researcher conducts more than one longitudinal study over a given period of years. This design is essentially the same as the cohort-sequential strategy of Schaie, but the inferences made are different. The researcher can determine whether the sequence of developmental changes are the same for more than one cohort. This design overcomes the limitation of a traditional longitudinal study, in which only one cohort is followed over one time period. If the results comparing one age to the other are different, this suggests that social time is interacting with personal aging. Without this check, there would be no way of knowing whether the longitudinal results generalize over time or not. Similarly, in what Baltes calls the "cross-sectional sequences" design, the researcher conducts more than one cross-sectional study. The time-sequential design of Schaie fits this description. The researcher can determine whether cross-sectional findings observed at one time of measurement are comparable to those obtained at another time. If they are not, then the researcher must suspect that social time is influencing the results. There is no design in the Baltes framework that corresponds to the cross-sequential design proposed by Schaie. This design, according to Baltes, is redundant with the other two, as indeed may be apparent from the earlier discussion.

Implications

Although the concepts of age, cohort, and time of measurement are easy to translate into numerical values, it is easy to see how quickly they become interwoven and a researcher can lose track of what exactly is being measured. These are the difficulties faced by researchers who try to make sense out of developmental data. In reading published findings, it is also important to look for possible threats to the validity of a study's findings. Some of these threats may be based on fairly subtle considerations regarding the comparability of findings across periods of social time. A finding based on research conducted in the 1970s may not hold up to testing in the 1990s. A single-sample cross-sectional or longitudinal design cannot tell you whether the effects observed would apply to more than the sample who were studied. Replications of findings, within the same study (as in research using sequential designs) or across studies conducted in different years, adds credence to the results of any given published article.

The necessity for researchers to test their findings on various populations is another factor to consider. Many of the results about the "human aging process," turn out, on closer inspection, to be descriptive of processes taking place within a culturally narrow group. As the field of gerontology matures, it will be increasingly important for researchers to think "sequentially" with respect not only to social time, but also to socially diverse groups.

Finally, multivariate methods have become increasingly important in developmental research. Methodologies based on new statistical procedures are revamping the strategies of data collection so that multiple measures are being collected on multiple occasions, and the data subjected to highly sophisticated analysis. In particular, the application of structural modeling (such as LISREL) is making it possible for researchers to draw causal inferences about underlying developmental processes and multiple effects on outcomes (Bentler, 1980). Using structural modeling, researchers can estimate the contributions of multiple personality and demographic variables thought to be related to age effects in physical health, personality, and intelligence over the adult years.

REFERENCES

Aldwin, C. M., Levenson, M. R., & Spiro, A. (1994). Vulnerability and resilience to combat exposure: Can stress have lifelong effects? *Psychology and Aging, 9,* 34–44.

Baltes, P. B. (1968). Longitudinal and cross-sectional sequences in the study of age and generation effects. *Human Development, 11,* 145–171.

Bentler, P. M. (1980). Multivariate analysis with latent variables: Causal modeling. *Annual Review of Psychology, 31,* 419–456.

Chown, S. M. (1959). Rigidity— A flexible concept. *Psychological Bulletin, 56,* 353–362.

Elder, G. H., Jr., Shanahan, M. J., & Clipp, E. C. (1994). When war comes to men's lives: Life-course patterns in family, war and health. *Psychology and Aging, 9,* 5–16.

Field, D., & Millsap, R. E. (1991). Personality in advanced old age: Continuity or change? *Journal of Gerontology: Psychological Sciences, 46,* P299–308.

Fraser, W. T. (1987). *Time: The familiar stranger.* Amherst, MA: University of Massachusetts Press.

Irion, J. C., & Blanchard-Fields, F. (1987). A cross-sectional comparison of adaptive coping in adulthood. *Journal of Gerontology, 42,* 502–504.

Kastenbaum, R. J., Derbin, V., Sabatini, P., & Artt, S. (1972). "The ages of me": Toward personal and interpersonal definitions of human aging. *Journal of Aging and Human Development, 3,* 197–211.

Labouvie-Vief, G., Hakim-Larson, J., DeVoe, M., & Schoeberlein, S. (1989). Emotions and self-regulation: A life-span view. *Human Development, 32,* 279–299.

Lachman, M. E., Weaver, S. L., Bandura, M., Elliott, E., & Lewkowicz, C. J. (1992). Improving memory and control beliefs through cognitive restructuring and self-generated strategies. *Journal of Gerontology: Psychological Sciences, 47,* P293–299.

Schaie, K. W. (1965). A general model for the study of developmental change. *Psychological Bulletin, 64,* 92–107.

Schaie, K. W., & Willis, S. L. (1991). Adult personality and psychomotor performance: Cross-sectional and longitudinal analyses. *Journal of Gerontology: Psychological Sciences, 46,* P275–284.

Whitbourne, S. K., & Waterman, A. S. (1979). Psychosocial development in young adulthood: Age and cohort comparisons. *Developmental Psychology, 15,* 373–378.

3

Aging of Appearance and Mobility

The physiological changes associated with the aging process occur as the result of an inexorable process that moves the individual ultimately toward death. The cause of aging is not yet known, and there are many theories that attempt to address the underlying mechanism that manifests itself in the aging of the body. Yet, the human body is remarkable in its ability to make many physiological changes in its functioning and integrity over time. Rather than simply progressing downward until the end of life, the body actively attempts to integrate the deleterious changes in its tissues into new levels of organization to preserve life and functioning for as long as possible. In reviewing the changes in the body with age, it is important to keep this point in mind, as the aging of the body is not synonymous with the aging of a machine (Whitbourne, 1985). In examining these age-related changes at the system or organ level, it is also important to keep in mind that the level of discussion here is at the descriptive rather than the explanatory level. Ultimately, the cause of aging will almost invariably be found to occur at the level of the genes, but until then theories of aging run a wide gamut involving many possible mechanisms (Hayflick, 1994).

In each of the areas of bodily functioning, I develop themes regarding the interaction of physical aging with psychological processes, and the way that individuals can affect the physical aging process through their own behaviors.

To help organize the information presented in these chapters, a summary chart of age-related changes is presented here (Table 3.1). This chart includes changes in the major organ systems in the body, the UIOLIs that can help

TABLE 3.1 Summary Chart of Age-Related Changes

System	Summary of changes	UIOLI	Bad habits	Risks	Possible identity changes
Appearance and mobility	Wrinkles Gray hair Changes in body mass and proportions Loss of bone strength	Exercise to strengthen muscles and bone	Sun exposure Smoking Sedentary lifestyle	Falling	Feeling of "looking old" Loss of confidence and perceived frailty
Cardiovascular and respiratory	Lower aerobic capacity Decreased ventilatory efficiency	Exercise to maintain aerobic capacity and respiratory efficiency	Smoking Poor diet Sedentary lifestyle Exposure to toxins	Overexertion	Inner feelings of morality
Digestive	Reduced gastric acid secretion Some changes in large intestine	Monitor intake of fiber and essential nutrients	Overuse of laxatives Poor eating habits	Malnutrition	Incontinence or constipation as inevitable features of aging
Excretory	Reduced functioning of kidneys Loss of bladder capacity	Behavioral methods of bladder control	Reliance on adult diapers	Dehydration Toxicity to medications Incontinence	Feelings of "senility"
Central nervous system	Loss of neurons Growth of dendrites on surviving neurons	Mental activity	Loss of interest in activities and disengagement	Early loss of cognitive abilities	Feelings of "senility"
Immune system	Decreased effectiveness of T-Cells Increased autoimmunity	Adequate coping strategies, e.g., social support	Use inappropriate coping strategies	Lowered resistance to infection	Feelings of lower competence due to illness
Reproductive	Some slowing of sexual responsiveness	Remain sexually active	Inflexibility regarding sexual involvement	Secondary impotence	Feelings of inadequacy and loss of attractiveness
Autonomic nervous system	Reduced temperature regulation Changes in sleep patterns	Adopt healthy sleep habits	Take daytime naps Anxiety over sleep changes	Hypothermia Reduced responsivness to heat Insomnia	

to preserve functioning in these systems, the bad habits that accelerate the aging process, the risks that come from failing to take advantage of UIOLIs or from not attending to these changes, and the possible influence on identity of these changes.

APPEARANCE

The outward signs of aging are most apparent in the aging of the individual's appearance. Contributing to the aging of appearance are changes in the skin, hair, facial structures, and body build. For the most part the effect of these changes is cosmetic; however, there are ramifications of the aging of these structures for the individual's overall physical functioning. Furthermore, as described in Chapter 1, the aging of appearance is for many individuals a critical threshold. It is known that many in Western society show prejudice and stereotyping toward those who appear old (Pruzinsky & Cash, 1990). Perhaps as a consequence, many older people would prefer to appear younger than they are, although men and women may be sensitive to different manifestations of their aging appearance (Harris, 1994).

The effects of aging on appearance begin to appear at a relatively early age in adulthood. The average person associates features such as gray hair, wrinkles, and a stooping posture with the changes of later life, but the bodily changes that ultimately cause the person to appear old begin as early as the 20s and 30s. These are changes that involve the skin, hair, fatty tissue, and muscle throughout the body. Degenerative changes that eventually alter the shape of the skeleton affect the individual's body build and stature. Most of these changes occur in a very gradual fashion and can be accommodated to over a period of years, even decades. In keeping with the multiple threshold model of aging, though, a point will be reached in later life when these changes become obvious to the individual. Perhaps the person takes a quick look when passing by a mirror or store window and sees the reflection of someone "old." Or the individual may notice that long-time friends have started to look middle aged or elderly, and start to realize that this label now hits home.

The media, of course, add immeasurably to the individual's sensitivity to the effects of aging on appearance. Interestingly, television commercials and magazine advertisements in which "anti-aging" products are promoted are increasingly being targeted to younger and younger consumers. Women in their 30s are warned that they must use these products now to stop or reverse the deleterious effects of aging on the skin. Clearly, these cosmetics manufacturers have found a receptive audience to their message, and have profited by preying on the desire of the young to avoid the ravages of age on appearance.

Skin

The development of creases, discoloration, furrows, sagging, and loss of resiliency are the most apparent age changes that occur in the skin. These changes are caused by a combination of alterations in the skin cells and the cells found throughout the structure of the skin as well as damage from photoaging, or exposure to the sun (Kligman, Grove, & Balin, 1985). Individuals vary widely in the rate at which the skin ages due to physiological variations among the older adult population and the differences associated with occupation, geographic location, and recreational exposure to the outside elements. Given the tremendous media and social attention given to the appearance of the skin as an indicator of age, it may seem suprising to learn that there is not an abundance of research on the aging of this organ system.

The cause of wrinkling, for example, one of the most widespread indicators of aging, is not fully known. There are a number of changes in the skin layers, however, that almost certainly contribute to the development of wrinkles. The epidermis, the outer layer of the skin, becomes flattened (Kligman et al. 1985). Further, as epidermal cells are replaced through cell renewal, they form less organized patterns, becoming less regularly arranged. These microscopic changes are reflected in visible changes of the geometric furrows visible on the surface of exposed areas of the skin, which become less orderly (Lavker, Kwong, & Kligman, 1980).

The sagging and wrinkling of the skin may be explained further by changes in the middle, dermal layer of the skin. Some of these changes involve collagen, a connective tissue making up a large part of the dermis that prevents tearing of the skin when it is stretched. A decrease in collagen in the dermis, in addition to loss of its flexibility, may contribute to the loosening of the dermis (Kligman et al., 1985). Elastin, which makes up a small but important proportion of the cells of the dermis, is responsible for maintaining the normal tension of the skin as well as allowing it to stretch to accommodate the movement of joints and muscles. Beginning at about age 30 and with increasing age in adulthood, the elastin fibers become more brittle so that the ability of the skin to conform to the moving limbs is greatly reduced. The skin is therefore more likely to sag, since when it is stretched out through movement, it cannot return to its original tension. Furthermore, although the amount of elastin in the skin increases, particularly in older persons with sun-damaged skin, this tissue is not structurally normal, so that it loses resiliency after being stretched.

In addition to these changes in the skin cells themselves, there are significant changes in the sweat and oil-producing glands within the dermis (Balin & Pratt, 1989; Kurban & Bhawan, 1990). The sweat glands in areas such as the palm of the hands and the underarms become less active, and although there may be some advantages in terms of a decrease in the discomfort sometimes caused by sweating, there is a significant drawback in that the older adult is less able to adapt physiologically to heat. The sebaceous glands lubricate the skin with the oil they secrete, and in older adults, these glands become less active. Consequently, the skin becomes dryer, rougher, and more likely to be damaged when rubbed by clothing or exposed to the elements. These changes lead not only to heightened risk of medical problems such as dermatitis (Grove, 1989) and pruritis (excessive itching), but they can lead the older individual to feel considerable discomfort (Kligman, 1989).

Subcutaneous fat, which is stored in the innermost layer of the skin, ordinarily provides an underlying padding that smooths out the curves of the arms, legs, and face and provides opacity to the color of the skin. As individuals age, the subcutaneous fat on the limbs decreases and instead collects in areas of fatty deposits, such as around the waist and hips. A decrease in muscle mass, as will be discussed later, further adds to the loss of firmness in the skin's appearance.

Other age-related alterations affecting the appearance of the skin occur on the skin surface. The coloring of light-skinned people becomes altered as the result of changes in the melanocytes, pigment-containing cells in the epidermis. There are reductions in the total number of melanocytes, and those that remain have fewer pigment granules so that the older adult is less likely to develop a tan when exposed to the sun. Irregular areas of dark pigmentation ("age" or "liver" spots, technically called *lentigo senilus*) often develop, as do pigmented outgrowths ("moles"), skin tags (small uncolored outgrowths), and angiomas, consisting of elevations of small blood vessels on the surface of the skin. Some capillaries and small arteries become dilated, creating small irregular colored lines on the skin. Varicose veins may appear on the skin of the legs, consisting of knotty, bluish, and cordlike irregularities of blood vessels. Capillary loss can lead fair-skinned people to look paler, and in general the blood vessels and bones become more visible under an apparently thinner skin surface.

The changes described so far have a negative effect on the protective functions of the skin as there is less of a barrier against environmental agents that can irritate the skin. Some of the age changes in the skin itself combine with changes in the blood vessels to have the effect of limiting the degree to which older adults can adapt to extremely hot and cold temperatures. The older adult sweats less in hot weather, and in cold weather conserves less heat due to thinning of the epidermis and the layer of subcutaneous fat. There are also alterations in the immune responsiveness of the skin and, along with a diminished blood supply to the skin, the immune system's response to surface inflammation is reduced (Balin & Pratt, 1989). Recovery from surface wounds to the skin and from surgical incisions is also impaired in the elderly (Kligman, Grove, & Balin, 1985).

Technically related to the skin, the nails also show signs of aging. They slow down in growth rate (Balin & Pratt, 1989; Kurban & Bhawan, 1990) and their appearance changes, as they become dull and yellow. Ridges and thickening also develop, particularly in the toenails, and the nails may appear to be hooked and curved (Kenney, 1989).

The Face

The face suffers a unique fate with respect to the aging process due to the fact that it is never (except perhaps in subzero temperatures) protected by clothing. Virtually any exposure to the outside air involves continuous contact with the potentially harmful effects of sun, wind, and various environmental toxins. The face, then, is particularly likely to undergo the deleterious changes associated with the effects of aging on the skin. In addition to damage from exposure to the elements, the skin on the face is stretched and furrowed in the course of everyday interactions, through the facial expressions of smiling, frowning, wrinkling the brow in concentration, and squinting the eyes. These expressions involve the use of certain muscle groups, which lead to characteristic wrinkling patterns from the pull of the muscles on the skin. Talking and eating, which involve movement of the jaw, can lead to the development of horizontal rings and vertical lines in the neck (Rossman, 1977).

The changes in the composition and amount of elastin in the dermis that lead to reduced flexibility of the skin have the effect of reducing the likelihood that the skin on the face will return to its original shape after being stretched along with the movement of facial muscles. Loss of subcutaneous fat and its shift to areas in which fat is deposited further accentuate the skin's sagging. This accumulation of fat and sagging is particularly noticeable under the chin, where the skin forms the infamous "double chin" of middle age and beyond. The loss of subcuntaneous fat also leads the skin on the face to develop a more translucent color.

There are also a series of changes in the underlying structure of facial features. The nose and ears become broader and longer (Damon, Seltzer, Stoudt, & Bell,

1972). The amount of bone in the jaw is reduced due to change in the bones (see pp. 61–62), an alteration that can shrink the lower part of the face. This process of bone loss is compounded by the deterioration and loss of teeth due, in large part, to years of poor dental hygiene practices in current cohorts of older adults. The need to wear dentures to replace diseased teeth can also change the older adult's facial appearance. The remaining teeth may become yellowed, cracked, and chipped, and the gums may recede markedly. As the enamel surface of the teeth wears down, they may become stained brown by substances such as food, tobacco, coffee, and tea.

Changes in the appearance of the eyes may also occur, beginning in the 40s, when adults increasingly need to wear eyeglasses. Even adults who have worn eyeglasses throughout their lives may now have to change to bifocals. The development of cataracts, which are pathological opacities in the lens of the eyes, may lead the individual to need to wear special eyeglasses that cause the eyes to look strangely magnified. An alternative to eyeglasses may be contact lenses, worn externally or surgically implanted, so that the older adult's appearance may not undergo the particular alterations due to the wearing of eyeglasses.

Other changes in the eyes occur due to changes in the surrounding structures. Wrinkles develop under and around the eyes, and there is the likelihood that the eyes will sag and accumulate fat and fluid (Mancil & Owsley, 1988). Dark pigment may accumulate around the eyes and eyelids, leading the eyes to develop a sunken appearance. The cornea may become duller and less translucent, and after the 70s, the individual may develop a condition known as *arcus senilus,* a white circle around the inside of the cornea. This change does not affect vision, but has a marked effect on appearance.

Hair

The most significant changes in the hair with age are that it becomes grayer and thinner. The appearance of gray hair is actually the outcome of the interspersing of pigmented hair and the white hair produced by the hair follicle after melanin production has ceased. The color of the individual's hair and the way it appears when mixed with white determines the shade of gray that appears on the head at any given point in the graying process. Eventually, all the pigment is lost and the overall hair color turns pure white, or white tinged with yellow or silver. The rate at which hair color changes varies from person to person in terms of the timing of its onset and the rate at which melanin production decreases across the scalp. Interestingly, although gray hair is thought to be universally associated with the aging process, the degree of hair grayness is not as reliable an indicator of a person's age as is the extent to which hair on the body (axillary and pubic) has turned gray (Kenney, 1989).

Gradual and general thinning of scalp hair occurs in both sexes over the years of adulthood, although loss of hair is popularly regarded as a problem for men only. Hair loss is the result of destruction or regression of the germination centers that produce hair follicles underneath the surface of the skin. However, the cause of hair loss is somewhat different in the case of pattern baldness, the most frequent form of baldness and the type that is genetically determined. In men with pattern baldness, the hair follicles do not die but change the type of hair they produce. Rather than producing course terminal hair, which is visible on the scalp, the hair follicles produce fine, almost invisible, hair called vellus hair. Men may also experience thinning of the hairs in the beard, but at the same time may develop longer and coarser hair on the eyebrows and inside the ear. Patches of coarse terminal hair may develop on the face of women, particularly around the area of the chin.

Body Build

Height. It is well-established that over the course of adulthood there is a consistent pattern of a reduction in standing height, occurring at a greater rate after the 50s and particularly pronounced in women (Adams, Davies, & Sweetname, 1970; Shephard, 1978). Qualifying this general statement, however, is the fact that most of what is known about the effects of aging on bodily stature is derived from cross-sectional studies comparing adults of different ages. These cross-sectional studies may present an overly negative view of age effects in adulthood because they involve comparing people who differ both in age and in exposure to early nutritional and other environmental influences. Although height is in large part genetically determined, it is also sensitive to the individual's intake of adequent vitamins and minerals during the years of bone development in childhood. Because the level of nutrition in the general population has become more favorable throughout the 20th century, younger cohorts are likely to be taller than older ones. What appears to be a "decrease" in height in older age groups may reflect the fact that the earlier cohorts did not grow to the same height as have later cohorts of adults. Some evidence in favor of a general decline in height in later adulthood, however, comes from a longitudinal study of a small but randomly selected sample of adults ranging from 55 to 64 years of age who were followed over a period of 11 years (Adams, Davies, & Sweetname, 1970). There was a slight decrease of height (one inch for women; half an inch for men) observed over the course of the study; this decrease is less than is generally reported on the basis of cross-sectional studies. To the extent that a height decrease does occur, the main reason appears to be loss of bone mineral content in the vertebrae, leading to their collapse and a compression of the length of the spine (Garn, 1975). Changes in the joints and flattening of the arches of the feet can further contribute to height loss (Kenney, 1989).

Weight. Information on the effects of aging on body weight is subject to the same criticism as is true for studies on height; namely, that the results are based on cross-sectional studies and therefore potentially confound generational differences with the true effects of aging on height. In the case of weight, however, the problem takes on a different configuration because generational differences in nutritional status can affect weight throughout adulthood, not only in the formative years of childhood and adolescence as is the case for height. Cohorts of adults who are currently considered elderly are more likely to be living according to the eating habits of the early and middle 20th century, a time when Americans were almost oblivious to the fat and carbohydrate content of the foods they consumed. A further confound is presented by the factors that might affect food intake in the elderly, whose eating patterns may reflect social and psychological changes associated with the eating process that cause them to become undernourished. Consequently, it is not known whether the apparent effects of aging on body weight are due to intrinsic aging changes or to social, cultural, and personality influences on eating patterns.

These considerations in mind, current cross-sectional data on the effects of aging on body weight indiate a pattern of weight gain throughout the period of middle adulthood followed by a dropping off of weight through the later years of old age (Parizkova, 1974; Shephard, 1978). In part, this apparent pattern of age changes in weight may be an artifact of the tendency for the overweight and obese to die at earlier ages. The survivors represent a group whose weight has remained low throughout their adult years and now that the heavier individuals are no longer around, the average weight of older adults more closely reflects the lighter weight of this segment of the population. (McArdle, Katch, & Katch, 1991).

Body composition. Most of the initial weight gain observed in middle adulthood is due to an accumulation of body fat, particularly around the waist and hips (the proverbial "middle-aged spread"). The weight loss that occurs in the later years of adulthood is not due to a slimming down of the torso but to a loss of lean body mass consisting of muscle and bone (Chien, et al., 1975; Ellis, Shukla, Cohn, & Pierson, 1974). This loss continues throughout the decades of the 70s and 80s, at least as indicated cross-sectionally (Baumgartner, Stauber, McHugh, Koehler, & Garry, 1995). Consequently, very old adults may have very thin extremities but fatty areas in the chin, waist, and hips. Middle-aged and older women are particularly likely to experience this accumulation of body fat around the torso, with a gain of abdominal girth amounting to 25%–35% across the adult years compared to 6%–16% for men over a comparable time period (Shephard, 1978). Recent changes in lifestyle and improved nutrition may be altering this trend, with current cohorts of older women showing a decrease rather than an increase in body fat (Rico, Revilla, Hernandez, Gonzalez-Riola, & Villa, 1993).

Psychological Interactions

A person's appearance is highly individualized, and the way the individual's face and body look provide important cues to the self and others regarding personal identity. As the individual's appearance changes in later adulthood, the potential exists for his or her identity to change in corresponding ways, some of them negative. Comparisons of present appearance with pictures or memories of early adulthood may be painful and damaging to self-esteem for people who valued their youthful image (Fenske & Albers, 1990; Kleinsmith & Perricone, 1989). At the same time, young people may be repulsed by the wrinkles, discolorations, and white hair of the older person, causing the aged individual to feel rejected and isolated (Kligman, 1989). These changes involve primarily the face, but can also include changes in exposed areas of the body. With regard to body build, changes in body fat and muscle tone that lead to the appearance of a sagging or heavier body shape can result in increased identification of the self as moving away from the figure of youth. The development of middle-aged spread may be one of the first occurrences to trigger recognition of the self as aging, even before the first gray hairs have made their presence known. The changes brought about by aging are likely to be of heightened concern in America and many parts of Europe, where social values equate youth with attractiveness, particularly for women. Consequently, the threshold for recognizing the effects of aging on appearance is likely to be low, because individuals beginning at a very early age are primed to watch for what they are socialized to regard as the erosion of their youthful appearance by the aging process.

Compensatory Measures

Fortunately, despite the low threshold for recognizing age effects on appearance, there are many possible routes that individuals can take to compensate for the aging of the face and body. The most radical alternative is cosmetic surgery, including such procedures as face lifts and liposuction. The average adult is unlikely to sacrifice the expense and time needed to take such drastic action. More realistic are the preventative and compensatory steps that are available to ordinary individuals involving the use of particular cosmetic products, the UIOLI of exercise, and the avoidance of bad habits.

The primary method that individuals can use to prevent the effects of aging on the skin is for fair-skinned people to start early in life to avoid the worst bad habit of all—direct exposure to the sun, and to use sunblocks when exposure cannot be avoided (Gilchrest, 1989). Cigarette smoke can also be harmful to the skin. Increasingly, young people are being educated about the dangers of both of these sources of premature aging, both in the context of avoiding the harmful effects of aging and to reduce the risk of developing cancer.

Once age changes in the skin have become manifest, however, there are still many possible ways for the individual to take compensatory measures. To counteract the fragility, sensitivity, and dryness of the skin, the individual can use sunscreens, emollients, and fragrance-free cosmetics. As it is traditional for women to use facial cosmetics, the proper choice of color and coverup techniques can enhance the individual's appearance (O'Donoghue, 1991). Men tend not to use these commercial preparations, although hair dyes for men are becoming increasingly popular. Hair loss is a problem more easily compensated by women, who can more subtly wear a wig or hairpiece than men, who must either find a way to camouflage a toupee or seek costly hair replacement therapy.

Even with these compensatory measures, men and women eventually reach a point where their face and hair have become distinctly "old," at least as recognized by others. Short of maintaining continuous coverage of the face to protect it from the environmental hazards of exposure to the sun, there is little that the individual can do to reverse the effects of aging on the appearance of the face and hair.

By contrast, changes in body build can be compensated, often in remarkable ways, by regular involvement in activities and exercise that maintain muscle tone and reduce fat deposits around the waist and hips. It is well established that participation in active sports and exercise activity can offset the deleterious effects of aging on the accumulation of body fat. Unlike the general population, endurance athletes do not gain weight and they maintain their muscular physiques throughout adulthood for as long as they continue to train (Grimby & Saltin, 1966; Kavanagh & Shephard, 1978; Suominen, Heikkinen, Parkatti, Forsberg, & Kiiskinen, 1980). Participation in exercise training programs by middle-aged and elderly adults who were sedentary throughout their lives can also be of value in reducing body fat and increasing muscle mass. By engaging in vigorous walking, jogging, or cycling for 30 to 60 minutes a day for 3 to 4 days a week, the sedentary adult can expect to achieve positive results in a period as short as 10–20 weeks (Whitbourne, 1985). Heavy resistance training is another compensatory measure that can "defy certain aspects of the normal aging process" in terms of body fat and muscle mass (McArdle, Katch, & Katch, 1991, p. 707). Ironically, identity can interact in potentially damaging ways with the need to exercise. Individuals who feel that their bodies are unattractive may stay away from the gym, thus depriving themselves of valuable exercise opportunities. If they can be encouraged to overcome this reluctance, they can experience improvement both in physical functioning and bodily identity (McAuley, Bane, Rudolph, & Lox, 1995).

It is also quite probable that the effects of aging on appearance occur below the level of awareness for the individual whose threshold for recognizing such changes is high. Aged individuals whose identity has never hinged on their outward appearance may not give a second thought to their white hair and wrinkles. Others, due to their cultural or ethnic background, might regard their aging appearance with pride and the gray hair and wrinkles as badges signifying their success in living to a ripe maturity. For these individuals, aging is not equivalent to unattractiveness. Conversely, older individuals who unrealistically hold onto a youthful self-image that no longer is appropriate may appear comical if not pathetic to others. In this case, the threshold of awareness needs to be brought closer to objective reality so that the older individual avoids ridicule and perhaps even ostracism by older adult peers.

MOBILITY

The individual's ability to move around in the physical environment is a function of bone strength, the strength and flexibility of the joints between the bones, integrity of the tendons and ligaments that connect muscle to bone, and contractility of the muscles that control flexion and extension. Mobility changes in important ways over the course of the adult years as each component that contributes to it undergoes significant losses. Consequently, movement becomes more difficult, more painful, and often less effective for the older adult. For many individuals, thresholds of aging become painfully crossed with each newly-discovered joint ache or mobility restriction, sometimes beginning in the 40s. It is possible, however, for the older adult to find ways to compensate for potentially debilitating age-related losses, largely through the UIOLI of active participation in various forms of exercise.

Muscles

Researchers who study the physical effects of aging focus on the skeletal muscles, which are controlled by the motoneurons in the central nervous system and hence respond to external stimulation and cortical efforts to control their operation. The skeletal muscles make movement possible because as they contract, they exert a force on the bones to which they are attached via the tendons. Researchers who study the aging process are interested in both the structure of the muscles, quantified by number and size, as well as muscle function, which is measured in terms of muscle strength and endurance.

Age effects. The functional variable having the greatest direct relevance to aging is muscle strength, and although it is commonly held that muscle strength decreases linearly and uniformly across adulthood, there are individual variations that can lead to important deviations from such a general pattern of decline. The effects of aging vary according to which gender is being tested, the general level of activity in which the individual has typically engaged, and the particular muscle group being tested. Whether the type of muscle strength being assessed is static (isometric) or dynamic is another influence on the extent to which age effects are manifest. Taking these considerations into account, the general statement can be made that there is little reduction in muscle strength until at least ages 40 or 50 years with a loss of approximately 10% to 20% through ages 60 or 70. More severe losses of 30% to 40% become apparent after ages 70 to 80, losses that are more pronounced in the muscles of the lower extremities (McArdle et al., 1991; Whitbourne, 1985). By contrast, aging is kinder to eccentric strength, which is preserved through the 70s and 80s in men and women (Hortobágyi, Zheng, Weidner, Lambert, Westbrook, & Houmard, 1995). This is the type of strength involved in lowering arm weights, slowing down while walking, and going down the stairs.

In attempting to account for this pattern of diminishing muscle strength, researchers have focused on the loss of muscle mass due to atrophy of muscle fibers, particularly the "fast twitch" fibers important in developing the rapidly accelerating powerful contractions normally associated with strength. The "slow twitch" fibers involved in maintaining posture and muscular contractions over protacted periods of exertion remain constant over the adult years. The atrophy of fast-twitch fibers is thought to result from the loss of the motoneurons that activate the muscles. After the muscle fiber dies, it is replaced initially by connective tissue and in its final stages, by fat (Fiatrone & Evans, 1993; Whitbourne, 1985). However, declines in muscle strength are not completely accounted for by loss of muscle mass, and there are other influences on age effects on muscle strength as yet to be determined (Kallman, Plato, & Tobin, 1990; Overend, Cunningham, Kramer, Lefcoe, & Paterson, 1992). Furthermore, changes in muscle mass have no apparent effect on eccentric strength (Hortobágyi et al., 1995).

Psychological interactions. Virtually every activity carried out in the routine course of a day requires the effective use of muscles, even what might otherwise be regarded as the sedentary activities of reading (holding a book and turning the pages), watching television (pushing those buttons on the remote control), or using a computer (pushing down the keys). Adaptation to one's physical environment requires, on a very basic level, the ability to have one's motions be accurate and efficient. The skeletal muscles make it possible for the individual to perform necessary activities in the home, at work, and during recreational activities. Even if these activities do not require strength or exertion, they very often depend on muscular coordination. To feel competent in performing these actions, the individual must be able to complete these activities within a small range of error, with some degree of accuracy and effectiveness, and without undue fatigue. The more demanding the individual's range of activities and the more central they are to the individual's sense of competence, the more it might be expected that the individual will be vigilant for the first signs of loss of power and effectiveness due to aging.

The threshold for aging of the muscles, then, may involve separate but related components of strength, endurance, and coordination. In addition, the individual's threshold for aging of the muscles may involve physical appearance. Those adults who value a muscular physique (and this is becoming an increasing number of people) may be particularly affected by the sense that they have crossed the threshold from having a muscular body to one that has turned to fat. In order to retain their muscular appearance, they will have to work much harder at controlling their diet and carrying out their exercise regimes. Loss of muscular coordination, however, may be more difficult to monitor and control, and perhaps even more difficult to accommodate to. It is socially awkward to be in a situation where one cannot effectively walk, run, or carry a cup of coffee down the hall without spilling it. Missing a step and falling, being unable to connect a broken wire, and failing to button one's coat can create distress when others are present. Although such losses are not inevitable and may even be reversed or at least slowed down with exercise and precautionary measures, they have the potential to stimulate significant changes in the older adult's feelings of physical competence and identity.

Compensatory measures. Counteracting what might appear to be a picture of inevitable decline in muscle strength is evidence, accruing from the 1970s, that a regular program of exercise can serve as a significant UIOLI, helping the aging person compensate substantially for the loss of fast-twitch muscle fibers. Although there is nothing that can be done to stop the deafferation and loss of muscle cells, the remaining fibers can be strengthened and work efficiency increased through exercise training even in persons as old as 90 years (Fiatarone et al., 1990; Grimby & Saltin, 1983). Inactivity, conversely, is one of those bad habits that can accelerate the loss of muscle strength (Bortz, 1982a; Rikli & Busch, 1986; Sallis, Haskell, Wood, & Fortman, 1985). However, even a previously sedentary individual can gain signifcantly in strength as the result of participation in a short-term exercise training study, amounting to a relative increase comparable to that achieved by a young adult in a similar program. This training, however, must be relatively intense and adjusted continuously to take advantage of training improvements as they occur (McArdle et al., 1991). Resistance training, rather than aerobic exercise alone, also appears to be critical for preserving muscle fiber size and strength, as demonstrated both in endurance athletes (Klitgaard et al., 1990) and previously sedentary men and women (Charette, McEvoy, Pyka, Snow-Harter, & Guido, 1991; Pyka, Lindenberger, Charette, & Marcus, 1994).

Exercise training is the mode of compensation for muscular deterioration in adulthood that is most readily accessible to the average adult. If the individual has access to a weight training facility, so much the better, but even without special machines activities such as walking, light jogging, and lifting small hand weights can counteract the process of muscle atrophy. As mentioned earlier in the context of appearance, experimental studies of the effects of exercise training provide clearcut evidence for the effectiveness of this important compensatory mechanism. With regard to muscle functioning in particular, exercise training enhances the metabolic efficiency of muscles, decreased accumulation of lactate during exercise (the major source of muscular cramps and discomfort), greater fiber size, and more widespread recruitment of motor units so that the remaining muscle fibers in general become more "fit" . Furthermore, neural activation of muscle fibers can be augmented by exercise so that a primary source of muscle loss may be countered (Whitbourne, 1985).

Bones

The bones provide the rigid strength that supports muscular movement, posture, and the structural framework of the body. Bone consists of living cells, called osteocytes, suspended in a matrix of collagen and inorganic salts made up primarily of calcium, an inorganic mineral. Collagen provides resilience and flexibility to the bone, and the calcium salts make it firm. The bone matrix includes two types of bone that vary in structure and location within the skeleton. Compact (or cortical) bone, which comprises the majority of the skeleton, is located in the outer layer of the bones. It is very dense and provides the bone with mechanical strength. Trabecular (or cancellous) bone is located in the interior of bones and at the articular or joint ends. It is spongy in quality, with many large openings interspersed through it.

Age effects. Bone development in early life is marked by two processes. One is the increase in the thickness and length of the bones through the growth of temporary or woven bone which is characterized by loosely organized collagenous fiber bundles. As the bone reaches its adult size, the woven bone is replaced by lamellar bone, in which the collagen matrix is organized into layers or lamellae. The second process of bone development is ossification, the replacement of the cartilage that is the main component of bone in early childhood with the mature calcified bone matrix. Once the bones have fully developed, however, they are constantly in a state of flux through the process of remodeling, an internal reconstruction of the bone tissue. The lifespan of osteocytes is limited to approximately 25 years, and they do not replace themselves through cell division. Bone substance containing dying osteocytes must therefore be removed and replaced by bone containing new osteocytes. Removal of old bone substance is accomplished by osteoclasts, and new osteocytes are created by cells called osteoblasts, which are the precursors of the new osteocytes. This remodeling process operates throughout adulthood under the influence of the circulatory system, the endocrine system, and the mechanical pressures placed on the bone through the activity of the muscles (Rogers, 1982).

Nutrition, overall physical health (freedom from infection), and psychological well-being contribute to the maintenance of bone strength in later adulthood. Overall, however, the thrust of bone development in adulthood is the loss of bone strength, resulting in diminished ability of the bones to withstand mechanical pressure and to show greater vulnerability to fracture (Whitbourne, 1985). The decrease in various measures of bone strength ranges from 5% to 12% per decade from the 20s through the 90s (McCalden, McGeough, Barker, & Court-Brown, 1993).

The loss of bone strength in adulthood is generally explained as a function of the loss of bone mineral content, so that with increasing porosity, the bone becomes weakened so that it cannot support the loads it must bear (McCalden et al., 1993). The extent to which bone mass decreases over the years of adulthood amounts to approximately 20 to 30 percent of total bone mineral content in women, and approximately half that amount in men (Mazess, 1982; Riggs, et al., 1981). The period of maximum bone loss is between the 50s and the 70s (Sparrow, Beausoleil, Garvey, Rosner, & Silbert, 1982), with greater loss in the trabecular than in the compact bone (Avioli, 1982).

The progressive decline in bone strength and bone mineral content in adulthood is difficult to separate from the disease known as osteoporosis, in which bones become brittle and weak to the point of breaking with little or no apparent stress placed upon them. The explanation of the underlying process that causes loss of bone mineral content is that the rate of resorption exceeds that of new bone growth in later adulthood, giving a net result of a reduction in bone mass (Cohn, Vaswani, Zanzi, & Ellis, 1976; Sherman et al., 1992). In part, bone density and the loss of bone mass in the later years of adulthood may be a function of genetic factors (Dargent & Breart, 1993; Kelly et al., 1993). Lifestyle also seems to play a role, however, including factors such as physical activity, smoking, alcohol use, and diet which can account for 50%-60% of the variation in bone density (Krall & Dawson-Hughes, 1993). There are also hormonal influences on bone mass, as indicated by the observation that bone mineral loss in women proceeds at a higher rate in post-menopausal women who are no longer producing estrogen in monthly cycles (Nuti & Martini, 1993). Researchers have also been intrigued by the fact that growth hormone production declines in later adulthood, a change that parallels the decline of bone mineral content (Slootweg, 1993). However, the experimental administration of growth hormone as a stimulant to bone growth has not proven to be effective in increasing bone mass (Corpas, Harman, & Blackman, 1993; Marcus, Holloway, & Butterfield, 1993). The osteoblasts of older adults do not seem to be able to take advantage of increased levels of growth hormone, suggesting that the deficiency is more than hormonal (Pfeilschifter, et al., 1993).

Psychological interactions. Given the importance of the integrity of the bones to every move that an individual makes, it would seem to follow that aging of the bones would have the potential to have a particularly significant impact on the quality of the older adult's daily life. However, these effects are probably difficult for the older person to differentiate from the general effects of aging on the musculoskeletal system as a whole. Of greater significance to the aging adult is the threat or actuality of bone fractures due to the reduced resistance of the bones to mechanical stresses or pressure. For the older adult, particularly a woman, the experience of breaking a limb is highly probable due to reduced bone mass (Dargent & Breart, 1993), and it is likely that the fracture will occur in association with a fall.

Estimates of the prevalence of falling in the over-65 community-dwelling population estimates range from a low of approximately one-third (Tinetti, Speechley, & Ginter, 1988) to as many as 40% (Downton & Andrews, 1990), to one-half of all older adults (Walker & Howland, 1991). These rates of falling translate into a figure of over 250,000 individuals who are hospitalized each year in the U.S. for treatment of a fractured hip (Allegrante, MacKenzie, Robbins, & Cornell, 1991). In addition to the need for hospitalization, a fall often has a permanent effect on the older individual's everyday life. Of those who experience a fall, it is estimated that about one-quarter significantly restrict their daily activities to avoid future accidents (Tinetti et al., 1988). Those who break their hip, a misfortune that disproportionately afflicts women, are more likely to suffer long-term disability and dependency (Roberto, 1992).

As impressive as these statistics are, it is nevertheless true that not all older adults are victims of falling. There are a number of interacting age-related processes that operate to increase the older adult's likelihood of suffering from a disabling fall, including musculoskeletal and changes and sensory losses (Woollacott, 1993). Those elderly who are most at risk of falling include people who suffer from visual impairment in addition to bone loss, neurological deficits, gait disturbance, and loss of muscle strength and coordination (Craven & Bruno, 1986; Felson, Anderson, Hannan, Milton, Wilson, & Kiel, 1989; Kelsey & Hoffman, 1987, Lord, Clark, & Webster, 1991; Morse, Tylko, & Dixon, 1987). Cognitive impairments, particularly those associated with Alzheimer's disease, contribute further to heightened risk of falling (Morris, Rubin, Morris, & Mandel, 1987; Spar, la-Rue, Hewes, & Fairbanks, 1987; Tinetti, Speechley, & Ginter, 1988). Psychological factors, such as anxiety and depression, also increase the older individual's risk of falling (Tinetti, Richman, & Powell, 1990; Vetter & Ford, 1989). Disability and a history of smoking are two final contributing risk factors (Vetter & Ford, 1989).

The experience of falling can lead to a vicious cycle in which one fall leads the individual to become fearful of more falls, and as a result, to walk less securely and confidently. This loss of a sense of security can serve to increase the risk that the older person will lose his or her balance and actually make him or her more likely to fall in the future. The experience of falling can also lead the individual to develop a low "self-efficacy" as being unable to avoid a fall, further impairing her balance and gait (Downton & Andrews, 1990; Tinetti, Richman, & Powell, 1990).

Apart from the physical risk factors that increase the likelihood of falling, there exist psychological variables related to the elderly person's attitudes toward his or her abilities and sense of security (Tinetti & Powell, 1993). Even without a fall or actual bone fracture, then, the older adult may experience some of the psychological consequences associated with lessened mobility (Myers et al., 1996). Furthermore, necessary daily activities that were previously conducted with little concern, such as descending a steep flight of stairs or walking on icy pavement, may create fear and hence avoidance. The experience of falling, in this sense, might precipitate rapid crossing of a threshold regarding the fragility of the bones and lead to a premature loss of autonomy and sense of competence.

Given the high psychological and physical cost of falling, it might be expected that elderly individuals, particularly women, have a low threshold for age changes that might make them vulnerable to this problem. The further lowering of the threshold after a fall may be an expectable response. There is some indication that such awareness of the possibility of falling can be ultimately of some benefit if the older adult develops problem-oriented coping strategies rather than trying to pretend that the fall or fracture never occurred. Confronting the problem directly is a useful coping strategy if it leads the older person to take advantage of activities that can benefit recovery or aid in prevention (Roberto, 1992).

Compensatory mechanisms. The main implication of research on the effects of aging on structural and functional properties of bone is that the reason for loss of strength with adult age is a decrease in skeletal mass, reflected in loss of bone mineral content. It is well known that activity levels directly influence bone mass as is reflected, for example, in the fact that astronauts lose relatively large amounts of bone mineral during their period of weightlessness in space when no stress is placed on the bones. Under less extreme conditions of inactivity, such as prolonged bed rest, even young adults can suffer significant bone loss. Without mechanical pressures provided by moving limbs, the rate of destruction of old bone exceeds the rate of new bone growth.

Following this line of reasoning, it would seem that a logical way to compensate for bone loss in the aged is to take advantage of the UIOLI provided by resistance training, in which the individual lifts weights under controlled conditions that place stress on particular muscles and, hence, the bones that are connected to those muscles. In the 1980s, as the effectiveness of this intervention was explored, evidence began to accumulate in support of the advantages of weight training as a means of compensating for bone loss (Dalsky, 1988; Krolner, 1982; Rikli & McManis, 1990; Smith, 1981). In addition to its effects on muscle mass, then, resistance training can prove beneficial, particularly for women, to help offset the effects of aging on bone.

Joints

The smooth functioning of the joints of the body is accomplished by the strength and elasticity of the tendons and ligaments and the synovial fluid, which enables frictionless movement of the bones as they rub against each other within the protective encasement of the joint capsule.

Age effects. Although the aging of joints is most commonly associated with the later years of life, degenerative processes that reduce the functional efficiency of the joints begins to take effect even before the individual reaches skeletal maturity. Restrictions of movement and discomfort are therefore a potential problem for adults of any age, but they occur with increasing frequency as age progresses. Joint functioning peaks in efficiency in the 20s and decreases continuously thereafter (Bortz, 1982b).

The decline in joint functioning can be accounted for by age losses in virtually every structural component of the joint. The articular surfaces of the ends of the bones at the joints are ordinarily protected by clear cartilage from the frictional damage that direct bone-to-bone contact would create. Starting in the 20s and 30s, the arterial cartilage begins to thin, fray, shred, and crack (Adrian, 1981; Chung, 1966a). Unprotected by cartilage, the underlying bone eventually begins to wear away. At the same time, outgrowths of cartilage develop and these interfere with the smooth movement of the joint.

The articular surfaces of the joints are enclosed within a sac formed by connective tissue called bursa. The bursa is filled with synovial fluid, a lubricant secreted by the bursal membranes. This lubricant allows the articular surfaces to glide freely against each other. A series of age-related changes in the connective tissue throughout the bursa result in increasing restriction of joint movement (Adrian, 1981). These changes include the growth of calcified and fibrous tissue that make the connective tissue less pliable and easily flexed (Chung, 1966b), causing the individual to feel that the joints are "stiffening." These results of normal aging are similar to osteoarthritis, a common disease afflicting the elderly in which excessive bone substance develops in the joints, limiting the individual's range of movement and causing joint pain (Rogers, 1982). As a result of joint stiffening, greater muscle strength is required to activate or move the joint. Age-related weakening of the muscles further contributes to restrictions in range of movement due to changes in the joints themselves (Vandervoort et al., 1992).

In finding a cause for deteriorative changes in the joints, researchers have not been able to single out one primary factor. There are almost certainly changes at the cellular level in the structure of collagen and elastin comparable to those that occur in the tissues within the dermis. Such changes are likely to contribute to loss of flexibility, strength, and resiliency of connective tissue. Diminished efficiency of circulation may contribute further to deteriorative changes. Since the cartilage receives little vascular supply to begin with, any reductions in adulthood due to aging or arterial disease will further reduce its reparative ability.

The most commonly accepted implicit model for the aging of the joints is the "wear and tear" theory (Brooks & Fahey, 1984), and although this is not generally considered a good explanation of the aging process, it appears to have some value in explaining the aging of the joints. These bodily areas are subjected to an extreme amount of trauma throughout life, due partly to the constant stresses placed upon them during movement. Over the course of the adult years, the individual is also likely to experience many major and minor strains and sprains encountered during everyday activities and during strenuous exercise. Unlike the muscles, the joints do not seem to benefit from their continued use. On the contrary, the joints seem to be victim to reparative processes that ultimately prove to be detrimental. For example, in response to the repair processes that stimulate growth of new fibrous tissue and bone at the sites of the joints, excess material accumulates that interferes with the effective working of the joints. Rather than a simple wear-and-tear model, which seems more appropriate for machines than humans, a more useful model incorporates the reparative processes of living organisms: a wear, tear, and repair process. Unfortunately, for the majority of elderly persons, the repair process of the joints is a faulty one.

Psychological interactions. Degenerative changes in the joints, whether due to osteoarthritis or the normal aging process, have many pervasive effects on the individual's life and are a major source of disability (Hughes, Cordray, & Spiker, 1984; Hughes, Edelman, Singer, & Chang, 1993). Restriction of movement in the upper limbs rules out many enjoyable leisure activities such as handcrafts, racquet sports, and playing musical instruments such as the piano, and can make it difficult for the individual to perform occupations that require finely tuned motor skills and repetitive movements of the hand and arm. Pain and lack of flexibility in the legs and feet can slow the individual's pace when walking. Restricted movement of the hip leads to a number of restrictions, such as limping, difficulty climbing stairs, and rising from a chair or sofa. Involvement of the knee adds to these difficulties. Degenerative changes in the spine, in addition, often result in back pain which, if not restrictive in and of itself, has the constant potential to detract from the individual's enjoyment of both occupational and recreational activities. This restriction of activities, combined with the experience of pain, may lead the individual to suffer from clinical symptoms of depression (Williamson & Schulz, 1992).

Given that the joints must move to perform almost any action, it is difficult for the individual with pain or stiffness to avoid being confronted with the effects of aging. Joint pain has the dubious distinction of being impossible to ignore, forget, or disguise. The ache of a sore shoulder, elbow, or knee is not very easily dismissed by the individual who experiences it. As a result, the adult who would rather disregard the physical aging process will be hard-pressed to overcome the feelings of pain and restriction that accompany movement problems. The threshold for joint changes is likely to be very low, then, with age changes readily perceived and not readily dismissed.

Compensatory mechanisms. If the continuous use of the joints is a factor responsible for the deleterious effects of aging, it would follow that the older adult would be well advised to refrain from the strain involved in excess exercise. Nevertheless, there are decided benefits of exercise training in terms of alleviating some of the more distressing aspects of joint deterioration such as pain and restriction of movement. For positive outcomes to result from exercise training, however, there must be progressive increments built into the program so that at no one point is a joint hyperextended or overstressed (Shephard, 1982). Muscle and joint problems can be reduced through aerobic exercise training, but if the purpose of training is to enhance joint flexibility and range of movement, the program should be adapted to suit this objective.

The types of exercise that appear to offset the effects of aging on joint functioning include light jogging (Buccola & Stone, 1975), finger lifting (Chapman, deVries, & Swezey, 1972), flexibility exercises (Frekany & Leslie, 1975), rhythmic exercise (Lesser, 1978), dance (Munn, 1981), and strengthening (Blanpied & Smidt, 1993). It would be unrealistic to claim that these exercise programs can undo the damage to joints that has accumulated over a lifetime. Nevertheless, these programs can ameliorate restrictions on the older adult's life caused by limited flexibility and joint pain (Brooks & Fahey, 1984). Perhaps the greatest benefit of these programs is strengthening of the muscles that support the joints so that less stress is placed upon impaired tendons, ligaments, and arterial surfaces.

Secondary, movement stimulates cardiovascular activity, enhancing the vascular supply that promotes healthy reparative processes in the exercising joints.

OVERALL IMPLICATIONS FOR IDENTITY

Given the significance of age-related changes in appearance and movement for many adults, and the likelihood of changes in these systems becoming significant aging thresholds, it is difficult to comprehend the relative lack of research in either area. We can assume, however, that on the basis of the few studies identifying fears of aging with regard to loss of independence and changes in appearance that these are some of the most salient identifiers of aging to individuals in the general population. Interestingly, some very able individuals may be extremely resilient to the effects of aging on physical strength and mobility. Although one might suspect that people who were star athletes in their young adult years would be most sensitive to the limitations presented by the aging process, it is possible that early success in this realm may insulate the individual from crossing the threshold as early or as harshly as more sedentary individuals (McGue, Hirsch, & Lykken, 1993). An individual whose identity is based on the self-perception of being athletically competent may retain this identity through assimilation for many years into adulthood, particularly as the individual compares the self to others who are less athletically inclined. As long as the individual continues to maintain a high level of physical activity, there is no reason for this identity to be challenged or for negative adaptational consequences to occur. However, such an individual may be vulnerable to more extremely negative effects of a discrepancy between this identity as competent and the reality of an accident or physical failure. The threshold will be crossed with a vengeance, and the individual may resort to the opposite extreme of accommodation and hopelessness.

REFERENCES

Adams, P., Davies, G. T., & Sweetname, P. (1970). Osteoporosis and the effect of aging on bone mass in elderly men and women. *Quarterly Journal of Medicine, 39,* 601–615.

Adrian, M. J. (1981). Flexibility in the aging adult. In E. L. Smith & R. C. Serfass (Ed.), *Exercise and aging: The scientific basis* (pp. 45–58). Hillsdale, NJ: Enslow.

Allegrante, J. P., MacKenzie, C. R., Robbins, L., & Cornell, C. N. (1991). Hip fracture in older persons: Does self-efficacy-based intervention have a role in rehabilitation? *Arthritis Care and Research, 4,* 39–47.

Avioli, L. V. (1982). Aging, bone, and osteoporsis. In S. G. Korenmann (Ed.), *Endocrine aspects of aging.* New York: Elsevier Biomedical.

Balin, A. K., & Pratt, L. A. (1989). Physiological consequences of human skin aging. *Cutis, 43,* 431–436.

Baumgartner, R. N., Stauber, P. M., McHugh, D., Koehler, K. M., & Garry, P. J. (1995). Cross-sectional age differences in body composition in persons 60+ years of age. *Journal of Gerontology: Medical Sciences, 50A,* M307–316.

Blanpied, P., & Smidt, G. L. (1993). The difference in stiffness of the active plantarflexors between young and elderly human females. *Journal of Gerontology: Medical Sciences, 48,* M58–63.

Bortz, W. M. I. (1982a). Disuse and aging. *Journal of the American Medical Association, 248,* 1203–1208.

Bortz, W. M. I. (1982b). Disuse and aging. *Journal of the American Medical Association, 248,* 1203–1208.

Brooks, G. A., & Fahey, T. D. (1984). *Exercise physiology: Human bioenergetics and its applications.* New York: Wiley.

Buccola, V., & Stone, W. J. (1975). Effects of a jogging and cycling program on physiological and personality variables in aged men. *Research Quarterly, 46,* 134–139.

Chapman, E. A., deVries, H. A., & Swezey, R. (1972). Joint stiffness: Effects of exercise on old and young men. *Journal of Gerontology, 27,* 218–221.

Charette, S. L., McEvoy, L., Pyka, G., Snow-Harter, C., & Guido, D. (1991). Muscle hypertrophy response to resistance training in older women. *Journal of Applied Physiology, 70,* 1912–1916.

Chien, S., Peng, M. T., Chen, K. P., Huang, T. F., Chang, C., & Fang, H. S. (1975). Longitudinal studies on adipose tissue and its distribution in human subjects. *Journal of Applied Physiology, 39,* 825–830.

Chung, E. B. (1966a). Aging in human joints: I. Articular cartilage. *Journal of the National Medical Association, 58,* 254–260.

Chung, E. B. (1966b). Aging in human joints: II. Joint capsule. *Journal of the National Medical Association, 58,* 87–95.

Cohn, S. H., Vaswani, A., Zanzi, I., & Ellis, K. J. (1976). Effect of aging on bone mass in adult women. *American Journal of Physiology, 230,* 143–148.

Corpas, E., Harman, S. M., & Blackman, M. R. (1993). Human growth hormone and human aging. *Endocrinology Reviews, 14,* 20–39.

Craven, R., & Bruno, P. (1986). Teach the elderly to prevent falls. *Journal of Gerontological Nursing, 12,* 27–33.

Dalsky, G. P. (1988). Weight-bearing exercise, training, and lumbar bone mineral content in post-menopausal women. *Annals of Internal Medicine, 108,* 824–828.

Damon, A., Seltzer, C. C., Stoudt, H. W., & Bell, B. (1972). Age and physique in healthy white veterans at Boston. *Journal of Gerontology, 27,* 202–208.

Dargent, P., & Breart, G. (1993). Epidemiology and risk factors of osteoporosis. *Current Opinions in Rheumatology, 5,* 339–45.

Downton, J. H., & Andrews, K. (1990). Postural disturbance and psychological symptoms amongst elderly people living at home. *International Journal of Geriatric Psychiatry, 5,* 93–98.

Ellis, F. P., Shukla, K. K., Cohn, S. H., & Pierson, R. N. J. (1974). A predictor for total-body potassium based on height, weight, sex, and age: Application in medical disorders. *Journal of Laboratory and Clinical Medicine, 83,* 716–727.

Felson, D. T., Anderson, J. J., Hannan, M. T., Milton, R. C., Wilson, P. W., & Kiel, O. P. (1989). Impaired vision and hip fracture: The Framingham Study. *Journal of the American Geriatrics Society, 37,* 495–500.

Fenske, N. A., & Albers, S. E. (1990). Cosmetic modalities for aging skin: what to tell patients. *Geriatrics, 45,* 59–60.

Fiatarone, M. A., & Evans, W. J. (1993). The etiology and reversibility of muscle dysfunction in the aged. *Journal of Gerontology, 48 (Special Issue),* 77–83.

Fiatarone, M. A., Marks, E. C., Ryan, N. D., Meredith, C. N., Lipsitz, L. A., & Evans, W. J. (1990). High-intensity strength training in nonagenarians. Effects on skeletal muscle. *Journal of the American Medical Association, 263,* 3029–3034.

Frekany, G., & Leslie, D. K. (1975). Effects of an exercise program on selected flexibility measurements of senior citizens. *Gerontology, 15,* 182–183.

Garn, S. M. (1975). Bone loss and aging. In R. Goldman & M. Rockstein (Ed.), *The physiology and pathology of aging* (pp. 39–57). New York: Academic Press.

Gilchrest, B. A. (1989). Skin aging and photoaging: An overview. : *Journal of the American Academy of Dermatology, 21,* 610–613.

Grimby, G., & Saltin, B. (1966). Physiological analysis of physically well-trained middle-aged and old athletes. *Acta Medica Scandinavica, 179,* 513–526.

Grimby, G., & Saltin, B. (1983). The aging muscle. *Clinical Physiology, 3,* 209–218.

Grove, G. L. (1989). Physiologic changes in older skin. : *Clinics in Geriatric Medicine, 5,* 115–25.

Harris, M. B. (1994). Growing old gracefully: Age concealment and gender. *Journal of Gerontology: Psychological Sciences, 49,* P149–158.

Hayflick, L. (1994). *How and why we age.* New York: Ballantine Books.

Hortobágyi, T., Zheng, D., Weidner, M., Lambert, N. J., Westbrook, S., & Houmard, J. A. (1995). The influence of aging on muscle strength and muscle fiber characteristics with special reference to eccentric strength. *Journal of Geronotology: Biological Sciences, 50B,* B399–406.

Hughes, S. L., Cordray, D. S., & Spiker, V. A. (1984). Evaluation of a long-term home care program. *Medical Care, 22,* 460–475.

Hughes, S. L., Edelman, P. L., Singer, R. H., & Chang, R. W. (1993). Joint impairment and self-reported disability in elderly persons. *Journal of Gerontology: Social Sciences, 48,* S84–92.

Kallman, D. A., Plato, C. C., & Tobin, J. D. (1990). The role of muscle loss in the age-related decline of grip strength: Cross-sectional and longitudinal perspectives. *Journal of Gerontology: Medical Sciences, 45,* M82–88.

Kavanagh, T., & Shephard, R. J. (1978). The effects of continued training on the aging process. *Annals of the New York Academy of Science, 301,* 356–370.

Kelly, P. J., Nguyen, T., Hopper, J., Pocock, N., Sambrook, P., & Eisman, J. (1993). Changes in axial bone density with age: A twin study. *Journal of Bone Mineral Research, 8,* 11–17.

Kelsey, J. L., & Hoffman, S. (1987). Risk factors for hip fracture. *New England Journal of Medicine, 316,* 404–406.

Kenney, A. R. (1989). *Physiology of aging* (2nd ed.). Chicago: Year Book Medical.

Kleinsmith, D. M., & Perricone, N. V. (1989). Common skin problems in the elderly. *Clinics in Geriatric Medicine, 5,* 189–211.

Kligman, A. M. (1989). Psychological aspects of skin disorders in the elderly. *Cutis, 43,* 498–501.

Kligman, A. M., Grove, G. L., & Balin, A. K. (1985). Aging of human skin. In C. E. Finch & E. L. Schneider (Ed.), *Handbook of the biology of aging.* New York: Van Nostrand Reinhold.

Klitgaard, H., Mantoni, M., Schiaffino, S., Ausoni, S., Gorza, L., Laurent-Winter, C., Schnohr, P., & Saltin, B. (1990). Function, morphology and protein expression of ageing skeletal muscle: A cross-sectional study of elderly men with different training backgrounds. *Acta Physiological Scandanavica, 140,* 41–54.

Krall, E. A., & Dawson-Hughes, B. (1993). Heritable and life-style determinants of bone mineral density. *Journal of Bone Mineral Research, 8,* 1–9.

Krolner, B. (1982). Bone mass of the axial and the appendicular skeleton in women with Colles' fracture: Its relation to physical activity. *Clinical Physiology, 2,* 147–157.

Kurban, R. S., & Bhawan, J. (1990). Histologic changes in skin associated with aging. *Journal of Dermatology and Surgical Oncology, 16,* 908–914.

Lavker, R. M., Kwong, F., & Kligman, A. M. (1980). Changes in skin surface patterns with age. *Journal of Gerontology, 35,* 348–354.

Lesser, M. (1978). The effects of rhythmic exercise on the range of motion in older adults. *American Corrective Therapy Journal, 32,* 118–122.

Lord, S. R., Clark, R. D., & Webster, I. W. (1991). Physiological factors associated with falls in an elderly population. *Journal of the American Geriatrics Society, 39,* 1194-1200.

Mancil, G. L., & Owsley, C. (1988). "Vision through my aging eyes" revisited. *Journal of the American Optometric Association, 59,* 288–294.

Marcus, R., Holloway, L., & Butterfield, G. (1993). Clinical uses of growth hormone in older people. *Journal of Reproduction and Fertility Supplement, 46,* 115–118.

Mazess, R. B. (1982). On aging bone loss. *Clinical Orthopaedics and Related Research, 165,* 239–252.

McArdle, W. D., Katch, F. I., & Katch, V. L. (1991). *Exercise physiology: Energy, nutrition, and human performance* (3rd ed.). Philadelphia: Lea & Febiger.

McAuley, E., Bane, S. M., Rudolph, D. L., & Lox, C. L. (1995). Physique anxiety and exercise in middle-aged adults. *Journal of Geronotology: Psychological Sciences, 50B,* P229–P235.

McCalden, R. W., McGeough, J. A., Barker, M. B., & Court-Brown, C. M. (1993). Age-related changes in the tensile properties of cortical bone. The relative importance of changes in porosity, mineralization, and microstructure. *Journal of Bone and Joint Surgery, 75,* 1193–1205.

McGue, M., Hirsch, B., & Lykken, D. T. (1993). Age and the self-perception of ability: A twin study analysis. *Psychology and Aging, 8,* 72–80.

Morris, J. C., Rubin, E. H., Morris, E. J., & Mandel, S. A. (1987). Senile dementia of the Alzheimer's type: An important risk factor for serious falls. *Journal of Gerontology, 42,* 412–417.

Morse, J. M., Tylko, S. J., & Dixon, H. A. (1987). Characteristics of the fall-prone patient. *Gerontologist, 27,* 516–522.

Munn, K. (1981). Effects of exercise on the range of motion in elderly subjects. In E. Smith & R. Serfass (Ed.), *Exercise and aging: The scientific bases* (pp. 167–186). Hillside, NJ: Enslow.

Nuti, R., & Martini, G. (1993). Effects of age and menopause on bone density of entire skeleton in healthy and osteoporotic women. *Osteoporosis International, 3,* 59–65.

O'Donoghue, M. N. (1991). Cosmetics for the elderly. *Dermatology Clinics, 9,* 29–34.

Overend, T. J., Cunningham, D. A., Kramer, J. F., Lefcoe, M. S., & Paterson, D. H. (1992). Knee extensor and knee flexor strength: Cross-sectional areas ratio in young and elderly men. *Journal of Gerontology: Medical Sciences, 47,* M204–210.

Parizkova, J. (1974). Body composition and exercise during growth and development. In G. L. Rarick (Ed.), *Physical activity: Human growth and development* (pp. 98–104). New York: Academic Press.

Pfeilschifter, J., Diel, I., Pilz, U., Brunotte, K., Naumann, A., & Ziegler, R. (1993). Mitogenic responsiveness of human bone cells in vitro to hormones and growth factors decreases with age. *Journal of Bone Mineral Research, 8,* 707–717.

Pruzinsky, T., & Cash, T. F. (1990). Integrative themes in body-image development, deviance, and change. In T. Pruzinsky & T. F. Cash (Ed.), *Body images: Development, deviance and change* (pp. 337–349). New York: Guilford.

Pyka, G., Lindenberger, E., Charette, S., & Marcus, R. (1994). Muscle strength and fiber adaptations to a year-long resistance training program in elderly men and women. *Journal of Gerontology: Medical Sciences, 49,* M22–27.

Rico, H., Revilla, M., Hernandez, E. R., Gonzalez-Riola, J. M., & Villa, L. F. (1993). Four-compartment model of body composition of normal elderly women. *Age and Ageing, 22,* 265–268.

Riggs, B. L., Wahner, W. H., Dunn, W. L., Mazess, R. B., Offord, K. P., & Melton, L. J. (1981). Differential changes in bone mineral density of the appendicular and axial skeleton with agin. *Journal of Clinical Investigation, 67,* 328–335.

Rikli, R., & Busch, S. (1986). Motor performance of women as a function of age and physical activity level. *Journal of Gerontology, 41,* 645–649.

Rikli, R. E., & McManis, B. G. (1990). Effects of exercise on bone mineral content in postmenopausal women. *Research Quarterly in Exercise of Sport, 61,* 243.

Roberto, K. (1992). Coping strategies of older women with hip fractures: Resources and outcomes. *Journal of Gerontology: Psychological Sciences, 47,* P21–26.

Rogers, S. L. (1982). *The aging skeleton: Aspects of human bone involution.* Springfield, IL: Charles C. Thomas.

Rossman, I. (1977). Anatomic and body composition changes with age. In C. E. Finch & L. Hayflick (Ed.), *Handbook of the biology of aging.* New York: Van Nostrand Reinhold.

Sallis, J., Haskell, W., Wood, P., & Fortman, S. (1985). Physical activity assessment methodology for the Five City project. *American Journal of Epidemiology, 121,* 91–106.

Shephard, R. J. (1978). *Physical activity and aging.* Chicago: Yearbook Medical.

Shephard, R. J. (1982). *Physiology and biochemistry of exercise.* New York: Praeger.

Sherman, S. S., Tobin, J. D., Hollis, B. W., Gundberg, C. M., Roy, T. A., & Plato, C. C. (1992). Biochemical parameters associated with low bone density in healthy men and women. *Journal of Bone and Mineral Research, 7,* 1123–1130.

Slootweg, M. C. (1993). Growth hormone and bone. *Hormone and Metabolic Research, 25,* 335–43.

Smith, E. L. (1981). Physical activity: A preventive and maintenance modality for bone loss with age. In F. J. Nagle & H. J. Montoye (Ed.), *Exercise in health and disease* (pp. 196–202). Springfield, IL: Charles C. Thomas.

Spar, J. E., la-Rue, A., Hewes, C., & Fairbanks, L. (1987). Multivariate prediction of falls in elderly inpatients. *International Journal of Geriatric Psychiatry, 2,* 185–188.

Sparrow, D., Beausoleil, N. I., Garvey, A. J., Rosner, B., & Silbert, J. E. (1982). The influence of cigarette smoking and age on bone loss in men. *Archives of Environmental Health, 37,* 246–249.

Suominen, H., Heikkinen, E., Parkatti, T., Forsberg, S., & Kiiskinen, A. (1980). Effect of lifelong physical training on functional aging in men. *Scandanavian Journal of the Society of Medicine, 14 (Suppl.),* 225–240.

Tinetti, M. E., & Powell, L. (1993). Fear of falling and low self-efficacy: A cause of dependence in elderly persons. *Journals of Gerontology (Special Issue), 48,* 35–58.

Tinetti, M. E., Richman, D., & Powell, L. (1990). Falls efficacy as a measure of fear of falling. *Journals of Gerontology: Psychological Sciences, 45,* p. 239–243.

Tinetti, M. E., Speechley, M., & Ginter, S. F. (1988). Risk factors for falls among elderly persons living in the community. *New England Journal of Medicine, 319,* 1701–1707.

Vandervoort, A. A., Chesworth, B. M., Cunningham, D. A., Paterson, D. H., Rechnitzer, P. A., & Koval, J. J. (1992). Age and sex effects on mobility of the human ankle. *Journal of Gerontology: Medical Sciences, 47,* M17–21.

Vetter, N. J., & Ford, D. (1989). Anxiety and depression scores in elderly fallers. *International Journal of Geriatric Psychiatry, 4,* 159–163.

Walker, J. E., & Howland, J. (1991). Falls and fear of falling among elderly persons living in the community: Occupational therapy interventions. *American Journal of Occupational Therapy, 45,* 119–122.

Whitbourne, S. K. (1985). *The aging body: Physiological changes and psychological consequences.* New York: Springer Verlag.

Williamson, G. M., & Schulz, R. (1992). Pain, activity restriction, and symptoms of depression among community-residing adults. *Journal of Gerontology: Psychological Sciences, 47,* P367–372.

Woollacott, J. H. (1993). Age-related changes in posture and movement. *Journal of Gerontology, 48 (Special Issue),* 56–60.

4

Cardiovascular and Respiratory Systems

The aging of the body's appearance and ability to move through the environment has, as was discussed in Chapter 3, widespread effects on the individual's psychological adaptation, identity, and social functioning. In addition to effects in these domains, the aging of the body's vital organ systems has major implications for the individual's survival. Short of chronic or acute diseases which can terminate life within a matter of minutes to years, aging processes in these systems can compromise basic life functions, affecting the quality of life as well as its length.

As was discussed in Chapter 1, the aging of the cardiovascular and respiratory systems has the greatest relevance to the component of physical identity relevant to mortality. Individuals know that deleterious changes in the functioning of the heart and lungs in particular can ultimately have fatal consequences. Furthermore, although early age-related changes in these systems may proceed without being noticed by the individual, when the threshold is crossed and age effects are observed, they can be extremely frightening.

CARDIOVASCULAR FUNCTIONING

The heart's sole functional requirement is to pump blood continuously through the circulatory system at a rate that provides adequate perfusion of the body's cells during rest and exertion, both mental and physical. The aging process results in significant limitations of this function and, consequently, can have the effect of reducing the individual's ability to enjoy and participate in a wide range of strenuous activities. Although an entity distinct from aging in terms of underlying processes, fatal cardiovascular diseases do become more probable with advancing age in adulthood. These diseases can have widespread effects on daily life in addition to providing constant sources of reminders of the individual's mortality. For example, the chest pains associated with angina, a chronic cardiac illness, are not only uncomfortable but provide clear warning signals of the heart's impending failure.

Age Effects

The structural characteristics of the heart and arteries that have the greatest importance in terms of age changes and also heart disease are the contractility of the heart's left ventricle walls (the largest chamber of the heart and the one from which blood is pumped into the aorta) and the ability of the arteries to distend in response to the heart's pumping action. The heart's ventricle walls affect the heart's pumping capacity because their ability to contract quickly and fully determines the force and rate at which blood is pumped into the arteries. The more quickly and fully the ventricle walls contract, the more force they can apply to the ejection of blood as it is ejected from the heart into the arteries. It seems fairly clear, at least from autopsy studies, that the pumping capacity of the heart is reduced in increasingly older adult individuals due to a variety of changes affecting the structure and function of the heart muscle walls, particularly in the area of the left ventricle (Gerstenblith, 1980; Weisfeldt & Gerstenblith, 1986). The interior wall of the left ventricle becomes thicker with each progressive decade in adulthood (Kitzman, Scholz, Hagen, Ilstrup, & Edwards, 1988). The number of myocardial (heart muscle) cells decreases, and the remaining cells become hypertrophied (Olivetti, Melissari, Capasso, & Anversa, 1991). The muscle cells contract at a slower rate, reducing the force that is applied at each pump. There is also a decrease in the amount of heart muscle itself and a corresponding increase in fat and connective tissue. The pericardium, composed of bundles of collagen, becomes stiffer, contributing further to the decrease in compliance of the left ventricle wall (Kitzman & Edwards, 1990). Another important set of changes involves the degree to which the heart is filled during the diastolic (filling) phase of the cardiac cycle. In general, the more the heart's muscle cells are stretched as the ventricles fill, the greater the pressure that will be applied to the blood when the heart muscle eventually contracts and spews the blood into the aorta. The decreased capacity of the ventricle walls to expand less during diastole results in a reduced and delayed filling of the left ventricle. During the systolic (emptying) phase of the cardiac cycle, the muscles in the left ventricle contract less and eject less blood. Finally, the cardiac muscle becomes less responsive to the neural stimulation of the "pacemaker" cells in the heart that initiate each contraction (Montamat & Davies, 1989; Schulman & Gerstenblith, 1989).

In addition to these changes in the heart muscle itself are effects of aging on the arteries that further compromise the system's ability to distribute blood to the body's cells. Although it is difficult to separate the effects of aging from those of atherosclerosis (a disease in which the arteries become rigid and narrowed by fatty accumulation), or prior history of heart disease, there appear to be changes in the aorta and arteries that have independent causes due to intrinsic aspects of the aging process (Shimojo, Tsuda, Iwasaka, & Inada, 1991). One important set of changes involves the aorta, the chamber into which blood is ejected at each contraction of the heart muscle. The wall of the aorta becomes less flexible, so that the blood leaving the left ventricle of the heart is faced by more resistance and cannot travel as far into the arteries. The walls of the arteries throughout the body become thicker so that they, too, are less flexible. Impedence of blood flow through the arteries is further influenced by the accumulation of lipids that occurs over the individual's lifetime. The normal effects of aging include an increase in the concentrations of total plasma cholesterol, triglycerides, and the low and very low density lipoproteins (LDLs and VLDLs) that transport these substances through circulation of the blood O (Heiss et al., 1980). Adding to these changes are greater impediments provided by the capillaries, through which blood perfuses the body's tissues at the cellular level (Gerstenblith, 1980; Weisfeldt & Gerstenblith, 1986; Yin, 1980).

These structural changes in the heart and arteries are reflected in important changes that take place in various indices of physiological functioning. Three functions in particular are of relevance to the aging process, both in terms of how it is studied and in terms of the individual's personal experience of aging. The first function of interest pertains to the maximum amount of blood that can be delivered from the heart to the body's tissues. This function can be measured either as cardiac output, which is the output of blood pumped per minute, or as aerobic power, the amount of oxygen made available to the body's tissues through the flow of blood. As indices of aging, these measures are usually calculated at the maximum level, when the person being tested is exercising aerobically (bicycling or running) at peak capacity. Determination of this measure depends on the subject's and experimenter's willingness and confidence in pushing the levels of performance to a point where the subject has reached exhaustion, or when the measures being taken reach a plateau. Such a method clearly presents difficulties in testing elderly respondents. Experimenter and respondent alike are reluctant to push the test to its maximum level. Further, the measurement of cardiac output involves arterial puncture and catheterization, a procedure that is very invasive and risky. For these reasons, the cardiac output and aerobic power in aged respondents are often predicted from the heart rate at levels of less than maximum exertion. Regardless of measurement technique, the findings from a large range of both cross-sectional and longitudinal studies are in agreement that maximum cardiac output and aerobic capacity are negatively related to age, decreasing in a linear fashion throughout the adult years, so that the average 65- year-old individual has 30%–40% of the aerobic capacity of the young adult (McArdle et al., 1991). The second cardiovascular function is maximum heart rate, which is the heart rate achieved at the point when no further increase in maximum oxygen consumption is observed despite increases in the intensity of the work load. This measure is usually taken along with indices of cardiac output or aerobic power, and like those functions, also shows a linear decrease across age groups of adults.

There is considerably less agreement regarding age effects on blood pressure, another measure of cardiovascular efficiency that provides important information regarding the individual's overall health status. Although many researchers have reported that blood pressure is characteristically heightened among older adults (Gerstenblith, 1980), other evidence suggests that there are no effects of aging on this index of cardiovascular functioning in healthy individuals (Ordway & Wekstein, 1979; Tzankoff, Robinson, Pyke, & Brown, 1972), or when physiological indicators of physical fitness are statistically controlled (Gardner & Poehlman, 1995). A lack of consistency across different investigations is most likely related to variations across samples in the incidence of hypertension, a chronic cardiovascular disorder that involves elevated blood pressure. The inclusion of individuals with this chronic illness in samples of older adults tested for normal aging effects presents an obvious confound of the effects of aging with the effects of disease.

Changes in the ventricular muscles and arterial walls can be seen as accounting in large part for the more reliable reports of effects of aging on cardiac output, aerobic capacity, and maximum attainable heart rate. Also contributing to the observed reductions in these indices is the fact that there is less of a demand for oxygen by the tissues due to the reduction in muscle mass that occurs generally throughout the body. According to this explanation, less oxygen is extracted from the blood by the muscles because there are fewer skeletal muscles requiring a supply of oxygen during exercise (Brooks & Fahey, 1984; Fleg & Lakatta, 1988).

Effects of Exercise

Given the importance of cardiovascular functioning to the overall health and longevity of the individual, there has been a wealth of research pointing to the effectiveness of exercise as one of the most potent UIOLIs for slowing or reversing the effects of the aging process on the system (Morey et al., 1989; Sidney & Shephard, 1976). The majority of research on exercise training and aging is focused on the effects of short- and long-term participation in programs of bicycling, jogging, swimming, and indoor ball sports on aerobic power in otherwise sedentary adults. The short-term effects are usually evaluated in training studies spanning a 10–12- week period, during which participants meet three to five times a week, for about one hour or less per session. Long-term training studies are conducted for periods ranging from 1 to 15 years, and involve the same weekly rate of participation. The degree of intensity the individual needs to reach so that the exercise will be considered "training" rather than recreation is 60%–75% of the individual's maximum capacity, which is perceived as strenuous but not totally exhausting. If you have ever used aerobic training equipment yourself, or attended aerobic classes, you are probably aware of the need to exercise for at least 20 to 30 minutes within your "training zone." This type of exercise has a number of effects beyond those that affect the cardiovascular system, including the increased metabolism of body fat.

The major dependent variable in research on the effectiveness of exercise training is aerobic capacity and, secondarily, maximum attainable heart rate. The goal of this type of exercise training, which is called "aerobic" exercise, is to reach a state of dynamic exercise in which the large muscle groups are contracting rhythmically at a steady of state of maximal activity and relying on aerobic (oxygen-consuming) muscle metabolism. The exercise equipment used in this research is usually either a stationary bicycle ergometer, in which work load can be quantified in terms of the tension applied against the pedals, or a treadmill, which can be varied in the speed and incline of the belt that passes under the feet of the walking exerciser. Measurements taken on these machines can be made at the submaximal level, in which the oxygen uptake at given work loads is set at a fixed amount. The determination of maximum oxygen consumption (aerobic capacity) can be predicted from submaximal levels, as mentioned earlier, or can be assessed through direct performance evaluations of the highest oxygen consumption the individual can achieve at a steady state. Maximum heart rate can be evaluated by placing sensors on the individual's pulse points or hands.

Long-term training effects. Early studies on aerobic exercise training were conducted in the Scandinavian countries of Norway and Sweden, where a large percentage of the population participates in endurance sports such as cross-country skiing and long-distance running. Investigators were able to capitalize on the popularity of these sports to evaluate the effects of lifelong exercise on cardiovascular functioning. In many cases, the individuals in these studies were extremely well-trained endurance athletes who competed in track and field sports at the world- or national-class levels throughout their adulthood. With the growth of the fitness industry in the United States, contemporary research includes respondents who only recently became interested in aerobic exercise, and may constitute a more representative segment of the aging population.

The original studies on Scandanavian endurance athletes proved to be extremely encouraging in that they demonstrated consistently favorable effects of lifetime patterns of aerobic exercise on aerobic capacity (Anderson & Hermansen, 1965). This effect amounts to cutting in half the normal age-related loss in maximum oxygen consumption and can enhance the ability to perform a strenuous task when the situation demands sudden exertion (Hodgson & Buskirk, 1977; Shephard, 1978). However, even though these unusual individuals have larger aerobic capacity than their sedentary peers, endurance athletes still experience age-related losses in their cardiovascular functioning.

Interestingly, a history of athletic involvement in adolescence or early adulthood does not serve as protection against the effects of aging unless the individual sustains a regular pattern of aerobic exercise. In studies of middle-aged adults who were physical education majors in college, no general advantage has appeared in their cardiovascular functioning compared to that of their age-matched peers. In fact, because they were so well-trained when young, some of these athletes may be especially susceptible to a decrease in aerobic capacity after they stop exercising: the "detraining" effect. Those who did continue hard physical training demonstrated improved cardiovascular fitness. Current levels of training, then, rather than past athletic involvement, seems to be the determinant of aerobic functioning in middle-aged adults (Asmussen, Fruensgaard, & Norgaard, 1975; Kanstrup & Ekblom, 1978).

It seems to be that continued exercise throughout the middle adult years makes it possible for individuals to avoid substantial age losses in aerobic power and perhaps even reverse them. For example, gains in aerobic capcity in the 13 years between testings in one longitudinal study were demonstrated only for those men who continued a regular program of exercise throughout the period.

By contrast, the men who had trained in youth and then discontinued had the same rate of loss of aerobic power compared to the others in the longitudinal sample (Robinson, Dill, Tzankoff, Wagner, & Robinson, 1973).

The athlete who continues to participate in competitive endurance sports throughout adulthood into old age is a special case of great interest to researchers in exercise physiology. This individual should theoretically provide the most extreme test case to prove that exercise can offset the effects of aging on aerobic capacity. The sport called "orienteering," practiced mainly in Scandinavian countries, has produced such a set of endurance athletes, as does cross-country skiing. In orienteering, competitors run from 4 to 10 miles (depending on age) in a wooded area in which the runner encounters various artificial and natural landmarks such as fences, hills, swamps, and streams. The orienteer must navigate through this area with a map. Training for this sport involves at least 1–1.5 hr of running from two to six times per week. A number of investigators have confirmed that master athletes who participate in orienteering, as well as skiers and long-distance runners, have much larger aerobic capacities than their sedentary counterparts, even those who are considerably younger (Anderson & Hermansen, 1965; Grimby & Saltin, 1966; Pollock, Foster, Knapp, Rod, & Smith, 1987; Suominen, Heikkinen, Parkatti, Forsberg, & Kiiskinen, 1980). Similarly, the champion or master athlete who continues to compete in special events such as track and field meets, is able to maintain a higher level of aerobic capacity through continued involvement in his or her sport well into the later adult years (Heath, Hagberg, Ehseni, & Holloszy, 1981).

A major benefit of long-term involvement in endurance training is enhanced function of the heart's left ventricle, such that the diastolic filling index in master athletes approximates that of healthy young adults (Forman et al., 1992). Even these experienced and active older athletes, however, experience some age-related reduction in aerobic power.

There are fewer empirical investigations involving "ordinary" or nonathletic participants in long-term endurance training activities. Kasch and his colleagues followed one group of 15 men over a 20-year period, from the ages of 45 to 65 years (Kasch, Wallace, Van Camp, & Verity, 1988). These long-term exercisers had kept up their involvement in long-distance running or swimming and were found to have greater aerobic power than their age peers who were not in training. Additional studies on adults who remain active during their middle years support the finding of the advantage offered by continued exercise participation. These active men and women function at the level of sedentary people who are 10 to 20 years younger (Morley & Reese, 1989; Plowman, Drinkwater, & Horvath, 1979; Wright, Zauner, & Cade, 1982). Furthermore, it is aerobic exercise specifically that seems to provide this protection from the effects of aging. A physically active occupation is not sufficient to ensure that the individual will be able to stave off the decline in aerobic capacity that ordinarily accompanies the aging process; what is necessary is participation in leisure activities that specifically involve the elements of aerobic training (Brunner & Meshulam, 1970).

Short-term training effects. The conclusion that long-term patterns of exercise involvement can reduce but not reverse the effects of aging on aerobic power is consistent with the findings of short-term training studies in which previously sedentary average individuals are exposed to a systematic program of aerobic exercise. Evidence from short-term experimental training studies has certain advantages over the findings reported from studies of highly conditioned athletes in that the lifelong athlete is not representative of the general population. Further, a short-term training study offers the opportunity to impose strict experimental controls, including random assignment, over the independent variable of exercise training. This is not to say that the short-term training study is without its drawbacks. Although respondents may be randomly assigned to treatment versus no-treatment conditions, there is still a volunteer bias in the sample as a whole. These individuals may have unusually high motivation to participate in exercise at this point in their lives, and are perhaps in better physical shape than non-volunteers. Once enrolled in the study, the respondents may differentially drop out due to lack of motivation, low morale, or dislike of the type of training modality. In studies in which investigators either fail to take into account the need to provide incentives or make the training regimen so rigorous that unfit sedentary subjects become injured, the drop-out rate may reach as high as 50%. The remaining subjects, then, do not constitute a representative sample of the original sample which, as noted already, may not have been representative of the general population in the first place. Despite these qualifications, the short-term training study has proven to have considerable value in establishing the possibility that even sedentary, nonconditioned, older adults can experience the benefits enjoyed by long-term endurance athletes.

The major dependent variable that is examined in short-term exercise training studies is maximum oxygen consumption or aerobic power. If a subject's aerobic power is increased by training, it means that the oxygen transport system is better able to support the maximum amount of work being performed by the muscles. The main advantage that exercise seems to hold as a means of retaining a higher level of cardiovascular functioning is that it provides a continued potent stimulus for the muscle cells of the heart to undergo strong contractions so that they retain or gain contractile power. The greater strength of the myocardial muscle improves the functioning of the left ventricle and as a result, more blood can be ejected from the left ventricle during the systolic phase of the cardiac cycle (Ehsani, Ogawa, Miller, Spina, & Jilka, 1991). The other advantage of exercise training is that it makes it possible for the individual to "save" energy during aerobic work that is less than maximal by fulfilling the demands of the work load but placing less stress on the heart. Due to the fact that more blood is ejected with each cardiac muscle contraction, the same output of blood can be pumped per minute but at a lower heart rate. The effects of training on cardiac functioning under submaximal conditions are of interest in that these performance situations are closer to the conditions under which people exert themselves in their daily lives. Exercise training also has favorable effects on the body's performance by increasing the efficiency of metabolism in the working muscles (Meredith et al., 1989).

The findings of short-term exercise training studies have consistently revealed improved aerobic power in previously sedentary adults. If the normal loss of aerobic power is figured at 1% per year or a total of 40% between ages 25 and 65 years, the loss can be reduced by up to one-half in a 2- to 3-month training study in which the participants meet at least 3 hr a week and exercise at training levels of 60%–75% of maximum capacity. This positive effect of training has been consistently demonstrated in middle-aged and elderly men and women, including individuals in their 70s and 80s (McArdle, Katch, & Katch, 1991; Whitbourne, 1985), and can approximate the improvement in fitness levels achieved by younger adults (Govindasamy, Paterson, Poulin, & Cunningham, 1988; Hagberg et al., 1989). Even moderate or low intensity exercise can have beneficial effects on healthy sedentary elderly men and women (Foster, Hume, Byrnes, Dickinson, & Chatfield, 1989; Hamdorf, Withers, Penhall, & Haslam, 1992). Further, aerobic exercise training has the additional positive effect of lowering the heart rate and improving work load intensity and duration in submaximal exercise (Morey et al., 1989; Morey et al., 1991; Poulin, Paterson, Govindasamy, & Cunningham, 1988) ultimately placing less stress upon the heart during exertion.

Short-term exercise training studies also have demonstrated beneficial effects on the peripheral vasculature, another important site of age-related decrements in cardiovascular functioning (Blumenthal et al., 1989). Middle-aged and elderly participants in training seem to benefit from the favorable effect that exercise has on enhancing lipid metabolism (Tamai et al., 1988). This effect is due to the increase in the fraction of high-density lipoproteins (HDLs), the plasma lipid transport mechanism responsible for carrying lipids from the peripheral tissues to the liver where they are excreted or synthesized into bile acids (Haskell, 1984). Training thereby counteracts the normal deleterious effects of aging on cholesterol metabolism throughout the body. The more favorable rate of lipid and triglyceride catabolism that results from training therefore diminishes the chances for lipid accumulation in the arteries. These changes, in turn, should lower the peripheral resistance caused by normal changes in the arteries as well as those associated with atherosclerosis. A similar process may account for the beneficial effect that exercise training has on reducing blood pressure during or immediately after maximum exertion (Buccola & Stone, 1975; Tzankoff et al., 1972; Webb, Poehlman, & Tonino, 1993). A reduction of blood pressure during dynamic exercise reduces the load placed on the heart that is otherwise caused by age-related heightened resistance to blood flow in the arteries.

Still unclear from this otherwise impressive list of benefits to be derived from exercise is whether such training actually increases longevity, although there is some evidence for the converse, that lack of exercise is associated with heightened mortality (Rakowski & Mor, 1992). A prime motivating factor for improving the individual's health status in the later adult years seems to be the reduced risk of developing chronic circulatory disorders such as atherosclerosis and hypertension and even cancer (Blair et al., 1989; Mersy, 1991). Apart from these practical benefits, the fact that exercise can have such beneficial effects on physical functioning in old age, even if it is begun after a lifetime of sedentary patterns, provides strong evidence in favor of the view that the rate of the aging process can be significantly altered through active lifestyle choices made by the individual.

Psychological Interactions

Although researchers have not specifically explored the psychological consequences of the aging of the cardiovascular system, there is a considerable body of research pertinent to the psychological processes involved in exercise participation in middle and late adulthood. This research is oriented toward the psychological correlates of exercise participation and, to a lesser extent, the psychological attributes of athletes who specialize in endurance training and performance. From these two sources of evidence, it is possible to begin to make inferences about what is important to adults about the aging of their cardiovascular systems as well as the psychological consequences of the reductions in aerobic capacity associated with the aging process.

Motivational factors in exercise training. The reasons that adults have for partcipating in aerobic exercise training can provide insight into the concerns that are salient to adults regarding the aging of the cardiovascular system. One primary initial motivation, particularly characteristic of men in their 50s (who traditionally have served as the primary target group for exercise training studies) is to reduce the risk of developing cardiovascular disease by getting into "shape," a desire for companionship offered by group exercise experiences, or an interest in seeking a change in routine or new form of recreation (Fuchs, Heath, & Wheeler, 1992; Heinzelman, 1973; Heinzelman & Bagley, 1970; Keller & Woolley, 1991; Stiles, 1967; Teraslina, Parten, Oja, & Koskela, 1970). These reasons can be considered "extrinsic" sources of motivation, as they do not pertain to a direct desire to participate in the activity itself because it constitutes an enjoyable activity or provides a sense of mastery and bodily competence. Although social motivators can still serve as incentives (Heinzelman & Bagley, 1970), as can the opportunity to watch television or listen to music while exercising, it is these "intrinsic" sources of motivation that, over the long-term, will determine whether the individual continues to participate in the activity (McPherson, 1980).

Once this level of involvement is achieved, it is likely that the individual will experience a positive spiraling effect in which the activity leads to positive effects on mood, a lowering of anxiety levels, and enhanced feelings of mastery, control, self-efficacy, and self-esteem (Blumenthal et al., 1989; Hill, Storandt, & Malley, 1993; McAuley, Lox, & Duncan, 1993; Sidney & Shephard, 1976). These affective changes seem to occur independently of changes in beta-endorphins (Hatfield, Goldfarb, Sforzo, & Flynn, 1987), the neurotransmitters that some researchers have argued produce some of the favorable effects of exercise on mood. Consequently, as the individual begins to see benefits to accrue from exercise training, the activity becomes more intrinsically involving and satisfying, so that he or she no longer questions the possibility of continued participation. The effects of exercise training also seem to be favorable in other domains, such as work attitudes and performance, improved sleep and less need for sleep, and even enhanced sexual relations (Donohue, 1977; Hanson & Nedde, 1974; Heinzelman & Bagley, 1970; Hellerstein, 1973). Furthermore, some researchers have demonstrated there to be positive effects of exercise on cognitive functioning (Chodzko-Zajko, Schuler, Solomon, Heinl, & Ellis, 1992; Dustman et al., 1984; Stevenson & Topp, 1990; Stones & Kozma, 1988), although this effect is not consistently observed (Blumenthal et al., 1991; Hill et al., 1993).

Psychological consequences of aging. Looking at the finding that exercise enhances feelings of competence and mastery, it may then be inferred that the loss of aerobic capacity associated with the aging process can detract from the individual's sense of personal control and competence in situations demanding physical exertion. As pointed out earlier, it is a basic fact of life that the efficiency of the cardiovascular system is essential to maintaining one's existence. Threats to the integrity of this system caused by aging or disease constitute threats to life itself. Age changes in the cardiovascular system, when they are perceived as physical strain during exertion or the inability to perform a desired task, serve as reminders of one's mortality. The fact that individuals will go to considerable time and expense for the sake of preserving their cardiac functioning is an indication of the importance of this system's functioning in daily life and its centrality to physical identity.

Through exercise, the middle-aged and older adult can regain lost skills needed to perform strenuous daily activities or recreational involvements. Further, this experience allows the individual to receive continuous assurances that the body is capable of working effectively in response to the demands placed upon it and that shape, fitness, and appearance are being restored (King, Taylor, Haskell, & DeBusk, 1989). Although such a model of mastery and competence may be too simplistic to account for the psychological benefits of exercise (Folkins & Sime, 1981), many researchers believe that these are two essential elements in interpreting the psychological benefits of exercise (Sonstroem, 1984). Furthermore, such a model provides a useful framework for understanding the psychological interactions in the aging of other bodily systems.

RESPIRATORY SYSTEM

The respiratory system functions to permit a process of gas exchange in the air sacs of the lungs in which the blood that passes through the lungs is perfused with oxygen and cleansed of carbon dioxide. The lungs are like bellows in that they sequentially fill and empty the air sacs (called alveoli), pulling the alveoli open during inspiration and collapsing them during expiration. If the lungs are to perform their function efficiently, the alveoli must be pulled open enough so that the blood becomes maximally oxygenated and collapsed sufficiently so that as much carbon dioxide as possible is extracted from the blood before it begins to recirculate through the body. The aging process compromises these functions, reducing the efficiency of gas exchange in the lungs, and further compounding limitations on the body's performance caused by changes in the muscles and cardiovascular system.

The effects of aging on the lungs are readily equated by the general public and even by researchers with the disease processes of emphysema and chronic obstructive pulmonary disease that can impair respiratory functioning at any age. Lifetime habits of cigarette smoking and exposure to environmental pollutants cause significant limitations of respiratory functioning but are extrinsic to the aging process per se. Nevertheless, these sources of respiratory problems have cumulative effects and are therefore more likely to be encountered in older adults.

Another factor that tends to confound age effects in the study of respiratory functioning is the fact that some measures of the lung's efficiency are related to bodily height (taller people have larger lungs). Since there are cohort-related and possibly true age differences in height in later adulthood, age effects may be exaggerated when cross-sectional adult samples are not equated on this variable. Apart from these extraneous factors, there remain some important independent contributions of the aging process to the efficiency of the respiratory system.

Age Effects

The major outcome of the aging process in the lung expressed in functional terms is a reduction in the amount of oxygen delivered from the outside air to the blood within the arteries. Researchers measure the efficiency of this oxygenation process by calculating the difference between the oxygen pressure of the arterial blood after passing through the lungs compared to the oxygen pressure that reached the alveoli from the outside air. Numerous cross-sectional studies document the drop in the efficiency of this oxygenation process, expressed both in terms of absolute arterial oxygen pressure as well as in terms of the difference between the alveolar and the arterial oxygen levels (Begin, Renzetti, Bigler, & Watanabe, 1975). Corroborating this finding is the consistent observation that ventilatory efficiency, an index of oxygen transport, decreases across adulthood (Robinson, Dill, Tzankoff, Wagner, & Robinson, 1975). At the same time, it is a well-established finding that the maximum level of ventilatory efficiency that can be achieved is reduced in older adults (Norris, Shock, & Yiengst, 1955), meaning that older adults are less able to provide sufficient oxygen to meet the body's demands at maximal levels of exertion.

The efficiency of the respiratory system is also indexed by measures of the amount of air taken in by the lungs under various conditions of physical exertion. Total lung capacity is the maximum amount of air that can be held by all structures of the lung. This measure can be broken down into two components. Vital capacity is the volume of air moved into and out of the lungs when the individual is ventilating at maximal levels. The volume of air remaining in the airways and alveoli at the end of the maximal expiration the individual can produce is called residual volume. The most consistent finding across both cross-sectional and longitudinal studies regarding measures of lung volumes is that vital capacity decreases and residual volume increases across the years of adulthood (Asmussen et al., 1975; Drinkwater, Horvath, & Wells, 1975; Muiesan, Sorbini, & Grassi, 1971). This process begins at around the age of 40 and amounts to a 40% loss of vital capacity between the ages of 20 and 70 years (Lynne-Davies,

1977), a figure interestingly comparable to the loss of aerobic power over adulthood. Yet a third set of indices of respiratory function involve the amount of air brought into the lung per unit of time. One of these measures is the ventilatory rate, which is equal to the volume of air (in liters) inspired during a normal breath (called the "tidal volume") multiplied by the frequency of breaths per minute. This measure of respiratory efficiency also shows cross-sectional decreases into old age, as indicated by the finding that older individuals are less able to maintain a high ventilatory rate at maximal levels of exercise (Daly, Barry, & Birkhead, 1968). Since there are no apparent age effects on tidal volume (Montoye, 1982), a decrease in maximum breathing frequency would seem to be the major factor responsible for the age effects on maximum ventilatory rate.

Another widely used measure of ventilatory flow is the forced expiratory volume, which is the amount of air that can be breathed out during a specified short interval of time (such as 1 sec). There is a fairly consistent downward linear trend across different cross-sectional studies in this measure (Kannel & Hubert, 1982; Smith, Cunningham, Patterson, Rechnitzer, & Koval, 1992).

The cause of reductions in respiratory functioning is the apparent result of anatomical changes in a number of pulmonary structures. The primary cause of decreased oxygenation of the blood lies in the nonuniform distribution of air through the lungs. This is important because a major element in the efficiency of gas exchange in the lungs is the matching of the rate of blood flow through the pulmonary capillaries with the rate of air that is supplied to the alveoli. When these rates are matched, oxygen is available from the alveoli at precisely the moment that the blood is there to participate in the process of gas exchange. If the blood flows too slowly, the air is wasted, or if the air supply is cut off, the blood passes through without gas exchange taking place. The result of nonuniform air distribution through the lungs is to create many zones in which there is a mismatch between blood flow and air supply. As a result, the blood becomes insufficiently oxygenated as it passes through the lungs. A certain disparity between blood and air flow rates occurs even in healthy young adults due to the fact that gravity pulls more blood to the lower part of the lungs than to the upper portions. However, this inequality does not have serious consequences. The gravitational pull on the lower part of the lung turns out to have a significant impact on the oxygenation of the blood in older adults. It is the lower portion of the lung that is more likely to be poorly ventilated by air due to structural changes in the lung tissue (discussed later). Since there is more blood flowing through this less well-oxygenated portion, there is disproportionate amount of non-oxygenated blood that leaves the lung of the older person.

Reduced ventilation in the lower portion of the lungs occurs due to a general age-related change that affects the entire lung but hits particularly hard on the lower, larger portion. This change involves the elastic recoil of the lung, the tendency of lung tissue to resist expansion as it becomes filled with air. The loss of elastic recoil of lung tissue is not unlike what happens to balloons as they become used and less resilient. It takes more energy to blow up a new balloon than one that has been filled and emptied many times. In the case of the lungs, elastic recoil provides a crucial function in ventilation. During the inspiratory phase of the respiratory cycle, the airways are held open for a longer period of time when there is sufficient elastic recoil to create positive pressure across the lung surface. During expiration, the elastic recoil of lung tissue helps keep the airways open until the last possible moment when they are forced to collapse due to the pressure of the respiratory muscles. If the airways close prematurely due to loss of elastic recoil, air will be trapped inside them and the lungs will not be able to empty completely. On the next inspiration, less air can be inhaled because the old, unexpired air, remains in the airways. Gravity again proves to be a negative factor in the aging of the lung as the loss of elastic recoil with age affects the lower portion of the lung differentially. The lower portion of the lung ordinarily has less elastic recoil, and the loss associated with the aging process reduces it even further compared to the upper lung portion. A complementary finding involves lung compliance, the increase in volume in the lung associated with an increase in pressure. This measure increases in older adults, reflecting the loss of resistance with age to distention of the lung as it is filled with air.

Age changes in lung structures that account for decreased elastic recoil and increased compliance are alterations in the composition and structure of the elastin and collagen composition of lung tissue (Brandstetter & Kazemi, 1983; D'Errico et al., 1989; Lynne-Davies, 1977). Changes in the chest wall resulting in increased rigidity further lowers the lung's ability to be fully compressed during expiration and fully expanded during inspiration (Lynne-Davies, 1977; Mahler, Rossiello, & Loke, 1986; Shephard, 1978). These changes mean that less than the maximal amount of air can be brought into and out of the lungs, particularly under conditions of exertion (Teramoto, Fukuchi, Nagase, Matsuse, & Orimo, 1995). The greater rigidity of the chest wall also increases the amount of work that must be performed by the respiratory muscles during the inspiratory and expiratory phases of the ventilation cycle.

Effects of Exercise

The main requirement of the respiratory system for adequate functioning during aerobic exercise is to supply enough oxygen to the working muscles at a rate sufficient to support their metabolism. If the respiratory system fails to function efficiently, the individual will experience dyspnea, the technical term for the state of feeling "winded." Fatigue rapidly develops in this state as the muscles lose a primary source of energy. Without training, elderly individuals are more likely to experience these sensations, particularly when they are working at submaximal levels of exertion, such as when they begin an exercise session on a bicycle ergometer (McConnell & Davies, 1992). The purpose of exercise training is to reverse the negative effects of aging on the rates of oxygenation and ventilation. The variables that are most commonly used to examine the effects of exercise are vital capacity and ventilatory efficiency.

Given the structural differences between the composition of the lungs and the composition of the heart, it would seem sensible to expect exercise training to have less potential to improve the respiratory system's function than is the case for the cardiovascular system. The only muscular tissues in the respiratory system that can be strengthened by exercise training are the muscles that control breathing. By contrast, the heart is composed primarily of muscle tissue, which is amenable to strengthening through the stimulation to contract provided by aerobic exercise. Nevertheless, conditioning of the chest wall muscles may prove beneficial in giving these muscles increased strength to move the chest wall structures more effectively.

The number of long- and short-term training studies that are focused specifically on respiratory functioning is far smaller than is the case for cardiovascular training studies. In part, this may be due to the fact that the respiratory system tends to be less a focus of positive intervention activities. Instead, attempts to improve respiratory functioning seem to involve the cessation of "bad habits," the most serious of which, obviously, is smoking. To the extent possible, exposure to environmental toxins should also be avoided (Webster & Kadah, 1991). Methodological problems among the samples also present themselves in conducting intervention research on aging of the respiratory system. The studies that exist tend to involve a wide variety of measures of respiratory functioning, and the samples tend to be very diverse in terms of age, gender, degree of physical activity and, especially, smoking habits. While the frequency of smoking is an important control in any study of physiological functioning, it is of particular relevance in the area of the respiratory system. In a training study, it is difficult to control for smoking experience because as part of getting involved in the study, the participants may "get religion" and change many of their lifestyle habits, especially smoking (Morgan & Pollock, 1978). As a result, the effects of the training program itself cannot be separated from the effects of these changed habits.

Given the difficulties involved in drawing conclusions from exercise training studies, it can be said that there are some ameliorative effects of long-term participation in endurance sports. Athletes and even former athletes show less of a decline in vital capacity with age than do sedentary adults and, in some cases, to show no decline over the course of a longitudinal study (Asmussen et al., 1975; Grimby & Saltin, 1966; Hagberg, Yerg, & Seals, 1988; Kanstrup & Ekblom, 1978; Plowman et al., 1979; Robinson et al., 1973). A favorable effect on vital capacity of aerobic training has been more difficult to substantiate in short-term training studies (Niinimaa & Shephard, 1978). If vital capacity is amenable to exercise, it therefore seems that it requires many years of continued participation as well as adherence to a set of UIOLIs associated with an active and healthy lifestyle. Moreover, as of yet it appears that the benefits of exercise on respiratory functioning do not extend past the age of 50 or 60 at the most.

A somewhat more positive picture in terms of short-term training appears when the measure being tested is ventilatory rate, at least at maximum levels of exertion. Training raises the maximum rate of ventilation that can be attained during dynamic exercise (Astrand, Astrand, Hallback, & Kilbom, 1973; Barry et al., 1966; Cunningham, Rechnitzer, Howard, & Donner, 1987; deVries, 1970; Kanstrup & Ekblom, 1978; Wessel & Van Huss, 1969). This increase can be attributed to an increase in the maximum rate of breathing the individual becomes able to attain (Saltin, Hartley, Kilbom, & Astrand, 1969) or to an increase in tidal volume (deVries, 1970). Measures of ventilatory flow are also enhanced by training in middle-aged and older adults (Grimby & Saltin, 1966; Saltin et al., 1969). Findings of these effects further implicate the improved ability to move the chest in and out to increase air flow through the lungs as a mechanism for exercise training's effect. This enhanced air flow, in turn, makes it possible for a greater volume of air per unit of time to be available to oxygenate the blood. However, the fact that more air can be moved into and out of the lungs as a result of training does not necessarily improve the oxygenation of the blood. Training studies which evaluate the effect of exercise on ventilatory efficiency or oxygen uptake do not indicate positive effects on these indices of how much oxygen is actually reaching the blood (deVries, 1970; Grimby & Saltin, 1966; Shephard, 1978). The fact that the trained individual is breathing in more air but oxygenating the blood less fully may be due to the irreversible changes to the lung tissue and airways within the lung that are not amenable to training effects.

Psychological Interactions

Compared to the attention given to cardiovascular functioning, the concern shown among the general population with respiratory functioning is quite minimal. Media coverage regarding health, for example, rarely focuses on respiratory variables in comparison to blood pressure, cholesterol levels, or aerobic power. In the absence of specific respiratory ailments or diseases, most adults probably worry very little about whether their vital capacity or ventilatory rates will change with age. Yet, the distress associated with dyspnea and fatigue can cause alarm and is probably the major psychological consequence of reduced respiratory functioning in the later years of adulthood. This distress is not unlike that which occurs when the cardiovascular system is strained during physical exertion in that it provokes the sudden realization of one's physical limitations in a vitally important area of life. The ability to breathe easily is one of the body's maintenance activities that healthy persons invariably take for granted. The perception of respiratory insufficiency during a strenuous task can produce frightening sensations and rapidly propel the individual across a threshold of sensitivity to respiratory system dysfunctioning.

Fortunately, in most everyday activities, the loss of respiratory function that occurs in normal aging will not approach the point at which dyspnea is experienced. Dyspnea will be more likely to occur, however, at lower degrees of activity than was true when the individual was younger, such as trying to catch a bus or crossing the street before the light changes (Cunningham, Nancekievill, Paterson, Donner, & Rechnitzer, 1985). Particularly serious or novel episodes of dyspnea may provoke such an unpleasant reaction that the individual vows never to engage in that activity again. In some cases, this might be an adaptive reaction, leading the individual away from potentially detrimental involvement in work, recreational, or family tasks. The individual may also react to such an event by giving up the "bad habit" of cigarette smoking, if this is part of the individual's life style. The danger in overreacting to an isolated episode of dyspnea is that, as might also be true in cardiovascular functioning, the individual avoids physical activity that might otherwise be beneficial. A panicky reaction to dyspnea or strain after a particularly rigorous tennis game, or after the first time one has ridden a bicycle in some years, might lead the individual to give up trying these activities entirely. Such an occurrence would represent an overaccommodation that would not be adaptive. Instead, graded re-engagement in the activity would allow the individual to avoid overexertion without closing off the opportunity to develop improved cardiac or respiratory functioning.

In terms of the association between training and psychological well-being, it would not be unreasonable to speculate that training which reduces the likelihood of experiencing dyspnea during the course of daily activities would have a comparable effect on feelings of well-being and competence that accompany reductions in the perception of cardiovascular strain or gains in aerobic endurance. Moreover, even though the motivation that stimulates a middle-aged or older adult to participate in exercise training may be the desire to enhance cardiac functioning, the outcome may be a desirable improvement in respiratory efficiency that adds to gains achieved in the cardiovascular system. The same argument can also be made regarding the relationship between cardiovascular functioning and feelings of bodily competence. Reduced respiratory efficiency may be hypothesized to have psychologically negative effects due to its influence on feelings of bodily competence. The perception that one is "out of shape," which accompanies the feeling of dyspnea, may have the effect of reducing the individual's sense of well-being because of the implications that this experience has for the aging body's ability to adapt to the demands of the environment.

REFERENCES

Anderson, K. L., & Hermansen, L. (1965). Aerobic work capacity in middle-aged Norwegian men. *Journal of Applied Physiology, 20,* 432–436.

Asmussen, E., Fruensgaard, K., & Norgaard, S. (1975). A follow-up longitudinal study of selected physiologic functions in former physical education students—after 40 years. *Journal of the American Geriatrics Society, 10,* 379–387.

Astrand, I., Astrand, P. O., Hallback, I., & Kilbom, A. (1973). Reduction in maximal oxygen uptake with age. *Journal of Applied Physiology, 35,* 649–654.

Barry, A. J., Daly, J. W., Pruett, E. D. R., Steinmetz, J. R., Page, H. F., Birkhead, N. C., & Rodahl, K. (1966). The effects of physical conditioning on older individuals. *Journal of Gerontology, 21,* 182–191.

Begin, R., Renzetti, A. D., Bigler, A., & Watanabe, S. (1975). Flow and age dependence of airway closure and dynamic compliance. *Journal of Applied Physiology, 38,* 199–207.

Blair, S. N., Kohl, H. W., Paffenbarger, R. S., Jr., Clark, D. G., Cooper, K. H., & Gibbons, L. W. (1989). Physical fitness and all-cause mortality: A prospective study of healthy men and women. *Journal of the American Medical Association, 262,* 2395–2401.

Blumenthal, J. A., Emery, C. F., Madden, D. J., Schniebolk, S., Walsh-Riddle, M., George, L. K., McKee, D. C., Higginbotham, M. B., Cobb, F. R., & Coleman, R. E. (1991). Long-term effects of exercise on psychological functioning in older men and women. *Journal of Gerontology: Psychological Sciences, 46,* P352–361.

Blumenthal, J. A., Emery, C. F., Madden, D. J., George, L. K., Coleman, R. E., Riddle, M. W., McKee, D. C., Reasoner, J., & Williams, R. S. (1989). Cardiovascular and behavioral effects of aerobic exercise training in healthy older men and women. *Journal of Gerontology: Medical Sciences, 44,* M147–157.

Brandstetter, R. D., & Kazemi, H. (1983). Aging and the respiratory system. *Medical Clinics of North America, 67,* 419–431.

Brooks, G. A., & Fahey, T. D. (1984). *Exercise physiology: Human bioenergetics and its applications.* New York: Wiley.

Brunner, D., & Meshulam, N. (1970). Physical fitness of trained elderly people. In D. Brunner & E. Jokl (Ed.), *Medicine and Sport: Vol. 4. Physical activity and aging* (pp. 80–88). Baltimore, MD: University Park Press.

Buccola, V., & Stone, W. J. (1975). Effects of jogging and cycling program on physiological and personality variables in aged men. *Research Quarterly, 46,* 134–139.

Chodzko-Zajko, W. J., Schuler, P., Solomon, J., Heinl, B., & Ellis, N. R. (1992). The influence of physical fitness on automatic and effortful memory changes in aging. *International Journal of Aging and Human Development, 35,* 265–285.

Cunningham, D. A., Nancekievill, E. A., Paterson, D. H., Donner, A. P., & Rechnitzer, P. A. (1985). Ventilation threshold and aging. *Journal of Gerontology, 40,* 703–707.

Cunningham, D. A., Rechnitzer, P. A., Howard, J. H., & Donner, A. P. (1987). Exercise training of men at retirement: A clinical trial. *Journal of Gerontology, 42,* 17–23.

D'Errico, A., Scarani, P., Colosimo, E., Spina, M., Grigioni, W. F., & Mancini, A. M. (1989). Changes in the alveolar connective tissue of the ageing lung. An immunohistochemical study. *Virchows Archives A, Pathologial Anatomy and Histopathology, 415*(2), 137–44.

Daly, J. W., Barry, A. J., & Birkhead, N. C. (1968). The physical working capacity of older individuals. *Journal of Gerontology, 23,* 134–139.

deVries, H. A. (1970). Physiological effects of an exercise training regimen upon men aged 52–88. *Journal of Gerontology, 25,* 325–336.

Donohue, S. (1977). The correlation between physical fitness, absenteeism, and work performance. *Canadian Journal of Public Health, 68,* 201–203.

Drinkwater, B. L., Horvath, S. M., & Wells, C. L. (1975). Aerobic power of females ages 10 to 68. *Journal of Gerontology, 30,* 385–394.

Dustman, R. E., Ruhling, R. O., Russell, E. M., Shearer, D. E., Bonekat, H. W., Shigeoka, J. W., Wood, J. S., & Bradford, D. C. (1984). Aerobic exercise training and improved neurophysiological function of older individual. *Neurobiology of Aging, 5,* 35–42.

Ehsani, A. A., Ogawa, T., Miller, T. R., Spina, R. J., & Jilka, S. M. (1991). Exercise training improves left ventricular systolic function in older men. *Circulation, 83*(1), 96–103.

Fleg, J. L., & Lakatta, E. G. (1988). Role of muscle loss in the age-associated reduction in $\dot{V}O_2$ max *Journal of Applied Physiology, 65,* 1147–1151.

Folkins, C. H., & Sime, W. E. (1981). Physical fitness training and mental health. *American Psychologist, 36,* 373–389.

Forman, D. E., Manning, W. J., Hauser, R., Gervino, E. V., Evans, W. J., & Wei, J. Y. (1992). Enhanced left ventricular diastolic filling associated with long-term endurance training. *Journal of Gerontology: Medical Sciences, 47,* M56–58.

Foster, V. L., Hume, G. J. E., Byrnes, W. C., Dickinson, A. L., & Chatfield, S. J. (1989). Endurance training for elderly women: Moderate vs low intensity. *Journal of Gerontology: Medical Sciences, 44,* M184–188.

Fuchs, R., Heath, G. W., & Wheeler, F. C. (1992). Perceived morbidity as a determinant of health behavior. *Health Education Research, 7*(3), 327–334.

Gardner, A. W., & Poehlman, E. T. (1995). Predictors of the age-related increase in blood pressure in men and women. *Journal of Gerontology: Medical Sciences, 50A,* M1–6.

Gerstenblith, G. (1980). Noninvasive assessment of cardiovascular function in the elderly. In M. L. Weisfeldt (Ed.), *Aging: Vol. 12. The aging heart: Its function and response to stress.* New York: Raven Press.

Govindasamy, D., Paterson, D. H., Poulin, M., & Cunningham, D. A. (1988). The time course of cardiorespiratory adaptations in elderly men. *Canadian Journal of Sport Sciences, 13,* 53–54P.

Grimby, G., & Saltin, B. (1966). Physiological analysis of physically well-trained middle-aged and old athletes. *Acta Medica Scandinavica, 179,* 513–526.

Hagberg, J. M., Graves, J. E., Limacher, L., Woods, D. R., Leggett, S. H., Cononie, C., Gruber, J. J., & Pollock, M. L. (1989). Cardiovascular responses of 70- to 79-year-old men and women to exercise training. *Journal of Applied Physiology, 66,* 2589–2594.

Hagberg, J. M., Yerg, J. E., & Seals, D. R. (1988). Pulmonary function in young and older atheletes and untrained men. *Journal of Applied Physiology, 65,* 101–105.

Hamdorf, P. A., Withers, R. T., Penhall, R. K., & Haslam, M. V. (1992). Physical training effects on the fitness and habitual activity patterns of elderly women. *Archives of Physical Medicine and Rehabilitation, 73,* 603–608.

Hanson, J. S., & Nedde, W. H. (1974). Long-term physical training effect in sedentary females. *Journal of Applied Physiology, 37,* 112–116.

Haskell, W. L. (1984). The influence of exercise on the concentrations of triglyceride and cholesterol in human plasma. *Exercise and Sports Sciences Reviews, 12,* 205–244.

Hatfield, B. D., Goldfarb, A. H., Sforzo, G. A., & Flynn, M. G. (1987). Serum betaendorphin and affective responses to graded exercise in young and elderly men. *Journal of Gerontology, 42,* 429–431.

Heath, G. W., Hagberg, J. M., Ehseni, A. A., & Holloszy, J. O. (1981). A physiological comparison of young and old endurance athletes. *Journal of Applied Physiology, 51,* 634–640.

Heinzelman, F. (1973). Social and psychological factors that influence the effectiveness of exercise programs. In J. Naughton & H. Hellerstein (Ed.), *Exercise testing and exercise training in coronary heart disease.* New York: Academic Press.

Heinzelman, F., & Bagley, R. W. (1970). Response to physical activity programs and their effects on health behavior. *Public Health Reports, 85,* 905–911.

Heiss, G., Tamir, I., Davis, C. E., Tyroler, H. A., Rifkind, B. M., Schonfeld, G., Jacobs, D., & Frantz, I. D. J. (1980). Lipoprotein-cholesterol distributions in selected North American populations: The Lipid Research Clinics Program Prevalence Study. *Circulation, 61,* 302–315.

Hellerstein, H. K. (1973). Exercise therapy in coronary disease. Rehabilitation and secondary prevention. In J. H. d. Hass, H. C. Hemker, & H. A. Snellen (Ed.), *Ischaemic heart disease* (pp. 406–429). Baltimore, MD: Williams & Wilkins.

Hill, R. D., Storandt, M., & Malley, M. (1993). The impact of long-term exercise training on psychological function in older adults. *Journal of Gerontology: Psychological Sciences, 48,* P12–17.

Hodgson, J. L., & Buskirk, E. R. (1977). Physical fitness and age, with emphasis on cardiovascular function in the elderly. *Journal of the American Geriatrics Society, 25,* 385–392.

Kannel, W. B., & Hubert, H. (1982). Vital capacity as a biomarker of aging. In M. E. Reff & E. L. Schneider (Ed.), *Biological markers of aging* (pp. 145–160): (NIH Publication No. 62-2221).

Kanstrup, I. L., & Ekblom, B. (1978). Influence of age and physical activity on central hemodynamics and lung function in active adults. *Journal of Applied Physiology, 45,* 709–717.

Kasch, F. W., Wallace, J. P., Van Camp, S. P., & Verity, L. (1988). A longitudinal study of cardiovascular stability in active men aged 45 to 65. *Physical Sportsmedicine, 16,* 117–124.

Keller, M. J., & Woolley, S. M. (1991). Designing exercise programs with older adults: Theory and practice. *Activities, Adaptation and Aging, 16*(2), 1–17.

King, A. C., Taylor, C. B., Haskell, W. L., & DeBusk, R. F. (1989). Influence of regular aerobic exercise on psychological health: A randomized, controlled trial of healthy middleaged adults. *Health Psychology, 8,* 305–324.

Kitzman, D. W., & Edwards, W. D. (1990). Age-related changes in the anatomy of the normal human heart. *Journal of Gerontology: Medical Sciences, 45,* M33–39.

Kitzman, D. W., Scholz, D. G., Hagen, P. T., Ilstrup, D. M., & Edwards, W. D. (1988). Age-related changes in normal human hearts during the first ten decades. Part II (Maturity): A quantitative anatomic study of 765 specimens from subjects 20 to 99 years old. *Mayo Clinic Proceedings, 63,* 137–146.

Lynne-Davies, P. (1977). Influence of age on the respiratory system. *Geriatrics, 32,* 57–60.

Mahler, D. A., Rossiello, R. A., & Loke, J. (1986). The aging lung. *Clinics in Geriatric Medicine, 2,* 215–225.

McArdle, W. D., Katch, F. I., & Katch, V. L. (1991). *Exercise physiology: Energy, nutrition, and human performance* (3rd ed.). Philadelphia: Lea & Febiger.

McAuley, E., Lox, C., & Duncan, T. E. (1993). Long-term maintenance of exercise, self-efficacy, and physiological change in older adults. *Journal of Gerontology: Psychological Sciences, 48,* P218–224.

McConnell, A. K., & Davies, C. T. M. (1992). A comparison of the ventilatory responses to exercise of elderly and younger humans. *Journal of Gerontology, 47,* B137–141.

McPherson, B. D. (1980). Social factors to consider in fitness programming and motivation: Different strokes for different groups. In R. R. Danielson & K. F. Danielson (Ed.), *Fitness motivation* (pp. 8–17). Toronto: Orcol Publications.

Meredith, C. N., Frontera, W. R., Fisher, E. C., Hughes, V. A., Herland, J. C., Edwards, J., & Evans, W. J. (1989). Peripheral effects of endurance training in young and old subjects. *Journal of Applied Physiology, 66,* 2844–2849.

Mersy, D. J. (1991). Health benefits of aerobic exercise. *Postgraduate Medicine, 90,* 103–107.

Montamat, S. C., & Davies, A. O. (1989). Physiological response to isoproterenol and coupling of beta-adrenergic receptors in young and elderly human subjects. *Journal of Gerontology: Medical Sciences, 44,* M100–105.

Montoye, H. J. (1982). Age and oxygen utilization during submaximal treadmill exercise in males. *Journal of Gerontology, 37,* 396–402.

Morey, M. C., Cowper, P. A., Feussner, J. R., DiPasquale, R. C., Crowley, G. M., Sullivan, R., Jr., & Kitzman, D. W. (1991). Two-year trends in physical performance following supervised exercise among community-dwelling older veterans. *Journal of the American Geriatrics Society, 39,* 549–554.

Morey, M. C., Cowper, P. A., Feussner, J. R., DiPasquale, R. C., Crowley, G. M., Sullivan, R., Jr., & Kitzman, D. W. (1989). Evaluation of a supervised exercise program in a geriatric population. *Journal of the American Geriatrics Society, 37,* 348–354.

Morgan, W. P., & Pollock, M. L. (1978). Physical activity and cardiovascular health: Psychological aspects. In F. Landry & W. Orban (Ed.), *Physical activity and human well-being* (pp. 163–181). Miami: Symposium Specialists.

Morley, J. E., & Reese, S. S. (1989). Clinical implications of the aging heart. *American Journal of Medicine, 86,* 77–86.

Muiesan, G., Sorbini, C. A., & Grassi, V. (1971). Respiratory function in the aged. *Bulletin de Physio-Pathologie Respiratoire, 7,* 973–1009.

Niinimaa, V., & Shephard, R. J. (1978). Training and oxygen conductance in the elderly. I. The respiratory system. *Journal of Gerontology, 33,* 354–361.

Norris, A. H., Shock, N. W., & Yiengst, M. J. (1955). Age differences in ventilatory and gas exchange responses to graded exercise in males. *Journal of Gerontology, 10,* 145–155.

Olivetti, G., Melissari, M., Capasso, J. M., & Anversa, P. (1991). Cardiomyopathy of the aging human heart. Myocyte loss and reactive cellular hypertrophy. *Circulation Research, 68,* 1560–1568.

Ordway, G. A., & Wekstein, D. R. (1979). Effect of age on cardiovascular response to static (isometric) exercise. *Proceedings of the Society for Experimental Biology and Medicine, 161,* 189–192.

Plowman, S. A., Drinkwater, B. L., & Horvath, S. (1979). Age and aerobic power in women: A longitudinal study. *Journal of Gerontology, 34,* 512–520.

Pollock, M. L., Foster, C., Knapp, D., Rod, J. L., & Smith, D. H. (1987). Effects of age and training on aerobic capacity and body composition of masters atheletes. *Journal of Applied Physiology, 62,* 725–731.

Poulin, M., Paterson, D. H., Govindasamy, D., & Cunningham, D. A. (1988). Endurance training of elderly men. Responses to submaximal exercise. *Canadian Journal of Sport Sciences, 13,* 78–79P.

Rakowski, W., & Mor, V. (1992). The association of physical activity with mortality among older adults in the Longitudinal Study of Aging (1984–1988). *Journal of Gerontology: Medical Sciences, 47,* M122–129.

Robinson, S., Dill, D. B., Ross, J. C., Robinson, R. D., Wagner, J. A., & Tzankoff, S. P. (1973). Training and physiological aging in man. *Federation Proceedings, 32,* 1628–1634.

Robinson, S., Dill, D. B., Tzankoff, S. P., Wagner, J. A., & Robinson, R. D. (1975). Longitudinal studies of aging in 37 men. *Journal of Applied Physiology, 38,* 263–267.

Saltin, B., Hartley, L. H., Kilbom, Ä., & Åstrand, I. (1969). Physical training in sedentary middle-aged and older men. II. Oxygen uptake, heart rate, and blood lactate concentration at submaximal and maximal exercise. *Scandanavian Journal of Clinical Laboratory Investigations, 24,* 323–334.

Schulman, S. P., & Gerstenblith, G. (1989). Cardiovascular changes with aging: The response to exercise. *Journal of Cardiopulmonary Rehabilitation, 9,* 12–16.

Shephard, R. J. (1978). *Physical activity and aging.* Chicago: Yearbook Medical.

Shimojo, M., Tsuda, N., Iwasaka, T., & Inada, M. (1991). Age-related changes in aortic elasticity determined by gated radionuclide angiography in patients with systemic hypertension or healed myocardial infarcts and in normal subjects. *American Journal of Cardiology, 68,* 950–953.

Sidney, K. H., & Shephard, R. J. (1976). Attitudes toward health and physical activity in the elderly: Effects of a physical training program. *Medicine and Science in Sports and Exercise, 246,* 246–252.

Smith, W. D. F., Cunningham, D. A., Patterson, D. H., Rechnitzer, P. A., & Koval, J. J. (1992). Forced expiratory volume, height, and demispan in Canadian men and women aged 55–86. *Journal of Gerontology: Medical Sciences, 47,* M40–44.

Sonstroem, R. J. (1984). Exercise and self-esteem. *Exercise and Sports Sciences Reviews, 12,* 123–155.

Stevenson, J. S., & Topp, R. (1990). Effects of moderate and low intensity long-term exercise by older adults. *Research in Nursing and Health, 13*(4), 209–218.

Stiles, M. H. (1967). Motivation for sports participation in the community. *Canadian Medical Association Journal, 96,* 889–892.

Stones, M. J., & Kozma, A. (1988). Physical activity, age and cognitive/motor performance. In M. L. Howe & C. J. Brainerd (Ed.), *Cognitive development in adulthood: Progress in cognitive development research* (pp. 273–321). New York: Springer.

Suominen, H., Heikkinen, E., Parkatti, T., Forsberg, S., & Kiiskinen, A. (1980). Effect of lifelong physical training on functional aging in men. *Scandanavian Journal of the Society of Medicine, 14 (Suppl.),* 225–240.

Tamai, T., Nakai, T., Takai, H., Fujiwara, R., Miyabo, S., Higuchi, M., & Kobayashi, S. (1988). The effects of physical exercise on plasma lipoprotein and apolipoprotein metabolism in elderly men. *Journal of Gerontology: Medical Sciences, 43,* M75–79.

Teramoto, S., Fukuchi, Y., Nagase, T., Matsuse, T., & Orimo, H. (1995). A comparison of ventilation components in young and elderly men during exercise. *Journal of Gerontology: Biological Sciences, 50A,* B34–39.

Teraslina, P., Parten, T., Oja, P., & Koskela, A. (1970). Some social characteristics and living habits associated with willingness to participate in a physical activity intervention study. *Journal of Sports Medicine and Physical Fitness, 10,* 138–144.

Tzankoff, S. P., Robinson, S., Pyke, F. S., & Brown, D. A. (1972). Physiological adjustments of work in older men as affected by training. *Journal of Applied Physiology, 33,* 346–350.

Webb, G. D., Poehlman, E. T., & Tonino, R. P. (1993). Dissociation of changes in metabolic rate and blood pressure with erthrocyte Na-K pump activity in older men after endurance training. *Journal of Gerontology: Medical Sciences, 48,* M47–52.

Webster, J. R., & Kadah, H. (1991). Unique aspects of respiratory disease in the aged. *Geriatrics, 46,* 31–34.

Weisfeldt, M. L., & Gerstenblith, G. (1986). Cardiovascular aging and adaptation to disease. In J. W. Hurst (Ed.), *The heart.* New York: Macmillan.

Wessel, J. A., & Van Huss, W. D. (1969). The influence of physical activity and age on the exercise adaptation of women. *Journal of Sports Medicine and Physical Fitness, 9,* 173–180.

Whitbourne, S. K. (1985). *The aging body: Physiological changes and psychological consequences.* New York: Springer-Verlag.

Wright, T. W., Zauner, C. W., & Cade, R. (1982). Cardiac output in male middle aged runners. *Journal of Sports Medicine and Physical Fitness, 22,* 17–22.

Yin, F. C. P. (1980). The aging vasculature and its effects on the heart. In M. L. Weisfeldt (Ed.), *Aging: Vol. 12. The aging heart: Its function and response to stress.* New York: Raven Press.

5

Physiological
Control Systems

The vital functions served by the systems described in Chapter 4 are central to the maintenance of life. Additional controls provided by the digestive, excretory, endocrine, and immune systems also play essential roles in the individual's adaptive ability and health. The body's cells require a stable internal environment in which to carry out their functions despite variations in the external environment to which the body is exposed. This stable environment is regulated by complex regulatory devices involving these physiological systems. The aging of the digestive and excretory systems may be seen as most relevant to the component of physical identity involving the body's competence. Although the actual extent of changes in these systems tends not to be of great magnitude, individuals may be highly sensitive to cues that their body's ability to perform these vegetative functions is on the wane. Changes within these systems can also interact with personality and social functioning, as will be discussed, and distress caused by an inabilty to cope with whatever changes do occur can interfere with and reduce the efficiency of functioning to a significant degree. The endocrine system permits the individual to respond quickly to the requirements for increased energy use that occur when the situation demands mobilization of the body's resources. The immune system protects the body's cells from the threat of infection. Furthermore, this system is highly sensitive to the individual's degree of psychological stress, and therefore the processes involved in coping are extremely relevant to its functioning. The reproductive system involves a set of controls that interact with the endocrine system as a whole. Further, the reproductive system in mature adults serves to make it possible for them to have their own children and to derive pleasure from sexual relations. The feelings connected with sexuality are important contributors to the individual's overall well-being, and form a significant component of intimate relationships. Changes with age in the reproductive system have important implications on a day-to-day basis in terms of the individual's sense of sexuality as well as the interactions that exist between the reproductive hormones and other control systems of the body.

Disturbances caused by the aging process in any of these systems can have significant effects on the individual's daily life. The aspects of physical identity most likely to be affected by age-related changes involve feelings of competence to the extent that the individual is less able to perform valued functions. Furthermore, changes in sexual and reproductive functioning may be seen as interacting with the impact of aging on the appearance component of physical identity.

DIGESTIVE SYSTEM

The digestive system functions to extract nutrients from the various types of foods that enter the body, and then to pass these nutrients into the bloodstream. The components of food that cannot be used by the body are eliminated through the excretory system and lower digestive tract. The two critical features necessary for normal digestive functioning, then, are the transformation of food into usable form, and the movement of food through the digestive tract.

Age Effects

In the area of digestive functioning, the distinction between normal aging and disease is essential but difficult to make. There are numerous gastrointestinal diseases that interfere with the efficiency of digestion and must be ruled out before considering the possibility that a particular problem or symptom that the individual experiences is clearly the result of aging. Diseases that are not caused by specific gastrointestinal disturbances may also create difficulties for the individual, and the contributions of these must be considered before interpreting a given abnormality or symptom as a reflection of the aging process. Lifetime habits of alcohol ingestion serve as an additional factor to consider, as excess use of alcohol can create gastrointestinal problems if not life-threatening diseases. The fact that individuals vary so much in digestive habits further complicates the analysis of aging effects. There are a host of psychological, cultural, and economic factors whose cumulative effects on diet over a lifetime interact with whatever changes are intrinsic to the aging process.

It is easiest to consider the effects of age by dividing the digestive process into phases that correspond to the movement of food from the mouth through the intestines. The initial digestive processes occur in the oral phase, with the chewing of food by the teeth and the dissolution of food by the saliva. Early investigations in salivary functioning yielded evidence of diminished secretions by the parotid glands (Kamocka, 1970). However, these investigations failed to exclude participants with diagnosed medical problems, and they were based exclusively on cross-sectional data. When healthy individuals only are studied, and are followed over time, there is no diminution reported to occur in parotid gland flow (Ship, Nolan, & Puckett, 1995; Ship, Patton, & Tylenda, 1991; Wu, Atkinson, Fox, Baum, & Ship, 1992) or in the antibacterial function of saliva secreted by the parotid gland (Fox et al., 1987). Secretion by the submandibular gland, however, has been found to show an age-related decrease (Wu, Baum, & Ship, 1995).

The next point in the digestive process studied in relation to age involves the transporting of food (which has been processed into a food bolus at the end of the oral phase) down the esophagus (primary peristalsis), and into the stomach (secondary peristalsis). Some investigators have described as a normal function of aging the condition called "presbyesophagus," literally meaning "old" esophagus, defined as a diminution of primary peristalsis and an increase in secondary peristalsis. The cause, presumably, of this condition is a reduction in strength of the esophageal muscles. The attribution of this condition to the aging process is considered controversial because it was first described among elderly persons whose health was not at all good, including some older persons who suffered from esophageal disease. Researchers studying the healthy elderly, screened for disease, have found that primary peristalsis remains intact in old age. However, secondary peristalsis does seem to be negatively affected by aging, as indicated by reduced intensity of the peristaltic wave propelling food into the stomach and a higher resting esophageal pressure (Khan, Shragge, Crispin, & Lind, 1977). This age effect does not have a significant functional impact, however, and so it seems reasonable to conclude that esophageal motility is relatively well preserved into old age.

The gastric phase, which is the next point in the digestive process, involves the transformation of the food bolus into a liquid form, called "chyme." This job is accomplished through the secretion of gastric juice which, when agitated with food in the stomach, dissolves the bolus and prepares it to enter the small intestine. Aging appears to affect the secretion of gastric juice, with estimates of its decrease amounting to approximately 25% by the time a person reaches the age of 60 years compared to the earlier adult years (Bernier, Vidon, & Mignon,

1973). The reduction in gastric juice secretion has several effects on the digestion of specific nutrients. Protein, iron, calcium, Vitamin B_{12}, and folic acid are less completely digested, and there is in addition increased bacterial growth in the intestinal tract (Bowman & Rosenberg, 1983). Interestingly, there is evidence that the "advantage" that men have over women in the capacity to digest alcohol shifts to favor women in later adulthood. The metabolism of alcohol by stomach enzymes occurs at a higher rate for elderly women compared to men, a reversal of the findings for young adults (Pozzato et al., 1995).

Within the small intestine, the chyme is moved forward through a process of segmentation, involving the contraction of circular muscles in the wall of the small intestine. The absorption of nutrients into the bloodstream takes place in fingerlike projections called villi, which are composed of epithelial cells. There are some structural changes in the small intestine that have the potential to impair the absorption process, particularly a reduction in its surface area through alterations in the shape and number of villi (Minaker & Rowe, 1982). However, these changes have little functional impact, because the epithelial cells are so numerous that their altered shape does not present a significant loss, and they turn over so rapidly (they replace themselves completely every few days) that they do not "age." Nevertheless, there appear to be some notable age-related changes, including reduction in the absorption of fats, calcium, Vitamin B_{12}, folic acid, iron, and Vitamin B_6 (Eastell et al., 1991; Hsu & Smith, 1984; Lynch, Finch, Monsen, & Cook, 1982; Minaker & Rowe, 1982). These changes are exacerbated by the lack of compliance shown by many older adults with maintaining adequate dietary intakes of magnesium, viamins A and E, calcium, and zinc (Costello & Moser-Veillon, 1992; Ryan, Craig, & Finn, 1992).

The entry of chyme into the small intestine stimulates digestive hormones and enzymes that stimulate other digestive enzymes in the stomach and pancreas as well as the release of bile from the liver. Blood levels of the two major pancreatic enzymes are not altered in later adulthood (Carrere et al., 1987) and there are no significant changes in the structure of this organ (Kreel & Sandin, 1973). Conflicting reports about structural changes in the liver exist, with some evidence suggesting increasing abnormalities with age. The best estimate though is that liver function is unimpaired in normally functioning elderly adults who are free of alcohol-related disease (Kampmann, Sinding, & Møller-Jørgensen, 1975). For example, there are no age differences or short-term longitudinal age effects in albumin, the major protein produced by the liver (Campion, deLabry, & Glynn, 1988). This lack of correspondence between structural and functional changes in the liver appears to be due primarily to the large margin of safety built into this organ. Up to 80% of the liver can be removed without interfering significantly with its functioning. Furthermore, the liver has tremendous regenerative capacity, and so it can compensate for whatever normal structural losses may occur in later adulthood (Cohen, Gitman, & Lipshutz, 1960). Gallbladder problems can arise at any point in adulthood in connection with other physiological disorders, and although gallbladder disease is more prevalent in the elderly, this seems to reflect lifelong dietary patterns of fat intake rather than significant alterations in this structure (Bowman & Rosenberg, 1983; Wedmann et al., 1991).

At the point that it enters the large intestine, digestion of nutrients from the chyme is essentially complete. The major task performed by the large intestine is the absorption of water to solidify digestive waste products and to expel these as feces from the body. After the fecal material is propelled by the large intestine into the rectum, it is stored until it can be expelled by relaxation of the anal sphincter, a muscle under voluntary control. The natural frequency for defecation ranges from 3 times a day to once every 3 days. Although the media constantly push the need for laxatives in the middle-aged and older populations, there is no evidence that apart from some changes in the lining of the large intestine and atrophy of muscles responsible for moving fecal material through it (Yamagata, 1965), age changes in the functioning of this organ are minimal (Brauer, Slavin, & Marlett, 1981; Brocklehurst, 1978; Minaker & Rowe, 1982). When constipation occurs in the elderly individual, it is more likely to be caused by factors related to diet and lifestyle, as will be discussed below. Fecal incontinence, the loss of control over anal sphincters, is more likely to occur in women after the age of 50 compared to men, perhaps related to estrogen changes associated with the menopause (Haadem, Dahlstrom, & Ling, 1991).

Psychological Interactions

The psychological significance of food is certainly a well-recognized feature of life, and activities and concerns surrounding the processes of intake and digestion occupy considerable significance in the everyday life of virtually all cultures around the world. In addition to the interest that many people have in their eating and digestive habits, health and well-being are often tied in with the adequacy of a person's state of hunger or satiety and freedom from or discomfort caused by gastrointestinal symptoms. Excessive hunger or fullness interfere with the performance of daily activities as do pain, heartburn, gas, cramps, or constipation. On the basis of physiological evidence alone, there is little to suggest that older adults should have particular difficulty in this area of functioning as long as they are economically secure and maintain reasonable eating habits (Altman, 1990). Nevertheless, many older persons seek medical help for a variety of digestive ailments. Psychological factors, then, must be seen as playing an important role in understanding these complaints.

Physiologically speaking, the relationship between psychological functioning and the quality of digestion is mediated by the autonomic nervous system. Under periods of intense stress, adults of any age can suffer from impairments in digestive functioning due to the contribution of autonomic nervous system stimulation. In the case of the elderly, stress-provoked responses of this kind exacerbate what would otherwise be subtle alterations caused by the normal aging process. For example, anxiety can inhibit salivary and gastric juice secretion, which are at least partly affected by aging. The processes involved in the elimination of feces are also highly sensitive to emotional factors which, in turn, can lead to harmful daily habits of eating and elimination. Defecation acquires a particular significance for the elderly person who has been taught the importance of "regularity" (one bowel movement a day) and who has had this impression carved in stone by daily exposure to endless advertisements for laxatives and dietary supplements. Any deviation from this set pattern of elimination is perceived, by the older individual who has bought into this view, as in need of correction. It is no small irony that the very steps taken to correct what might be a temporary bout of constipation are exactly those that can lead to a more chronic problem. There is general agreement in the literature that the major factor leading to constipation in the elderly is overuse of laxatives (Brocklehurst, 1978; Minaker & Rowe, 1982) and that the perception in an otherwise healthy older person of constipation is probably exaggerated compared to the existence of a diagnosable condition (Holt, 1991).

There are other meanings attached to the process of defecation in the elderly that can be attributed to its association with feared diseases and institutionalization in later life (Wald, 1990). Symptoms of constipation are associated with cancer of the gastrointestinal tract, the most frequent form of malignant disease affecting the elderly (Brocklehurst, 1978). Loss of fecal continence is a major factor leading to the need to institutionalize an elderly person (Holt, 1991), and this undesirable outcome heightens the concern over incontinence. Fear over loss of control over defecation is another concern, based on fact that fecal incontinence is a known occurrence in the advanced stages of Alzheimer's disease. Older persons who believe that "senility" is an inevitable feature of aging may regard with alarm any indication that their patterns of elimination are changing, seeing in such changes a more ominous significance that can risk putting them over the threshold. The anxiety created by this concern may contribute further to gastrointestinal problems so that what originates as a temporary problem comes to have a more prolonged course.

We can see, then, that what is basically one of the most mundane features of everyday life has the potential to assume great magnitude in the identities of elderly adults. The significance of digestive function extends far beyond its actual scope within the body. As a component of physical identity, digestive function may be seen as relating to the body's competence, but it may also involve a component of autonomy and independence. The need to rely on others for help, particularly in elimination, is a condition that many elders fear. Not only does it involve shame and embarrassment of the highest degree, but it symbolizes a return to earlier childlike states of dependency.

It is also the case that poor dietary habits can lead to constipation, particularly the insufficient consumption of natural food fibers as are found in grain products and many fruits and vegetables. Elderly people may stay away from these sources of food fiber because they have been exposed to outdated medical advice from the 1950s and 1960s which recommends the avoidance of any sort of roughage in the diet. The physical inactivity that is part of the sedentary lifestyle engaged in by older people who are unable to or who fear that they cannot exert themselves contributes further to constipation (Brocklehurst, 1978). Here is a case where emotion-focused coping and identity accommodation can have very deleterious effects, as a negative cycle is triggered by improper diet and exercise to create conditions involving further loss of abilities or the incentive to try to maintain functioning.

In addition to these psychological interactions involving elimination, there are a host of other physical changes as well as cognitive, emotional, motivational, and social factors that contribute to changes in eating patterns (Fischer & Johnson, 1990). Reduced mobility, for example, can interfere with the older adult's ability to shop for groceries, and to complete the many complex physical tasks needed to prepare food at home. Reaching around the back of the refrigerator can present a significant challenge to a older adult with limited range of movement in the upper body and arms. Visual losses may interfere with the older individual's ability to read the grocery list, food coupons, and recipes (Wantz & Gay, 1981) and other sensory losses in taste and smell can reduce the enjoyment of food. Problems with teeth and dentures are another source of possible loss of eating pleasure and, ultimately, nutritional deficiencies (Posner, Jette, Smigelski, Miller, & Mitchell, 1994). In the cognitive domain, memory problems and difficulties processing information can make it more difficult for the older individual to take the necessary steps for healthy and satisfying food preparation (see Chapter 8). Changes in family patterns, particularly the loss of a spouse, can cause older individuals to lose the incentive to cook, and the emotional associations to family mealtimes of the past that no longer can take place may lead to depression and disinterest in eating (Rosenbloom & Whittington, 1993). Men living alone are particularly vulnerable to poor nutrition (Davis, Murphy, & Neuhaus, 1988; Davis, Randall, Forthofer, Lee, & Margen, 1985). Adverse economic circumstances also can play a major role in affecting patterns of eating, as the individual may be working with such a limited budget that only the minimal, and perhaps unappetizing, necessities can be acquired.

Even though the digestive system itself suffers little from the aging process itself, then, there are continued threats to its functional integrity caused by psychological and social complications specific to later adulthood. Once a cycle of poor eating and elimination is established, particularly in combination with over-accommodation and emotion-focused coping, it may be very difficult to promote healthier habits so that food and all that goes with it can become a source of enjoyment and comfort. From a more positive perspective, the increased publicity in which older adults are encouraged to adopt problem-focused coping strategies of monitoring cholesterol levels through the lowering of fat content in food has already begun to exert positive effects on current cohorts of older adults and may be expected to increase further in the future.

EXCRETORY SYSTEM

The elimination of the chemical waste products of cellular metabolism is carried out by the excretory system, which keeps these substances from accumulating in harmful levels within the body. The blood passes through the kidneys, which extract these wastes and pass them on where they are stored in liquid form in the bladder until eliminated through the urethra. This elimination process is crucial for ensuring the consistency of the fluid environment surrounding the body's cells in terms of acidity and sodium content.

The nephron is the basic structural unit of the kidney, specialized to perform its function of extracting chemical wastes from the blood. It normally is surrounded by a fist-shaped cluster of blood vessels called the glomerulus. The blood reaches the nephron through the glomerulus, where it is rid of all its contents except proteins and red blood cells. The cleansed blood, which is now called the glomerular filtrate, passes through the tubule of the nephron, down and through the U-shaped loop of Henle, through another set of convolutions, and then into the collecting duct. The formation of urine from the filtrate begins in the tubule and collecting duct. In this conversion process, materials are added back into the blood by osmosis that the body needs to retain, such as water, sodium, minerals, glucose, and amino acids. In fact, one of the most crucial functions taking place in the kidney's tubules is the regulation of the amount of water lost from the body in the urine. Almost all of the water in the glomerular filtrate is taken back into the body's tissues through resorption across the tubular membrane. As a result, the urine becomes more concentrated than is the glomerular filtrate. This concentration is accomplished by a mechanism in the loop of Henle responsible for creating a high concentration of sodium in the tissues surrounding the tubule so that water will diffuse through osmosis from the highly dilute filtrate back into the tubules. More water reenters the tissues surrounding the tubule as the urine passes through the straight collecting duct that neighbors the loop of Henle. In this straight duct, there is a gradient of increasingly high sodium concentration, so that by the time the urine leaves this duct, it has become maximally concentrated. The now concentrated urine with the waste products that require elimination are finally excreted through the renal pelvis, down the ureters, into the bladder. The individual can eliminate the urine when it accumulates sufficiently in the bladder through voluntary control of the urethral spincters which forces it to exit through the urethra.

Research on the aging of the kidney has focused on structural changes in the nephron and its surrounding structures as well as on changes in the kidney's functioning as indicated by renal blood flow, the rate of glomerular filtrate formation, and the ability of the tubules to transport and concentrate the urine as it is being formed.

Age Effects on the Kidneys

The kidney was one of the first organs to receive thorough scrutiny by gerontological researchers. Early studies revealed many significant effects of aging on the structures of the kidney reflected, most simply, as a reduction of the kidney's volume and weight. The number of glomeruli is reduced, particularly in the inner part of the kidneys, beginning as early as the age of 45 years and continuing until almost all in this region are affected in some way by the age of 85 years (Takazakura et al., 1972). The remaining glomeruli, located in the outer region of the kidneys, show signs of partial degeneration, accumulation of scarlike tissue, and a smoothening of the surface and hence reduction of area where blood filtration can take place (Goyal, 1982; McLachlan, Guthrie, Anderson, & Fulker, 1977a; Sworn & Fox, 1972). The total number of nephrons decreases (Nakamaru et al., 1981), and those that remain increasingly acquire abnormalities, including a thickening of their membranes, degeneration into fatty tissue, shortening, the development of additional nonfunctional tubules, and a loss of functional convolutions (Darmady, Offer, & Woodhouse, 1973; Goyal, 1982). Adding to these changes in the nephron and its associated blood supply are abnormalities in the kidney's blood vessels, including a stiffening and narrowing seen in other parts of the circulatory system (Davidson, Talner, & Downs, 1969).

Corresponding to these significant and widespread changes in the structure of the kidneys is a well-established literature documenting age differences in cross-sectional studies in the direction of increasingly impaired efficiency in progressively older adults on every measure of renal functioning studied. Renal blood flow, an index of the amount of blood that passes through the kidneys per unit of time, remains stable until about age 50, but then shows a steady cross-sectional drop-off after that point (Wesson, 1969). An index of the efficiency of the nephrons themselves is the glomerular filtration rate, which is an indication of the amount of filtrate manufactured per unit of time. Over the course of adulthood, there is a gradual decrease beginning in the mid-30s and accelerating after the mid-60s (Rowe, Andres, Tobin, Norris, & Shock, 1976). The capacity of the tubules of the nephrons to exchange materials with their surrounding capillaries, as indicated by tubular transport, becomes less efficient in turn, with the loss estimated to be about 35%–45% between the ages of 20 and 90 (Davies & Shock, 1950).

A final index of kidney functioning at the level of the nephron is the adequacy of the urine concentration process. The outcome of this process is extremely important for maintaining the proper dilution of urine in response to the physiological status of the body. The urine must be dilute when there is an excess of fluid in the body, and highly concentrated when fluid levels are low due to dehydration or excess water loss through evaporation (sweating). Control of the urine's concentration is exerted in part by the hypothalamus, which contains osmoreceptors sensitive to the blood's water concentration. Local control of the urine concentration mechanism is influenced by the amount of sodium in the glomerular filtrate which in turn is related to the production of renin, an enzyme that reduces water content of the urine, and aldosterone, a hormone that further facilitates water loss from the tubule. With increasing age in adulthood, these mechanisms become deficient, impairing the urine concentrating ability of the kidneys under conditions of water deprivation (Rowe, Shock, & DeFronzo, 1976).

An overall estimate of the loss of various renal functions over adulthood was provided by one of the pioneer researchers in this area, Nathan Shock, who estimated that the kidney loses functioning at the approximate rate of 6% per decade from age 20 and continuing into the 90s. Although longitudinal studies report a picture of perhaps somewhat more stability when the same individuals are followed over time (Shock, Andres, Norris, & Tobin, 1978), later evidence has not seriously challenged this estimate. Having documented this extent of loss, the next question is why? Subsequent investigators have attempted to determine whether the nephron dies as a result of primary aging changes in its structure or whether, by contrast, it is the renal circulatory system that is to blame. The conclusion that the nephron loses function independently of the changes in the renal blood supply appears to have the weight of evidence behind it, given the frequent confound of age with cardiovascular disease, which clearly affects renal blood flow as well as other indicators of kidney function, the fact that nephron loss is not always associated with changes in renal blood supply (McLachlan, Guthrie, Anderson, & Fulker, 1977b), and the observation of independent losses in the urine concentrating mechanism (Rowe, 1982). The underlying cause of nephron loss, however, still has yet to be identified.

Implications of Age Effects on Renal Functioning

Before describing the changes in other areas of excretory functioning, there are several important implications of the aging of the kidneys that require explanation in terms of the daily life of the older adult. Although there is a gradual loss of function amounting to as much as 40% on some measures, the kidneys of healthy older persons are still able to meet their requirements as long as they are not placed under extreme physiological stress through unusual demands or in extreme situations (Rowe, 1982). One of these situations is aerobic exercise, activity which diverts blood to the working skeletal muscles, thereby causing further reduction in the renal blood flow. A more significant application pertains to the urine concentrating mechanism and its reaction to exercise or changes in temperature. Sodium and water become depleted during exercise or under extreme conditions of heat when the individual begins to perspire. Fatigue, changes in body chemistry, and potentially deleterious changes in bodily fluid levels will occur more rapidly in the older adult who cannot adequately conserve sodium and water under these conditions.

A third application of age effects on renal functioning has a more direct bearing on the individual's health, particularly for older adults who are taking certain types of medication. As described earlier, the tubules of the nephron operate less efficiently in the elderly individual. When an older person is given the same dosage of medication appropriate for a younger adult, whose tubular transport is operating more efficiently, more of the drug will remain in the bloodstream over the period of time between doses. With repeated dosages of the drug taken over a given interval of time, it is more likely that harmful levels will build in the blood. Unless the dosage is adjusted to take into account this lower rate of tubular transport, drugs may have an adverse impact instead of their intended benefits (Lamy, 1988; Montgomery, 1990). Surprisingly, although this fact is hardly kept secret within the gerontological community, there is nevertheless widespread inadvertent pharmacological abuse of the elderly commited by well-intended but uninformed health care practitioners.

Age Effects on the Bladder

The bladder is a sac-like muscular structure that functions to store the urine that passes from the kidneys through the ureters. The efficient operation of the bladder depends on its ability both to expand to hold the stored urine without discomfort and to empty completely when the individual is voiding. Both of these functions are compromised with increasing age in adulthood. Adults past the age of 65 years experience a reduction in the total amount of urine they can store before feeling a need to void, and more urine is retained in the bladder after the individual has attempted to empty it. These phenomena appear to be related to age changes in the connective tissue of the bladder causing the organ to lose its expandability and contractility somewhat like that which is seen in the case of the lung. Older adults also can experience some changes in the perception of the need to empty the bladder. The recognition of a need to void may not occur until the bladder is almost or even completely filled. This means that the individual has less or perhaps no time to reach a lavatory before leakage or spillage occurs. Awakenings during the night stimulated by a need to void are also more frequent in the elderly, but this age effect apparently occurs without direct correspondence to changes in the kidney or bladder (Goldman, 1977).

The most significant effect of changes with age in the bladder is on patterns of urinary incontinence. The prevalence of incontinence among the population 60 years and older is estimated to be 19% for women and 8% for men (Herzog, Diokno, Brown, Normolle, & Brock, 1990) but can reach as high as 36% among community-dwelling elderly with dementia (Ouslander, Zarit, Orr, & Muira, 1990). Women are more likely to suffer from stress incontinence, which refers to loss of urine at times of exertion such as when one is laughing, sneezing, lifting, or bending. This condition is the result of weakness of the pelvic muscles. Urge incontinence is more prevalent in men, and involves urine loss following an urge to void or lack of control over voiding with little or no warning (Diokno, Brock, Brown, & Herzog, 1986). For men, incontinence is related to prostatic disease or incomplete emptying of the bladder. Among the community-dwelling elderly, each of these conditions, particularly urge incontinence, is reversible and may disappear within a year or two of its initial development (Herzog et al., 1990).

Psychological Consequences of Aging of the Excretory System

Most adults probably tend not to be concerned about or even aware of the aging of the kidneys compared to the effects of aging on other bodily systems. You may have been surprised to learn that so much research attention has been devoted to uncovering the causes of aging of the ill-fated nephron. More apparent to the individual in terms of psychological functioning are changes in the bladder that lead to altered patterns of urination. This concern stems partly from the fact that it is annoying to have to take time out of daily activities to urinate and, conversely, it is uncomfortable to have to hold one's urine when there is no easy access to a lavatory. Embarrassment is also associated with the frequent need to urinate, particularly when there are others present in the situation. Needless to say, any type of incontinence, involving either leakage or spillage, is highly distressing to the individual under any circumstances (Hunskaar & Vinsnes, 1991; Ouslander & Abelson, 1990; Wyman, Harkins, & Fantl, 1990; Yu, 1987). Not only do such occasions involve shame, but they feed into the association in many people's minds between "senility" and urinary incontinence. Other horrors of incontinence may also loom in the mind of the older person, such as the need for institutionalization, and loss of self-respect and respect from eyes of family and friends. Given the many associations to urinary continence, it would not be unreasonable to suppose that even a single episode of stress incontinence could create a significant threshold experience for the individual.

Unfortunately, annoyingly frequent television and print advertisements for adult diapers communicate the message that such changes are expectable aspects of aging and that there is no other form of prevention. Ironically enough, once identified, incontinence is a condition that in many cases can be managed if the individual is able to muster the resources to use problem-focused coping strategies rather than assuming that all is lost. Through behavioral techniques, sometimes involving only very simple exercises, the problem can be held in check if not reversed (Baigis-Smith, Smith, Rose, & Newman, 1989; Burgio & Engel, 1990; Burns et al., 1993). Thus, although the psychological damage is potentially very high from changes in urinary functioning, this can be offset by the individual's experience of success in learning problem-focused behavioral management techniques that can work with impressive success.

ENDOCRINE SYSTEM

The release of hormones into the bloodstream by the glands in the endocrine system is a process governed by various feedback mechanisms involving metabolic and other needs of various cells throughout the body. The endocrine system regulates such cellular activities as protein synthesis, storage and release of glucose, sodium retention, and the reduction of inflammation at the site of tissue injury. The hypothalamus controls many of these functions; others are carried out by glands within the pancreas.

It was once thought (and still thought by some) that the endocrine system held the key to finding the cause of aging by virtue of its dominant control over the body's organ systems. When scientists first discovered hormones in the late 19th century, some believed that they would eventually prove to be the "elixirs of youth." Although this belief has failed to be realized, there remains a tremendous interest among present-day researchers in elucidating the role played by hormones in the aging process. Each of the components of the endocrine system has at one time or another been nominated as the main protagonist in the aging process. Currently, researchers are more circumspect, restricting their investigations to the contributions made by particular hormone systems to the regulation of specific bodily systems rather than searching for the ultimate cause of aging in the body as a whole. Whether or not such specific changes have a role in the bigger picture, they are important because they influence the use of energy by the body at rest and during exercise, and can have widespread significance for the individual's sense of well-being.

Hypothalamus and Pituitary Gland

The hypothalamus secretes hormones into the pituitary gland, and this hormonal system forms the core of a network that has a broad range of control over the body. The functions of this system are best understood in terms of the anterior and posterior divisions of the pituitary gland. Although there is no available research on humans regarding the effects of age on the hormones released by the hypothalamus (the hypothalamic-releasing factors, or HRFs), there are extensive data on the effects of age on pituitary gland functioning. The pituitary hormones studied with regard to age are the thyroid-stimulating hormone (TSH), adrenocorticotropic hormone (ACTH), and growth hormone (GH). The other pituitary hormones are prolactin, follicle-stimulating hormone (FSH), and luteinizing hormone (LH), are primarily involved in the reproductive system.

Anterior pituitary gland. Given the central role of the anterior pituitary gland in regulating many of the body's functions, age-related changes in this organ were once thought to play an especially key role in the aging of the body. There are documented age effects in the structure and weight of this gland (Lockett, 1976; Verzar, 1966); however, these structural changes have little apparent functional impact. The response of the anterior pituitary gland to hypothalamic stimulation remains intact (Lewis, Alessi, Imperial, & Refetoff, 1991), and the anterior pituitary hormone reserves do not undergo significant reductions (Blichert-Toft, 1975). As will be shown in the following discussion, there are scattered reports of age effects in various anterior pituitary hormones, but often the findings are difficult to evaluate because of possible variations across samples in health status.

TSH. There are conflicting reports on the existence of age effects in thyroid-stimulating hormone with some evidence of no age differences in blood levels of TSH or TSH responsiveness to hypothalamic thyrotropin-releasing factor (Azizi et al., 1979; Blichert-Toft, Hummer, & Dige-Petersen, 1975; Greenspan, Klibanski, Rowe, & Elahi, 1991); other reports reveal a variable or inconsistent pattern of age differences (Robuschi, Safran, Braverman, Gnudi, & Roti, 1987; Runnels, Garry, Hunt, & Standefer, 1991; Sawin et al., 1991). Investigators have postulated that although TSH levels in the blood may not show decreases with age, a portion of circulating TSH may be biologically inactive, thereby reducing its effective levels (Runnels et al., 1991). The existence of subclinical levels of hypothyroidism in elderly individuals may also complicate the picture regarding the effects of age (Minaker, Meneilly, & Rowe, 1985).

ACTH. Age-related reductions in the levels of ACTH would have widespread significance on bodily functioning because this hormone plays a crucial mediating role in preparing the body to react to stressful situations. However, there are no apparent age effects on levels of ACTH in the blood or the pituitary gland. The normal responses are maintained into old age of increasing ACTH levels in response to decreased blood levels of glucocorticoids and blood glucose and lowered ACTH following the administration of steroids (Blichert-Toft, 1975; Lockett, 1976; Waltman, Blackman, Chrousos, Riemann, & Harman, 1991).

GH. The function of growth hormone and its role in aging are topics that have intrigued researchers for a number of years. The primary importance of this hormone is the regulation of growth during the maturation process. It was therefore believed at one time that maintenance of high levels of GH could ultimately slow down the rate of aging. This hypothesis, however, was not consistent with the fact that excessive GH production in an adult leads to premature death. The effects of GH on adults, then, have remained a puzzle.

GH has a number of other functions, however, that are more clearly relevant to the aging process. Secretion of GH stimulates the liver to release larger amounts of glucose into the blood from its stored form as glycogen when blood glucose levels are low. Release of GH is also stimulated by exercise, which creates heavy glucose demands by the working muscles. GH secretion also plays an important role in defending the body against hypoglycemia, a condition that can have disastrous effects on the nervous system, which is a heavy consumer of glucose. Protein synthesis is another function maintained by GH secretion, as is the release of energy from fat tissue. All tolled, the metabolic actions served by GH make it a critical contributor to the availability of energy for the body's tissues, particularly during strenuous physical activity. It would seem important, then, to determine whether and how aging affects GH secretion. Complicating this assessment, however, is the fact that GH levels are very reactive to stressful stimuli such as pain, anxiety, and temperature changes. Further, GH levels show cyclical patterns during the day.

In general, the secretion of GH by the anterior pituitary gland appears to be maintained into old age. There is no decline in GH within the cells of this gland, nor a decrease in GH levels within the blood under baseline conditions. The clearance rate of GH through the body is maintained at normal levels into later adulthood. Moreover, and of particular importance in terms of physical functioning under conditions of stress, the extent to which GH increases in response to physiological stimulation seems to remain normal throughout the later years of adulthood (Blichert-Toft, 1975; Taylor, Finster, & Mintz, 1969). Variations across adulthood in GH secretion have been found to be related more to the relative degree of obesity of the individual rather than to age (Dudl, Ensinck, Palmer, & Williams, 1973; Elahi, Muller, Tzankoff, Andres, & Tobin, 1982).

Despite this overall picture of stability, there are some indications of selected areas of loss in GH secretion. The cyclical nature of GH secretion is such that in children and adults, GH secretion peaks during the nighttime hours, co-occurring with periods of slow wave sleep. The number of peaks during sleep decreases throughout the years from childhood to late adulthood (Prinz & Halter, 1983); for this reason, total GH secretion over a 24-hour period is lower in the aged compared to younger adults (Florini, Prinz, Vitiello, & Hintz, 1985; Kern, Dodt, Born & Fehm, 1996). Another area of loss, or at least abnormal functioning, involves the GH response to exercise. Under conditions of moderate (i. e., submaximal) exercise, older persons show attenuated GH responses (Hagberg et al., 1988). However endurance training can correct for attenuated GH responses to exercise in older adults, both over the short- and long-term (Hagberg et al., 1988; Sidney & Shephard, 1977; Szanto, 1975).

Glands controlled by the anterior pituitary. The hormones released by the anterior pituitary gland stimulate the secretion of hormones in the corresponding target glands. Apart from any effects of aging on the anterior pituitary hormones, changes in the target glands or the levels of hormones produced by those glands will have subsequent effects on the functions controlled by those glands such as muscle metabolism or glucose conversion.

Thyroid gland. Age effects on the thyroid gland are the center of considerable attention because of the instrumental role served by the thyroid hormones in controlling the expenditure of caloric energy by the body. However, it is difficult to pinpoint the effect of aging on the thyroid gland per se because of its feedback loop with the body's muscles. Thus, it is known that the basal metabolic rate (BMR) slows with age as indexed by cross-sectional studies, and this decrease is regarded as being due to lower oxygen uptake by the muscle cells (Tzankoff & Norris, 1977). The diminished oxygen uptake is, in turn, accounted for by a reduction in the number of actively metabolizing muscle cells and hence, less of a demand for the thyroid hormones. Lowered activity levels in middle and old age can further contribute to a lowered BMR due to a reduction of energy expenditure (McGandy et al., 1966). The decline in energy expenditure can, in turn, reduce the output of the thyroid gland due to a diminution in the bodily demands that it must meet.

Initial indications of the involution of the thyroid gland (Lasada & Roberts, 1974) were countered by the finding that apparent age differences in loss of volume were due to a confound of age and body weight (Hegedus et al., 1983). In terms of function, it appears that the secretion of thyroid hormones is not negatively affected by aging, including the responsiveness of the thyroid gland to externally administered TSH (Azizi et al., 1979). Circulating levels of free T_4 are also unchanged in older adults (Greenspan, Klibanski, Rowe, & Elahi, 1991; Rubenstein, Butler, & Werner, 1973; Sawin, Chopra, Azizi, Mannix, & Bacharach, 1979). From these findings, it would seem evident that the thyroid gland itself is unaltered by aging and that reductions in the BMR are consequent to alterations in the muscles and the body's energy demands. This conclusion must be moderated by the fact that there are small but reliable age effects on blood levels of another thyroid hormone, T_3 (Minaker, Meneilly, & Rowe, 1985), although to some extent this decrease might be caused by disease and not aging (Olsen, Laurberg, & Weeke, 1978). In any case, the changes in thyroid functioning itself appear to be minor and cannot account for the more substantial reductions that occur in the body's metabolic rate across the adult years.

Adrenal cortex. The cells in the cortex of the adrenal glands produce several types of corticosteroids: glucocorticoids (primarily cortisol), mineralocorticoids (primarily aldosterone), and sex steroids (primarily androgens and estrogens). ACTH is released by the anterior pituitary gland in response to bodily demands for glucose and protein. Release of ACTH in turn stimulates secretion of the adrenal hormones, which in turn stimulate the liver to release glucose and protein. Of the adrenal hormones, cortisol has received the greatest attention with regard to the effects of aging. Cross-sectional studies have revealed that there are structural changes with age in the adrenals, but these changes do not detract from the functional capacity of the adrenal cortex. Blood levels of cortisol generally remain stable across adulthood (Barton et al., 1993), as does the adrenal gland's response to stimulation by ACTH (Roberts, Barton, & Horan, 1990).

Pancreas. Outside the realm of the hypothalamic control is the endocrine gland component of the pancreas, located in the islets of Langerhans. The endocrine pancreas is the primary regulator of glucose availability to the other cells of the body, via the secretion of insulin (by the beta cells) and glucagon (by the alpha cells). Insulin facilitates the conversion of glycogen to glucose in the liver, other energy-storing reactions in muscle and fat tissues, and the uptake of glucose from the blood by the muscles. When the glucose level of the blood becomes low, glucagon is stimulated, and the glucose-producing reactions are stimulated throughout the body, including the liver. Insulin and glucagon also regulate the metabolism of other nutrients by the body's tissues. Insulin inhibits the breakdown and promotes the synthesis of proteins, fats, nucleic acids, and glycogen, so that more energy is stored in muscle and fat tissue. Glucagon stimulates the converse reactions, liberating stored energy from muscle and fat tissues.

Within the over-65 population, there is a high proportion of diabetes mellitus (a disease characterized by abnormally low insulin levels in the blood). This fact alone has stimulated considerable research directed at understanding pancreatic functioning in old age. Furthermore, many aged men and women who do not show clinical symptoms of diabetes are found to have abnormally high scores on laboratory tests of glucose tolerance. Ordinarily, the insulin produced by the pancreas reduces glucose levels in the blood between 1 to 3 hours after glucose is ingested. Decreased glucose tolerance, that is less of a reduction in blood glucose levels, is almost universally observed in progressively older age groups of adults (Minaker et al., 1985; Shimokata et al., 1991), although there are rare exceptions to this overall trend (Bourey et al., 1993). An important factor related to the maintenance of glucose tolerance is the amount of exercise in which the individual participates as well as amount of body fat (Rogers, King, Hagberg, Ehsani, & Holloszy, 1990; Sparrow, Borkan, Gerzof, Wisniewski, & Silbert, 1986). Fatty tissue, particularly in the intra-abdominal regions, is associated with higher glucose tolerance. Exercise, to the extent that it reduces body fat, may help to prevent age-associated decreases in glucose tolerance (Kirwan, Kohrt, Wojta, Bourey, & Holloszy, 1993).

There is good evidence that independently of age-related changes in glucose tolerance, insulin levels are maintained in older adults (Minaker et al., 1985), leading to the question of whether there are differences in insulin secretion and clearance or whether the body's tissues present increasing resistance to the effects of insulin on glucose uptake and conversion to glycogen. It is generally found that insulin secretion is diminished in progressively older samples of adults (Beccaro, Pacini, Velerio, Nosadini, & Crepaldi, 1990; Gumbiner et al., 1989), and that insulin clearance also diminishes (Minaker, Rowe, Pallotta, & Sparrow, 1982). The result of these changes would be unaltered levels of insulin in the bloodstream. The next question, then, is whether there are changes in the tissue resistance to insulin, and a number of findings support this interpretation (Broughton, James, Alberti, & Taylor, 1991; Davidson, 1979; DeFronzo, 1979; Ratzmann, Witt, Heinke, & Shulz, 1982; Reed, Reaven, Mondon, & Zahar, 1993). Even older individuals with normal glucose tolerance show this impaired insulin sensitivity (Fink, Kolterman, Griffin, & Olefsky, 1983; Rowe, Minaker, Pallotta, & Flier, 1983). The reduced insulin sensitivity, it is postulated, is particularly evident in muscle tissue (DeFronzo, 1982).

Another perspective on the issue of insulin sensitivity in later life is provided by the growing number of investigations yielding no age-related decrease in insulin sensitivity when body fat of the respondents is taken into account or controlled (Kalant, Leiborici, Leibovici, & Fukushima, 1980; Pacini et al., 1988; Shimokata et al., 1989). Level of activity also appears to be an important factor, as reduced physical activity has been shown to reduce insulin sensitivity in older persons (Hollenbeck, Haskell, Rosenthal, & Reaaven, 1984; Seals et al., 1984). Conversely, exercise training or even regular involvement in leisure-related physical activity can have favorable effects on insulin levels and sensitivity (Allen, Seals, Hurley, Ehsani, & Hagberg, 1985; Kahn et al., 1990; Kirwan et al., 1993; Reaven, Barrett-Connor, & Edelstein, 1991; Seals, Hagberg, Hurley, Ehsani, & Holloszy, 1984; Tonino, 1989).

Implications of Age Effects on Endocrine Functioning

In virtually all systems studied with regard to age, it appears that the complex feedback loops involved in the hormonal control of bodily systems are maintained to a large extent throughout the later adult years. Yet, in almost every subsystem studied, there appear to be changes in the hormone's effectiveness in acting on its target cells. In some cases, such as T_3 and cortisol, the alteration might be due to a loss of tissue mass so that less of the hormone is required to achieve the necessary effect. In the case of insulin, it might be argued that the body's tissues are less responsive, leading to a need for more insulin to be produced to achieve the adequate storage of glucose.

Given that the endocrine glands underlie so many aspects of functioning in everyday life, the stability that is shown in this system may be seen as contributing to the individual's ability to adapt to situations in which energy reserves must be used or stored. For example, the fact that the functioning of the anterior pituitary gland and the pancreatic glands that produce insulin remain fairly stable allows for some stability in the individual's ability to draw on bodily reserves during times of exertion. Such stability means that any threshold with regard to the endocrine system is likely to be crossed relatively late in the grand scheme of the aging process.

It must be recognized, however, that there is tremendous diversity in the composition of the samples of adults who have participated in the research on aging in factors that may have profound relationships to hormonal functioning. One of these is body fat, shown in several instances to be more strongly related than age to various aspects of metabolic functioning. Degree of physical activity is another important influence, with sedentary individuals exhibiting less of a hormonal response to exercise than well-trained adults throughout adulthood (Silverman & Mazzeo, 1996). Other factors that might serve as confounds with age include gender, nutritional status, and overall health. Although researchers usually attempt to solicit subjects who are in good physical health, this is not always the case, so that age groups may differ in some very important physiological characteristics or lifestyle habits that could affect endocrine functioning. Another factor that could confound the results of studies on aging is the individual's level of stress due to the unfamiliarity of the test situation. Stress can influence the levels of many of the hormones studied in relation to age, and extraneous influences of settings and procedures may throw off, in differential ways across age groups, some of the delicate balances in the systems being investigated. Fortunately, researchers are increasingly sensitive to these problems, and future studies should contain far more reliable data than has been true in the past. However, to the extent that individuals suffer from conditions that could negatively influence the functioning of the endocrine system, they may find that they approach a threshold experience, particularly under conditions of exertion.

IMMUNE SYSTEM

The function of the immune system is to protect the cells of the body from harm caused by foreign, "non-self" substances that invade the body. As was true for the endocrine system, a case has been made for the idea that the aging of the immune system is the ultimate biological cause of aging (Walford, 1969). Roy Walford, who still stands by this theory of aging, drew national attention when he became a member of the crew of the Biosphere II. Although his theory is still not generally accepted, there is nevertheless convincing evidence of important changes in this major bodily system. Furthermore, the immune system is of interest to the aging process because of the increased prevalence with age of certain immune-related diseases particularly cancer (Newell, Spitz, & Sider, 1989).

The immune system operates through the actions of a variety of cells that respond to foreign substances or organisms introduced into the body ("antigens"). There are essentially two types of responses made by the immune system in these situations: cell-mediated immune responses and humoral (blood-related) responses. Each of these types of responses shows different aging effects.

Cell-Mediated Immunity

Cell-mediated immune responses involve the activation of specialized cells that respond directly with and ultimately destroy the antigen-bearing cells that have entered the body. This type of immune response is involved in the body's reaction to viruses, cells from foreign tissue in grafts or organs, and cancer cells. There are several types of immune cells involved in this type of response: cytotoxic T lymphocytes (T-cells), natural killer cells (NK cells), and lymphokine-activated killer cells (K cells). These cells target particular antigens in a selective fashion, and when they bind with these antigens, produce proteins that destroy the target. Accessory cells consisting of leucocytes (white blood cells) and macrophages also participate in cell-mediated immunity. These cells destroy antigens by engulfing and digesting them.

The most consistent finding regarding cell-mediated immunity is that although T-cells show no change in absolute number, they become decreasingly effective over the years of adulthood (Bloom, 1994; Globerson, Eren, Abel, & Ben-Menahem, 1990; Heidrick, 1987; Thoman & Weigle, 1989). In part, this age effect is due to diminished ability of T-cells to respond to their target antigens, by being less able to destroy them and less able to interfere with mitogens, substances that induce division of the antigen cells. The effect of age on T-cell functioning is also due to changes that occur in the thymus gland (Hirokawa, Utsuyama, & Kasai, 1990). T-cells develop from stem cells in the bone marrow that travel to the thymus, where a portion of them mature into what are called "immunocompetent" cells, that have the ability to destroy their target cells. Fewer of these mature T-cells are produced in the thymus gland of the older individual due to severe involutional changes in this organ. Autopsy studies have revealed that the deterioration of the thymus gland begins shortly after sexual maturity is reached, so that by the time the individual is 45–50 years old, the thymus retains only 5% to 10% of its peak mass. As a result of these changes, there are more immature T-cells present both within the thymus gland and in the bloodstream. Along with the decreased ability to stimulate differentiation and development of the T-cells, the thymus gland produces fewer of its thymic hormones, which are also involved in stimulating the production of mature T-cells (Hausman & Weksler, 1985). Evidence regarding NK cells, K cells, and macrophages indicates that these cells retain their functioning into old age (Bloom, 1994; Kutza, Kaye, & Murasko, 1995).

Humoral-Mediated Immunity

The second line of defense represented within the immune system is mediated through the production of antibodies (immunoglobulins), molecules that circulate through the blood and neutralize specific antigens by binding to them. The antibody-antigen bond leads to engulfment and destruction of the antigen by phagocytes, activating complement blood proteins that further enable the process. The primary cells involved in humoral immunity are the B-cells (signifying that their differentiation is within the bone marrow) that produce the antibodies; however, T-cells play an important role in this immune resonse as well. The so-called "helper" T-cells interact with B-cells to enhance their destruction of antigens. "Suppressor" T-cells reduce the effectiveness of B-cells.

Findings with regard to age in humoral-mediated immunity indicate that older individuals show impairment in this aspect of immune functioning, primarily as the result of diminished activity of helper T-cells (Bloom, 1994; Hausman & Weksler, 1985). At the same time, there may be increases in autoimmune responses, such that antibodies are produced to the body's own cells rather than to foreign antigens. The greater prevalence of certain "autoimmune" diseases in older populations is regarded as support for this interpretation. Another line of support comes from the fact that although specific antibody responses are impaired with age, the number of antibody-producing cells shows no decline nor does the total amount of antibody formed. It is also possible that suppressor T-cell activity increases with age, interfering with the ability of B cells to destroy their target antigens (Hausman & Weksler, 1985).

Psychological Interactions

Research on immune system functioning is limited in large part to studies of nonhuman species, although enough investigations with humans have been conducted to warrant conclusions regarding age effects on T-cell activity. Recent lines of investigation into the role of the immune system in psychological functioning of humans have been stimulated by progress in the field of psychoneuroimmunology, in which the intricate connections are explored between affective states such as stress and depression, nervous system functioning, and the operation of the immune system (O'Leary, 1990; Vollardt, 1991). It has long been known that people are more vulnerable to illness when emotionally stressed, and discoveries in the past few decades have begin to provide empirical support for this common-sense notion. For example, elderly individuals with high levels of life stress have been found experience lower T-cell functioning than individuals not experiencing adversity (McNaughton, Smith, Patterson, & Grant, 1990). Conversely, social support, at least among women, was found in one large-scale study to be postively related to competence of immune functioning measured in terms of lymphocyte numbers and response to mitogens (Thomas, Goodwin, & Goodwin, 1985).

It is believed that emotional stress stimulates hypothalmic hormones that in turn lower immune system activity (Rabin, Cohen, Ganguli, Lysle, & Cunnick, 1989), making the individual more susceptible to physical disorders that can affect individuals of a variety of ages, including bronchial asthma, rheumatoid arthritis, ulcerative colitis, and cancerous conditions such as leukemia and lymphomas (Schleifer, Scott, Stein, & Keller, 1986). Conversely, activation of the immune system alters levels of norepinephrine in the hypothalamus and stimulates the release of corticotropin releasing factor from the hypothalamus. Changes in these neural and endocrine substances are found in individuals with depression (Stein, Miller, & Trestman, 1991), as are decreased levels of T-cell function (Schleifer, Keller, Siris, Davis, & Stein, 1985). Older individuals are at least as susceptible to stress as younger adults in terms of increases in T-suppressor cells and NK cell numbers, although not in terms of increased NK activity (Naliboff et al., 1991). Stress also seems linked to the release of beta-endorphin, an opioid peptide released from the pituitary gland that has an analgesic effect. This process may play an important role in mediating the effects of emotions on the immune system (Antoni, 1987).

Although there are no compensatory measures that can be taken to offset age-related changes in the thymus, compensation for age-related decreases in immune functioning may be possible through exercise. It is known that exercise has a positive effect on T-cell numbers and functioning in younger adults (Kanonchoff et al., 1984). Although this research has not been replicated on older individuals, there is suggestive evidence that healthy aged adults can increase NK cell functioning through exercise to the extent comparable to younger persons (Fiatarone et al., 1989).

Apart from changes in the immune system that interact with psychological functioning, the lowered effectiveness of the immune system in older adults has important implications for health. The aging immune system has been linked to increased vulnerability to influenza, infections, cancer, and certain age-associated autoimmune disorders such as diabetes and possibly atherosclerosis and even Alzheimer's disease. Although there are other factors that affect the development of each of these conditions, particularly cancer (Ershler, 1993), a less competent immune system can put the elderly individual at higher risk at least to certain forms of cancer and influenza (Ershler, 1990; Miller, 1993). And clearly, the development of severe health problems can have significant effects on the individual's psychological well-being.

Although the point may be apparent to the reader by now, there are many possible interactions between identity and immune system functioning. The crossing of an aging threshold in any salient area of functioning, to the extent that it triggers a stressful reaction not adequately coped with, can have deleterious effects on the immune system. The individual then becomes more susceptible to immune-related conditions. This may be a case in which overassimilation has some beneficial aspects, particularly if it is combined with coping strategies that minimize the extent of stress the individual experiences without putting the individual at risk.

REPRODUCTIVE SYSTEM AND SEXUALITY

The ability of the sexually mature individual to reproduce constitutes one of the most important components of human functioning. Furthermore, there are important interactions of the endocrine features of the reproductive system with other bodily control systems as these are affected by the aging process.

Female Reproductive System

Throughout the decade of the 40s, a woman's capacity to have children gradually diminishes, until it ceases altogether by the time she reaches the age of 50 to 55 years. This gradual reduction of reproductive capacity, the climacteric, ends in the menopause, when menstruation eventually ceases altogether. Associated with the ending of the monthly phases of ovulation and menstruation is a reduction of the hormones produced by the main reproductive organs, the ovary and uterus. Changes in these hormones affect the functioning of other reproductive structures and secondary sex characteristics, and have a more widespread impact on other systems within the body. The aging of the reproductive system is also affected by age-related changes in other bodily systems, including the connective tissues and circulatory system.

Physiological changes associated with the menopause. Beginning with the menarche during puberty, the female experiences monthly cycles during which the ovarian follicles produce ova and the uterus develops an endometrial lining to serve as nutritive tissue for a developing embryo. The monthly cycle's regulation occurs under the influence of the pituitary hormones, follicle-stimulating hormone (FSH) and luteinizing hormone (LH), as well as the estrogen and progesterone produced by the ovary.

The changes involved in the climacteric occur gradually over a period of at least 10 years preceding the actual cessation of menstruation. One of the major changes to occur in the climacteric is a shortening of the monthly cycle, so that instead of 30 days (at about age 30), it decreases to 25 by age 40 years, and 23 by the late 40s. There are also more cycles of irregularly long or short duration in the years prior to menopause, and more cycles during which no ovulation occurs (Harman & Talbert, 1985; Treloar, Boynton, Benn, & Brown, 1967). Beginning at about age 35 years and increasing rapidly after then, the ova released each month are more likely to have defects so that if they were fertilized, they would produce infants with severe abnormalities (Kram & Schneider, 1978).

Associated with the changes that lead toward menopause are alterations in the female reproductive hormones. There is a decrease in levels of estradiol, the primary estrogen produced by the ovaries (Sherman, West, & Korenmann, 1976). The lower levels of estradiol stimulate, in turn, increased production of FSH, the anterior pituitary hormone that ordinarily stimulates the ovarian follicles to secrete more estradiol when blood levels become low. A similar process leads to heightened production of LH, which also plays a role in stimulating the production of ovarian hormones (Harman & Talbert, 1985). There is also a decrease in blood levels of prolactin, a hormone produced by the anterior pituitary gland that stimulates the mammary glands (Vekemans & Robyn, 1975). The reduction in estradiol eventually leads to the end of the menstruation, as the uterus is no longer stimulated to develop an endometrial lining. Following menopause, estradiol production drops even further and no longer shows cyclical variations (Judd & Korenmann, 1982). At the same time, there are rises in the blood levels of estrone, another estrogen, as the result of increased production by the ovaries and the adrenal cortex (Judd, Judd, Lucas, & Yen, 1974; Suiteri & MacDonald, 1973). However, the increased estrone does not compensate for the loss of estradiol. The consequences of estrogen loss include changes in the reproductive and secondary sex organs, as well as heightened risk of osteoporosis and heart disease. Estrogen appears to play an important protective role in both of these areas.

Changes in sexual functioning. Although the loss of reproductive capacity does not have a direct impact on the woman's ability to enjoy sexual relations, there are a variety of changes associated with the menopause in appearance and functioning of the reproductive organs that can require adjustments in previous patterns of sexual behavior.

One important set of changes related both to the menopause and to the aging process in general involves the appearance of the woman's body. Although these changes do not lessen her ability to benefit from sexual activities, they may change a woman's physical identity with regard to the way she looks to her sexual partner. For example, the skin loses its elasticity in later adulthood, and as a result, fat-containing areas of the torso, arms, and legs begin to sag. The fact that mammary gland tissue has become replaced with fat means that the breasts are likely to droop. The alveoli become smaller, and eventually disappear altogether, and the nipples do not become as firmly erect when stimulated. Changes in the face and hair contribute further to these bodily changes to alter the woman's appearance throughout the aging years.

The genitals also show significant alterations in appearance and functioning following the menopause. The pubic hair becomes thinner and coarser, and the labia become thinner and wrinkled. As occurs throughout the body, the dermal and epidermal layers of the skin in the vulva undergo atrophy. Estrogen loss changes the biochemical environment of the vagina, and infections become more likely to occur. Within the vaginal wall, the surface cells become thin, dry, pale, and smooth and the vagina itself becomes narrower and shorter. These changes increase the likelihood of discomfort or pain during sexual intercourse.

Changes in sexual functioning. Although conducted over three decades ago, the landmark research of Masters and Johnson (Masters & Johnson, 1966) remains a primary source for understanding the effects of aging on female sexual functioning. Pre- and post-menopausal women were compared in their sexual responses while under the scrutiny of laboratory observations. The main finding to emerge from this investigation was that although the phases of the sexual response cycle might be progressed through at a slower rate, there is nevertheless no physiological basis for alterations in sexual enjoyment for older women in good health. The main limitation on a woman's sexual activity was the presence of a willing and desirable male partner. Subsequent longitudinal research confirmed this finding, indicating that the availability of a partner for women remains a key factor in determining the frequency of sexual activity for older adult women (Marsiglio & Donnelly, 1991; Pfeiffer, Verwoerdt, & Davis, 1974).

Male Reproductive Syste

The aging of the male reproductive system occurs gradually over the later years of adulthood, lacking the dramatic markers that characterize changes in women. During the male climacteric, sperm cells continue to be produced, but their number diminishes. However, men retain the ability to father children well into old age. The gerontological literature on this topic frequently includes reference to a legendary 94-year-old man who successfully fathered a child at this advanced age (Seymour, Duffy, & Koerner, 1935).

Changes in reproductive capacity. The testes are the primary site of both sperm production and the secretion of testosterone. The production of sperm takes place in the seminiferous tubules; testosterone is produced in the nearby Leydig cells. Both processes are under the control of FSH and LH, the same hormones produced by the anterior pituitary gland that stimulate the production of female reproductive hormones.

The weight of the testes remains stable into later adulthood, but there is a reduction beginning in the 40s and 50s in the proportion of normal viable sperm produced in the seminiferous tubules (Harman & Talbert, 1985). The remaining sperm show reduced motility after the age of 50 (Schwartz et al., 1983). A thickening of connective tissue around the inside of the tubules appears to be the main factor responsible for these changes in sperm production. Some of the tubules become nonfunctional, degenerating to the point of collapse. This reduction in sperm count sets off an increase in FSH production by the anterior pituitary (Swerdloff & Heber, 1982), an increase that is maintained as there are not enough sperm produced to turn off the control gland.

Changes in accessory structures. There are a number of structures within the male reproductive system that serve as accessories to the main reproductive activities of the testes. Two of these structures, the seminal vesicles and prostate gland, have been studied with respect to aging.

The seminal vesicles produce a thick fluid that contributes to the volume of the semen, providing nutrients to the sperm to give them energy after ejaculation to travel through the vagina and into the fallopian tubes. With increasing age in adulthood, the vesicles develop deposits of amyloid and there are various degenerative changes in the epithelium, mucosal lining, and muscle fiber.

The amount of fluid that can be retained within them drops by as much as 50% in men over the age of 60 years (Harman & Talbert, 1985; Pitkanen, Wester-mack, Cornwell, & Murdoch, 1983).

There are extensive data available describing age changes within the prostate gland, not so much because of its role in reproduction, but because of the frequency and seriousness of the medical problems that can develop in this structure in later adulthood. The normal role of the prostate is to discharge a thin, milky, and highly alkaline fluid that protects the sperm as it passes through the acidic areas within the vagina. This fluid is constantly being produced, and in between episodes of sexual activity, is discharged into the urine. By the time later adulthood is reached, the prostate loses secretory activity and shows signs of deterioration. Hard masses may appear in some of its glandular sacs. These masses constitute stagnant secretions that have not been eliminated through the ducts. Changes also occur in the connective tissue, which loses elasticity and contractility. The consequence of these changes are reduced volume and pressure of expelling semen during ejaculation. A condition known as benign prostatic hypertrophy develops in many men over the age of 50, rising to an estimated incidence of 50% in men over the age of 80 years. As the prostate enlarges, it places pressure on the penile urethra, and urinary retention may occur. If this condition becomes chronic, kidney problems may develop.

Changes in testosterone production. The primary male sex hormone is testosterone, produced by the Leydig cells in the testes. This hormone has numerous effects on the development and maintenance of male sexual characteristics, including the size and appearance of the penis and other reproductive structures, as well as the maintenance of facial and body hair, muscle growth, and the deepness of the male voice. There appear also to be some links in men between testosterone and sexual desire as well as aggressive or hostile behavior.

For many years it had been taken as a given that testosterone levels diminished in increasingly older age groups of men (Vermuelen, 1976), until contradictory evidence emerged from well-controlled studies in which health status and living situation (community vs. institutional residence) were controlled. Many of the earlier studies documenting so-called age-related declines in testosterone involved samples of aged men living in chronic care institutions, undergoing surgery, or under medical care for chronic diseases compared with healthy younger men living on their own in the community. More recent data indicate that obesity is another factor to control when comparing age groups in testosterone levels (Gray, Feldman, McKinlay, & Longcope, 1991). Age differences in testosterone levels do not appear when samples of older men are selected according to the criteria of living independently and having no major health problems, (Harman, 1978; Nieschlag, Kley, & Wiegelmann, 1982; Sparrow, Bosse, & Rowe, 1980). Even in those cases when age differences in testosterone have been reported, the researchers acknowledge that there are wide individual variations across samples of adult men, with frequent overlap between the young and old groups.

Changes in sexual functioning. As is true for aging women, there is a general slowing down associated with the aging process that affects how men progress through the phases of the human sexual response cycle. For older as compared to younger men, orgasm is shorter, involving fewer contractions of the prostate, and a smaller amount of seminal fluid is ejected (Masters & Johnson, 1970). These findings are consistent with the physiological data on changes in the male reproductive system, and possibly carry some negative implications for the aging male's sexual relations. However, the older man may find an enhanced ability to enjoy sexuality. He may feel less driven toward the pressure to ejaculate, be able to prolong the period of sensual enjoyment prior to orgasm, and have the control to coordinate his pleasure cycle to correspond more to that of his partner.

A man's pattern of sexual activity in the earlier years of adulthood is by far the best predictor of his sexual activity in old age (George & Weiler, 1985). The sexually active middle-aged man, given good health, has the potential to remain sexually active well into his later years.

Psychological Interactions

The feelings connected with sexuality, both in terms of reproduction and the expression of sexual drives, are important contributors to the adult's overall well-being and form an important component of intimate relationships with partners. In addition, the individual's sense of competence and self-worth is related to continued participation in sexual activities through later adulthood (Marsiglio & Donnelly, 1991).

The impact of reproductive changes in later adulthood depends heavily on how the individual interprets the significance of this transition. The menopause, perhaps one of the most heralded threshold events, may be met with relief or it may serve as a reminder of the inevitability of aging and one's own mortality. Discomfort from symptoms associated with the climacteric, such as "hot flashes" (feelings of rapid increases in body temperature) and mood changes related to hormonal imbalances may make it difficult to adapt to the transition. Age-related changes leading to a slowing of sexual response may have a negative impact on the individual's enjoyment of sexual relations. The man may write himself off as a sexual partner, believing that his masculine prowess has failed. Furthermore, the changes in sexual functioning may serve as signs that one's body is deteriorating and death is around the corner. As is true regardless of age, depression, heavy alcohol use, or late-life career pressures and disappointments may also interfere with the ability to enjoy sexual relations in later adulthood. Illness, particularly cardiovascular disease, can be another important factor causing the older individual to feel the need to discontinue sexual activity (Persson & Svanborg, 1992).

If the aging individual is distressed about changes in appearance, he or she can use various problem-focused coping strategies, including the creative use of clothing, to disguise or compensate for them. However, changes in one's sexual appearance that are visible only to oneself or one's intimate partner may constitute a different set of challenges. It may be embarrassing for the aging person to seek the emotional support and reassurance of a partner or same-sex peers about the changing appearance of the body. On the other hand, as the partners in a relationship age together, seeing the changes that both undergo as a result of the aging process may bolster the emotion-focused strategy of deriving a sense of comfort and companionship from sharing each other's experience.

Difficulties in adjusting to age changes in the sexual response cycle may present a problem if the partners are unfamiliar with the fact that sexual responsivity naturally becomes altered in later adulthood. Overaccommodation here can have disastrous consequences, given the very delicate balance of physical and psychological factors in this area of functioning. The aging individual may be sent into an overaccommodative tailspin, worrying about loss of orgasmic capacity because it takes longer to become aroused, excited, and stimulated. Adding to these concerns may be the belief that it is wrong and unnatural for older people to harbor sexual desires, and that it is inappropriate for them to maintain an interest in sexual relations (Weg, 1983). If one's partner is infirmed, or if the individual is widowed, the older individual in current society, raised during a sexually more conservative period of history, is unlikely to seek other outlets of sexual stimulation such as masturbation, homosexual partnerships, or liasons outside the marriage (Croft, 1982). Increasingly, the individual may come to view oneself as an asexual creature when, in fact, he or she possesses a considerable reserve of potential sexual enjoyment. Educational programs that inform the older individual or couple about normal age-related changes in sexual functioning can help break what would otherwise be a negative cycle of loss of sexual interest and capacity (Goldman & Carroll, 1990).

REFERENCES

Allen, W. K., Seals, D. R., Hurley, B. F., Ehsani, A. A., & Hagberg, J. M. (1985). Lactate threshold and distance-running performance in young and older endurance athletes. *Journal of Applied Physiology, 58,* 1281–1284.

Altman, D. F. (1990). Changes in gastrointestinal, pancreatic, biliary, and hepatic function with aging. *Gastroenterology Clinics of North America 19,* 227–234.

Antoni, M. H. (1987). Neuroendocrine influences in psychoimmunology and neoplasia: A review. *Psychology and Health, 1,* 3–24.

Azizi, F., Vagenakis, A. G., Portnay, G. I., Rapoport, B., Ingbar, S. H., & Braverman, L. E. (1979). Pituitary-thyroid responsiveness to intramuscular thyrotropin-releasing hormone based on analyses of serum thyrozine, tri-iodothyronine, and thyrotropin concentrations. *New England Journal of Medicine, 292,* 273–277.

Baigis-Smith, J., Smith, D. J., Rose, M., & Newman, D. K. (1989). Managing urinary incontinence in community-residing elderly persons. *Gerontologist, 29,* 229–233.

Barton, R. N., Horan, M. A., Weijers, J. W. M., Sakkee, A. N., Roberts, N. A., & Van Bezooijen, F. A. (1993). Cortisol production rate and the urinary excretion of 17-hydroxycorticosteroids, free cortisol, and 6 beta-hydroxycortisol in healthy elderly men and women. *Journal of Gerontology: Medical Sciences, 48,* M213–218.

Beccaro, F., Pacini, G., Velerio, A., Nosadini, R., & Crepaldi, G. (1990). Age and glucose tolerance in healthy adults. *Aging, 2,* 277–282.

Bernier, J. J., Vidon, N., & Mignon, M. (1973). The value of a cooperative multicenter study for establishing a table of normal values for gastric acid secretion and as a function of sex, age, and weight. *Biologie et Gastr-Enterologie (Paris), 6,* 287–296.

Blichert-Toft, M. (1975). Secretion of corticotrophin and somatotrophin by the senescent adenohypophysis in man. *Acta Endocrinologica (Supp.), 195,* 15–154.

Blichert-Toft, M., Hummer, L., & Dige-Petersen, H. (1975). Human serum thyrotrophin level and response to thyrotrophin-releasing hormone in the aged. *Gerontologica Clinica, 17,* 191–203.

Bloom, E. T. (1994). Natural killer cells, lymphokine-activated killer cells, and cytolytic T lymphocytes: Compartmentalization of age-related changes in cytolytic lymphocytes? *Journal of Gerontology: Biological Sciences, 49,* B85–92.

Bourey, R. E., Kohrt, W. M., Kirwan, J. P., Staten, M. A., King, D. S., & Holloszy, J. O. (1993). Relationship between glucose tolerance and glucose-stimulated insulin response in 65-year-olds. *Journal of Gerontology: Medical Sciences, 48,* M122–127.

Bowman, B. B., & Rosenberg, I. H. (1983). Digestive function and aging. *Human Nutrition: Clinical Nutrition, 37C,* 75–89.

Brauer, P. M., Slavin, J. L., & Marlett, J. A. (1981). Apparent digestibility of neutral detergent fiber in elderly and young adults. *American Journal of Clinical Nutrition, 34,* 1061–1070.

Brocklehurst, J. C. (1978). The large bowel. In J. C. Brocklehurst (Ed.), *Textbook of geriatric medicine and gerontology.* New York: Churchill Livingstone.

Broughton, D. L., James, O. W. F., Alberti, K. G. M. M., & Taylor, R. (1991). Peripheral and hepatic insulin sensitivity in healthy elderly human subjects. *European Journal of Clinical Investigation, 21,* 13–21.

Burgio, K. L., & Engel, B. T. (1990). Biofeedback-assisted behavioral training for elderly men and women. *Journal of the American Geriatrics Society, 38,* 338–340.

Burns, P. A., Pranikoff, K., Nochajski, T. H., Hadley, E. C., Levy, K. J., & Ory, M. G. (1993). A comparison of effectiveness of biofeedback and pelvic muscle exercise treatment of stress incontinence in older community-dwelling women. *Journal of Gerontology: Medical Sciences, 38,* M167–174.

Campion, E. W., deLabry, L. O., & Glynn, R. J. (1988). The effect of age on serum albumin in healthy males: Report from the Normative Aging Study. *Journal of Gerontology: Medical Sciences, 43,* M18–20.

Carrere, J., Serre, G., Vincent, C., Croute, F., Soleilhavoup, J.-P., & Figarella, C. (1987). Human serum pancreatic lipase and trypsin 1 in aging: Enzymatic and immunoenzymatic assays. *Journal of Gerontology, 42,* 315–317.

Cohen, T., Gitman, L., & Lipshutz, E. (1960). Liver function studies in the aged. *Geriatrics, 15,* 824–836.

Costello, R. B., & Moser-Veillon, P. B. (1992). A review of magnesium intake in the elderly. A cause for concern? *Magnesium Research, 5,* 61–7.

Croft, L. H. (1982). *Sexuality in later life: A counseling guide for physicians.* Boston: John Wright.

Darmady, E. M., Offer, J., & Woodhouse, M. A. (1973). The parameters of the aging kidney. *Journal of Pathology, 109,* 195–207.

Davidson, A. J., Talner, L. B., & Downs, W. M. (1969). A study of the angiographic appearance of the kidney in an aging normotensive population. *Radiology, 92,* 975–983.

Davidson, M. B. (1979). The effect of aging on carbohydrate metabolism: A review of the English literature and a practical approach to the diagnosis of diabetes mellitus in the elderly. *Metabolism, 28,* 688–705.

Davies, D. F., & Shock, N. W. (1950). Age changes in glomerular filtration rate, effective renal plasma flow, and tubular excretory capacity in adult males. *Journal of Clinical Investigation, 29,* 496–507.

Davis, M. A., Murphy, S. P., & Neuhaus, J. M. (1988). Living arrangements and eating behaviors of older adults in the United States. *Journal of Gerontology: Social Sciences, 43,* S96–98.

Davis, M. A., Randall, E., Forthofer, R. N., Lee, E. S., & Margen, S. (1985). Living arrangements and dietary patterns of older adults in the United States. *Journal of Gerontology, 40,* 434–442.

DeFronzo, R. A. (1979). Glucose intolerance and aging: Evidence for tissue sensitivity to insulin. *Diabetes, 28,* 1095–1101.

DeFronzo, R. A. (1982). *Glucose intolerance and aging* (No. 82-2221, pp. 98–119). Washington, DC: National Institute of Health.

Diokno, A. C., Brock, B. M., Brown, M. B., & Herzog, A. R. (1986). Prevalence of urinary incontinence and other urological syptoms in the noninstitutionalized elderly. *Journal of Urology, 136,* 1022–1025.

Dudl, R. J., Ensinck, J. W., Palmer, H. E., & Williams, R. H. (1973). Effect of age on growth hormone secretion in man. *Journal of Clinical Endocrinology and Metabolism, 37,* 11–16.

Eastell, R., Yergey, A. L., Vieira, N. E., Cedel, S. L., Kumar, R., & Riggs, B. L. (1991). Interrelationship among vitamin D metabolism, true calcium absorption, parathyroid function, and age in women: evidence of an age-related intestinal resistance to 1,25-dihydroxyvitamin D action. *Journal of Bone Mineral Research, 6,* 125–32.

Elahi, E., Muller, D. C., Tzankoff, S. P., Andres, R., & Tobin, J. E. (1982). Effect of age and obesity on fasting levels of glucose, insulin, glucagon, and growth hormone in man. *Journal of Gerontology, 37,* 385–391.

Ershler, W. B. (1990). Influenza and aging. In A. L. Goldstein (Ed.), *Biomedical advances in aging* (pp. 513–521). New York: Plenum.

Ershler, W. B. (1993). The influence of an aging immune system on cancer incidence and progression. *Journal of Gerontology, 48,* B3–7.

Fiatarone, M. A., Morley, J. E., Bloom, E. T., Benton, D., Solomon, G. F., & Makinodan, T. (1989). The effect of exercise on natural killer cell activity in young and old subjects. *Journal of Gerontology: Medical Sciences, 44,* M37–45.

Fink, R. I., Kolterman, O. G., Griffin, J., & Olefsky, J. M. (1983). Mechanisms of insulin resistance in aging. *Journal of Clinical Investigation, 71,* 1523–1525.

Fischer, J., & Johnson, M. A. (1990). Low body weight and weight loss in the aged. *Journal of the American Dietetic Association, 90,* 1697–1706.

Florini, J. R., Prinz, P. N., Vitiello, M. V., & Hintz, R. L. (1985). Somatomedin-C levels in healthy young and old men: Relationship to peak and 24-hour integrated levels of growth hormone. *Journal of Gerontology, 40,* 2–7.

Fox, P. C., Heft, M. W., Herrera, M., Bowers, M. R., Mandel, I. D., & Baum, B. J. (1987). Secretion of antimicrobial proteins from the parotid glands of different aged healthy persons. *Journal of Gerontology, 42,* 476–481.

George, L. K., & Weiler, S. J. (1985). Sexuality in middle and late life. In E. Palmore, J. Nowlin, E. Busse, I. Siegler, & G. Maddox (Ed.), *Normal aging III.* Durham, NC: Duke University Press.

Globerson, A., Eren, R., Abel, L., & Ben-Menahem, D. (1990). Developmental aspects of T lymphocytes in aging. In A. L. Goldstein (Ed.), *Biomedical advances in aging* (pp. 363–373). New York: Plenum.

Goldman, A., & Carroll, J. L. (1990). Educational intervention as an adjunct to treatment in erectile dysfunction in older couples. *Journal of Sex and Marital Therapy, 16,* 127–141.

Goldman, R. (1977). Aging of the excretory system: Kidney and bladder. In C. E. Finch & L. Hayflick (Ed.), *Handbook of the biology of aging.* New York: Van Nostrand Reinhold.

Goyal, V. K. (1982). Changes with age in the human kidney. *Experimental Gerontology, 17,* 321–331.

Gray, A., Feldman, H. A., McKinlay, J. B., & Longcope, C. (1991). Age, disease, and changing sex hormone levels in middle-aged men: results of the Massachusetts Male Aging Study. *Journal of Clinical Endocrinology and Metabolism, 73,* 1016–1025.

Greenspan, S. L., Klibanski, A., Rowe, J. W., & Elahi, D. (1991). Age-related alterations in pulsatile secretion of TSH: role of dopaminergic regulation. *American Journal of Physiology, 260,* E486–491.

Gumbiner, B., Polonsky, K. S., Beltz, W. F., Wallace, P., Brechtel, G., & Fink, R. I. (1989). Effects of aging on insulin secretion. *Diabetes, 38,* 1549–1556.

Haadem, K., Dahlstrom, J. A., & Ling, L. (1991). Anal sphincter competence in healthy women: clinical implications of age and other factors. *Obstetrics and Gynecology, 78,* 823–827.

Hagberg, J. M., Seals, D. R., Yerg, J. E., Gavin, J., Gingerich, R., Premachandra, B., & Holloszy, J. O. (1988). Metabolic responses to exercise in young and older athletes and sedentary men. *Journal of Applied Physiology, 65,* 900–908.

Harman, S. M. (1978). Clinical aspects of the male reproductive system. In E. L. Schneider (Ed.), *Aging: Vol. 4. The aging reproductive system.* New York: Raven Press.

Harman, S. M., & Talbert, G. B. (1985). Reproductive aging. In C. E. Finch & E. L. Schneider (Ed.), *Handbook of the biology of aging* (pp. 457–510). New York: Van Nostrand Reinhold.

Hausman, P. B., & Weksler, M. E. (1985). Changes in the immune response with age. In C. E. Finch & E. L. Schneider (Ed.), *Handbook of the biology of aging* (pp. 414–432). New York: Van Nostrand Reinhold.

Hegedus, L., Perrild, H., Poulson, L. R., Anderson, J. R., Holm, B., Schnohr, P., Jensen, G., & Hansen, J. M. (1983). The determination of thyroid volume by ultrasound and its relationship to body weight, age, and sex in normal subjects. *Journal of Clinical Endocrinology and Metabolism, 56,* 260–263.

Heidrick, M. L. (1987). Immune cells. In G. L. Maddox (Ed.), *Encyclopedia of aging* (pp. 344–346). New York: Springer.

Herzog, A. R., Diokno, A. C., Brown, M. B., Normolle, D. P., & Brock, B. M. (1990). Two-year incidence, remission, and change patterns of urinary incontinence in noninstitutionalized older adults. *Journal of Gerontology: Medical Sciences, 45,* M67–74.

Hirokawa, K., Utsuyama, M., & Kasai, M. (1990). Role of the thymus in aging of the immune system. In A. L. Goldstein (Ed.), *Biomedical advances in aging* (pp. 375–384). New York: Plenum.

Hollenbeck, C. B., Haskell, W., Rosenthal, M., & Reaaven, G. M. (1984). Effect of habitual physical activity on regulation of insulin-stimulated glucose disposal in older males. *Journal of the American Geriatrics Society, 33,* 273–277.

Holt, P. R. (1991). General perspectives on the aged gut. *Clinics in Geriatric Medicine, 7,* 185–189.

Hsu, J. M., & Smith, J. C., Jr. (1984). B-Vitamins and ascorbic acid in the aging process. In J. M. Ordy, D. Harman, & R. B. Alfin-Slater (Ed.), *Aging: Vol. 26. Nutrition in gerontology* (pp. 87–118). New York: Raven Press.

Hunskaar, S., & Vinsnes, A. (1991). The quality of life in women with urinary incontinence as measured by the Sickness Impact Profile. *Journal of the American Geriatrics Society, 39,* 378–382.

Judd, H. L., Judd, G. E., Lucas, W. E., & Yen, S. S. C. (1974). Endocrine function of the postmenopausal ovary: Concentrations of androgens and estrogens in ovarian and peripheral vein blood. *Journal of Clinical Endocrinology and Metabolism, 39,* 1020–1024.

Judd, H. L., & Korenmann, S. G. (1982). Effects of aging on reproductive function in women. In S. G. Korenmann (Ed.), *Endocrine aspects of aging.* New York: Elsevier Biomedical.

Kahn, S. E., Larson, V. G., Beard, J. C., Cain, K. C., Fellingham, G. W., Schwartz, R. S., Veith, R. C., Stratton, J. R., Cerqueira, M. D., & Abrass, I. B. (1990). Effect of exercise on insulin action, glucose tolerance, and insulin secretion. *American Journal of Physiology, 258,* E937–943.

Kalant, N., Leiborici, D., Leibovici, T., & Fukushima, N. (1980). Effect of age on glucose utilization and repsonsiveness to insulin in forearm muscle. *Journal of the American Geriatrics Society, 28,* 304–307.

Kamocka, D. (1970). Cytological studies of parotid gland secretion in people over 60 years of age. *Excerpta Medica, Section 20, 13,* 412.

Kampmann, J. P., Sinding, J., & Møller-Jørgensen, I. (1975). Effect of age on liver function. *Geriatrics, 30,* 91–95.

Kanonchoff, A. D., Cavanaugh, D. J., Mehl, V. L., Bartel, R. L., Penn, G. M., & Budd, J. A. (1984). Changes in lymphocyte subpopulations during acute exercise. *Medicine in Science and Sports, 16,* 175.

Kern, W., Dodt, C., Born, J., & Fehm, H. L. (1996). Changes in cortisol and growth hormone secretion during nocturnal sleep in the course of aging. *Journal of Gerontology: Medical Sciences, 51A,* M3–9.

Khan, T. A., Shragge, B. W., Crispin, J. S., & Lind, J. F. (1977). Esophageal motility in the elderly. *American Journal of Digestive Diseases, 22,* 1049–1054.

Kirwan, J. B., Kohrt, W. M., Wojta, D. M., Bourey, R. E., & Holloszy, J. O. (1993). Endurance exercise training reduces glucose-stimulated insulin levels in 60- to 70-year-old men and women. *Journal of Gerontology: Medical Sciences, 48,* M84–90.

Kram, D., & Schneider, E. L. (1978). An effect of reproductive aging: Increased risk of genetically abnormal offspring. In E. L. Schneider (Ed.), *Aging: Vol. 4. The aging reproductive system.* New York: Raven Press.

Kreel, L., & Sandin, B. (1973). Changes in pancreatic morphology associated with aging. *Gut, 14,* 962–970.

Kutza, J., Kaye, D., & Murasko, D. M. (1995). Basal natural killer cell activity of young versus elderly humans. *Journal of Gerontology: Biological Sciences, 50A,* B110–116.

Lamy, P. P. (1988). Actions of alcohol and drugs in older people. *Generations, 12,* 9–13.

Lasada, K., & Roberts, P. (1974). Variation in the morphometry of the normal human thyroid in growth and aging. *Journal of Pathology, 112,* 161–168.

Lewis, G. F., Alessi, C. A., Imperial, J. G., & Refetoff, S. (1991). Low serum-free thyroxine index in ambulating elderly is due to a resetting of the threshold of thyrotropin feedback suppression. *Journal of Clinical Endocrinology and Metabolism, 73,* 843–849.

Lockett, M. F. (1976). Aging of the adenophypophysis in relation to renal aging. In A. V. Everitt & J. A. Burgess (Ed.), *Hypothalamus, pituitary and aging.* Springfield, IL: Charles C. Thomas.

Lynch, S. R., Finch, C. A., Monsen, E. R., & Cook, J. D. (1982). Iron status of elderly Americans. *American Journal of Clinical Nutrition, 36,* 1032–1045.

Marsiglio, W., & Donnelly, D. (1991). Sexual relations in later life: A national study of married persons. *Journal of Gerontology: Social Sciences, 46,* S338–344.

Masters, W. H., & Johnson, V. E. (1966). *Human sexual response.* Boston: Little, Brown.

Masters, W. H., & Johnson, V. E. (1970). *Human sexual inadequacy.* Boston: Little, Brown.

McGandy, R. B., Barrows, C. H., Jr., Spanias, A., Meredith, A., Stone, J. L., & Norris, A. H. (1966). Nutrient intake and energy expenditure in men of different ages. *Journal of Gerontology, 21,* 581–587.

McLachlan, M. S. F., Guthrie, J. C., Anderson, C. K., & Fulker, M. J. (1977a). Vascular and glomerular changes in the aging kidney. *Journal of Pathology, 121,* 65–78.

McLachlan, M. S. F., Guthrie, J. C., Anderson, C. K., & Fulker, M. J. (1977b). Vascular and glomerular changes in the aging kidney. *Journal of Pathology, 121,* 65–78.

McNaughton, M. E., Smith, L. W., Patterson, T. L., & Grant, I. (1990). Stress, social support, coping resources, and immune status in elderly women. *Journal of Nervous and Mental Disease, 178,* 460–461.

Miller, R. A. (1993). Aging and cancer—Another perspective. *Journal of Gerontology: Biological Sciences, 48,* B8–9.

Minaker, K. L., Meneilly, G. S., & Rowe, J. W. (1985). Endocrine systems. In C. E. Finch & E. L. Schneider (Ed.), *Handbook of the biology of aging* (pp. 433–456). New York: Van Nostrand Reinhold.

Minaker, K. L., & Rowe, J. W. (1982). Gastrointestinal system. In J. W. Rowe & R. W. Besdine (Ed.), *Health and disease in old age*. Boston: Little, Brown.

Minaker, K. L., Rowe, J. W., Pallotta, J., & Sparrow, D. (1982). Clearance of insulin: Influence of steady state insulin level and age. *Diabetes, 31,* 132–135.

Montgomery, S. A. (1990). Depression in the elderly: Pharmacokinetics of antidepressants and death from overdose. *International Clinical Psychopharmacology, 5,* 67–76.

Nakamaru, M., Ogihara, T., Hata, T., Maruyama, A., Mikami, H., Naka, T., Iwanaga, K., & Kumahara, Y. (1981). The effect of age on active acryoactivatable inactive plasma renin in normal subjects and patients with essential hypertension. *Japanese Circulation Journal, 45,* 1231–1235.

Naliboff, B. D., Benton, D., Solomon, G. F., Morley, J. E., Fahey, J. L., Bloom, E. T., Makinodan, T., & Gilmore, S. L. (1991). Immunological changes in young and old adults during brief laboratory stress. *Psychosomatic Medicine, 53,* 121–132.

Newell, G. R., Spitz, M. R., & Sider, J. G. (1989). Cancer and age. *Seminars in Oncology, 16,* 3–9.

Nieschlag, E., Kley, K. H., & Wiegelmann, W. (1982). Age dependence of the endocrine testicular funciton in adult men. *Acta Endocrinological (Suppl.), 177,* 122.

O'Leary, A. (1990). Stress, emotion, and human immune function. *Psychological Bulletin, 108,* 363–382.

Olsen, T., Laurberg, P., & Weeke, J. (1978). Low serum triiodothyronine and high serum reverse triiodothyronine in old age: An effect of disease not age. *Journal of Clinical Endocrinology and Metabolism, 47,* 1111–1115.

Ouslander, J. G., & Abelson, S. (1990). Perceptions of urinary incontinence among elderly outpatients. *Gerontologist, 30,* 369–372.

Ouslander, J. G., Zarit, S. H., Orr, N. K., & Muira, S. A. (1990). Incontinence among elderly community-dwelling dementia patients: Characteristics, management, and impact on caregivers. *Journal of the American Geriatrics Society, 38,* 440–445.

Pacini, G., Valerio, A., Beccaro, F., Nosadini, R., Cobelli, C., & Crepaldi, G. (1988). Insulin sensitivity and beta-cell responsivity are not decreased in elderly subjects with normal OGTT. *Journal of the American Geriatrics Society, 36,* 317–323.

Persson, G., & Svanborg, A. (1992). Marital coital activity in men at the age of 75: Relation to somatic, psychiatric, and social factors at the age of 70. *Journal of the American Geriatrics Society, 40,* 439–444.

Pfeiffer, E., Verwoerdt, A., & Davis, G. C. (1974). Sexual behavior in aged men and women. In E. Palmore (Ed.), *Normal aging II* (pp. 243–251). Durham, NC: Duke University Press.

Pitkanen, P., Westermack, P., Cornwell, C. G., III, & Murdoch, W. (1983). Amyloid of the seminal vesicles: A distinctive and common localized form of senile amyloidosis. *American Journal of Pathology, 110,* 64–69.

Posner, B. M., Jette, A., Smigelski, C., Miller, D., & Mitchell, P. (1994). Nutritional risk in New England elders. *Journal of Gerontology: Medical Sciences, 49,* M123–132.

Pozzato, G., Moretti, M., Franzin, F., Croce, L. S., Lacchin, T., Benedetti, G., Sablich, R., Stebel, M., & Campanacci, L. (1995). Ethanol metabolism and aging: The role of "first pass metabolism" and gastric alcohol dehydrogenase activity. *Journal of Gerontology: Biological Sciences, 50A,* B135–141.

Prinz, P. N., & Halter, J. (1983). Sleep disturbances in the elderly: Neurohormonal correlates. In E. D. Weitzman & M. Chase (Ed.), *Advances in sleep research* (Vol. 8, pp. 463–501). New York: Spectrum.

Rabin, B. S., Cohen, S., Ganguli, R., Lysle, D. T., & Cunnick, J. E. (1989). Bidirectional interaction between the central nervous system and immune system. *Critical Reviews in Immunology, 9,* 279–312.

Ratzmann, K. P., Witt, S., Heinke, P., & Shulz, B. (1982). The effect of ageing on insulin sensitivity and insulin secretion in non-obese healthy subjects. *Acta Endocrinologica, 100,* 543–549.

Reaven, P. D., Barrett-Connor, E., & Edelstein, S. (1991). Relation between leisure-time physical activity and blood pressure in older women. *Circulation, 83,* 559–565.

Reed, M. J., Reaven, G. M., Mondon, C. E., & Zahar, S. (1993). Why does insulin resistance develop during maturation? *Journal of Gerontology: Biological Sciences, 48,* B139–144.

Roberts, N. A., Barton, R. N., & Horan, M. A. (1990). Ageing and the sensitivity of the adrenal gland to physiological doses of ACTH in man. *Journal of Endocrinology, 126,* 507–513.

Robuschi, G., Safran, M., Braverman, L. E., Gnudi, A., & Roti, E. (1987). Hypothyroidism in the elderly. *Endocrinological Reviews, 8,* 142–153.

Rogers, M. A., King, D. S., Hagberg, J. M., Ehsani, A. A., & Holloszy, J. O. (1990). Effect of 10 days of inactivity on glucose tolerance in master athletes. *Journal of Applied Physiology, 68,* 1833–1837.

Rosenbloom, C. A., & Whittington, F. J. (1993). The effects of bereavement on eating behaviors and nutrient intakes in elderly widowed persons. *Journal of Gerontology: Social Sciences, 48,* S223–229.

Rowe, J. W. (1982). Renal function and aging. In M. E. Reff & E. L. Schneider (Ed.), *Biological markers of aging.* Bethesda, MD: National Institutes of Health, Publication Number 82-2221.

Rowe, J. W., Andres, R. A., Tobin, J. D., Norris, A. H., & Shock, N. W. (1976). The effect of age on creatinine clearance in man: A cross-sectional and longitudinal study. *Journal of Gerontology, 31,* 155–163.

Rowe, J. W., Minaker, K. L., Pallotta, J. A., & Flier, J. S. (1983). Characterization of the insulin resistance of aging. *Journal of Clinical Investigation, 71,* 1581–1587.

Rowe, J. W., Shock, N. W., & DeFronzo, R. A. (1976). The influence of age on the renal response to water deprivation in man. *Nephron, 17,* 270–278.

Rubenstein, H. A., Butler, V. P., & Werner, S. C. (1973). Progressive decrease in serum triiodothyronine concentrations with human aging: Radioimmuno-assay following extraction of serum. *Journal of Clinical Endocrinology and Metabolism, 37,* 247–253.

Runnels, G. L., Garry, P. J., Hunt, W. C., & Standefer, J. C. (1991). Thyroid function in a healthy elderly population: Implications for clinical evaluation. *Journal of Gerontology: Biological Sciences, 46,* B39–44.

Ryan, A. S., Craig, L. D., & Finn, S. C. (1992). Nutrient intakes and dietary patterns of older Americans: A national study. *Journal of Gerontology: Medical Sciences, 47,* M145–150.

Sawin, C. T., Chopra, D., Azizi, F., Mannix, J. E., & Bacharach, P. (1979). The aging thyroid: Increased prevalence of elevated serum thyrotropin levels in the elderly. *Journal of the American Medical Association, 242,* 247–250.

Sawin, C. T., Geller, A., Kaplan, M. M., Bacharach, P., Wilson, P. W., & Hershman, J. M. (1991). Low serum thyrotropin (thyroid-stimulating hormone) in older persons without hyperthyroidism. *Archives of Internal Medicine, 151,* 165–168.

Schleifer, S. J., Keller, S. E., Siris, S. G., Davis, K. L., & Stein, M. (1985). Depression and immunity. *Archives of General Psychiatry, 42,* 129–133.

Schleifer, S. J., Scott, B., Stein, M., & Keller, S. E. (1986). Behavioral and developmental aspects of immunity. *Journal of the American Academy of Child Psychiatry, 26,* 751–763.

Schwartz, D., Mayaux, M.-J., Spira, A., Moscato, M., Jouannet, P., Czyglik, F., & David, G. (1983). Semen characteristics as a function of age in 833 fertile men. *Fertility and Sterility, 39,* 530–535.

Seals, D. R., Hagberg, J. M., Allen, W. K., Hurley, B. F., Dalsky, G. P., Ehsani, A. A., & Holloszy, J. O. (1984). Glucose tolerance in young and older athletes and sedentary men. *Journal of Applied Physiology, 56,* 1521–1525.

Seals, D. R., Hagberg, J. M., Hurley, B. F., Ehsani, A. A., & Holloszy, J. O. (1984). Effects of endurance training on glucose tolerance and plasma lipids in older men and women. *Journal of the American Medical Association, 252,* 645–649.

Seymour, F. I., Duffy, C., & Koerner, A. (1935). A case of authenticated fertility in a man of 94. *Journal of the American Medical Association, 105,* 1423–1424.

Sherman, B. M., West, J. H., & Korenmann, S. G. (1976). The menopausal transition: Analysis of LH, FSH, estradiol, and progesterone concentrations during menstrual cycles of older women. *Journal of Clinical Endocrinology and Metabolism, 42,* 629–636.

Shimokata, H., Muller, D. C., Fleg, J. L., Sorkin, J., Ziemba, A. W., & Andres, R. (1991). Age as independent determinant of glucose tolerance. *Diabetes, 40,* 44–51.

Shimokata, H., Tobin, J. D., Muller, D. C., Elahi, D., Coon, P. J., & Andres, R. (1989). Studies in the distribution of body fat: I. Effects of age, sex, and obesity. *Journal of Gerontology: Medical Sciences, 44,* M66–73.

Ship, J. A., Nolan, N. E., & Puckett, S. A. (1995). Longitudinal analysis of parotid and submandibular salivary flow rates in healthy, different-aged adults. *Journal of Gerontology: Medical Sciences, 50A,* M285–289.

Ship, J. A., Patton, L. L., & Tylenda, C. A. (1991). An assessment of salivary function in healthy premenopausal and postmenopausal females. *Journal of Gerontology: Medical Sciences, 46,* M11–15.

Shock, N. W., Andres, R., Norris, A. H., & Tobin, J. D. (1978, August 20–25). *Patterns of longitudinal changes in renal function.* Paper presented at the Proceedings XII International Congress of Gerontology, Tokyo. Amsterdam: Excerpta Medica.

Sidney, K. H., & Shephard, R. J. (1977). Growth hormone and cortisol—age differences, effects of exercise training. *Canadian Journal of Applied Sports Sciences, 2,* 190–193.

Silverman, H. G., & Mazzio, R. S. (1996). Hormonal responses to maximal and submaximal exercise in trained and untrained men of various ages. *Journal of Gerontology: Biological Sciences, 51A,* B30–37.

Sparrow, D., Borkan, G. A., Gerzof, S. G., Wisniewski, C., & Silbert, C. K. (1986). Relationship of fat distribution to glucose tolerance: Results of computed tomography in male participants of the Normative Aging Study. *Diabetes, 35,* 411–415.

Sparrow, D., Bosse, R., & Rowe, J. W. (1980). The influence of age, alcohol consumption and body build on gonadal function in men. *Journal of Clinical Endocrinology and Metabolism, 51,* 508–512.

Stein, M., Miller, A. H., & Trestman, R. L. (1991). Depression, the immune system, and health and illness. *Archives of General Psychiatry, 48,* 171–177.

Suiteri, P. K., & MacDonald, P. C. (1973). Role of extragrlandular estrogen in human endocrinology. In R. O. Greep & E. B. Astwood (Ed.), *Handbook of physiology (Vol. 2, Part 1).* Baltimore, MD: Williams & Wilkins.

Swerdloff, R. S., & Heber, D. (1982). Effects of aging on male reproductive function. In S. G. Korenman (Ed.), *Endocrine aspects of aging.* New York: Elsevier Biomedical.

Sworn, M. J., & Fox, M. (1972). Donor kidney selection for transplantation. *British Journal of Urology, 44,* 377–383.

Szanto, S. (1975). Metabolic studies in physically outstanding elderly men. *Age and Ageing, 4,* 37–42.

Takazakura, E., Sawabu, N., Handa, A., Takada, A., Shinoda, A., & Takeuchi, J. (1972). Intrarenal vascular changes with age and disease. *Kidney International, 2,* 224–230.

Taylor, A. L., Finster, J. L., & Mintz, D. H. (1969). Metabolic clearance and production rates of human growth hormone. *Journal of Clinical Investigation, 48,* 2349–2358.

Thoman, M. L., & Weigle, W. O. (1989). The cellular and subcellular bases of immunosenescence. *Advances in Immunology, 46,* 221–261.

Thomas, P. D., Goodwin, J. M., & Goodwin, J. W. (1985). Effect of social support on stress-related changes in cholesterol, uric acid level, and immune function in an elderly sample. *American Journal of Psychiatry, 142,* 735–737.

Tonino, R. P. (1989). Effect of physical training on the insulin resistance of aging. *American Journal of Physiology, 256,* E352–356.

Treloar, A. E., Boynton, R. E., Benn, B. G., & Brown, B. W. (1967). Variation of the human menstrual cycle throughout reproductive life. *International Journal of Fertility, 12,* 77–126.

Tzankoff, S. P., & Norris, A. H. (1977). Effect of muscle mass decrease on age-related BMR changes. *Journal of Applied Physiology, 43,* 1001–1006.

Vekemans, M., & Robyn, C. (1975). Influence of age on serum prolactin levels in women and men. *British Medical Journal, 4,* 738–739.

Vermuelen, A. (1976). Leydig-cell function in old age. In A. V. Everitt & J. A. Burgess (Ed.), *Hypothalamus, pituitary, and aging.* Springfield, IL: Charles C. Thomas.

Verzar, F. (1966). Anterior pituitary function in age. In B. T. Donovan & G. W. Harris (Ed.), *The pituitary gland* (Vol. 2). Berkeley: University of California Press.

Vollardt, L. T. (1991). Psychoneuroimmunology: A literature review. *American Journal of Orthopsychiatry, 61,* 35–47.

Wald, A. (1990). Constipation and fecal incontinence in the elderly. *Gastroenterology Clinics of North America, 19,* 405–418.

Walford, R. (1969). *The immunologic theory of aging.* Baltimore, MD: Williams and Wilkins.

Waltman, C., Blackman, M. R., Chrousos, G. P., Riemann, C., & Harman, S. M. (1991). Spontaneous and glucocorticoid-inhibited adrenocorticotropic hormone and cortisol secretion are similar in healthy young and old men. *Journal of Clinical Endocrinology and Metabolism, 73,* 495–502.

Wantz, M. S., & Gay, J. E. (1981). *The aging process: A health perspective.* Cambridge, MA: Winthrop.

Wedmann, B., Schmidt, G., Wegener, M., Coenen, C., Ricken, D., & Althoff, J. (1991). Effects of age and gender on fat-induced gallbladder contraction and gastric emptying of a caloric liquid meal: a sonographic study. *American Journal of Gastroenterology, 86,* 1765–1770.

Weg, R. B. (1983). *Sexuality in the later years.* New York: Academic Press.

Wesson, L. G. (1969). *Physiology of the human kidney.* New York: Grune & Stratton.

Wu, A. J., Atkinson, J. C., Fox, P. C., Baum, B. J., & Ship, J. A. (1992). Cross-sectional and longitudinal analyses of stimulated parotid salivary constituents in healthy, different-aged subjects. *Journal of Gerontology: Medical Sciences, 48,* M219–224.

Wu, A. J., Baum, B. J., & Ship, J. A. (1995). Extended stimulated parotid and sub-
    mandibular secretion in a healthy young and old population. *Journal of Gerontol-
    ogy: Medical Sciences, 50A,* M45–48.
Wyman, J. F., Harkins, S. W., & Fantl, J. A. (1990). Psychosocial impact of urinary incon-
    tinence in the community-dwelling population. *Journal of the American Geriatrics
    Society, 38,* 282–288.
Yamagata, A. (1965). Histopathological studies of the colon in relation to age. *Japanese
    Journal of Gastroenterology, 62,* 229–235.
Yu, L. C. (1987). Incontinence Stress Index: Measuring psychological impact. *Journal of
    Gerontological Nursing, 13,* 18–25.

6

The Nervous System

The nervous system is composed of the central nervous system, which includes the brain and spinal cord, and the peripheral nervous system, which includes the autonomic nervous system and the somatic nervous system. Moving into the study of the effects of aging on the nervous system, brings the discussion increasingly close to the realm of behavior. This chapter, begins with a discussion of the autonomic nervous system which in some ways forms a crucial link between the control processes discussed in Chapter 5 and the behavioral functions served by the central nervous system. The activities of the somatic system, as they pertain to sensory and perceptual functioning, will be covered in Chapter 7.

AUTONOMIC NERVOUS SYSTEM

Regulation of diverse bodily systems involved in many life support functions is the function of the autonomic nervous system (ANS). Like the endocrine system, the work of the ANS goes on continuously and outside the conscious control of the individual. The ANS performs its function not through release of hormones but through the activation of neurons that lie in close physical proximity to their target tissues. The subdivisions of the ANS are the parasympathetic nervous system (PNS) and the sympathetic nervous system (SNS). These components of the autonomic nervous system operate in complementary fashion to regulate features of the body's internal environment critical to life, such as respiration, digestion, excretion, and the circulation of blood. The hypothalamus is a major contributor to this process, serving as a lynchpin within the brain to regulate many autonomic activities independently, coordinate information from the autonomic and endocrine systems, and communicate with other parts of the brain regarding the status of various bodily systems.

Sympathetic Nervous System (SNS) Activity

As many readers will have learned in their introductory psychology classes, the SNS is most easily thought of as responsible for the "fight or flight" syndrome. More specifically, the SNS has a primary role in controlling the body's response to stressful and energy-demanding activities. The neurotransmitter released by most SNS neurons onto their targets or effectors is norepinephrine. This neurotransmitter has an excitatory effect, leading to energization of bodily reserves, including a rise in oxygen consumption and cardiac output, release of glucose from the muscles and liver, secretion of sweat and oil from the exocrine glands in the skin, and the diversion of the blood from internal organs toward the skeletal muscles. SNS stimulation also causes the adrenal gland to secrete glucocorticoids, leading to further release of stored energy.

The starting point for describing the effects of age on the SNS is the almost universal finding from a large number of studies indicating that the level of norepinephrine in the blood is progressively higher across age groups of adults, when subjects are tested at rest in a recumbent position (Esler et al., 1981; Featherstone et al., 1987; Pfeifer et al., 1983; Veith, Featherstone, Linares, & Halter, 1986; Wilkie et al., 1985). Rising to an upright position, which normally results in heightening the levels of norepinephrine, has a more pronounced effect on older adults (Saar & Gordon, 1979), as do other activities and sources of sympathetic stimulation such as isometric exercise (Sowers, Rubenstein, & Stern, 1983), exposure to cold (Palmer, Ziegler, & Lake, 1978; Wagner, Horvath, Kitagawa, & Bolduan, 1987), ingestion of large amounts of glucose (Young, Rowe, Pallotta, Sparrow, & Landsberg, 1980), and being placed in a stressful learning situation (Barnes, Raskind, Gumbrecht, & Halter, 1982).

Given that many people associate aging with a "calming down" rather than a "revving up" process, this increase in an excitatory neurotransmitter may seem paradoxical. Indeed, researchers have proposed that the increase in norepinephrine results from higher levels of SNS activity in older persons, leading to a situation in which the neurotransmitter "spills over" from the sympathetic neurons to their neighboring capillaries, and from there into the general circulation (Pfeifer et al., 1983). Another possibility, and one that is more in keeping with the "calming down" view of aging, is that the SNS is working overtime in order to arouse a set of less responsive tissues. More norepinephrine is produced by the SNS but its effectiveness is compromised by lower tissue responsivity to sympathetic stimulation. Nevertheless, the SNS keeps producing norepinephrine in response to feedback that the tissues require more stimulation. This explanation appears to help explain findings in the cardiac system in which it has been found that the cardiac muscles in the left ventricle of older adults have lower contractile force (Kendall, Woods, Wilkins, & Worthington, 1982). According to this argument, the norepinephrine increase is a compensatory mechanism to offset the reduction of myocardial muscle effectiveness (Vestal, Wood, & Shand, 1979).

Another explanation for the effects of age on the SNS comes from observations regarding the baroreceptor reflex. Baroreceptors are stretch receptors in the large arteries leaving the heart. They are sensitive to sudden changes in arterial pressure, and react to such changes by stimulating the ANS to respond either by inhibiting or stimulating cardiac activity so as to maintain an adequate cardiac output. One of the most important functions served by the baroreceptor reflex is to maintain blood flow to the brain despite changes in head position. Across the agespan of adulthood, the baroreceptor reflex becomes progressively less effective (Lindblad, 1977; Mader, 1989) due, it is thought, to age-related changes in the heart's pumping capacity (Minaker et al., 1991) or changes in the arteries that limit their capacity to respond to ANS instructions either to constrict or dilate. Higher levels of norepinephrine, reflecting greater SNS activity, might help compensate for these arterial changes, particularly in the critical situation when the person moves to an upright position from recumbancy. The observation that norepinephrine increases more in older than in younger adults when moving position in this way supports this view (Rowe & Troen, 1980).

These findings regarding the SNS are consistent with the observations made with respect to the endocrine system in which age effects occur at the level of the tissues rather than in the control mechanisms themselves. In the case of norepinephrine, the higher levels in the blood may be seen as an adaptive response directed toward maintaining and prolonging the function of critical life support activities. Again, as was the case for the endocrine system, it is unlikely that individuals are generally aware of crossing an aging threshold in this aspect of physical functioning.

Parasympathetic Nervous System (PNS) Activity

The PNS is the division of the autonomic nervous system that controls restorative processes when the body is in a quiescent state. Some of the PNS functions include slowing the heart rate, stimulating the secretion of salivary and other digestive fluids, increased motility by the muscles in the digestive tract, and relaxation of the anal and urethral sphincters. Acetylcholine is the major neurotransmitter in this system.

There is suprisingly little information on the functioning of the PNS across adulthood. Although the data on age differences are not entirely consistent, there is support for the interpretation that the PNS is maintained with relative stability into old age (Finch, 1977). One exception is the baroreceptor reflex. Age differences in the sensitivity of the baroreceptors could be partially accounted for by alterations in PNS activity as well as by changes in sensitivity to stimulation by the SNS.

REGULATORY ACTIVITIES OF THE ANS

In addition to the functions of the autonomic nervous system described so far are the autonomic regulatory mechanisms involving temperature control and sleep patterns. These two areas of autonomic control have considerable importance in influencing the individual's daily sense of well-being and are areas where the ANS plays a much more important role in the crossing of aging thresholds. Furthermore, in the area of sleep in particular, the reactions that individuals have to whatever age-related changes they experience can play a significant role in daily life in altering the further development of problems associated with aging.

Body Temperature Control

The regulatory mechanisms of the ANS maintain a core temperature of the body that fluctuates within an optimal temperature range for cellular metabolism of 98.6°F to 100.4°F. This control is accomplished through integration by the hypothalamus of sensory information concerning the outside temperature. The hypothalamus acts like a thermostat, initiating actions in the body's periphery that raise or lower the body's core temperature. Contractions of the skeletal muscles produce heat (experienced as shivering), and the raising of the hairs in the skin and constriction of capillaries in the dermis conserves heat. To produce the opposite effect of temperature reduction, the capillaries are stimulated to dilate, and the sweat glands to secrete fluid that cools the body's surface temperature. Conscious steps taken by the individual to regulate body temperature include changing clothes, adjusting the heat or air conditioning, seeking a change in environment, or immersing the body in water. If the individual is to take advantage of these measures, the thermal sensory abilities must be operating efficiently, producing accurate readings of the outside temperature.

There is substantial evidence from population surveys indicating that persons over the age of 65 years are impaired in their abilities to adapt to extremely hot and cold temperatures. In fact, in the summer of 1995, hundreds of people, many of whom were elderly, lost their lives during a massive heat wave that hit the midwest portions of the U.S. This loss of the individual's adaptive mechanisms actually appears fairly early in adulthood, but it does not reach threshold levels or have serious consequences until advanced old age. However, given the generally high level of attention the media places on deaths of the elderly during heat or cold spells, it is quite probable that older individuals become vigilant to changes in their ability to adapt to temperature extremes much earlier than they otherwise would.

Responses to cold. The diminished adaptation of the elderly to cold outside temperatures reflects a combination of factors, including a reduction in the awareness of a lower core body temperature (Fox, MacGibbon, Davies, & Woodward, 1973) and an inability to take advantage of the various mechanisms that raise the core body temperature when the temperature of the body's periphery is low (Collins et al., 1977). Women appear to be better able to maintain core body temperatures during cold exposure due to greater protection by higher levels of body fat (Wagner & Horvath, 1985) and by altered hormonal responses perhaps related to the menopause (Wagner et al., 1987).

Responses to heat. The primary reason given for reduced adaptability of elderly adults to heat is a diminution in sweat gland production (Ellis, Exton-Smith, Foster, & Weiner, 1976; Hellon & Lind, 1956). The decreased rate of sweating is related, in turn, to diminished input from the ANS to sweat glands (Foster, Ellis, Dore, Exton-Smith, & Weiner, 1976). These changes are reflected in a diminished ability of older adults to adjust to prolonged heat exposure, such as that involved in work in the heat during the summer months (Wagner, Robinson, Tzankoff, & Marino, 1972). An active lifestyle may mitigate somewhat against age losses in the ability to adapt to heat, at least for women (Drinkwater, Bedi, Loucko, Roche, & Horvath, 1982).

The observation that older persons are less able to cool themselves by sweating in hot environments is not easily reconciled with the frequently reported clinical observation that older adults often feel cold, even in warm weather. This phenomenon seems to reflect impaired cardiovascular efficiency rather than normal age-related changes in ANS functioning.

Sleep Patterns

Unlike other autonomic mechanisms, the function of sleep to the individual's survival is not known. One hypothesis is that sleep serves a restorative function for the various organ systems of the body including the brain. The function of sleep in everyday life is clearly crucial to the individual's sense of well-being and there is a strong relationship between quality of sleep and psychological symptoms (Bliwise, 1992). Given the sensitivity of sleep patterns to psychological distress, this is an area where identity–age change relationships might very profitably be investigated. Those older adults who overreact through accommodation to slight sleep change patterns are perhaps the ones fated to experience the most significant changes in their ability to get a good night's sleep.

During sleep, the brain's arousal patterns show marked shifts, reflected in four distinct patterns of electrophysiological activity: Stage 1 or drowsiness, Stages 2 and 3, which correspond to deeper levels of sleep, and Stage 4, which is deep sleep. These stages appear as different patterns on electroencephalograms (EEGs), which are neurophysiological measures of brain activity. Stage 4 sleep is characterized by a pattern of large and peaked brain waves on the EEG. No dreaming takes place during this stage, and most bodily functions slow significantly.

Approximately every 90–100 minutes, paradoxical sleep emerges. This type of sleep is called paradoxical because although the EEG pattern resembles that of the more active Stage 1, it is more difficult to awaken the sleeper than from any of the slow wave sleep stages. During paradoxical sleep, dreaming occurs, accompanied by "rapid eye movements" (REMs), movements of the eyeballs that can be seen underneath the person's closed eyelids. Other significant characteristics of paradoxical sleep include decreased muscle tone, irregular heart beat and respiration rate, and in men, penile erections. The relative length of time spent in a period of paradoxical sleep increases from the early part of the night until morning.

There is a fairly consistent picture from the literature of the features that characterize the sleep of adults in middle and late adulthood. Across age groups of adults, there is an increase in the amount of time spent lying awake in bed (Coleman et al., 1981). Although the total amount of time spent in bed shows a cross-sectional increase after 60 years, the amount of time spent sleeping remains constant into old age (Williams, Karacan, & Hursch, 1974). As a consequence, the proportion of time asleep to time in bed, an index of sleep efficiency, shows a cross-sectional decrease across adulthood, beginning after 30 years for men and 50 for women. The increased time in bed is due to a longer period of time needed to fall asleep when first retiring for the night, more frequent periods of wakefulness, and time spent lying awake before arising in the morning. In one investigation of older adults, an average of 21 awakenings per night were recorded (Hayashi & Endo, 1982). Men are more likely than women to suffer from sleep disturbances in the years between 40 and 70, possibly due to increased disruptions by REM sleep and its associated penile erections (Williams et al., 1974). By the 70s and 80s, these gender differences disappear. It has been suggested that in old age, the primary causes of sleep disruptions are sleep apnea, involuntary periodic leg movements, gastric distress, and more frequent needs to urinate (Coleman et al., 1981). Although almost one-half of all elderly persons are estimated to have either sleep apnea or leg movements (Ancoli-Israel & Kripke, 1991; Ancoli-Israel, Kripke, Mason, & Kaplan, 1985), the role of these symptoms in causing sleep problems has been debated by sleep researchers (Bliwise, 1992).

Sleep disturbances seem to have a physiological basis, or at least a correlation to electroencephalogram (EEG) measurements of brain activity during sleep. EEG sleep patterns show distinct changes in old age, at least as revealed by cross-sectional studies (Feinberg, 1974). Related, perhaps, to the phenomenon of increased wakefulness is a rise across adulthood in Stage 1 sleep (drowsiness without actual sleep). There are some decreases after age 60 years in Stages 2 and 3 sleep, but the most pronounced pattern is a large decrease of Stage 4 sleep. By the later years of adulthood, this stage is not even detectable in the EEGs of many of the persons studied. Total REM sleep (both amount and percent) remains fairly stable until the 60s and 70s, at which point it diminishes. At the same time, the observable behaviors associated with REM sleep become less apparent. These age differences, combined with information on wakefulness, suggest that the sleep of older adults is less restful, with more time awake and less time spent in deep, dreamless sleep or REM sleep. At all stages of sleep, older adults awaken more readily.

These patterns of age effects on sleep and EEG patterns may have their source in age effects on SNS activity. Increased amounts of norepinephrine in the blood in older persons is associated with more periods of wakefulness and less REM and Stage 4 sleep (Prinz, Halter, Benedetti, & Raskind, 1979; Prinz, Vitiello, Smallwood, Schoene, & Halter, 1984). Changes in the central nervous system structures responsible for controlling sleep may be another source of age effects on sleep patterns (see Chapter 7).

There are also a number of behavioral concomitants associated with the physiological changes in sleep and EEG patterns in later life. In particular is the finding that older adults spend more time in bed but sleep for about the same number of hours as do younger adults. It is possible that older adults need to spend more time in bed so that they reach the nightly total of 7 hr of sleep (the average number of hours sleeping by adults of all ages). Such a strategy would therefore be adaptive. Conversely, it is also possible that older adults change their sleep habits so that they inappropriately spend more awake time in bed. The changes in sleep patterns can be seen as maladaptive responses to altered daily schedules associated with retirement, misconceptions about age-related sleep needs, or overaccommodation to slight sleep changes. Older people may spend more time in bed because they feel they should have more sleep, but because the physiological need for sleep remains at 7 hr, the time in bed is spent less efficiently. The expectation that they should be getting more sleep than they do may lead to the development of insomnia as preoccupation with sleep develops into a serious concern that actually interferes with sleep (Morin & Gramling, 1989). As sleep problems develop, a vicious cycle may ensue in which concern over increased wakefulness leads the individual to seek sleep medications such as sedative-hypnotics, which can ultimately create more sleep problems (Kales & Kales, 1984).

Another vicious cycle may develop in which poor sleep at night leads the individual to take more daytime naps, further exacerbating nighttime insomnia. Finally, psychological symptoms such as anxiety and thought disturbances are related to chronic sleep problems in the elderly; reflecting either the influence of poor sleep on well-being or the influence of psychopathology on sleep disturbances (Bliwise, 1992). Fortunately, sleep problems are not irreversible and behavioral treatments can prove effective in reducing periods of wakefulness. Stimulus control is one of the most effective methods, involving correction of maladaptive sleep habits such as eliminating non-sleep inducing stimuli from the bedroom (Morin & Azrin, 1988).

Implications of Age Effects on Autonomic Functioning

The everyday life of the average person is influenced in crucial ways by the adequacy of functioning of the ANS. In particular, the ability to adjust the circulation of the blood, body temperature, and sleep patterns to the demands of the situation are critical for engaging in a variety of recreational and work-related activities and for feelings of well-being on a day-to-day basis. To the extent that aging brings with it perceptible changes from otherwise stable adult levels of functioning, it may be speculated that feelings of restriction and distress will arise as each new threshold is crossed. For example, the knowledge that one's body is less adaptable to outside temperatures means that adults living in geographical areas with cold winters will restrict their outdoor activities and spend more time at home. Outdoor exposure during the summer must also be limited to the extent that the individual's ability to adapt to the heat becomes restricted. Discomfort caused by difficulties in making postural adjustments can also be distressing in that they cause the individual to feel weak and enfeebled. Awareness of this variety of changes is likely to be heightened by the fact that regulatory systems over the body's circulation and temperature are designed to be salient to the individual, serving as warning of danger or imminent harm. As has been mentioned on several occasions, overaccommodation to the threshold experience of aging in this domain is a very real threat to the well-being of the older adult. Conversely, overassimilation can have deleterious effects as well, particularly when the older adult does not take precautions during physical exertion or when venturing out into very hot or cold weather.

Cyclical processes have also been described in which a response to crossing an aging threshold in this area triggers a maladaptive pattern that exacerbates the problem. Fear and apprehension associated with changes in the autonomic control mechanisms over temperature, blood pressure, and sleep can in themselves contribute to further impairment of functioning beyond that which is dictated by the aging process. Anxiety increases the level of sympathetic arousal and therefore interferes with the functions regulated by this system such as norepinephrine, blood pressure, sleep patterns, and sweat gland activity. On the more positive side, it is also possible for older individuals to use the changes signalled by the autonomic nervous system as stimuli for altering their patterns of behavior, making necessary adjustments to compensate for changes in cold or heat responses, sleep patterns, and postural adjustments. In some cases, increased participation in physical exercise and activity can help offset age-related changes. Fortunately, the changes in the autonomic nervous system described here occur gradually over a period of many years. Consequently, there are numerous opportunities for the individual to learn to adjust to the effects of aging and find new behavioral accommodations as these become necessary.

CENTRAL NERVOUS SYSTEM

The activities of the central nervous system are the basis for the individual's entire range of complex thoughts, actions, and emotions. This system coordinates all sensory information from within the body and from the outside environment, preparing and instructing the body's efforts to make complex integrated responses. The size and complexity of the central nervous system, particularly the cerebral cortex, is what most biologists believe differentiates humans from lower animal species and gives us our unique potential for having a "mind." Age differences in this system can be seen as underlying many of the age differences observed in cognitive functioning, including memory, information processing and the general quality we refer to as intelligence.

In this part of the chapter, I will focus on the "normal" aging of the central nervous system; specifically, changes at the level of the neuron and changes at the level of brain structures. Changes due to Alzheimer's disease, and theories regarding its cause, will be brought into the discussion at the end of the chapter.

Models of the Aging Nervous System

The effects of aging in the central nervous system are in some ways unique compared to other bodily systems. When a neuron dies, it does not have an identical replacement, because no new neurons are formed once the nervous system has completed the early stage of development in infancy. As a result, the loss of neurons, along with their synaptic connections to other neurons, can result in permanent loss. For many years, the irreversible nature of neuronal death formed the basis for major approaches to understanding the aging of the nervous system. However, as shall be seen here, there now are contrasting and less pessimistic explanations of how the brain ages.

Neuronal fallout model. The loss of neurons due their death without replacement is the basis for the so-called longstanding "neuronal fallout" model of aging (Hanley, 1974). Researchers who work within this model attempt to document the rate and extent of neuronal loss across different brain regions. The psychological counterpart to this model can be thought of as a behavioral fallout model, used by researchers attempting to demonstrate the extent and timing of loss of various cognitive functions.

Researchers working within the neuronal fallout model assume that although there is some redundancy across sites in the brain so that the loss of a single neuron or synapse, or even groups of neurons perhaps, is not necessarily significant. Ultimately, however, it is assumed that progressive neuron loss leads to irreversible changes in behavior, as the brain's reserve capacity erodes (Henderson, Tomlinson, & Gibson, 1980). A variant of the neuronal fallout model involves the assumption that the loss of certain cells is more crucial than of others. Where there is little redundancy, the loss of even small numbers of neurons may have quite serious consequences (Finch, 1982). In other cases, the loss of "pacemaker" cells that control the functioning of other neurons can lead to a cascade effect of more widespread degeneration so that the harmful effects spread far beyond the damaged areas (Greenough & Green, 1981; Ordy, 1981). Minor insults to pathways of the brain, which accumulate over time, could thereby come to have progressively damaging effects on the structural integrity of the central nervous system as a whole.

Plasticity model. An alternative to the neuronal fallout model is the plasticity model, in which it is assumed that growth and regeneration are vital features of the brain throughout life (Cotman & Peterson, 1990). Plasticity in the nervous system refers to the growth of new structures and functions in response to loss or damage of neurons or synapses. Although parts of the nervous system are composed of "nonplastic" genetically programed circuits or highly specialized cells and synpases, there are millions of neurons that are able to sprout new axons or enrich their dendritic trees when other neurons are damaged through injury or degeneration. Plasticity is not only a reactive quality, according to this model. Stimulation from the environment in the form of opportunities to process new information can lead to the growth of new dendritic connections (Diamond, 1990). The neurologically based plasticity model corresponds to psychological models of intellectual development in later adulthood, according to which continued acquisition of new skills and information can occur as the result of training or experience (Willis & Schaie, 1994). In Chapter 9, the implications of this model for behavior will be explored in more depth.

The proposal that plasticity can compensate for or even outstrip the rate of neuronal fallout counters decades of literature grimly aimed at demonstrating and documenting the precise rate of neuron death throughout the nervous system. Part of the reason for discrepancies between these approaches pertains to the target of research. Neuronal fallout researchers count total numbers of neurons but do not examine the structure of existing neurons. By contrast, plasticity researchers conduct careful analyses of the extent and branching of dendritic trees. Another factor has been the familiar confound between aging and disease. Researchers who intend to document the effects of normal aging may inadvertently be providing data on the damaging effects on brain tissue of diseases such as Alzheimer's disease or circulatory problems affecting the blood supply to the brain. For example, one set of researchers included older respondents with known symptoms of cerebral disease and although specific lesions could not be identified, there remains the possibility that the findings of increased brain atrophy with age reflected the results of disease rather than normal aging (Takeda & Matsuzawa, 1985). Evidence of failure to separate healthy older adults from those with a dementing disease is found throughout the aging literature. One example is a well-known and frequently reproduced report on the progressive degeneration of dendrites in neurons within the aging nervous system in which six out of the nine cases included in the sample were diagnosed with Alzheimer's disease

(Scheibel, Lindsay, Tomiyasu, & Scheibel, 1976). Generalizations from this type of research can lead to an overly pessimistic view of the aging of the nervous system. Given the significance of findings in this field, and the race to find the genetic cause or causes of Alzheimer's disease, it would seem crucial for the gerontological optimists and pessimists to reach consensus on their research methods!

The inappropriateness of research focusing on neuron death alone, particularly among unhealthy samples, was highlighted in a landmark study by Buell and Coleman (Buell & Coleman, 1979). This investigation was the first in a series of studies (Flood, Buell, Horwitz, & Coleman, 1987; Flood & Coleman, 1988) designed to demonstrate plasticity in the nervous system of aged humans and, furthermore, to contrast the effects of normal aging with those of Alzheimer's disease. In this research, dendritic growth in neurons was quantified in brains taken from adults ranging in age from the 40s to the 90s. A separate analysis involved dendritic branching in neurons taken from the brains of individuals given a definitive diagnosis of Alzheimer's disease. The surprising finding to emerge from this study that of the growth of neurons in normal aged compared to middle aged individuals. It was not that the older adults grew "new" neurons, but that their existing neurons were greatly and more densely elaborated along their dendritic branches. This was true in the area that has served as a major focus for Alzheimer's researchers as well as researchers interested in the normal aging of memory functions: the hippocampal region within the limbic system. The dendrites of those elderly adults with Alzheimer's disease were significantly reduced compared to the other two groups. These findings point out the importance of separating normal aging from disease, and convincingly documented the prospect that growth in the nervous system can occur throughout the later years of adulthood.

The findings regarding neural plasticity provide encouragement for the potential of continued growth into old age of the neurons within the central nervous system. Another important finding of the Buell and Coleman research is the fact that throughout the adult years studied, dying neurons were found to co-exist with those showing plasticity. While affirming the plasticity model, these findings reinforce the need to understand the cause of neuronal fallout.

The "Normal" Aging Neuron

As the basic unit of structure and function within the nervous system, the neuron is a central focus of researchers studying the aging of the brain. Not all neurons degenerate and die as a function of time or aging, as was just pointed out. For convenience, those that do will be referred to here as "aging neurons."

Some of the abnormalities seen in aging neurons are the same as those that characterize neurons affected by Alzheimer's disease but are observed with less frequency or to a lesser degree. As in many other areas of physiological aging, it is difficult to place into completely separate categories the changes caused by diseases more prevalent in the aged from those changes due to the normal aging process.

Hypothesized causes of neuron loss. Why do neurons die? This seemingly simple question has stimulated several promising lines of investigation into hypothesized causes of neuron loss. There is as yet no one clear-cut explanation that emerges, and at present each possibility provides a description of an age-related process, or at least age differences established cross-sectionally that remain a potentially important cause of the death of neurons.

Lipofuscin hypothesis. A frequently cited observation in research on aging is that neurons accumulate a yellowish pigment known as lipofuscin within their cell bodies. According to the lipofuscin hypothesis, it is this accumulation that causes the malfunctioning and eventual death of neurons by interfering with protein metabolism (Mann & Yates, 1974). This position is disputed, as other researchers have claimed that lipofuscin has benign (Bondareff, 1981) or even beneficial effects (Davies & Fotheringham, 1981) on the nervous system. The strongest evidence used to refute the lipofuscin hypothesis is that the inferior olive, a structure in the midbrain with neurons rich in lipofuscin, does not show age-related deficits in structure, number, or function.

Circulatory deficit hypothesis. A second proposed cause of neuron loss is that circulatory deficits associated with the aging process lead to deprivation of the cerebral blood supply and ultimately cause the neuron to die through starvation. This explanation takes the primary locus of neuronal aging away from factors intrinsic to the nervous system and places it onto factors that affect how well blood is pumped to the brain. As is true for research on cardiovascular functioning, a major concern in this area is differentiating normal age changes in the circulatory system from coronary heart disease.

The primary evidence used to support the circulatory deficit hypothesis is based on measures of cerebral blood flow (CBF), the rate of blood circulation in the brain. A reduction in CBF leads to the death of neurons whose metabolic needs cannot be supported. However, this is not such a clear-cut determination. If neurons have died due to intrinsic aging changes then the CBF would be reduced because there are fewer metabolizing neurons present in the system. A decrease in CBF may reflect an adjustment made by the microcirculation of the brain to the diminished metabolic needs of a reduced neuron population. In fact, the weight of evidence appears to support this latter interpretation. Although CBF is reduced among healthy older individuals (Hagstadius & Risberg, 1989; MacInnes, Paull, & Quaife, 1989), there is also a reduction in oxygen uptake by nervous system tissue, indicating that there is less metabolizing tissue in the brains of older persons (Frackowiak, Jones, Lenzi, & Heather, 1980). A parallel trend is observed for data on neuronal glucose uptake, again signifying a reduction in metabolizing tissue (Dekoninck, Jacquy, Jocquet, & Noel, 1976). These findings, although suggestive, are not definitive. What remains to be shown is the temporal progression of neuron loss occurring first followed by a commensurate reduction in CBF.

Regardless of the cause of lowered CBF in later adulthood, there is evidence that participation in aerobic exercise can increase the circulation of blood to the brain and hence improve behavioral functions such as psychomotor performance (Baylor & Spirduso, 1988; Spirduso, 1980). This evidence cannot determine whether circulatory deficiency is the cause of neuron death, but provides additional support for the position that the nervous system maintains plasticity in old age. Furthermore, the advantages of aerobic exercise as a means of compensation for the effects of aging once again is shown to extend into behavioral realms.

Cellular changes in the neuron. Other, less well-investigated sources of neuron loss involve changes at the cellular level within the neuron. One hypothesis is that there are metabolic changes in protein kinase activity, which would indicate diminished neural responsiveness to neurotransmitter or neurohormonal stimulation. Another proposed metabolic change is a reduction in carbonic anhydrase activity, which would signify that glycolitic turnover (involving the conversion of glycogen to glucose) is impaired (Meier-Ruge, Hunziker, Iwangoff, Reichlmeier, & Schulz, 1980).

A more generic hypothesis at the molecular level of the neuron is the proposal that protein synthesis within the nucleus of the neuron is increasingly subject to error over time (Lynch & Gerling, 1981). Since there is no neuron turnover, these errors are more likely to accumulate over the lifespan, as contrasted with cells that replace themselves on a continuous basis. Moreover, since neurons do not replicate themselves these errors would not be erased when new neurons take over for the old, error-ridden ones, as occurs in cells that replace themselves by division.

Structural changes in the neuron. Apart from the ultimate cause of neuron loss, it remains the case that a number of significant changes occur within the aging neuron that can influence its structure and function.

Cell body. Processes that support the cellular activity of the neuron take place within the cell body. Although the size and shape of the cell body in neurons within the cortex does not change, at least up until the mid-70s (Schulz & Hunziker, 1980), various abnormalities appear within the cell body of the aging neuron. These abnormalities include distortions in the surface of the membrane surrounding the nucleus, and deteriorative changes of organelles within the cell body (Duara, London, & Rapoport, 1985). The accumulation of lipofuscin within the cell body constitutes another feature of the aging neuron.

Other changes in the cell body have been investigated in comparisons of normal aging and Alzheimer's disease, focusing particularly on the cells of the hippocampus. (Tomlinson & Henderson, 1976). A process called granulovacuolar degeneration involves the development of spaces, or vacuoles, in the intracellular fluid outside the nucleus. These vacuoles accumulate small granules of unknown matter and the impact of their presence is not known. Another change observed within cells of the hippocampus is the development of neurofibrillary tangles, in which the cellular material within the cell bodies of neurons becomes replaced by densely packed, twisted protein microfibrils, or tiny strands. The effect of neurofibrillary tangles is not clear, but it is thought possible that their presence obstructs the flow of cellular fluids within the cell body.

Dendrites. Dendrites are tree-like extensions of the cell bodies whose function is to receive information from other neurons. Their branches often form elaborate and intricate patterns, and may be covered with dendritic spines. The more extensive this network of branches and spines, the greater the receptive surface of the neuron.

Initial investigations of the effects of aging on the dendrite provided a picture of dramatic losses in dendritic elaboration in the later adult years (Scheibel, 1982; Scheibel, Lindsay, Tomiyasu, & Scheibel, 1975; Scheibel, Lindsay, Tomiyasu, & Scheibel, 1976; Scheibel, Tomiyasu, & Scheibel, 1977). This finding was based on judgments made by the researchers in the appearance of dendrites stained by the "rapid Golgi" method rather than by quantitative measurement. From their observations, Scheibel and associates concluded that dendrites are lost in progressive fashion from the aging neuron, beginning in the outermost sections of the tree and eventually spreading toward the cell body of the neuron. The final stage of deterioration was the complete loss of dendrites, so that the neuron appeared to be a stump with no branches.

Scheibel's description of widespread dendritic degeneration throughout various regions of the brain contrasts sharply with the findings of Buell and Coleman described earlier; that, when quantitative measurements were used, there were more rather than fewer dendrites in the brains of nondemented aged persons. Although dying neurons similar to those described by Scheibel and associates were apparent, Buell and Coleman's (Buell & Coleman, 1979; Flood, Buell, Horwitz, & Coleman, 1987; Flood & Coleman, 1988) more systematic approach allowed them to detect healthy growth within the total population of neurons they studied. A further qualification that must be made in evaluating the Scheibel studies is the fact that the samples used in this research included patients with dementia whose data were not separated from the data of persons who showed no signs of neurological disease prior to death. Finally, a technical problem in the Scheibel studies was their use of a staining method that can create destroy neural tissue. Without a young control group to compare with the brains from older adults, the effects of the procedure could not be separated from the effects of the aging process.

The Environment of the Aging Neuron

The tissue of the nervous system is composed of a complex network of neurons, glial cells, and blood vessels. Communication among neurons and support of their metabolic activities are highly dependent on the adequate functioning within this extracellular environment. In part, this environment is altered by the presence of dying and degenerating neurons and in part by spontaneous age-related changes in the glia.

Amyloid plaques. As neurons die, their remnants collect around a central core of amyloid to form abnormal accumulations of hard tissue which are referred to as "senile" "neuritic," or, preferably, "amyloid plaques." These abnormalities are observed in the hippocampus and cerebral cortex with increasing frequency in old age (Tomlinson & Henderson, 1976). Because they are composed of the parts of dying neurons, it may seem logical to conclude that amyloid plaques are a product of the normal aging process. However, as these plaques accumulate, they may impede the functioning of intact neurons.

Glia. Glial cells are specialized cells found within the nervous system that serve as structural support and protection for neurons. In addition, glia interact actively in the metabolic and electrochemical activities of neurons. By virtue of their large number (they outnumber neurons in the brain by a ratio of 10 to 1) and their supportive role within the brain, the aging of these cells would have significant ramifications for the functioning of the nervous system as a whole.
Although the total number of glial cells remains constant into old age (Henderson, Tomlinson, & Gibson, 1980), there is a shift in the proportionate dis-

tribution of the two major types of cells. Astrocytes ordinarily link neurons and capillaries, but expand in size and number to form a scar after neurons are damaged or lost. There are more astrocytes, therefore, in parts of the brain that undergo neuron loss in old age such as the visual cortex and parts of the brain stem (Blinkov & Glezer, 1968; Devaney & Johnson, 1980). At the same time, there is an decrease in the proportion of the second type of glial cell, oligodendrites. These glial cells form the myelin sheath, and as myelinated neurons die, the oligodendrites die too (Brizzee, 1975).

In addition to changes in the proportions of glial cells are structural changes within the remaining astrocytes. These develop abnormalities and selected areas of deterioration (Ravens & Calvo, 1966) that can interfere with the process of suffusing neurons with blood from the surrounding capillaries.

Changes in Synapses

Communication among neurons is accomplished via the transmission of impulses from one neuron to another at the synapse. Through synaptic transmission, neurons form pathways along which information travels through the various parts of the nervous system. Each neuron can have many thousands of synapses, and given that there are at least one trillion neurons, the amount of information that can be carried through the system as a whole is virtually infinite. This fact is important when considering the effects of aging. With so much potential for information to be encoded in the nervous system, it takes either massive and widespread loss or the deterioration of a large piece of the system to have significant behavioral effects. That the nervous system shows a high degree of resiliency to loss is further reinforced by the nature of synaptic encoding of information. The formation of synapses forms the substrate for new learning, but it is typically the case that new information is represented diffusely across many synapses. Furthermore, there is a high degree of redundancy in the form of multiple representation of information throughout the central nervous system. This redudancy is key in offsetting the effects of loss of particular synapses involving aging neurons.

Synapse numbers. Counts of synapses in the brain of nondemented humans have been performed in areas of the frontal cortex, with the finding that age is associated with no change in total synapse number (Cragg, 1975; Huttenlocher, 1979). This stability is consistent with the position stated earlier that neurons showing plasticity compensate for whatever neuronal fallout occurs with age. Simple counts of synapse number do not, however, provide information regarding possible reorganization within the nervous system caused by loss of certain types of synapses within particular pathways. Changes in patterns of information transmission may occur, for example. if the loss of excitatory synapses is not compensated by loss of inhibitory synapses. Such alterations may have important implications for behavior regulated by complex patterns of relationships among neuronal pathways.

Neurotransmitters. The release and uptake of neurotransmitters across the synaptic cleft forms the basis for communication of information at the synapse. The presynaptic axon releases molecules of neurotransmitter from synaptic vesicles into the synaptic cleft. As these molecules diffuse across the cleft, they are taken up by receptors on the surface of the postsynaptic neuron. If the neurotransmitter has an excitatory effect, the postsynaptic neuron will become more likely to trigger an impulse. Inhibitory synapses reduce the likelihood of an impulse in postsynaptic neurons.

There are a large number of types of neurotransmitters in the central nervous system. Pathways of neurons are identified in terms of the neurotransmitter that passes through them. One of the most well-researched pathways in terms of the effects of aging is the pathway that carries acetylcholine. This pathway, called the cholinergic pathway, travels through the hippocampus and is identified with the consolidation of short-term memory. Because of its role in memory and suggested links to the development of Alzheimer's disease (Mann, 1991), researchers have been interested in the role of acetylcholine in normal aging, which is also associated with memory loss. Although not establishing a direct link between aging and reductions in acetylcholine, researchers have found that the administration of scopolamine, a drug that briefly blocks acetylcholine transmission, leads to deficits in short-term memory among young adults that are comparable to those shown by healthy aged individuals (Drachman & Leavitt, 1974; Drachman & Sahakian, 1980; Flicker, Serby, & Ferris, 1990). Scopolamine causes an even more severe impairment when administered to healthy elderly persons (Flicker, Ferris, & Serby, 1992).

Support of the "cholinergic" hypothesis that memory loss in the aged is caused by deficits in acetylcholine pathways is provided by anatomical studies showing a reduction of hippocampal cells in later adulthood (Ball, 1977; Mouritzen Dam, 1979), and lowered activity of cholinergic neurons and receptor binding sites (Nordberg, Adolfsson, Marcusson, & Winblad, 1982; Perry, Perry, Gibson, Blessed, & Tomlinson, 1977). Taken together, this evidence suggests that cholinergic neurons in the hippocampus are particularly vulnerable to the effects of aging so that even the redundancy within the system cannot compensate for loss of these pathways.

Another area of selected loss in a particular neurotransmitter pathway occurs in the dopaminergic pathway of the basal ganglia, a set of nuclei located deep within the brain that are responsible for controlling motor movements initiated by the cerebral cortex. The pathway connects the striatum of the basal ganglia with the substantia nigra, a structure within the midbrain. The striatum receives input directly from sensory receptors throughout the body, and this input is used as the basis for specific movement programs. Dopamine, one of several monoamines, is the primary neurotransmitter involved in this pathway.

Reductions of dopaminergic activity are documented throughout the substantia nigra-striatal pathway, along with a reduced number of binding sites for dopamine (Carlsson et al., 1980; McGeer & McGeer, 1980). A severe reduction of dopaminergic activity is the cause of Parkinson's disease, a disorder that results in widespread loss of motor control involving the face, hands, gestures, and feet. The relationship between normal aging and Parkinson's disease is not clear, but it is possible that the more moderate losses shown in normal aging can be compensated by the redundancy present within this pathway.

Changes in the levels and activity of other monoamines also appear in the brain stem (Frolkis & Bezrukov, 1979). Reductions in norepinephrine in particular can have widespread deleterious effects on a number of functions, including postural balance, muscle tone, regulation of behavioral arousal, and sleep functions. Changes in monoamine oxidase and acetylcholine activity in the reticular activating formation may add to these effects, further interfering with sleep functions as can a reduction in serotonin in the raphe nucleus, another sleep control center. Alterations with age in the levels of norepinephrine in the hypothalamus and other limbic system structures may have effects on emotional reactivity.

The overall picture of the available findings is of reductions in a variety of major neurotransmitter pathways affecting a variety of behavioral functions. However, balancing this view of decline are data that reflect stability of some of the same neurotransmitters in other brain regions or even within the same pathways as those in which decline is documented. For example, although acetylcholine shows decreases in hippocampal pathways, it does not show consistent declines in the cerebral cortex or basal ganglia (McGeer & McGeer, 1980). Similarly, although a reduction in gamma amino butyric acid (GABA) activity is in the thalamus, this effect is specific to this brain structure, and other neurotransmitters in the thalamus are stable into old age. Even in the hippocampus, reports are not consistent regarding declines in cholinergic activity (Carlsson et al., 1980).

There is confidence in the conclusion, then, that the areas of neurotransmitter functioning most severely affected by the normal aging process include cholinergic activity in the hippocampus, dopamine in the substantial nigra-striatal pathway, norepinephrine and serotonin in some parts of the brain stem, and GABA in the thalamus. The context for these changes is stability in the same neurotransmitters within other brain regions and other neurotransmitters in the same structures. The picture is not one of universal loss of neurotransmitter activity and thus the integrity of major brain pathways is maintained.

Aging of Major Brain Structures

The neurons within the central nervous system are organized into pathways, tracts, or structures. The major structural divisions of the central nervous system are organized so that the "higher" functions underlying "thought" and complex voluntary actions are served by structures within the cerebral cortex. The lower functions that serve the maintenance needs of the body or operate to feed information to and from the cerebral cortex are located within the subcortical structures located underneath the cortex toward the central core of the brain.

General age-related changes in structure. The weight, volume, and appearance of the brain reflects to a general extent its structural integrity. At maturity, the male brain weighs 1300–1400 g (about 3 pounds) and is somewhat lighter in the female (due, of course, to the fact that females tend to weigh less than males). Researchers interested in the overall effects of aging on the nervous system have taken as a measure the weight of the brain at autopsy. Numerous cross-sectional studies based on this measure indicate a loss of brain weight averaging 5% to 10% in the years between 20 and 90 (Dekaban & Sadowsky, 1978). The volume of the mature healthy brain is about 1300cm^3 in men and 1000cm^3 in women. A loss of 200cm^3 occurs between the ages of 20 and 80 years (Ordy, 1975), with a pronounced drop beginning after the age of 50 (Yamaura, Ito, Kubota, & Matsuzawa, 1980). Along with the shrinkage of brain tissue is a widening of space in the ventricles, and the surface of the brain changes in appearance as the *gyri* (swellings) become smaller and the *sulci* (valleys between gyri) become wider. One qualifying factor is that these findings are, of necessity, based on cross-sectional comparisons. Generational differences in nutritional patterns that influence height and weight can produce what might otherwise appear to be age-related differences in brain status. Furthermore, it is unknown the extent to which individuals included in these studies suffered from undiagnosed Alzheimer's disease, which is known to reduce areas of brain tissue.

Regional variations within the brain. The neuronal fallout and presence of aging neurons in the brain occur at different rates throughout the individual brain structures, and in some cases, no age-related losses are evident at all. There are also discrepancies in the literature on brain aging due to differences in measurement. Some researchers measure loss in terms of total neuron count in a given area (as estimated from fixated slices), and others measure packing density, the neuron count per unit of volume.

Brain stem. The brain stem remains relatively intact throughout the aging process, with little or no structural basis for impairment of the motor or arousal functions served by its structures. Of the nuclei within the brain stem, only the locus coeruleus shows neuronal fallout, and even within this structure, age effects, amounting to about 40%, do not appear until the mid-60s (Vijayashankar & Brody, 1979). A functional effect of this cell loss may be related to the behavioral reports of sleep problems in old age described earlier in the chapter.

Subcortical motor control structures. The cerebellum, which controls the finely tuned voluntary motor movements initiated by the motor cortex, has linkages throughout the brain stem and cerebral cortex. One of the specialized neurons within this structure responsible for this complex integrative function is the highly specialized Purkinje cell, which integrates large amounts of sensory information needed to evaluate the body's movement status. Over the course of the adult years, the number of Purkinje cells diminishes by 25%, a decline particularly noticeable after the age of 60 years (Hall, Miller, & Corsellis, 1975). The loss of these cells is significant because their numbers are relatively low to begin with, and because each one serves such a major integrative function.

The basal ganglia, described earlier in the context of dopaminergic pathways, show decreases in volume over the adult years. However, aging does not have a consistent effect on the number of neurons in the nuclei of the basal ganglia. Neurotransmitter alterations and loss of cortical cells in the motor area of the cortex may impair the quality of instructions for programming movement received by the basal ganglia. The structural integrity of these nuclei, however, is maintained into late adulthood.

Cerebral cortex. The cerebral cortex, the area of the brain responsible for higher level processing and programming of information, judgment, and analysis, consists of a very thin mantle of nervous tissue amounting to only 1.5 to 4.5 mm in thickness. However, this thin layer has virtually unlimited potential for information storage. There are an estimated 14–15 billion neurons in the cortex, and these form an estimated 1billion synapses per mm^3, meaning that the total number of synapses in the cortex could reach as high as 50 trillion. This enormously high potential for information storage is what serves in large measure as protection against the effects of aging on neuron loss.

Neuron loss has been documented throughout the cortex, but at different rates in different areas. In some cases, these losses appear to be very high. The primary visual area in the occipital cortex, primary somatosensory area in the parietal cortex, the secondary auditory area in the temporal cortex, the frontal pole, and motor areas of the frontol cortex are reported to show losses ranging to about 50% over the adult age span (Brody, 1955b; Devaney & Johnson, 1980; Henderson, Tomlinson, & Gibson, 1980). The association areas in the cortex appear to be less vulnerable to the process of neuronal fallout. No age differences in neuron number appear in the prefrontal region, and decreases amounting only to about 20% appear in the association areas located in the temporal lobe (Brody, 1955a; Henderson, Tomlinson, & Gibson, 1980; Higatsberger, Budka, & Bernheimer, 1982; Huttenlocher, 1979; Shefer, 1973).

Psychological Interactions

Aging appears to affect a variety of specific functions served by the central nervous system, effects that can have a wide-ranging impact on all aspects of behavior: from sensory functioning, to reaction time, to a variety of cognitive capacities, and emotion.

Losses in the sensory areas of the cortex add to changes in receptor structures with age for each of these systems (described in Chapter 7), to reduce the quality of input used in the association areas for higher order processing and integration with the programming of motor responses. Furthermore, losses of motor cells, particularly the large Betz cells which are relatively few in number, may play a role in causing motor disturbances such as diminished motor readiness and loss of fine control of the timing of movements (Mankovsky, Mints, & Lisenyuk, 1982; Rabbitt, 1980). Symptoms of muscle and joint discomfort may also be related to loss of these cells, including stiffening, slowness, joint pain, and leg cramps (Scheibel, 1982).

Countering these losses is the relative stability of the higher cortical functions served by neurons in the association regions of the cortex. The neuronal fallout demonstrated in these areas is not so high as to render impossible the regeneration of lost functions by the surviving neurons. This constancy may reflect increased activity by these surviving neurons as well as steady output from a constant number of active and healthy cells. It may be concluded, from an anatomical basis alone, that there is no reason for the aging process to impair the higher cortical functions of judgment, reasoning, foresight, and "wisdom."

Furthermore, it is important to emphasize once again that there is tremendous variation among adults in the ways in which the aging process (apart from disease) affects central nervous system functions. Some of these functions in later adulthood are, in addition, affected by the extent to which the individual developed and used them during the adult years. Exposure to stimulation in the areas of perception, cognition, and motor activity through mental and physical exercise can influence, throughout old age, the degree to which the abilities that depend on these functions are maintained. The importance placed by the individual on mental and physical abilities contribute further to the personal meaning of age changes in any of these areas.

Alzheimer's Disease as a Model of Normal Aging?

Up to this point, changes in the brain associated with Alzheimer's disease have not received attention, as the focus of the chapter is on "normal aging." However, with research in this area progressing at a dizzying pace, it seems important to bring the reader up to date on this disease and its implications for functioning. And if some investigators are correct in their speculations, the secrets of "normal" brain aging may someday be found within the laboratory of the Alzheimer's researcher.

Background of the disease. Alzheimer's disease was first reported in 1907 by a German psychiatrist and neuropathologist, Alois Alzheimer, who documented the case of a 51-year-old woman complaining of poor memory and disorientation to time and place (Alzheimer, 1907/1987). Alzheimer was unable to explain this process of deterioration until after the woman died when he observed upon autopsy that her brain had undergone what are now considered to be the classic characteristics of the disease: amyloid plaques, neurofibrillary tangles, and granuovacuolar degeneration. Currently, Alzheimer's disease is considered a form of "dementia," or progressive deterioration of cognitive functioning, associated with the widespread death of neurons throughout the cortex.

Although in about 10% of cases, Alzheimer's disease can have an early onset (age 65 and under), most cases are found in people over 60 to 65 years. The estimated incidence of Alzheimer's disease varies within the over-65 population from 0.6% for persons aged 65–69, 1% between 70 and 74 years, 2% in the 75–79-year bracket, 3.3% in the 80–84-year group, and 8.4% for those 85 years and over (Hebert et al., 1995). Although this figure represents only a small percentage of elderly people, the actual numbers of people potentially affected by Alzheimer's disease has increased as the number of people in the over-65 population has grown. Current estimates of the incidence of Alzheimer's indicate a rise from approximately 3 million people over the age of 65 with the disorder in 1980 to more than a projected 10 million by the year 2050 (Evans et al., 1989). Adding to the magnitude of the problem is the fact that Alzheimer's disease is more common among people over the age of 85. This is precisely the part of the population expected to show the greatest increase in size in the next half-century. As this oldest segment of the population grows, many chronic diseases, including Alzheimer's, will become significant public health problems.

Another possible cause of dementia is cardiovascular disease affecting the supply of blood to the brain. Such a condition is called *vascular dementia*. At one time it was thought that arteriosclerosis ("hardening of the arteries") was the major cause of Alzheimer's disease. It was then found that the degenerative changes in the brains of people with Alzheimer's disease were very different from changes due to vascular illness. Vascular dementia is caused by the death of selected groups of neurons in the cerebral cortex when clusters of capillaries in the brain are cut off by infarctions, acute forms of circulatory disease. Myocardial infarction is the technical term for what is commonly referred to as a "heart attack." The dementia caused by multiple infarctions in the brain is due to a series of minor strokes that cut off the blood supply to different regions of the cortex.

Symptoms of Alzheimer's disease. Alzheimer's disease progresses in stages that are marked by progressive deterioration of cognitive functioning along with changes in personality and interpersonal relationships. The behavioral symptoms of dementia due to Alzheimer's disease are memory loss, disorientation, decline of judgment, deterioration of social skills, and extreme flatness or changeability of affect. These symptoms evolve over time, but their rate of progress varies from person to person (Teri, Hughes, & Larson, 1990) and stage of the disease, with the most rapid deterioration occuring during the middle phase (Stern et al., 1994). Other psychological symptoms include agitation, wandering, hallucinations, delusions, aggressiveness, insomnia, demandingness, and an inability to adapt to new routines or surroundings (Ham, 1990).

The progression from early to late dementia in people with Alzheimer's usually occurs over a 5- to 10-year period, ending in death through the development of complicating diseases such as pneumonia. Those Alzheimer's patients who develop delusions are more likely to have severe overall cognitive impairment, a higher prevalence of hallucinations, and are generally more agitated and depressed. They are more likely to experience a number of psychosocial problems and are less able to care for themselves. Perhaps significantly, they are also likely to develop the disorder at an older age than individuals who are non-delusional (Rockwell, Jackso, Vilke, & Jeste, 1994).

Regrettably, no valid indicators currently exist for the certain diagnosis of Alzheimer's disease in its early stages. A definitive diagnosis of Alzheimer's disease can only be made after the person has died by studying microscopic changes in brain tissue. Because biopsies of the brain are dangerous and impractical, the best that can be done for a living person with the symptoms of dementia is to administer a variety of clinical and neurological tests and to infer a diagnosis of Alzheimer's if no other specific cause can be determined.

Theorized causes. Up until the late 1980s, biological theories focused on changes within levels of neurotransmitters or in particular structures that were thought to account for the degeneration of the brain and behavioral losses associated with Alzheimer's. One of the more prominent of these theories proposed that the primary disturbances involved in Alzheimer's disease are in the acetyl-choline neurotransmitter system, described earlier, as involved in processes of learning and memory (Coyle, Price, & DeLong, 1983). According to this view, people with Alzheimer's disease have insufficient amounts of choline acetyl-transferase (CAT), an enzyme essential for the synthesis of acetylcholine. As work in this area continues, researchers are also attempting to link changes at the bio-chemical level with the characteristic neurofibrillary tangles, amyloid plaques, and granulovacuolar degeneration that are associated with Alzheimer's disease (Geula & Mesulam, 1989). Whether these changes precede or follow changes at the biochemical level has yet to be discovered. Particularly important in this account of Alzheimer's disease is the fact that many of the biochemical and struc-tural changes found in the brains of people with this disorder are in the area of the hippocampus (Chui, 1989). Changes in this area of the brain are seen as playing a very strong role in causing the cognitive deficits associated with Alz-heimer's disease (Martin et al., 1987)

Another early line of biological research focused on diminished levels of cor-tical metabolism found in the temporoparietal region of the brains of people with Alzheimer's disease. This area of the brain plays an important role in lan-guage and cognitive functions. Metabolic changes in this area could reflect an actual abnormality in glucose metabolism or simply normal metabolism occur-ring in fewer neurons because of a loss of tissue in this part of the brain (Jagust, Budinger, Reed, & Conina, 1987). Abnormal EEG patterns have also been detected in this area of the brain (Rice et al., 1990). If the abnormality in glu-cose metabolism is a primary effect of the disease, then this could suggest a pos-sible mechanism for the degeneration of brain tissue caused by Alzheimer's.

Throughout the 1980s and into the 1990s, it became clear to Alzheimer's researchers that whatever changes may take place within the brain as a result of degenerative processes had to be triggered by some underlying defect in the genetic programming of neural activity. In the first place, there was increasingly strong evidence of a pattern of familial inheritance of the disorder. It became a well-established fact that relatives of people with Alzheimer's are three times as likely as others to develop this disease (Jarvik, 1988). Other suggestive evidence of genetic factors is the fact that there is an increased risk of Down syndrome within families of people who develop Alzheimer's at a relatively young age. Furthermore, Alzheimer's disease commonly develops in people with Down syndrome who survive into their 30s and 40s (Turkel & Nusbaum, 1986). The brain deficits of people with Alzheimer's resemble those of people with Down syndrome; in both disorders the areas of the brain that involve learning and memory are particularly affected (Schapiro & Rapoport, 1988). Evidence of a familial component also became clear from the identification of a form of the disease called "early-onset dementia" that strikes with particular vengeance between the ages of 30 and 60, progressing rapidly to death. This form of dementia accounts for 10% of all dementia cases, or approximately several hundred thousand people in the U.S. alone. People with this form of dementia are more likely to have relatives with the disease than those whose disease develops after the age of 70 years (Heun & Maier, 1995; Li et al., 1995; Silverman et al., 1994).

By studying the family lines of individuals with Alzheimer's using the newly developing genetics technology, researchers in the mid-90s have begun to close in on a set of genes that, when inherited, produce changes that cause the characteristic brain changes and death of neurons that ultimately lead to the behavioral symptoms of the disease. In 1995, a gene was positively identified on chromosome 14, whose mutations are responsible for 75% of cases of early-onset familial Alzheimer's (Sherrington et al., 1995). This gene (S182) codes a protein that is firmly embedded in a membrane of the neuron that might be involved in protein transport within neurons. These transport mechanisms could be connected with the amyloid plaques, one of the characteristic brain changes found in people with Alzheimer's disease and thought to be key factors in the progression of the disease. Following on the heels of this discovery was the identification of another defective gene (labelled STM2) on chromosome 1 (Levy-Lahad et al., 1995a; Levy-Lahad et al., 1995b). Mutations in this gene appear to be responsible for a familial form of early-onset Alzheimer's disease known to cluster in certain families. The ancestry of these families can be traced to the ethnic Germans living in the Volga valley of Russia in the 18th and 19th centuries. For years, researchers puzzled over the possible cause of the clustering of Alzheimer's disease in these families. The identification of this gene provided an important missing link in understanding not only these cases, but possibly a more general cause of Alzheimer's. This finding was particularly important because defects on the STM2 gene seem linked to the S182 gene located on chromosome 14.

The development of amyloid plaques has, since 1990, served as a major focus of genetics researchers in the Alzheimer's field (Behrouz, Defossez, Delacorte, & Mazzuca, 1991; Joachim & Selkoe, 1989; Yankner, Duffy, & Kirschner, 1990). These plaques are collections of ß-amyloid, a protein fragment clipped off a larger protein called amyloid precursor protein (APP). In 1991, defects were identified in the APP gene coded on chromosome 21 that could account for 2%–3% of early-onset cases. In healthy neurons, APP is transported to the outside membrane of the cell and broken down in a way that does not yield ß-amyloid proteins. Interference with this disposal mechanism for APP might lead to accumulation of ß-amyloid protein, which ultimately shows up as amyloid plaques. Unfortunately, hopes that abnormally high levels of amyloid protein in an individual's brain could serve as an early diagnostic test for the disease (Bissette et al., 1991) have led to disappointment, as the findings have failed to bear out the validity of such a screening test (Pirttila, Mehta, Frey, & Wisniewski, 1994).

The search for the Alzheimer's gene does not end there, however. Researchers have yet to account for the largest percentage (40%–50%) of Alzheimer's cases, those that arise after the age of 60 years. Progress toward the solution of this particular puzzle has come from investigations of defects in a gene (APOE) on chromosome 14 and the finding of the presence of a particular form of this gene, called APOE ε4 allele, among individuals who had the late-onset familial form of Alzheimer's disease (Strittmatter et al., 1993). Researchers have found that the risk for developing Alzheimer's disease was directly linked to the extent to which members of a family possessed the APOE ε4 allele (Corder et al., 1993; Tsai et al., 1994). Dramatic evidence for the role of this gene in the progression of the symptoms of late-onset Alzheimer's disease came from a longitudinal study at the Mayo Clinic. The possession of the APOE ε4 allele was associated with more severe cognitive deterioration over a 3–5-year period among Alzheimer's patients (Petersen et al., 1995).

The biochemical story behind εthis gene is a complex one, and involves the microtubules of the neurons and possibly amyloid plaques. Apolipoprotein E (Apo E), which is coded by the APOE gene, is one of the constituents of lipoproteins in the blood that transports cholesterol and other specific lipids throughout the body's cells. Apo E also appears to play a role in the transport of lipids as well as the degeneration and regeneration of neurons and it is thought that it might also be involved in the development of amyloid plaques (Wisniewski, Golabek, Matsubara, Ghiso, & Frangione, 1993).

The APOE gene has three common variants, ε2, ε3, and ε4, which code the main variants of Apo E, which are called "E2," "E3," and "E4." The presence of the ε4 allele codes for the E4 form of Apo E, which is thought to damage the microtubules within the neuron, small tubules that probably play an essential role in transport throughout the cell. Ordinarily, Apo E2 and Apo E3 protect a protein known as "tau," which helps to stabilize the microtubules. If the tau protein is unprotected by Apo E2 and Apo E3, as the theory goes, the microtubules will degenerate, eventually leading to the destruction of the neuron. Although promising the Apo E4 theory requires substantially more testing and will undoubtedly continue to be challenged by proponents of the role of ß-amyloid who see no connection between the two theories. Competition within the area of identifying genetic causes of Alzheimer's is fierce (McLoughlin & Lovestone, 1994), in part because of the huge implications of breakthrough findings, and in part because the solution to the Alzheimer's puzzle will most likely land the winning research team a Nobel Prize. These theories are important advances as they attempt to provide linkages between known patterns of genetic inheritance and events taking place within the biochemical environment of the neuron.

There are other theories that are considerably less well-established, but are interesting to think about as they indicate, in some ways, how researchers are sometimes willing to grasp at very thin straws in hopes of finding a cure for this dreaded disease. One of these tenuous theories proposed that a toxic accumulation of aluminum in the cells of the brain causes Alzheimer's (Schiffman, 1986; Ward, 1986). This controversial theory gained a great deal of media attention in the 1980s. According to this view, aluminum, a trace element in the environment, enters the brain through the nasal passages and damages the cortex, beginning with the olfactory cortex. It was even thought that aluminum pots and pans might be implicated in causing Alzheimer's. Aluminum is thought to be an important toxin because abnormal accumulations of it are often found inside neurons that have neurofibrillary tangles. Further, increased aluminum levels have been found in autopsies of the brains of people who had the disease. Although some researchers continue to investigate this theory (Good, Perl, Bierer, & Schmeidler, 1992), it seems relatively weak compared to the biochemical and genetic approaches. Interestingly, along these lines, is a report of an association between cigarette smoking (nicotine ingestion) and Alzheimer's disease, but not in the direction that one would expect. An epidemiological study identified a possible protective role of nicotine so that smokers were less likely to develop the disease (Lee, 1994). We might wonder, however, whether this finding is spurious, reflecting some other biological difference between those who choose to smoke from those who do not.

"Treatments." Researchers have desperately sought a cure for Alzheimer's, but at present only some minor symptomatic relief is available. A number of

medications have been used on an experimental basis, but none to date have provided anything approaching significant results (Satlin & Cole, 1988). These medications include vasodilators or metabolic enhancers that increase the blood flow to the brain and that affect neurotransmission and the metabolism of neurons. Choline-based substances also may be used to increase the activity of acetylcholine (Wecker, 1990).

Based in part on medical research that began with studies on laboratory animals in the 1970s, various methods of preventing the disease have attained a certain amount of popularity. As researchers began to focus their attention on CAT deficiencies, there was increased interest in lecithin, a natural substance that promotes the manufacturing of CAT in the nervous system. Controlled studies of drugs containing lecithin, however, failed to show any preventative or treatment effects (Becker & Giacobini, 1988). More recently, researchers have been experimenting with a drug called tetrahydroaminoacridine (or tacrine), which decreases the activity of cholinesterase, an enzyme that breaks down acetylcholine in the nervous system. After some initial enthusiasm about the beneficial effects of tacrine on cognitive functioning, a set of negative findings shattered the hope that these drugs could reverse the effects of Alzheimer's disease on memory dysfunction (Chatellier & Lacomblez, 1990). At best, tacrine can delay the progression of symptoms if given in high enough doses (Knapp et al,, 1994; Knopman & Gracon, 1994), but its benefits must be weighed against side effects that include serious liver function damage (Eagger, Richards, & Levy, 1994).

More success has been achieved in using medications to treat other symptoms, such as depression, in the early phases of the disorder (Teri & Gallagher-Thompson, 1991). Neuroleptics (antipsychotics) are used to treat the symptoms of paranoid thinking, hallucinations, and agitation that sometimes accompany Alzheimer's. Benzodiazepines can be given to treat agitation as well as anxiety. Although these medications can be useful, they must be administered with great care (Satlin & Cole, 1988; Teri & Gallagher-Thompson, 1991) particularly in light of the fact that the rate at which drugs are metabolized is slower in elderly persons than in younger adults, possibly leading to more toxic side effects in elderly people with Alzheimer's.

Psychological interactions. Alzheimer's disease is a devastating illness that ultimately destroys the intellect, personality, and social skills of the afflicted individual. As media attention on the search for its causes has grown, some elders may take heart in the fact that so much effort is being invested in bringing the tragedy of Alzheimer's to an end. However, it is just as likely that the impact of the news hype around Alzheimer's serves as a fearful reminder of what *might* happen to oneself or one's life partner, particularly given that the odds of being afflicted with the disease increase with increasing age.

There is ample evidence of the coexistence of depression with Alzheimer's disease in a number of elderly individuals (Merriam, Aronson, Gaston, Wey, & Katz, 1988), and though it is tempting to speculate that depression results from the knowledge that one has the disorder, it is also possible that there is a common underlying mechanism responsible for both sets of symptoms (Vanderploeg, Schinka, & Retzlaff, 1994). Rather than argue for psychological interactions of this nature (though they may very well exist) it seems clearer at this point to make the case for the fear of Alzheimer's as a significant dynamic in the aging individual's identity. As will be seen in Chapter 8, many elderly individuals fear that loss of memory signifies a step over the threshold into Alzheimer's disease. Consequently, they remain hypervigilant for its signs. Identity processes in conjunction with coping strategies, however, may provide an important basis for individual differences in the way that older adults approach and react to this threshold.

Another crucial dynamic in understanding the psychological interactions of Alzheimer's disease pertains to the burden or distress shown by caregivers of persons with the disorder. Research into this area began in earnest in the mid-1980s with the publication of key studies identifying the severe demands placed on Alzheimer's caregivers (Chenoweth & Spencer, 1986; George & Gwyther, 1986; Huckle, 1994; Pearlin, Mullan, Semple, & Skaff, 1990; Zarit, Todd, & Zarit, 1986). Since the identification of the problem, hundreds of publications have documented the devastating impact on spouses and adult children of individuals with Alzheimer's disease. Caregivers are likely to find themselves emotionally drained, exacerbating their own problems with aging (Vitaliano, Russo, Young, Teri, & Maiuro, 1991). The stress of caregiving may translate, for some individuals, into their own physical problems; in a fascinating application of research on the immune system, poorer immune system functioning has been identified in samples of elderly caregivers (Kiecolt-Glaser, Dura, Speicher, Trask, & Glaser, 1991). A strong sense of commitment by the spouse caregiver along with good health and positive marital interactions may help mitigate the burden associated with the role, when caregiving takes place over a prolonged period, strain on the spouse becomes more or less inevitable (Wright, 1994).

Researchers have suggested that caregivers may need to employ a variety of coping strategies to ward off depression (Williamson & Schulz, 1993). Active coping strategies may be particularly well suited for situations in which the caregiver can have some direct effect. Thus, caregivers who are feeling depressed about memory loss in their loved ones may feel better once they have taken practical steps to help the family member remain as independent as possible. In situations that are not subject to change, such as sadness at witnessing the decline of a loved one, acceptance may be a more effective coping strategy.

As demoralizing as the situation may sound, there may actually be some positive aspects to caring for relatives with Alzheimer's (Schulz, Visintainer, & Williamson, 1990; Talkington-Boyer & Snyder, 1994). It may be emotionally rewarding to see the relative respond positively to the caregiver's efforts, or for the caregiver to feel supported by other family members and friends (Kinney & Stephens, 1989). The presence of role rewards from caregiving may actually be related to improved well-being in this otherwise highly distressed group (Stephens, Franks, & Townsend, 1994). Some caregivers may also interpret their burden in spiritual terms, regarding their role as consistent with the teachings of their religion. Prayer, spiritual reading materials, and a message of forgiveness may be important resources that caregivers turn to (Kaye & Robinson, 1994) that are as yet unexplored by researchers.

Along with burgeoning research interest in the experience of caregiving are the development of programs aimed at developing programs to help reduce caregiver burden. Researchers have demonstrated that caregivers can benefit from both brief psychodynamic cognitive-behavioral therapies for depression (Gallagher-Thompson & Steffen, 1994), and interventions targeted at helping caregivers develop more effective coping strategies (McNaughton, Patterson, Smith, & Grant, 1995). There may also be some value in understanding the ways that caregiving represents a threshold experience for older adults that, once crossed, interacts with identity processes as well as coping strategies.

REFERENCES

Alzheimer, A. (1907/1987). About a peculiar disease of the cerebral cortex. *Alzheimer's Disease and Associated Disorders, 1,* 7–8.

Ancoli-Israel, S., & Kripke, D. F. (1991). Prevalent sleep problems in the aged. *Biofeedback and Self Regulation, 16,* 349–359.

Ancoli-Israel, S., Kripke, D. F., Mason, W., & Kaplan, O. J. (1985). Sleep apnea and periodic movements in an aging sample. *Journal of Gerontology, 40,* 419–425.

Ball, M. J. (1977). Neuronal loss, neurofibrillary tangles and granuovacuolar degeneration in the hippocampus with ageing and dementia. *Acta Neuropathologica, 37,* 111–118.

Barnes, R. F., Raskind, M., Gumbrecht, G., & Halter, J. B. (1982). The effects of age on the plasma catecholamine response to mental stress in man. *Journal of Clinical Endocrinology and Metabolism, 54,* 64–69.

Baylor, A. M., & Spirduso, W. W. (1988). Systematic aerobic exercise and components of reaction time in older women. *Journal of Gerontology: Psychological Sciences, 43,* P121–126.

Becker, R. E., & Giacobini, E. (1988). Mechanisms of cholinesterase inhibition in senile dementia of the Alzheimer type: Clinical, pharmacological and therapeutic aspects. *Drug Development Research, 12,* 163–195.

Behrouz, N., Defossez, A., Delacorte, A., & Mazzuca, M. (1991). The immunohisto-chemical evidence of amyloid diffuse deposits as a pathological hallmark in Alzheimer's disease. *Journal of Gerontology: Biological Sciences, 46,* B209–212.

Bissette, G., Smith, W. H., Dole, K. C., Crain, B., Ghanbari, H., Miller, B., & Nemeroff, C. B. (1991). Alterations in Alzheimer's disease-associated protein in Alzheimer's disease frontal and tempral cortex. *Archives of General Psychiatry, 48,* 1009–1012.

Blinkov, S. M., & Glezer, I. I. (1968). *The human brain in figures and tables.* New York: Plenum and Basic Books.

Bliwise, N. G. (1992). Factors related to sleep quality in healthy elderly women. *Psychology and Aging, 7,* 83–88.

Bondareff, W. (1981). The neurobiological basis of age-related changes. In J. L. McGaugh & S. B. Kiesler (Ed.), *Aging: Biology and behavior.* New York: Academic Press.

Brizzee, K. R. (1975). Gross morphometric analyses and quantitative histology of the aging brain. In J. M. Ordy & K. R. Brizzee (Ed.), *Neurobiology of aging.* New York: Plenum.

Brody, H. (1955a). Organization of cerebral cortex. III. A study of aging in the human cerebral cortex. *Journal of Comparative Neurology, 102,* 511–556.

Brody, J. (1955b). Organization of cerebral cortex: III. A study of aging in the human cerebral cortex. *Journal of Comparative Neurology, 102,* 511–556.

Buell, S. J., & Coleman, P. D. (1979). Dendritic growth in the aged human brain and failure of growth in senile dementia. *Science, 206,* 854–856.

Carlsson, A., Adolfsson, R., Aquilonius, S.-M., Gottfries, C., Oreland, L., Svennerholm, L., & Winblad, B. (1980). Biogenic amines in human brain in normal aging, senile dementia, and chronic alcoholism. In M. Goldstein, D. B. Calne, A. Lieberman, & M. O. Thorner (Ed.), *Advances in biochemical psychopharmacology: Vol 23. Ergot compounds and brain function: Neuroendocrine and neuropsychiatric aspects.* New York: Raven Press.

Chatellier, G., & Lacomblez, L. (1990). Tacrine and lecithin in senile dementia of the Alzheimer type: A multicentre trial. *British Journal of Medicine, 300,* 495–499.

Chenoweth, B., & Spencer, B. (1986). Dementia: The experience of family caregivers. *The Gerontologist, 30,* 267–272.

Chui, H. C. (1989). Dementia: A review emphasizing clinicopathologic correlation and brain-behavior relationships. *Archives of Neurology, 46,* 806–814.

Cohen, G. (1988). *The brain in human aging.* New York: Springer.

Coleman, R. M., Miles, L. E., Guilleminault, C. C., Zarcone, V. P., van den Hoed, J., & Dement, W. C. (1981). Sleep-wake disorders in the elderly: A polysomnographic analysis. *Journal of the American Geriatrics Society, 29,* 289–296.

Collins, K. J., Dore, C., Exton-Smith, A. N., Fox, R. H., MacDonald, I. C., & Woodward, P. M. (1977). Accidental hypothermia and impaired temperature homeostasis in the elderly. *British Medical Journal, 1,* 353–356.

Corder, E. H., Saunders, A. M., Strittmatter, W. J., Schmechel, E. D., Gaskell, P. C., Small, G. W., Roses, A. D., Haines, J. L., & Pericak-Vance, M. A. (1993). Gene dose of apolipoprotein E Type 4 allele and the risk of Alzheimer's disease in late-onset families. *Science, 261,* 921–923.

Cotman, C. W., & Peterson, C. (1990). Synaptic plasticity and aging. In A. L. Goldstein (Ed.), *Biomedical advances in aging* (pp. 501–510). New York: Plenum.

Coyle, J. T., Price, D. L., & DeLong, M. R. (1983). Alzheimer's disease: A disorder of cortical cholinergic innervation. *Science, 219,* 1184–1190.

Cragg, B. G. (1975). The density of synapses and neurons in normal, mentally defective, and aging human brains. *Brain, 98,* 81–90.

Davies, I., & Fotheringham, A. P. (1981). Lipofuscin—Does it affect cellular performance? *Experimental Gerontology, 16,* 119–125.

Dekaban, A. S., & Sadowsky, D. (1978). Changes in brain weights during the span of human life: Relation of brain weights to body heights and body weights. *Annals of Neurology, 4,* 345–356.

Dekoninck, W. J., Jacquy, J., Jocquet, P., & Noel, G. (1976). Cerebral blood flow and metabolism in senile dementia. In J. S. Meyer, H. Lechner, & M. Reivich (Ed.), *Cerebral vascular disease.* Stuttgart: Thieme.

Devaney, K. O., & Johnson, H. A. (1980). Neuron loss in the aging visual cortex in man. *Journal of Gerontology, 35,* 836–841.

Diamond, M. C. (1990). An optimistic view of the aging brain. In A. L. Goldstein (Ed.), *Biomedical advances in aging* (pp. 441–449). New York: Plenum.

Drachman, D. A., & Leavitt, J. (1974). Human memory and the cholinergic system: A relationship to aging? *Archives of Neurology, 30,* 113–121.

Drachman, D. A., & Sahakian, B. M. (1980). Memory, aging, and pharmacosystems. In D. G. Stein (Ed.), *The psychobiology of aging: Problems and perspectives* (pp. 347–368). New York: Elsevier.

Drinkwater, B. L., Bedi, J. F., Loucko, A. B., Roche, S., & Horvath, S. M. (1982). Sweating sensitivity in capacity of women in relation to age. *Journal of Applied Physiology, 53,* 671–676.

Duara, R., London, E. D., & Rapoport, S. I. (1985). Changes in structure and energy metabolism of the aging brain. In C. E. Finch & E. L. Schneider (Ed.), *Handbook of the biology of aging* (pp. 595–616). New York: Van Nostrand Reinhold.

Eagger, S. A., Richards, M., & Levy, R. (1994). Long-term effects of tacrine in Alzheimer's disease: An open study. *International Journal of Geriatric Psychiatry, 9,* 643–647.

Ellis, F. P., Exton-Smith, A. N., Foster, K. G., & Weiner, J. S. (1976). Eccrine sweating and mortality during heat waves in very young and very old persons. *Israel Journal of Medical Science, 12,* 815–817.

Esler, M., Skews, H., Leonard, P., Jackman, G., Bobik, A., & Korner, P. (1981). Age-dependence of noradrenaline kinetics in normal subjects. *Clinical Science, 60,* 217–219.

Evans, D. A., Funkenstein, H. H., Albert, M. S., Scherr, P. A., Cook, N. R., Chown, M. J., Gevert, L. E., Hennekens, C. H., & Taylor, J. O. (1989). Prevalence of Alzheimer's disease in a community of population of older persons: Higher than previously reported. *Journal of the American Medical Association, 262,* 2551–2556.

Featherstone, J. A., Veith, R. C., Flatness, D., Murberg, M. M., Villacres, E. C., & Halter, J. B. (1987). Age and alpha-2 adrenergic regulation of plasma norepinephrine kinetics in humans. *Journal of Gerontology, 42,* 271–276.

Feinberg, I. (1974). Changes in sleep cycle patterns with age. *Journal of Psychiatric Research, 10,* 283–306.

Finch, C. E. (1977). Neuroendocrine and autonomic aspects of aging. In C. E. Finch & L. Hayflick (Ed.), *Handbook of the biology of aging.* New York: Van Nostrand Reinhold.

Finch, C. E. (1982). Rodent models for aging processes in the human brain. In S. Corkin, K. L. Davis, J. H. Growdon, E. Usdin, & R. J. Wurtman (Ed.), *Aging: Vol. 19, Alzheimer's disease: A report of progress.* New York: Raven Press.

Flicker, C., Ferris, S. H., & Serby, M. (1992). Hypersensitivity to scopolamine in the elderly. *Psychopharmacology, 107,* 437–441.

Flicker, C., Serby, M., & Ferris, S. H. (1990). Scopolamine effects on memory, language, visuospatial praxis and psychomotor speed. *Psychopharmacology, 100,* 243–250.

Flood, D. G., Buell, S. J., Horwitz, G. J., & Coleman, P. D. (1987). Dendritic extent in human dentate gyrus granule cells in normal aging and senile dementia. *Brain Research, 402,* 205–216.

Flood, D. G., & Coleman, P. D. (1988). Cell type heterogeneity of changes in dendritic extent in the hippocampal region of the human brain in normal aging and in Alzheimer's disease. In T. L. Petit & G. O. Ivy (Ed.), *Neural plasticity: A lifespan approach* (pp. 265–281). New York: Alan R. Liss.

Foster, K. G., Ellis, F. P., Dore, C., Exton-Smith, A. N., & Weiner, J. S. (1976). Sweat responses in the aged. *Age and Ageing, 5,* 91–101.

Fox, R. H., MacGibbon, R., Davies, L., & Woodward, P. M. (1973). Problem of the old and the cold. *British Medical Journal, 1,* 21–24.

Frackowiak, R. S. J., Jones, T., Lenzi, G. L., & Heather, J. D. (1980). Regional cerebral oxygen utilization and blood flow in normal man using oxygen-15 and positron emission tomography. *Acta Neurologica Scandinavica, 62,* 336–344.

Frolkis, V. V., & Bezrukov, V. V. (1979). *Aging of the central nervous system: Vol. II. Interdisciplinary topics in human aging.* New York: Karger.

Gallagher-Thompson, D., & Steffen, A. M. (1994). Comparative effects of cognitive-behavioral and brief psychodynamic psychotherapies for depressed family caregivers. *Journal of Consulting and Clinical Psychology, 62,* 543–549.

George, L. K., & Gwyther, L. P. (1986). Caregiver well-being: A multidimensional examination of family caregivers of demented adults. *The Gerontologist, 26,* 253–259.

Geula, C., & Mesulam, M. (1989). Special properties of cholinesterases in the cerebral cortex of Alzheimer's disease. *Brain Research, 498,* 185–189.

Good, P. F., Perl, D. P., Bierer, L. M., & Schmeidler, J. (1992). Selective accumulation of aluminum and iron in the neurofibrillary tangles of Alzheimer's disease: A laser microprobe (LAMMA) study. *Annals of Neurology, 31,* 286–292.

Greenough, W. T., & Green, E. J. (1981). Experience and the aging brain. In J. L. McGaugh & S. B. Kiesler (Ed.), *Aging: Biology and behavior.* New York: Academic Press.

Hagstadius, S., & Risberg, J. (1989). Regional cerebral blood flow characteristics and variations with age in resting normal subjects. *Brain and Cognition, 10,* 28–43.

Hall, T. C., Miller, A. K. H., & Corsellis, J. A. N. (1975). Variations in the human Purkinje cell population according to age and sex. *Neuropathology and Applied Neurobiology, 1,* 267–292.

Ham, R. J. (1990). Alzheimer's disease and the family: A challenge of the new millenium. In T. Zandi & R. J. Ham (Ed.), *New directions in understanding dementia and Alzheimer's disease* (pp. 3–20). New York: Plenum Press.

Hanley, T. (1974). "Neuronal fallout" in the aging brain: A critical review of the quantitative data. *Age and Ageing, 3,* 133–151.

Hayashi, Y., & Endo, S. (1982). All-night sleep polygraphic recordings of healthy aged persons: REM and slow-wave sleep. *Sleep, 5,* 277–283.

Hebert, L. E., Scherr, P. A., Beckett, L. A., Albert, M. S., Pilgrim, D. M., Chown, M. J., Funkenstein, H. H., & Evans, E. A. (1995). Age-specific incidence of Alzheimer's disease in a community population. *Journal of the American Medical Association, 273,* 1354–1359.

Hellon, R. F., & Lind, A. R. (1956). Activity of the sweat glands with reference to the influence of aging. *Journal of Physiology, 133,* 132–144.

Henderson, G., Tomlinson, B., & Gibson, P. H. (1980). Cell counts in human cerebral cortex in normal adults throughout life using an image analysing computer. *Journal of the Neurological Sciences, 46,* 113–136.

Heun, R., & Maier, W. (1995). Risk of Alzheimer's disease in first-degree relatives. *Archives of General Psychiatry, 52,* 317–318.

Higatsberger, M. R., Budka, H., & Bernheimer, H. (1982). Neurochemical investigations of aged human brain cortex. In S. Hoyer (Ed.), *The aging brain: Physiological and pathophysiological aspects.* New York: Springer-Verlag.

Huckle, P. L. (1994). Families and dementia. *International Journal of Geriatric Psychiatry, 9,* 735–741.

Huttenlocher, P. R. (1979). Synaptic density in human frontal cortex—developmental changes and effects of aging. *Brain Research, 163,* 195–205.

Jagust, W. J., Budinger, T. F., Reed, B. R., & Conina, M. (1987). Single-photon emission computed tomography in the cllinical evaluation of dementia. In G. G. Glenner & R. J. Wurtman (Ed.), *Advancing frontiers in Alzheimer's disease research* (pp. 217–233). Austin: University of Texas Press.

Jarvik, L. F. (1988). Aging of the brain: How can we prevent it? *The Gerontologist, 6,* 739–747.

Joachim, C. L., & Selkoe, D. J. (1989). Amyloid protein in Alzheimer's disease. *Journal of Gerontology: Biological Sciences, 44,* B77–82.

Kales, A., & Kales, J. D. (1984). *Evaluation and treatment of insomnia.* New York: Oxford University Press.

Kaye, J., & Robinson, K. M. (1994). Spirituality among caregivers. *Image: Journal of Nursing Scholarship, 26,* 218–221.

Kendall, M. J., Woods, K. L., Wilkins, M. R., & Worthington, D. J. (1982). Responsiveness to ß(beta)-adrenergic receptor stimulation: The effects of age are cardioselective. *British Journal of Clinical Pharmacology, 14,* 821–826.

Kiecolt-Glaser, J. K., Dura, J. R., Speicher, C. E., Trask, O. J., & Glaser, R. (1991). Spousal caregivers of dementia victims: Longitudinal changes in immunity and health. *Psychosomatic Medicine, 53,* 345–362.

Kinney, J. M., & Stephens, M. A. P. (1989). Hassles and uplifts of giving care to a family member with dementia. *Psychology and Aging, 4,* 402–408.

Knapp, M. J., Knopman, D. S., Soloman, P. R., Pendlebury, W. W., Davis, C. S., & Gracon, J. I. (1994). A 30-week randomized controlled trial of high-dose tacrine in patients with Alzheimer's disease. *Journal of the American Medical Association, 271,* 985–991.

Knopman, D., & Gracon, S. (1994). Observations on the short-term "natural history" of probable Alzheimer's disease in a controlled clinical trial. *Neurology, 44,* 260–265.

Lee, P. N. (1994). Smoking and Alzheimer's disease: A review of the epidemiological evidence. *Neuroepidemiology, 13,* 131–144.

Levy-Lahad, E., Wasco, W., Poorkaj, P., Romano, D. M., Oshima, J., Pettingell, W. H., Yu, C., Jondro, P. D., Schmidt, S. D., Wang, K., Crowley, A. C., Fu, Y.-H., Guenette, S. Y., Galas, D., Nemens, E., Wijsman, E. M., Bird, T. D., Schellenberg, G. D., & Tanzi, R. E. (1995a). Candidate gene for the chromosome 1 familial Alzheimer's disease locus. *Science, 269,* 973–977.

Levy-Lahad, E., Wijsman, E. M., Nemens, E., Anderson, L., Goddard, K. A. B., Weber, J. L., Bird, T. D., & Schellenberg, G. D. (1995b). A familial Alzheimer's disease locus on chromosome 1. *Science, 269,* 970–973.

Li, G., Silverman, J. M., Smith, C. J., Zaccario, M. L., Schmeidler, J., Mohs, R. C., & Davis, K. L. (1995). Age at onset and familial risk in Alzheimer's disease. *American Journal of Psychiatry, 152,* 424–430.

Lindblad, L. E. (1977). Influence of age on sensitivity and effector mechanisms of the carotid baroreflex. *Acta Physiologica Scandinavica, 101,* 43–49.

Lynch, G., & Gerling, S. (1981). Aging and brain plasticity. In J. L. McGaugh & S. B. Kiesler (Ed.), *Aging: Biology and behavior.* New York: Academic Press.

MacInnes, W. D., Paull, D., & Quaife, M. (1989). Longitudinal changes in regional cerebral blood flow in a normal elderly group. *Archives of Clinical Neuropsychology, 4,* 217–226.

Mader, S. L. (1989). Aging and postural hypotension: An update. *Journal of the American Geriatrics Society, 37,* 129–137.

Mankovsky, N. B., Mints, A. Y., & Lisenyuk, V. P. (1982). Age peculiarities of human motor control in aging. *Gerontology, 28,* 314–322.

Mann, D. M. (1991). Is the pattern of nerve cell loss in aging and Alzheimer's disease a real, or only an apparent, selectivity? [comment]. *Neurobiology of Aging, 12,* 340–343.

Mann, D. N. A., & Yates, P. O. (1974). Lipoprotein pigments—their relationship to aging in the human nervous system. I. The lipofuscin content of nerve cells. *Brain, 97,* 481–488.

Martin, E. M., Wilson, R. S., Penn, R. D., Fox, J. H., Clasen, R. A., & Savoy, S. M. (1987). Cortical biopsy results in Alzheimer's disease: Correlation with cognitive deficits. *Neurology, 37,* 1201–1204.

McGeer, E. G., & McGeer, P. L. (1980). Aging and neurotransmitter systems. In M. Goldstein, D. B. Calne, A. Lieberman, & M. O. Thorner (Ed.), *Advances in biochemical psychopharmacology: Vol 23. Ergot compounds and brain function: Neuroendocrine and neuropsychiatric aspects.* New York: Raven Press.

McLoughlin, D. M., & Lovestone, S. (1994). Alzheimer's disease: Recent advances in molecular pathology and genetics. *International Journal of Geriatric Psychiatry, 9,* 431–444.

McNaughton, M. E., Patterson, T. L., Smith, T. L., & Grant, I. (1995). The relationship among stress, depression, locus of control, irrational beliefs, social support, and health in Alzheimer's disease caregivers. *Journal of Nervous and Mental Disease, 183,* 78–85.

Meier-Ruge, W., Hunziker, O., Iwangoff, P., Reichlmeier, K., & Schulz, U. (1980). Effect of age on morphological and biochemical parameters of the human brain. In D. G. Stein (Ed.), *The psychobiology of aging: Problems and perspectives* (pp. 297–318). New York: Elseview.

Merriam, A. E., Aronson, M. K., Gaston, P., Wey, S., & Katz, I. (1988). The psychiatric symptoms of Alzheimer's disease. *Journal of the American Geriatrics Society, 36,* 7–12.

Minaker, K. L., Meneilly, G. S., Young, J. B., Landsberg, L., Stoff, J. S., Robertson, G. L., & Rowe, J. W. (1991). Blood pressure, pulse, and neurohumoral responses to nitroprusside-induced hypotension in normotensive aging men. *Journal of Gerontology: Medical Sciences, 46,* M151–154.

Morin, C. M., & Azrin, N. H. (1988). Behavioral and cognitive treatments of geriatric insomnia. *Journal of Consulting and Clinical Psychology, 56,* 748–753.

Morin, C. M., & Gramling, S. E. (1989). Sleep patterns and aging: Comparison of older adults with and without insomnia complaints. *Psychology and Aging, 4,* 290–294.

Mouritzen Dam, A. (1979). The density of neurons in the human hippocampus. *Neuropathology and Applied Neurobiology, 5,* 249–264.

Nordberg, A., Adolfsson, R., Marcusson, J., & Winblad, B. (1982). Cholinergic receptors in the hippocampus in normal aging and dementia of the Alzheimer type. In E. Giacobini, G. Filogano, & A. Vernadakis (Ed.), *Aging: Vol. 20. The aging brain: Cellular and molecular mechanisms of aging in the nervous system.* New York: Raven Press.

Ordy, J. M. (1975). The nervous system, behavior, and aging: An interdisciplinary approach. In J. M. Ordy & K. R. Brizzee (Ed.), *Neurobiology of aging.* New York: Plenum.

Ordy, J. M. (1981). Neurochemical aspects of aging in humans. In H. M. v. Praag, M. H. Lader, O. J. Rafaelson, & E. J. Sachar (Ed.), *Handbook of biological psychiatry.* New York: Marcel Dekker.

Palmer, G. J., Ziegler, M. G., & Lake, C. R. (1978). Response of norepinephrine and blood pressure to stress increases with age. *Journal of Gerontology, 33,* 482–487.

Pearlin, L. I., Mullan, J. T., Semple, S. J., & Skaff, M. M. (1990). Caregiving and the stress process: An overview of concepts and their measures. *The Gerontologist, 30,* 583–591.

Perry, E. K., Perry, R. H., Gibson, P. H., Blessed, G., & Tomlinson, B. E. (1977). A cholinergic connection between normal aging and senile dementia in the human hippocampus. *Neuroscience Letters, 6,* 85–89.

Petersen, R. C., Smith, G. E., Ivnik, R. J., Tangalos, E. G., Schaid, D. J., Thibodeau, S. N., Kokmen, E., Waring, S. C., & Kurland, L. T. (1995). Apolipoprotein E status as a predictor of the development of Alzheimer's disease in memory-impaired individuals. *Journal of the American Medical Association, 273,* 1274–1278.

Pfeifer, M. A., Weinberg, C. R., Cook, D., Best, J. D., Reenan, A., & Halter, J. B. (1983). Differential changes of autonomic nervous system function with age in man. *American Journal of Medicine, 75,* 249–258.

Pirttila, T., Mehta, P. D., Frey, H., & Wisniewski, H. M. (1994). a-sub-1-Antichymotrypsin and IL-1b are not increased in CSF or serum in Alzheimer's disease. *Neurobiology of Aging, 15,* 313–317.

Prinz, P. N., Halter, J., Benedetti, C., & Raskind, M. (1979). Circadian variation of plasma catecholamines in young and old men: Relation to rapid eye movement and slow wave sleep. *Journal of Clinical Endocrinology and Metabolism, 49,* 300–304.

Prinz, P. N., Vitiello, M. V., Smallwood, R. G., Schoene, R. B., & Halter, J. B. (1984). Plasma norepinephrine in normal young and aged men: Relationship with sleep. *Journal of Gerontology, 39,* 561–567.

Rabbitt, P. M. A. (1980). A fresh look at changes in reaction times in old age. In D. G. Stein (Ed.), *The psychobiology of aging: Problems and perspectives* (pp. 425–442). New York: Elsevier.

Ravens, J. R., & Calvo, W. (1966). Neurological changes in the senile brain. In F. Luthy & A. Bischoff (Ed.), *Proceedings of the Fifth International Congress of Neuropathology.* New York: Excerpta Medica Foundation, International Congress Series No. 100.

Rice, D. M., Buchsbaum, M. S., Starr, A., Auslander, L., Hagman, J., & Evans, W. J. (1990). Abnormal EEG slow activity in left temporal areas in senile dementia of the Alzheimer's type. *Journal of Gerontology: Medical Sciences, 45,* M145–151.

Rockwell, E., Jackso, E., Vilke, G., & Jeste, D. (1994). A study of delusions in a large cohort of Alzheimer's disease patients. *American Journal of Geriatric Psychiatry, 2,* 157–164.

Rowe, J. W., & Troen, B. R. (1980). Sympathetic nervous system and aging in man. *Endocrinological Review, 1,* 167–179.

Saar, N., & Gordon, R. D. (1979). Variability of plasma catecholamine levels: Age, duration of posture and time of day. *British Journal of Clinical Pharmacology, 8,* 353–358.

Satlin, A., & Cole, J. O. (1988). Psychopharmacologic interventions. In L. F. Jarvik & C. H. Winograd (Ed.), *Treatments for the Alzheimer patient.* New York: Springer.

Schapiro, M. B., & Rapoport, S. I. (1988). Alzheimer's disease in promorbidly normal and down's syndrome individuals: Selective involvement of hippocampus and neocortical associative brain regions. *Brain Dysfunction, 1,* 2–11.

Scheibel, A. B. (1982). Age-related changes in the human forebrain. *Neurosciences Research Progress Bulletin, 20,* 577–583.

Scheibel, M. E., Lindsay, R. D., Tomiyasu, U., & Scheibel, A. B. (1975). Progressive dendritic changes in aging human cortex. *Experimental Neurology, 47,* 392–403.

Scheibel, M. E., Lindsay, R. D., Tomiyasu, U., & Scheibel, A. B. (1976). Progressive dendritic changes in the aging human limbic system. *Experimental Neurology, 53,* 420–430.

Scheibel, M. E., Tomiyasu, U., & Scheibel, A. B. (1977). The aging human Betz cell. *Experimental Neurology, 56,* 598–609.

Schiffman, S. S. (1986). The nose as a port of entry for aluminosilicates and other pollutants: Possible role in Alzheimers disease (Special Issue: Controversial topics on Alzheimer's disease: Intersecting crossroads). *Neurobiology of Aging, 7,* 576–578.

Schulz, R., Visintainer, P., & Williamson, G. M. (1990). Psychiatric and physical morbidity effects of caregiving. *Journal of Gerontology: Psychological Sciences, 45,* P181–191.

Schulz, U., & Hunziker, O. (1980). Comparative studies of neuronal perikaryon size and shape in the aging cerebral cortex. *Journal of Gerontology, 35,* 483–491.

Shefer, V. F. (1973). Absolute number of neurons and thickness of the cerebral cortex during aging, senile and vascular dementia, and Pick's and Alzheimer's diseases. *Neuroscience and Behavioral Psychology, 6,* 319–324.

Sherrington, R., Rogaev, E. I., Liang, Y., Rogaeva, E. A., Levesque, G., Ikeda, M., Chi, H., Lin, C., Holman, K., Tsuda, T., Mar, L., Foncin, J.-F., Bruni, A. C., Montesi, M. P., Sorbi, S., Rainero, I., Pinessl, L., Nee, L., Chumakov, I., Pollen, D., Brookes, A., Sanseau, P., Polinsky, R. J., Wasco, W., Da Silva, H. A. R., Haines, J. L., Pericak-Vance, M. A., Tanzi, R. E., Roses, A. D., Fraser, P. E., Rommens, J. M., & St George-Hyslop, P. H. (1995). Cloning of a gene-bearing missense mutations in early-onset familial Alzheimer's disease. *Nature, 375,* 754–760.

Silverman, J. M., Li, G., Zaccario, M. L., Smith, C. J., Schmeidler, J., Mohs, R. C., & Davis, K. L. (1994). Patterns of risk in first-degree relatives of patients with Alzheimer's disease. *Archives of General Psychiatry, 51,* 577–586.

Sowers, J. R., Rubenstein, L. Z., & Stern, N. (1983). Plasma norepinephrine responses to posture and isometric exercise increase with age in the absence of obesity. *Journal of Gerontology, 38,* 315–317.

Spirduso, W. W. (1980). Physical fitness, aging, and psychomotor speed. *Journal of Gerontology, 35,* 850–865.

Stephens, M. A. P., Franks, M. M., & Townsend, A. L. (1994). Stress and rewards in women's multiple roles: The case of women in the middle. *Psychology and Aging, 9,* 45–52.

Stern, R. G., Mohs, R. C., Davidson, M., Schmeidler, J., Silverman, J., Kramer-Ginsberg, E., Searcey, T., Bierer, L., & Davis, K. L. (1994). A longitudinal study of Alzheimer's disease: Measurement, rate, and predictors of cognitive deterioration. *American Journal of Psychiatry, 1,* 390–396.

Strittmatter, W. J., Saunders, A. M., Schmechel, D., Pericak-Vance, M., Enghild, J., Salvesen, G. S., & Roses, A. D. (1993). Apolipoprotein E: High avidity binding to beta-amyloid and increased frequency of type 4 allele in late-onset familial Alzheimer disease. *Proceedings of the National Academicy of Science USA, 90,* 1977–1981.

Takeda, S., & Matsuzawa, T. (1985). Age-related brain atrophy: A study with computed tomography. *Journal of Gerontology, 40,* 159–163.

Talkington-Boyer, S., & Snyder, D. K. (1994). Assessing impact on family caregivers to Alzheimer's disease patients. *American Journal of Family Therapy, 22,* 57–66.

Teri, L., & Gallagher-Thompson, D. (1991). Cognitive-behavioral interventions of treatment of depression in Alzheimer's patients. *The Gerontologist, 31,* 413–416.

Teri, L., Hughes, J. P., & Larson, E. B. (1990). Cognitive deterioration in Alzheimer's disease: Behavioral and health factors. *Journal of Gerontology: Psychological Sciences, 45,* P58–P63.

Tomlinson, B. E., & Henderson, G. E. (1976). Some quantitative cerebral findings in normal and demented old people. In R. D. Terry & S. Gershon (Ed.), *Aging: Vol. 3. Neurobiology of Aging*. New York: Raven Press.

Tsai, M.-S., Tangalos, E. G., Petersen, R. C., Smith, G. E., Schaid, D. J., Kokmen, E., Ivnik, R. J., & Thibodeau, S. N. (1994). Apolipoprotein E: Risk factor for Alzheimer Disease. *American Journal of Human Genetics, 54*, 643–649.

Turkel, H., & Nusbaum, I. (1986). Down syndrome and Alzheimer's disease contrasted. *Journal of Orthomelecular Medicine, 1*, 219–229.

Vanderploeg, R. D., Schinka, J. A., & Retzlaff, P. (1994). Relationships between measures of auditory verbal learning and executive functioning. *Journal of Clinical and Experimental Neuropsychology, 16*, 243–25.

Veith, R. C., Featherstone, J. A., Linares, O. A., & Halter, J. B. (1986). Age differences in plasma norepinephrine levels in humans. *Journal of Gerontology, 41*, 319–324.

Vestal, R. E., Wood, A. J. J., & Shand, D. G. (1979). Reduced ß(beta)-adrenoreceptor sensitivity in the elderly. *Clinical Pharmacology and therapeutics, 26*, 181–186.

Vijayashankar, N., & Brody, H. (1979). A quantitative study of the pigmented neurons in the nuclei locus coeruleus and subcoeruleus in men as related to aging. *Journal of Neuropathology and Experimental Neurology, 38*, 490–497.

Vitaliano, P. P., Russo, J., Young, H. M., Teri, L., & Maiuro, R. D. (1991). Predictors of burden in spouse caregivers of individuals with Alzheimer's disease. *Psychology and Aging, 6*, 392–402.

Wagner, J. A., & Horvath, S. M. (1985). Influences of age and gender on human thermoregulatory responses to cold exposures. *Journal of Applied Physiology, 58*, 180–186.

Wagner, J. A., Horvath, S. M., Kitagawa, K., & Bolduan, N. W. (1987). Blood and urinary responses to cold exposures in young and older men and women. *Journal of Gerontology, 42*, 173–179.

Wagner, J. A., Robinson, S., Tzankoff, S. P., & Marino, R. P. (1972). Heat tolerance and acclimation to work in the heat in relation to age. *Journal of Applied Physiology, 37*, 562–565.

Ward, C. D. (1986). Commentary on "Alzheimer's disease may begin in the nose and may be caused by aluminosilicates" (Special Issue: Controversial topics on Alzheimer's disease: Intersecting crossroads). *Neurobiology of Aging, 7*, 574–575.

Wecker, L. (1990). Dietary choline: A limiting factor for the synthesis of acetylcholine by the brain. In R. J. Wurtman, S. Corkin, J. H. Growdon, & Ritter-Walker (Ed.), *Advances in neurology: Vol. 51 Alzheimer's disease* (pp. 139–145). New York: Raven.

Wilkie, F. L., Halter, J. B., Prinz, P. N., Benedetti, C., Eisdorfer, C., Atwood, B., & Yamasaki, D. (1985). Age-related changes in venous catecholamines basally and during epinephrine infusion in man. *Journal of Gerontology, 40*, 141–146.

Williams, R. L., Karacan, I., & Hursch, C. (1974). *Electroencephalography (EEG) of human sleep: Clinical applications*. New York: Wiley.

Williamson, G. M., & Schulz, R. (1993). Coping with specific stressors in Alzheimer's disease caregiving. *Gerontologist, 33,* 747–755.

Willis, S. L., & Schaie, K. W. (1994). Cognitive training in the normal elderly. In F. Boller (Ed.), *Cerebral plasticity in human aging*. New York: Springer-Verlag.

Wisniewski, T., Golabek, A., Matsubara, E., Ghiso, J., & Frangione, B. (1993). Apolipoprotein E: Binding to soluble Alzheimer's beta amyloid. *Biochemical and Biophysics Research Communication, 192,* 359–365.

Wright, L. K. (1994). Alzheimer's disease afflicted spouses who remain at home: Can human dialectics explain the findings? *Social Science and Medicine, 38,* 1037–1046.

Yamaura, H., Ito, M., Kubota, K., & Matsuzawa, T. (1980). Brain atrophy during aging: A quantitative study with computed tomography. *Journal of Gerontology, 35,* 492–498.

Yankner, B. A., Duffy, L. K., & Kirschner, D. A. (1990). Neurotrophic and neurotoxic effects of Amyloid beta protein: Reversal by tachykinin neuropeptides. *Science, 250,* 279–282.

Young, J. B., Rowe, J. W., Pallotta, J. A., Sparrow, D., & Landsberg, L. (1980). Enhanced plasma norepinephrine response to upright posture and oral glucose administration in elderly human subjects. *Metabolism, 29,* 532–539.

Zarit, S. H., Todd, P. A., & Zarit, J. M. (1986). Subjective burden of husbands and wives as caregivers: A longitudinal study. *The Gerontologist, 26,* 260–266.

7

Sensation and Perception

Throughout the years of adulthood and into old age, there are a multitude of changes in the ways that people experience their environments. These changes involve the processes of sensation and perception. In discussing these changes, the term "sensation" is used to refer to the transmission of the sights, sounds, smells, and feel of the internal (bodily) and external (physical and social) environments into terms that the central nervous system can use to decipher and interpret these signals. The term "perception," by contrast, refers to the interpretation process that takes in the brain as it integrates these signals with the individual's past experience and information coming in from the various senses. Both sensation and perception appear to be affected in significant ways by the aging process in the peripheral (sensory) and central (perceptual) components of the nervous system. In general, however, there is more information available on the aging of the structures responsible for sensation than on the aging of higher levels brain centers involved in perception. Furthermore, much of the available data on "perception" falls into the domain of attentional and control processes to be examined in more detail in Chapter 8.

There are profound effects on adaptation of the many age-related changes in the interpretation of sense information. Adults use sensory and perceptual processes in all of their daily activities, ranging from mundane routine affairs to challenging problem situations, and even to matters of life and death. Deleterious age-related changes in any of these systems can detract from the individual's ability to enjoy a variety of sensory experiences, move about in the environment, and participate comfortably in social interactions. Because of their centrality in everyday life, threshold effects for sensory and perceptual changes can be expected to be very significant for many adults.

BACKGROUND CONCEPTS

The Sensory Structures in Adulthood

Knowledge about the internal environment of the body and about the outside physical and social environment is communicated into neural signals via the process of sensation. The neural signals that register sense information are ultimately interpreted by the central nervous system into usable information about sight, sound, smell, taste, touch, temperature, and pain. This broad array of sensory information enables the individual to move about in the world and interact with other people, and it also contributes heavily to the sensual enjoyment of life. Without sensations of color, sound, taste, smell, and touch, the individual would have a vastly restricted range of enjoyable esthetic experiences. Sensory information also warns the individual about threats to bodily harm through the cues provided by vision, hearing, and touch or pressure on the skin's surface. Information about the outside temperature is essential to taking appropriate behavioral steps for seeking environments that are neither dangerously cold nor hot. Pain, although unpleasant, has a critical adaptive function in that it arouses the individual to seek ways of stopping or preventing harm to the body by agents that impinge on or can destroy the body's tissues.

The physical structures that initiate the sensory process are the sensory receptors, each of which is specially attuned to particular kinds of physical forces. The neurons that comprise the sensory receptors share the properties of being able to transduce physical energy into electrochemical signals that can travel through neural pathways, eventually going to the central nervous system. Each specialized receptor cell has a unique way of accomplishing its function, based on the nature of the type of stimulation to which it responds. For example, the light that triggers impulses in the cells of the eye's retina would be ineffective in stimulating responses in the hair cells of the cochlea within the ear.

Psychological Issues in Measuring Sensory Functioning in Adults

Documenting the effects of aging on the sensitivity of the sensory systems presents a unique challenge compared to studies of the other bodily organ systems.

Measures of efficiency of these structures depend entirely on the individual's self-report of sensory phenomena. In order to know how well a person can see, hear, feel pain, or smell, for instance, it is necessary to elicit a verbal or gestural response when a stimulus of known quantity is presented. The experimenter cannot place electrodes in selected receptor cells or neural pathways. Even if this process could be feasibly accomplished in living humans, it would still not provide information pertinent to the subjective quality of the individual's sensory experiences.

The functional efficiency of the sensory systems is indexed by thresholds, the ability to detect low levels of stimulation. The method that is most frequently used in cross-sectional studies of aging involves the determination of threshold values as these vary by age group. The absolute threshold is the least amount of stimulation that the individual can detect on half of the occasions that it is presented. Another commonly used index of sensitivity is discrimination, also called the difference threshold. Most studies on aging involve one or both of these threshold determinations. Using these methods, reduced sensitivity of the receptors to aging is indexed by higher threshold values (i.e., higher levels of intensity are needed to detect the presence of the stimulus or difference between two stimuli).

The dependence of experimental procedures on the self-report of experimental subjects is a problem that applies to the study of undergraduates, who are typically the subjects in most of the published sensory research in the nonaging literature. When studying older adults, an added difficulty is encountered due mainly to the fact that they represent a more varied group than are the average 18- to 22-year-old college students in terms of their past experiences, expectations, and attitudes toward testing. Adults are likely to have a wide range of familiarity with different sensory systems based on their occupational involvements. The proofreader's vision is likely to be very sharp in contrast to the piano tuner, who has a finely honed ear. Further complicating the situation is the fact that adults have a wide range of attitudes toward the experimental situation in which they are being tested. These attitudes may vary as a function of their sophistication with testing procedures independently of their age alone. People who have worn glasses all their lives would be more relaxed when having their vision tested than people who have managed to stay away from the optometrist's office. The instruments and questions would also be more familiar to people who know the routine of having their eyes examined.

Another source of variation among older adults in sensory performance is cautiousness. Individuals vary in the their willingness to report sensory experiences, and aged persons in particular may fear that they will make a mistake and appear to the examiner to be "senile." Therefore, even though a stimulus is accurately perceived, the older individual may not report its presence until absolutely sure that something is present. Greater cautiousness on the part of some elderly observers may create an artifact in test results causing apparent thresholds to be higher than they would be on the basis of sensory capacity alone.

A final psychological consideration pertains to the application of knowledge about aging of the sensory structures to everyday life. The psychological literature in general is most complete in the area of vision, somewhat less so in hearing, and far less in the area of touch, thermal sensitivity, pain, balance, taste, and smell. Information about age effects in later adulthood is roughly parallel to this order, although questions about possible age reductions in sensory functioning in each of the senses holds tremendous potential value. Part of this value lies in the interest of those who provide health care and social services to the aged population. The aging of sensory functioning has a large bearing on the quality of life of the elderly recipients of these services. There are also a number of commercial applications of knowledge regarding the aging sensory systems. In the area of vision, advertisers and consumer product manufacturers are interested in knowing the optimal size of print for advertisements, product labels, and product information, for example. Auditory information is of importance to television and radio advertisers who gear their marketing to an older audience. Producers of food, hygiene products, and medications also have an interest in determining the flavors and scents that are most appealing to older consumers.

Apart from these practical applications there are also questions of theoretical significance that are better addressed when information about many sensory areas is available. A classical issue in the aging literature on sensation concerns the locus of significant age effects. The main controversy in this field is whether the effects of aging are limited to the peripheral nervous system, which includes the structures containing the sensory receptors, the receptor cells themselves, the pathways leading directly to the spinal cord or brainstem, and in some cases, the primary sensory cortex (e.g., vision and somesthesis). Is the main effect of aging on the registration of sensory information to reduce the efficiency of these structures? Or, are these effects minimal compared to the effects of aging on the central processing of information that takes place in the higher levels of the cortex? Such processes include the interpretation of sensory data, its integration with data from other sources, and the preparation of a response. Here again, there are practical applications of knowledge on this issue. Presumably, peripherally based age losses, particularly those involving the sense organs themselves, would be easier to correct than losses that are based on higher order cortical processes. Prostheses such as hearing aids and eyeglasses can be provided for peripheral losses much more readily than corrective methods for centrally based losses. To correct for centrally based losses requires far more elaborate assessment and training procedures that are beyond the scope of most practitioners who work with the elderly.

A second theoretical concern is the relationship between the aging of the sensory systems and cognitive abilities. The quality of input brought in by the senses can influence the nature of the judgments that older people use as the basis for decision making. If one sees or hears a "V" instead of a "U" on a sign or label, for example, a wrong turn may be taken or the wrong name may be remembered. Furthermore, one might also argue that deprivation of sensory input as a system closes down or becomes unstable can lead to deterioration of cognitive skills that depend on new information from the environment. For these reasons, it is not surprising to learn that researchers investigating intelligence in old age have found that the qualities of vision, hearing, and somesthesis contribute to the maintenance of cognitive abilities (Lindenberger & Baltes, 1994). Although these researchers interpret the findings to mean that the quality of vision and hearing in particular are good indicators of the quality of the brain as a whole, it is just as likely that the findings demonstrate the crucial role of sensory functioning to the overall capacity of the individual to function effectively in the world.

The Nature of Perception

The process of perception involves integrating the sensory stimulation within the external and internal environment, and coordinating the information from multiple senses. Sensation, the translation of neural stimulation into information that can be of practical use to the individual, appears to be a locus of a variety of major age effects in adulthood. Age changes in sensation reduce the quality and quantity of information that the older individual has regarding the nature of the physical and social environment. Above and beyond these losses that originate at the sensory level are reductions in processing within the higher regions of the central nervous system, further compromising the individual's adaptation to the external environment. Of particular significance are the decisions that people make about the course of future actions. When these are based on less than adequate information, or information that is improperly interpreted, the individual will make erroneous decisions. Fortunately, compensating for the losses in sensory and perceptual abilities, are the years of experience that older adults have in making the types of routine decisions that dominate the course of everyday life. The ability to rely on past decisions when making current judgments allows the older individual to reduce the time and effort needed to process incoming information. In some cases, this past experience may eliminate age differences or even turn them in favor of the older experienced individual compared to the young novice.

Related to this point is the fact that many older adults spontaneously learn to compensate for losses in one sensory area by using intact processes in another. The case of balance provides a good illustration of this process. Visual cues can often serve as important compensatory measures when the sense receptors involved in judgments of joint position or movement are functioning less than optimally. Similarly, compensation for poor vision can be made by the use of hearing or touch, and people with hearing deficits may use visual cues to help them interpret what other people are saying to them. These adaptational processes are particularly essential for preserving the quality of life for adults in their 70s and beyond, but it is quite likely that they develop over a much longer period of time, beginning even in the 40s. Such gradual adaptation allows the individual to develop a repertoire of compensatory skills. Indeed, these skills may become so ingrained that the older individual hardly notices their existence. Consistency of environments can facilitate the process of compensation. It is easier to walk down the dark hallway of one's own home than it is to walk through a dimly lit hotel room, for example. It might be expected that for older people in particular, maximum perceptual performance occurs when the environment contains enough familiar cues so that the individual can take maximum advantage of well-tested and familiar compensatory strategies.

VISION

Awareness of the appearance of people and objects in one's surroundings is made possible by the visual sensory system. Within the eye, light energy is transformed into neural impulses that travel through the sensory pathways of the visual system to the central nervous system. When these impulses reach the cerebral cortex, they are further processed and refined into integrated perceptual judgments.

Age Effects on the Structure of the Eye

The structures of the eye transmit and focus the light reflected from stimuli in the environment onto the retina. Many of the effects of aging on these optical structures as well as the retina itself can explain, at least in part, the consistent pattern of age differences observed in studies of basic visual functions.

Cornea and sclera. Three concentric layers form the outside surface of the eyeball: the cornea and sclera, the uveal tract, and the retina. The outer layer protects the other layers and the soft interior of the eyeball. This coating is the cornea in the front part of the eye, and it is transparent to allow light to enter. The "white" part of the eye is the sclera. Alterations in the visible portions of the cornea and sclera lead to changes in the outward appearance of the eye in old age. These changes include loss of the cornea's luster, yellowing of the sclera, and development of translucent spots throughout the sclera so that some of the underlying blue and brown pigment shows through (Edelhauser, VanHorn, & Records, 1979; Mancil & Owsley, 1988; Scheie & Albert, 1977; Weale, 1963).

Other changes in the cornea have more significance due to their effects on vision. The cornea becomes increasingly translucent with age, leading to changes in the refractive power of the eye. In addition, light rays are more likely to become scattered as they pass through the cornea, which has a blurring effect on vision. The curvature of the cornea also changes, becoming flatter on the vertical than the horizontal plane, resulting in a form of astigmatism that is the opposite of that observed in younger adults.

Lens. One of the most significant structures in the eye to undergo changes with age is the lens, which serves as the main focusing mechanism for vision. Age-related changes in the lens throughout adulthood decrease its capacity to accommodate to necessary changes in focus as objects move closer to or further away from the individual.

The lens focuses light rays on the back of the retina by changing its shape in response to contraction and relaxation of the surrounding ciliary body. The lens is composed of transparent connective fibers arranged in concentric layers, like those of an onion. Lens fibers are continuously being formed around the outer rim, and as they are replaced, move toward the center of the lens. In later adulthood, the rate of new lens fiber growth slows, but the accumulation of old lens fibers continues to add to the increased density of the lens (Paterson, 1979). As the inner portion of the lens becomes denser, it grows increasingly more resistant to pressure from the ciliary body (Cotlier, 1981). In addition to becoming denser, the lens fibers become harder and less elastic (Fisher, 1969; Paterson, 1979).

The loss of accommodative power of the lens due to these changes is referred to as "presbyopia," and it is a condition that typically requires correction between the ages of 40 to 50. By the age of 60, the lens is completely incapable of accommodating to focus on objects at close distance (Moses, 1981). The lens also becomes yellowed due to an accumulation of yellow pigment, and as a result the older adult is less able to discriminate colors in the green-blue-violet end of the spectrum (Mancil & Owsley, 1988; Weale, 1963). Finally, opacities in the lens called cataracts may develop due to a disease process more likely to occur in later adulthood. Cataracts interfere further with vision loss by diffusing light as it passes through the lens, reducing the clarity of the image that reaches the retina.

Uveal tract. The middle layer of the eye, known as the uveal tract, serves both nutritive and optical functions. It contains the choroid, iris, and ciliary structures. The choroid, which is brown in color, contains blood vessels that carry nutrients and products of cellular metabolism to and from various parts of the eye. Beginning as early as the 30s, changes in the adult years in the choroid lead to unevenness in its surface. Most importantly, the inner membrane of the choroid adjacent to the retina becomes thicker, less elastic, and more easily torn (Weale, 1963). The quality of the visual image on the retina may also be reduced by the accumulation of thickened spots on the choroid, changes that can also interfere with the circulation of blood to the optical structures (Kuwabara, 1977; Scheie & Albert, 1977). The iris, the pigmented portion of the eye, controls the amount of light that reaches the retina. Atrophy of tissue in this structure contributes further to age changes in the cornea and sclera to altering the appearance of the eye. More significant in terms of the functions served by the iris is atrophy of the iris dilator, a process that continues from adolescence through the age of 60 years (Carter, 1982b; Loewenfeld, 1979). As a consequence of this atrophy, the size of the pupil is reduced, a condition known as senile miosis.

The final set of changes in the uveal tract involve the ciliary body—a mass of muscles, blood vessels, and connective tissue. It is this structure that indirectly controls the main focusing device of the eye, the lens. Age effects on the ciliary muscle reduce its effectiveness in adjusting the shape of the lens to adjust to changes in positioning of visual stimuli. Eventually, changes in the lens itself make it unresponsive to the mechanical forces placed upon it by the ciliary muscle which then atrophies from disuse (Weale, 1963). The ciliary body also produces aqueous, the nutritive and cleansing fluid distributed to the lens and cornea. This function also decreases into the later years of adulthood (Marmor, 1977).

The retina. The processing of visual stimuli begins in the retina, where specialized receptor cells, the rods and cones, trigger impulses when stimulated by light that are passed through the visual system. There is some evidence that the numbers of visual receptors shows significant age effects across adulthood, with decreases reported in the number of rods and cones, as well as the cells that organize information from the rods and cones at the retinal level, the bipolar and ganglion cells (Kuwabara, 1977; Ordy, Brizzee, & Johnson, 1982; Weale, 1982). A contrasting view is that there is no significant loss of photoreceptors with age, since the tips of the rods and cones constantly replace themselves in a process not deleteriously affected by aging (Young, 1976). It is also argued that there are so many receptor cells in the retina (over 130 million) that many can be lost without seriously affecting vision (Marmor, 1982). More serious, perhaps, is the accumulation of waste material shed from the rods and cones when they replace themselves in the outermost layer of the retina (the pigment epithelium) (Marmor, 1980).

Vitreous. The transparent gelatinous mass making up the inner part of the eye is the vitreous. Contained within the vitreous is the aqueous, a clear fluid that serves to nourish and carry away waste products to and from the parts of the eye that are not fed by blood. Beginning at about the age of 40 years, the vitreous begins to liquify, causing parts of the vitreous to shrink away from the surface of the retina and detach from it. As a result, visual disturbances begin to occur, such as the appearance of "floaters" and light flashes. In addition, light rays become scattered more diffusely before reaching the retina, making it more difficult for the older person to detect dim light (Balazs & Denlinger, 1982; Scheie & Albert, 1977; Weale, 1963).

Age Effects on Basic Visual Functions

The changes in the optical properties of the eye and the neural components of the visual system just described are fairly well established and may be understood as setting the stage for a variety of changes in critical visual functions. These include various "basic" functions that involve relatively direct applications of processing within the eye and the peripheral levels of the nervous system (including the primary visual cortex and structures within the subcortex). Many of these functional changes reflect fairly directly the changes already described, particularly senile meiosis and the thickening and yellowing of the lens. Some effects of age on visual functioning can be explained by more than one cause. Nonperceptual factors may also contribute to aging of visual functions. Further complicating the understanding of aging and visual functioning is the presence of individuals with uncorrected eye problems in a cross-sectional study. Although a distinction is often made between normal aging and visual changes due to disease, individuals with uncorrected visual disorders may still be present in the samples of studies comparing adults of different ages.

Visual acuity. The ability to detect details when objects are at varying distances is called visual acuity. Traditionally, the most common way to test visual acuity is with the Snellen chart, a method familiar to anyone who has been to an optometrist. Each row of the Snellen chart has letters that would subtend an angle of 5° if seen from the specified distance shown on the chart. Visual acuity as measured by this procedure is expressed in terms of the ratio of distance of the person from the chart divided by the smallest row of letters that can be read with ease. Acuity of 20/20 is considered normal (ideal) vision, meaning that the individual can see letters at the distance of 20 feet that subtend the 5° visual angle.

As measured by the Snellen chart, it is well-established that visual acuity shows a consistent cross-sectional pattern across the years of adulthood. There is an increase in acuity through about the age of 30, and this level is maintained until the decade of the 40s. After the 50s, there is a progressive decline until by the age of 85, there is an 80% loss compared to the level achieved in the 40s (Pitts, 1982; Weale, 1975). The loss of acuity is particularly severe when the levels of illumination are low, such as when the individual is driving on a dark road at night, and when viewing objects that are in motion (Panek, Barrett, Sterns, & Alexander, 1977; Richards, 1977).

Contrast sensitivity. Another measure of visual function that more closely approximates visual judgments made in the real world tests the individual's contrast sensitivity, or the amount of contrast needed for the individual to see stimuli of a fixed size. The contrast sensitivity function is based on the principle that as the lines of a black and white striped pattern are made narrower and narrower, it requires greater contrast between the stripes for the pattern to be reported as present by the observer. For example, a pin-striped oxford shirt has higher contrast sensitivity than the shirt of a professional football referee's uniform. In measuring visual acuity by the method of contrast sensitivity, the degree of contrast the observer needs to be able to discern the stripes is recorded while, at the same time, the width of the stripes is reduced.

Although the pattern of age-related results is not entirely consistent from study to study, it appears that older adults show a loss of contrast sensitivity, meaning that they are less able to discern contrast patterns involving medium to thin areas of dark and light (Elliott, Whitaker, & MacVeigh, 1990; Sekuler & Owsley, 1982).

Sensitivity to levels of illumination. People must be able to adapt their vision to constant changes in lighting. The processes of light and dark adaptation are based on the underlying fact that light reaching the retina bleaches pigment in the rods and cones so that they become temporarily unresponsive to further light stimulation. Changes in the structures of the eye rather than in the visual receptors themselves seem to be primarily responsible for age effects on adaptation to changing light conditions.

Older individuals appear to be particularly impaired when they must use dark adaptation, moving from a brighly lit situation, such as a sunny outdoor afternoon, to a dim environment, such as a movie theater. This impairment is due to the increased amount of time it takes for the rods to restore pigment bleached out by the light. However, even prolonged exposure to dim lighting does not result in completely adequate dark adaptation for the older adult. The reduced transmission of light through the lens and senile miosis can account for difficulties that the individual has in seeing in dimly lit situations (Pitts, 1982).

Adaptation to light involves achieving a balance between the production and degeneration of pigment under high levels of illumination. A major difficulty faced by older adults is adapting to lighting conditions in which there is a sudden burst of light, as when a flashbulb goes off in one's face or one is approaching the oncoming headlights of a car on a dark road. This situation is referred to as scotomatic glare, and is due to overstimulation of the photosensitive pigments in the rods and cones. Adults over the age of 40 are particularly susceptible to this kind of glare, due to senile miosis and greater density of the lens which results in overstimulation of the photosensitive pigments in the retinal receptors (Wolf, 1960; Wolf & Gardiner, 1965). In other cases, sensitivity to glare is caused by greater scatter as light passes through the lens. This condition, known as veiling glare, results in reduced contrast of the retinal image, and is more prevalent in the elderly who already suffer from greater diffusion of light across the retina (Carter, 1982b).

Color vision. The yellowing of the lens in adulthood has the direct effect of reducing the older adult's ability to discriminate colors at the green-blue-violet end of the spectrum. This effect is similar to what happens when an individual wears special yellow ("blue-block") sunglasses intended to block the sunlight. If you have ever tried such glasses, you know what an odd effect they have on your color vision. Adding to this change in the lens are reductions in the amount of light reaching the retina, so that the color-sensitive cones are less able to trigger impulses (Carter, 1982b). Senile miosis further restricts the amount of light entering the eye to the central region of the lens, its thickest and yellowest portion.

Perception of light flashes. As the individual is exposed to flashes of light from a flickering light source (such as the blinking of a street light), a process known as temporal summation accounts for the perception of these blinking lights as continuous. The point at which this occurs is called critical flicker fusion. The more sensitive the individual's vision, the less likely it is that a high frequency flicker will be perceived as continuous. Fusion is more likely to occur at lower levels of illumination. For older individuals, fusion occurs at lower frequency levels than is true for younger adults. Apart from changes in the lens and pupil contributing to this age effect are alterations in the visual pathways in the central nervous system and the observer's tendency to report the occurrence of fusion (Fozard, Wolf, Bell, McFarland, & Podolsky, 1977; Kline & Schieber, 1982).

Depth perception. To be able to maneuver successfully in the environment, the individual must be able to judge distances and relationships between objects in space. The factors that influence depth perception include monocular cues involving perspective, binocular cues involving stereopsis and intraocular convergence, past experience in the visual world, and motion parallax. Of these factors, only stereopsis has been studied in relation to age. This function appears to be maintained throughout the mid-40s but diminishes cross-sectionally thereafter (Hofstetter & Bertsch, 1976; Pitts, 1982).

Practical Implications of Changes in Vision

Many of the age effects on basic visual functions can be accounted for by the reduction of available light to the retina due to the diminishing size of the pupil and the increased thickness, opacity, and yellowness of the lens. Given these facts, you might think that perhaps the simplest form of compensation for the effects of aging on vision would be to increase the levels of illumination in the older adult's environment. Although the availability of more light can have some merits as a compensatory strategy, there is a serious drawback. With the increase of light in the environment comes the likelihood of more glare. Simply providing a brighter light for reading may fail to have the intended consequences if the reflection of light off the page is too bright. Appropriate increases in illumination require that the light provided be yellowish rather than bluish, since blue light is scattered more by the lens (which absorbs yellow light). Furthermore, it is necessary to take the environmental context into account when adjusting lighting conditions. Higher levels of illumination are particularly important in halls, staircases, entrances, and landings. Difficulties in dark adaptation can heighten the older adult's vulnerability to falls (McMurdo & Gaskell, 1991) and these are more likely to occur when there are difficult steps to negotiate in dimly lit settings.

Age effects on depth perception are another source of practical concern. The older adult may be more likely to trip and fall if altered depth perception leads to misjudgments of distance and height of obstacles and barriers in the environment (Felson et al., 1989). Such misjudgments are most likely to occur when the older individual is placed in a new setting, without familiar landmarks. Familiarizing an older adult with a new setting can help reduce the likelihood of falls due to faulty depth perception.

Another important set of practical applications of age changes in vision pertains to the older adult's ability to drive an automobile. With lower levels of light reaching the eye resulting in a less clear visual image, the older driver is often forced to make driving decisions with inaccurate or incomplete information (Panek et al., 1977). Such problems may be especially noticeable during twilight hours (Morgan, 1988). Although visual problems are not the only cause of driving problems in older adults, they contribute to attentional deficits that may have a more direct relationship to accident frequency (Owsley, Ball, Sloane, Roenker, & Bruni, 1991).

Other driving problems that may arise for the older individual pertain to visual difficulties experienced when night vision is required. After dark, it is more difficult to read road signs, avoid pedestrians, and veer away from obstacles in the road (Richards, 1977). The older adult's greater vulnerability to scotomatic glare reduces the ability to recover after the headlights of an oncoming car pass on a dark road at night. During the day, alternating spots of shade and sunlight in the road can create another set of hazards, as can tunnels and bridges. A loss of sensitivity to movement in the peripherpy of the visual field means, further, that the older driver will be less able to react to oncoming people and cars that emerge suddenly onto the road, because their approach was not observed by the driver .

Shifts of focus that are required between looking at the road and the dashboard of one's car can also be made more difficult by alterations in the accommodative power of the lens (Panek et al., 1977). Age-related alterations in color vision may create further difficulties. If the car has a tinted windshield (as most do), the ability to discriminate green, blue, and violet objects may be obscured. This problem is likely to be particularly troublesome at night.

In terms of absolute numbers, older adults are not more likely to have accidents than are drivers in the under-65 population. However, per driver, the figures tell a different story. Older adults have higher rates of traffic convictions, accidents, and fatalities per mile driven (National Highway Traffic Safety Administration, 1989). It is likely that older adults accommodate to changes they notice in their vision by voluntarily reducing their driving when they feel their visual or cognitive abilities are slipping, or at least do so under conditions known to create problems such as night driving. Other accommodative strategies may also be used such as driving more cautiously or relying on years of driving experience in many different types of situations to help guide judgments in difficult or ambiguous situations.

Psychological Consequences of the Aging of Visual Functions

Given the fundamental role of vision in daily activities, the changes with age in the basic functions of the eye can have a variety of profound psychological effects. In a practical sense, one set of problems involves the discomfort and frustration caused by poorer acuity and reduced focusing power. Even if the individual is able to correct visual problems with glasses or contact lenses, there are residual symptoms that may remain in special circumstances such as when the individual overworks or is trying to read small print. Older adults report experiencing as problems in daily life the types of changes detected clinically and in vision laboratories, including sensitivity to glare, difficulty seeing in dim light, and problems focusing on near objects (Kosnik, Winslow, Kline, Rasinski, & Sekuler, 1988). When these problems become more persistent, they may propel the individual toward a threshold experience.

Presbyopia, although reached after a gradual process of changes in the lens, is often perceived with relative suddenness by the individual (Carter, 1982a). The immediacy of this apparent change, given the association that many people have between presbyopia and the infirmities of age, makes it more likely that the change will be interpreted in a negative way. The fact that bifocals are generally needed to correct for presbyopia adds the complication of requiring the individual to adjust to a new and awkward way of using corrective lenses. You can often hear adults over 40 make reference to the approach of this particular threshold—either sadly announcing that they need bifocals or complaining about the fact that they have to wear them.

To the extent that changes in depth perception interfere with the person's mobility, the individual may additionally feel constrained and insecure within his or her living environment. Problems caused by impaired depth perception can be troubling as well. It is embarrassing, if not painful, to trip or stumble into furniture, on curbs, or on stairs. Such occurrences also have more ominous meaning, because they throw into relief the individual's heightened vulnerability to falls and subsequent injury and disability that may ensue. Consequently, the older adult may overaccommodate by limiting, perhaps unnecessarily, activities involving the risk of falling. As discussed in Chapter 3, such reductions not only lead to social isolation but can also influence in a negative way the individual's physical identity with regard to bodily competence. Vision loss can increase the individual's dependence on others (Hakkinen, 1984), interfering with the older adult's ability to complete basic tasks of living such as housekeeping, grocery shopping, and food preparation (Branch, Horowitz, & Carr, 1989; Rudberg, Furner, Dunn, & Cassel, 1993). Again, apart from the practical implications, these changes can permeate the individual's identity as a competent, able adult.

Finally, age changes in vision can have a variety of miscellaneous deleterious effects on daily life, including the older adult's ability to enjoy leisure and esthetic activities. The yellowing of the lens, which alters the perception of color, may make it more difficult to choose clothes that match, giving the individual an odd and disarrayed appearance. One author, reporting on the subjective experience of having "aging eyes," describes the difficulty he has in distinguishing pink from lavender (Morgan, 1988). Although not a serious problem compared to difficulties in driving, such changes can be annoying and perhaps lead to derision by others. In addition, the ability to appreciate works of art, movies, scenery, and design may be impaired by altered color vision. Other leisure activities involving the perception of color and fine detail may be interfered with, such as needlepoint, gardening, word puzzles, and painting. None of these changes, in and of themselves, are significant enough to have a major impact on the individual, but in combination they may very well reduce the ability to derive satisfaction from simple daily and recreational pleasures. Furthermore, they continue to hammer away at the threshold experience which may be replayed every time a new visual function is altered or affected by aging.

A number of changes in visual functioning can, fortunately, be compensated by corrective lenses, increases in the ambient lighting, and efforts to reduce glare and heighten contrast between light and dark. In cases of visual dysfunction caused by cataracts, corrective surgery can have a number of widespread positive effects on daily life (Brenner, Curbow, Javitt, Legro, & Sommer, 1993). In part, the success of these efforts depends on the willingness of the individual to experiment with new problem-focused coping strategies and persist in trying new ideas when the old methods no longer work. Nevertheless, a point may be reached within each sphere of functioning in which the individual's range of movement becomes compromised. Furthermore, when the situation does not permit compensation, as is true for night driving, the older adult may be forced to give up a formerly valued activity. Awareness of these restrictions along with the sense that one is more dependent on visual aids and forms of compensation may have the effect of detracting from the individual's sense of competence. Such an outcome is likely to be more pronounced for individuals whose eyesight has always been good, or who depend heavily on the use of their eyes for their work or leisure activities.

Age Effects on Higher Visual Functions

Age-related alterations in the structures of the eye are the basis for a number of observed age differences in basic visual functions. There are considerably less data available on the effects of age on the visual pathways in the brain. The functions that depend on processing in the visual cortex are less easily measured than functions such as acuity and dark adaptation (which in themselves may present complications). The kinds of visual functions that reflect the activity of the visual cortex rely more heavily on cognitive factors involving synthesis, expectancies, judgment, decision-making ability, and avoiding the effects of interference. The allocation of cognitive resources to a visual task involves other higher level processes that rely on the functioning of the visual cortex working in connection with other regulatory processes within the brain. Changes in the level above the eye, ranging from the optic nerve to the visual cortex, may play a role in affecting these perceptual processes (Balazsi, Rootman, Drance, Chulze, & Douglas, 1984; Devaney & Johnson, 1980; Weale, 1987; Werner, Peterzell, & Scheetz, 1990). Because these cognitive processes are pulled into the higher visual perceptual functions, they will be discussed in the context of attentional processing in Chapter 8.

HEARING

The auditory system plays a major role in making it possible for the individual to communicate with others and to appreciate the variety of sounds that form an essential part of everyday life. Located in the ears, the auditory sense organs convert energy from waves of sound pressure into neural impulses that are ultimately given meaning in the higher levels of the brain.

Age Effects on the Structures of the Ear

The aging process affects the sensory structures within the ear to differing degrees. In general terms, the aging process has a less pronounced effect on sound conduction through the ear than on the auditory structures themselves located within the inner ear.

A three-tiered set of structures located within the ear serves to transform sound into a form that is usable by the nervous system. Waves of sound pressure are conducted through an elaborate set of channels and moving parts.

When these pressure waves reach the cochlea, the auditory sensory organ, they serve to stimulate the transmission of neural impulses.

Outer ear. The outer ear is made up of the pinna, the visible part of the ear that sound waves reach first when they are encountered by the individual. The pinna is involved in localizing the source of sound, and so helps the individual make judgments regarding the direction from which the sound is coming. Moving into the ear, the concha is the outside opening of the external auditory canal and it is within this structure that sound waves are enhanced by resonance before they move into the ear for processing.

Apart from changes that affect hearing, aging affects the appearance of the pinna, so that with increasing age in adulthood, it becomes stiffer, longer, wider, and can develop freckles and long stiff hairs. The lining of the auditory canal may become brittle and dry, so that as a result, it is more susceptible to cracking and bleeding. Although these changes do not have a direct impact on hearing, they can have secondary effects that do lower auditory sensitivity. Cerumen (earwax) is secreted by cells located in the external auditory canal. Age-related changes such as the growth of hair, and thinning and dryness within the canal itself, can contribute to the accumulation of excessive amounts of cerumen (Anderson & Meyerhoff, 1982). The problem of cerumen build-up is exacerbated by the diminution of sweat gland activity, so that the cerumen is drier and less likely to dissipate on its own. The increase in cerumen accumulation can significantly lower the individual's ability to hear tones of low frequencies, a phenomenon that is estimated to be responsible for apparent cases of hearing loss in as many as one-third of older adults (Fisch, 1978).

Middle ear. Within the middle ear, sound energy is converted through a series of delicate transformations needed to "prepare" sound waves for the receptors located within the inner ear. The conversions that take place in the middle ear are necessary because sound waves travel more readily through the air of the external auditory canal than they do through the fluid environment of the inner ear. The vibrations of sound waves would be lost in the inner ear unless the middle ear structures equalized the differing resistance to movement presented by the environments of the outer and inner ears.

The process of sound wave conversion taking place in the middle ear occurs as sound waves passing through the outer ear reach the thin, elastic, and slightly tensed tympanic membrane, which is stretched across the end of the outer ear canal. As the tympanic membrane begins to vibrate, a small set of bones called the ossicles are set in motion. The ossicles include the tiny specialized bones that respond in highly specific ways to sound pressure. The "hammer" strikes the "anvil," which in turn causes the "stirrups" to displace fluid in the inner ear, starting a wave travelling down this structure. The stirrups actually hit a structure called the oval window, which is much smaller than the tympanic membrane, so that the same amount of energy now becomes concentrated into a smaller area. As a result, the energy from the original sound wave becomes amplified. When the oval window moves inward in response to pressure from the stirrups, a "relief valve" in the cochlea called the round window moves in a direction opposite to this pressure so that the fluid has a place into which to flow.

As might well be imagined, there are many possibilities for aging to alter the intricate set of steps involved in sound wave transmission within the middle ear. Surprisingly, age changes in the middle ear structures are not a major source of hearing problems in the aged, particularly compared to conduction deafness, a form of hearing loss due to structural defects in the middle ear. The age changes that do seem to have the most significant effect involve the tympanic membrane and the ossicles. To be maximally responsive to sound pressure waves, the tympanic membrane must be firm but elastic. With increasing age in adulthood, this membrane thins and becomes less resilient, a process compounded by loss of muscles and ligaments that support it and enable it to move (Schow, Christensen, Hutchinson, & Nerbonne, 1978). Calcification of the ossicular chain is another age-related change that can interfere with hearing, involving stiffening of the joints between the ossicles. However, the functional impact of these changes has not clearly been demonstrated (Etholm & Belal, 1974) or been the focus of recent investigation.

Inner ear. More dramatic in their impact on hearing than age effects on the outer and middle ear structures are changes in the inner ear, which is the location of the cochlea, or auditory sensory organ. The cochlea is a tightly coiled spiral encased in a bony core with three fluid-filled cavities. The width and elasticity of the cochlea decrease from its base (located nearest the middle ear) to its apex. Together, differences down the length of the cochlea in width and elasticity result in varying sensitivity of the sensory cells on the cochlea to high- and low-pitched sound. The wave that travels down the cochlear fluid in response to movement of the oval and round windows changes in amplitude as it moves from the base to the apex due to variations in the width and elasticity of the cochlear surface. High-frequency waves reach their maximum amplitudes at the base; waves of low frequency travel all through the spiral until they reach the apex. As a result, the base is most sensitive to high-frequency sounds and the apex to low-frequency sound waves.

One of the more general effects of aging on the sensory structures of the auditory system is degeneration of the sensory cells. This is most likely to occur near the base of the cochlea, causing the perception of high-frequency sound to be impaired. Other forms of hearing loss are the result of degeneration of the nerve fibers connecting the sensory structures to the auditory pathway leading to the central nervous system. The growth of bone tissue in the inner ear canal can lead to blockage of the holes through which the nerve fibers pass leading away from the cochlea, causing the nerve fibers to become compressed and eventually to degenerate. Atrophy within the vascular system supplying the sensory cells is another age-related effect. Finally, loss of elasticity or other mechanical damage to the surface of the cochlea is another potential source of age-related hearing loss.

Age Effects on Auditory Functions

The sensitivity of the auditory system is defined in terms of how soft a tone of given frequency can be and still be heard. For the normal listener, high frequency tones can be heard at very soft levels while low frequencies must be louder in order to be detected. To describe a person's auditory sensitivity, an audiogram is used. The individual being tested listens through headphones to pure tones at differing frequencies and the absolute threshold is determined. Normal listeners can detect sounds within a frequency range of 20 to 20,000 Hz.

Age-related changes within the inner ear are associated with various forms of presbycusis, or age-related hearing loss, reflected in loss of auditory sensitivity. Hearing loss begins gradually in early adulthood (the decade of the 30s) and continues progressively through the oldest ages measured (the decade of the 80s). In most cases, sensitivity to high-frequency tones is impaired earlier and more severely than is sensitivity loss involving low-frequency tones (Arlinger, 1991; Van-Rooij & Plomp, 1990). The loss of high-frequency pitch perception is particularly pronounced in men (Lebo & Reddell, 1972).

Forms of presbycusis. There are several forms of presbycusis, resulting from different age-related changes in the auditory structures (Corso, 1981). Sensory presbycusis results from degeneration of the sensory cells in the cochlea, and is closest to the form of hearing loss most commonly reported in older age groups. The audiograms of individuals with sensory presbycusis show a dramatic loss of hearing for high-frequency tones. Neural presbycusis is caused by degeneration of nerve fibers leading to the central nervous system. It is likely that the degeneration of neural pathways reduces the quality of neurally coded information used in the analysis of speech patterns, so that even though the sensory tissue may remain intact, higher level encoding is deleteriously affected. Atrophy of the blood supply to the cochlear surface is the cause of strial presbycusis, a loss of hearing that actually begins in early adulthood (the decade of the 20s). By the time the individual reaches middle age (50s to 60s), this degenerative process has significant cumulative effects. Unlike the other forms of presbycusis, which produce a graded loss of hearing for different frequencies of tones, strial presbycusis reduces sensitivity to all frequencies. Finally, mechanical presbycusis is the result of changes in the cochlear membrane that render it less able to vibrate in response to the pressure of the cochlear fluid. The audiogram of a person with this form of presbycusis resembles that of sensory presbycusis, with reduced sensitivity to high-pitched tones. However, rather than exhibiting a sharp drop-off of hearing for high tones, the audiogram of a person with mechanical presbycusis shows a gradual loss of sensitivity moving from low- to high-pitched tones.

Effects of Age on the Understanding of Speech

Speech perception, which is a major concern when considering the effects of aging on hearing in everyday life, is affected both by the various forms of presbycusis operating at the sensory level and by changes in the central processing of auditory information at the level of the brain stem and above (Van-Rooij & Plomp, 1992). As mentioned earlier, the most common effect of presbycusis is a reduction in sensitivity to high-frequency tones. Translated into speech discrimination, this means that older adults suffering from presbycusis have greater difficulty perceiving sibilants, which are consonants that have frequencies in the upper ranges of 3,000 to over 6,000 Hz. The sibilants include the underlined phonemes in these words: plus, xerox, ship, azure, wrench, and drudge. The English language is rich in these phonemes, particularly the s used in plurals, so that loss of the ability to hear these sounds can have a particularly damaging effect on everyday speech.

Research on speech understanding in conditions free of distractions reflects this loss of auditory sensitivity. Across the adult age range, there are cross-sectional losses in the ability to understand spondee words, two-syllable words with uniform emphasis on both syllables (e.g., "football," or "trumpet") (Corso, 1981). Similarly, the discrimination of phonetically balanced lists of single-syllable words decreases systematically across the years of adulthood, particularly after the decade of the 50s (Punch & McConnell, 1969). Age effects also appear in speech comprehension, particularly the perception of consonants (Revoile, Pickett, & Kozma-Spytek, 1991), and are more pronounced when background noise is present (Heller & Wilber, 1990). Under adverse listening conditions, when the speech signal is distorted or interfered with, age differences across adulthood become particularly pronounced. Beginning as early as the decade of the 40s, adults have difficulty understanding interrupted speech signals (Bergman, 1971; Bergman, Blumenfeld, Cascardo, Dash, Levitt, & Margulies, 1976). Increases in the rate of speech, compression of the speech signal, reverberation, and competition from background noise also interfere significantly with speech understanding among older adult age groups (Jerger & Hayes, 1977; Lutman, 1991; Plomp & Mimpen, 1979).

It is important to note that in many cases, age-related decreases in the ability to recognize speech occur beyond the point that would be predicted on the basis of pure-tone audiograms (Heller & Wilber, 1990; Humes & Christopherson, 1991; Lutman, 1991; Neils, Newman, Hill, & Weiler, 1991). This suggests that there are contributions of higher level cortical functions to age-related losses in speech understanding (Bergman, 1983). Difficulties discriminating tones of short duration and temporal intervals between words may interfere with word recognition (Cranford & Stream, 1991; McCroskey & Kasten, 1982). There may also be age-related losses in sequencing, memory, and rate of presentation of auditory material that contribute to speech perception problems (Neils et al., 1991).

In attempting to explain the factors contributing to altered speech understanding in the elderly, researchers have debated the relative contributions of sensory processes to those involving the integrative functions reflecting higher nervous system functioning. There is evidence to suggest that there are impairments with age in higher auditory centers of the brain (Hansen & Reske-Nielson, 1965; Henderson, Tomlinson, & Gibson, 1980). Such impairments can contribute central processing deficits to age-related difficulties in speech understanding.

Psychological Consequences of Aging of the Auditory System

The ability to hear plays a critical adaptive function in the individual's life. At the most basic level of survival, hearing provides the individual with cues of oncoming dangers that can only be heard, or that supplement visual cues. Examples of auditory cues within the environment include spoken warnings by others to avoid bumping into obstacles or going into a life-threatening situation such as stepping in front of a car on a crowded city street. Fire alarms, sirens, and emergency warning signals are other auditory signals that can save a person's life. Sound is also used to orient oneself in space and to locate the source of other people or objects. Apart from these directly adaptive functions of hearing is the role of auditory stimulation in enhancing the quality of life. Through hearing, the individual can enjoy music, theater, television, and radio. Social adaptation is also largely affected by hearing, which plays the almost irreplaceable role of making interpersonal communication possible. In addition to hearing's actual role in daily life is the subjective interpretation by the individual of the ability to hear adequately. As is the case of vision, psychological thresholds for hearing are likely to be highly significant as they are almost impossible not to notice (Slawinski, Hartel, & Kline, 1993). Threats to the individual's identity in terms of sense of competence can come from instances in which hearing failures cause one to fail to hear what someone else says or to commit an embarrassing faux pas through a misunderstanding of another person's speech.

Although individuals vary tremendously in the time of onset and degree of impairment they experience, the decade of the 60s involves, for the average adult, some loss of the ability to hear high-pitched sounds. This is a deficit that has a more pronounced impact on the comprehension of words containing sibilants (of which there are many), and will be greater when the listener hears a woman than a man. Under ideal conditions, these deficits may not seem significant, but most speaking takes place under less than ideal settings, with background noise, speech interruptions, variations in rate, and reverberations. In a practical sense, then, the speech understanding of the older adult is therefore likely to suffer noticeably. Furthermore, the older person's ability to hear sounds in the environment, such as the noise of a siren or a knock on the door, is likely to be reduced as well (Gatehouse, 1990).

There is some debate regarding the impact of hearing loss in later life on the individual's emotional state, with some claims made that hearing loss contributes to feelings of depression, social isolation, irritation, and even paranoia. Although empirical investigation does not support the long-held belief that hearing loss contributes to psychological disorder in later life, changes in communication ability can lead to strains in interpersonal relationships (Humes & Christopherson, 1991; Lindenman & Platenburg-Gits, 1991). Greater caution might also be expected on the part of the older person who wishes to avoid making inappropriate responses to uncertain auditory signals (Marshall, 1991). There is also some evidence linking hearing loss to impaired physical functioning (Bess, Lichtenstein, Logan, & Burger, 1989) and psychological difficulties including loneliness (Christian, Dluhy, & O'Neill, 1989) and depression (Kalayam et al., 1991). Depression is not consistently found to be related to hearing loss (Norris & Cunningham, 1981; Powers & Powers, 1978), though, and compared to visual changes, hearing loss has less of an impact on the individual's self-care abilities (Rudberg et al., 1993).

These effects notwithstanding, it remains the case that the majority of elderly adults do not suffer from hearing losses significant enough to interfere dramatically with their daily lives. Of those who are afflicted by hearing loss, a certain number compensate successfully, either by using problem-focused coping strategies such as obtaining hearing aids or by augmenting their auditory processing with knowledge gained from the other senses, particularly vision. By the same token, those who interact with hearing-impaired elders can benefit from learning ways to communicate that lessen the impact of age-related changes (Slawinski et al., 1993). Modulating one's tone of voice so that it is not too high, particularly for women, and avoiding distractions or interference can be important aids to communicating clearly with older adults.

SOMESTHETIC AND VESTIBULAR SYSTEMS

Information about touch, pressure, pain, and outside temperature is communicated by the somesthetic senses. It almost goes without saying that this information is essential for allowing the individual to judge the position and orientation of the body, the presence of threats to the body's integrity from harmful environmental conditions, and also to feel enjoyable sensations from comforting physical stimuli. Unlike the other senses, the somesthetic system has multiple types of receptors and sensory pathways, making the effects of aging on this system more complex to investigate and document.

The vestibular system adds information about movement and head position to the somesthetic system's input regarding body position and orientation. Awareness of the forces of gravitational pull and acceleration applied to the body is necessary for maintaining an upright position, or adjusting the body's position when moving or being moved. The vestibular system, located within the inner ear, contains receptors sensitive to these forces as they act upon the head. This system is vital for maintaining balance while moving and standing still.

Age Effects on Somesthesis

Many people are interested in the effects of aging on the somesthetic system, even if it is not a concern they can articulate. A common belief is that aging is associated with many "aches and pains" caused by stiffness in the joints and muscles. The threshold experiences of many middle-aged adults are undoubtedly marked by a "charley horse" in the calf, a knee that stiffens up during a long walk, or a stiff neck that will not go away. It might also be reasoned, however, that aging involves a diminished sensory experience in the area of somesthesis, just as aging reduces other aspects of sensory awareness. Unfortunately, research on aging of the somesthetic system does not permit resolution of this paradox. The existing research is sparse and thinly documented, with few indications of general trends, despite the practical significance of this area of functioning.

Touch. The skin contains a variety of specialized receptors that transmit neural signals when pressure is applied to them from mechanical displacement. One of the more well-established findings with regard to aging is that there are reductions across age groups of adults in the number of pacinian corpuscles and Meissner's corpuscles, receptors in the skin that respond to vibration (Bolton, Winkelmann, & Dyck, 1966). Another group of receptors that sense continuous pressure, the Merkel's discs, show little change in number or structure in later adulthood (Cauna, 1965).

Psychophysical evidence presents a mixed picture regarding the effects of aging on the functioning of the somesthetic receptors. Sensitivity to touch on the skin of the hand shows a clear diminution over the adult years, as indicated by higher absolute and difference thresholds to touch (Stevens, 1992; Thornbury & Mistretta, 1981). By contrast, touch sensitivity on the arm is maintained relatively intact (Stevens, 1992), as is sensitivity in other hair-covered parts of the skin. This finding is consistent with the observation that the number and structure of free-nerve endings and hair end-organs in the skin is not affected by aging (Kenshalo, 1977). Sensitivity to vibrations, reflecting the effectiveness of the pacinian and Meissner's corpuscles, also shows differential patterns of aging, with functioning maintained in the upper but not lower parts of the body. Changes in lower body sensitivity to vibration may be a function of alterations in the peripheral neural pathways in this part of the body rather than to changes in the sensory structures themselves (Kenshalo, 1977).

Position. Awareness of the degree of angular displacement between bones at the joints and the rate of joint movement are needed for the individual to monitor the location and movements of the arms and legs. Two pressure-sensitive touch receptors located deep in the joints monitor this type of information: the pacinian corpuscles and structures called Ruffini end-organs. Golgi endings are another type of position receptor, and are located within the ligaments at the joint. As the ligaments stretch, reflecting joint movement, the Golgi endings are stimulated to respond. Muscle spindle fibers also register movement and position, transmitting neural information when the muscle they are located in undergoes a stretch. The sensitivity of this group of receptors is indicated by the smallest degree of passive rotation of a joint that the individual can detect.

The information on sensitivity of position receptors in later adulthood is scattered and not very current. For example, early evidence suggested that older adults show diminished sensitivity to passive movement in some joints but not others (Laidlaw & Hamilton, 1937) and that individuals vary widely in passive movement perception (Howell, 1949). More recently, there are cross-sectional data indicating decreased sensitivity to passive movement (Skinner, Barrack, & Cook, 1984) and a loss of accuracy in reproducing and matching the angles of joint placement (Stelmach & Sirica, 1986). There are no available data on the sensitivity of muscle stretch receptors (Kenshalo, 1979), but the perception of muscular effort has been reported not to show age differences across adulthood (Landahl & Birren, 1959).

Temperature. As described in Chapter 6, the autonomic system plays an important role in maintaining the homeostasis of the body's internal environment. The perception of the outside temperature contributes to this process in that it signals the need for the individual to take necessary steps to protect the body from variations in the external environment. Although it is a well-known fact that older individuals are more vulnerable to the effects of extremes of heat and cold, age effects on the thermal receptors in the skin appear to have limited behavioral significance (Hensel, 1981; Kenshalo, 1979).

Pain. The subjective experience of pain arises when a stimulus applied to the skin or arising from within the body begins to damage tissue and in the process triggers impulses in free nerve endings located near the vicinity of the stimulus. The stimuli for pain can take the form of pressure, temperature, or chemical substances; most pain receptors are sensitive to more than one of these forms of stimulation. The question of whether aging causes more "aches and pains" in terms of sensitivity to pain has not been investigated within recent years. Over two decades ago, a review of the literature posed the possibility of alternatively, heightened, diminished, or unchanged sensitivity to pain across the later years of adulthood (Kenshalo, 1977). Perhaps complicating the picture is the role of the individual's attitude toward reporting pain, a factor that could easily confound whatever age differences are found to exist in actual pain thresholds (Clark & Meehl, 1971).

Psychological Consequences of Aging of the Somesthetic System

Although relatively little is known about the effects of aging on this system, the somesthetic system can be seen as having a number of crucial roles in the individual's daily life. Sensations from within the body can serve as warnings that the individual has placed excessive strain on muscles or joints, needs to take action to correct internal imbalances due to outside temperature variations, or is in need of rest after exertion. There are also pleasurable sensations communicated by this system associated with the "creature comforts" of sensuality, ranging from expressions of physical affection to the enjoyment of putting on a soft flannel shirt on a cold winter's day. The somesthetic system also provides information that may relate to the individual's identity with regard to physical competence, as it provides essential input about the adequacy of the body's functioning. It is through the actions of this system that the adult becomes aware of some of the dreaded signs of aging, such as muscular fatigue, joint pain, insufficiencies of the cardiovascular or respiratory system, or problems in digestion and elimination related to gastrointestinal or urinary pain. If in fact aging does not reduce pain sensitivity, then these signals can have a powerful impact on identity because they create the unavoidable realization that one's body is losing some of its vitality.

Apart from these unpleasant realizations related to the aging of the body, there may be an important function served by the relative preservation of the aging somesthetic system. The function of the perception of pain and effort is to warn the individual of danger caused by mechanical damage to the body's tissues or overexertion. It may be hypothesized that there is adaptive value in the somesthetic system's maintenance of function throughout the lifespan. Although awareness of reduced efficiency of the body's mobility and efficiency may be damaging to the aging individual's identity, this awareness can be of considerable value in ensuring that the individual does not engage in activity that could ultimately cause serious harm to the body. In this sense the somesthetic system may play an important role in maintaining the older adult's adaptation to the physical environment.

Age Effects on Balance

The body's orientation and movement in space is sensed by the vestibular system. From the information gained by this system regarding the gravitational and accelerational forces acting upon the head, knowledge of the whole body's position in space can be judged. The vestibular system is located within the inner ear, inside the same bony labyrinth in the skull that encloses the cochlea. This system includes two sets of spherical compartments called the utricle and saccule, and three looplike semicircular canals. The sensory cells in the utricle and saccule respond to linear movement and those in the semicircular canal respond to movement in a curved path. The signals provided by these motion detectors provide information to the central nervous system which then send messages to the muscles to make postural adjustments. It is through this process that the individual maintains balance.

In addition to stimulating postural reflexes, movement of the head initiates a response called nystagmus, a reflexive movement of the eyes in a direction equal and opposite to that of the head. Nystagmus serves to keep the eyes fixated on the visual field that was being observed before movement was initiated. Stability of the visual field despite changes in head position allows the person to maintain a constant visual input in tasks such as reading and talking, where random head movements would otherwise cause distracting changes in the visual field. In research on the functioning of the vestibular system, the nystagmus reflex is used to index sensitivity of the receptors to movement without actually rotating the individual. A common technique involves irritating the external ear canal with cool or warm water to produce "caloric" nystagmus. The change in temperature causes fluid in the semicircular canals to move, which in turn stimulates the sensory cells to respond.

With increasing age in adulthood, the number of sensory cells within the vestibular system is reported to be reduced (Rosenhall, 1973). The fluid surrounding the sensory cells in the utricle and saccule begins to deteriorate and may even disappear entirely (Ross, Johnsson, Peacor, & Allard, 1976). Neural degeneration also occurs in the nerves connecting the sensory receptors to the central nervous system pathways (Bergstrom, 1973) due to a process similar to that affecting the auditory nerves. Accumulation of bony tissue around the opening through which the vestibular nerves pass cause them to become compressed and eventually degenerate.

Malfunction due to age-related changes in the vestibular system seems to be manifested in the experience of dizziness and vertigo by elderly adults. Vertigo is the sensation that the self or one's surroundings are spinning. Dizziness is the feeling of floating, being lightheaded, or unsteady. Both of these sensations of disequilibrium are unpleasant to experience and can have serious consequences in that they can contribute to the risk of falling due to loss of balance. Although it is not possible to establish a direct link between age-related changes in the vestibular system and these sensations, it seems likely that differential loss of sensory receptors in the saccule and utricle canals results in distorted images of head position and linear movement. Loss of receptors within the semicircular canals can lead to lowered sensitivity to rotational movement. Interestingly, the loss of sensitivity of receptors in the semicircular canals appears to occur in non-linear fashion between the ages of 40 and 70 before diminishing more or less continuously into the 70s and beyond. Under a variety of conditions, sensitivity of the vestibular receptors as indicated by caloric nystagmus shows an inverted U-pattern across the middle and later decades of adulthood (Bruner & Norris, 1971; Karlsen, Hassanein, & Goetzinger, 1981). The peak in vestibular sensitivity in the middle adult years is difficult to explain, but the consistent decrease through the later decades of adulthood seems to reflect alterations in the receptor structures within the vestibular system.

It is important to point out, however, that structural changes in the vestibular system do not account entirely for the phenomena of dizziness and vertigo. There is considerable plasticity within the vestibular system so that loss of receptor cells in these structures may be compensated by the activity of structures in other sensory systems (Teasdale, Stelmach, & Breunig, 1991). For example, the positional receptors in the somesthetic system appear to be less vulnerable to aging effects (Babin & Harker, 1982). Conversely, the loss of information from more than one sensory system, such as the visual and the vestibular systems, can make it difficult for the older person to compensate successfully (Manchester, Woollacott, Zederbauer-Hylton, & Marin, 1989). Slowing of central integrative processes responsible for maintaining postural stability can also contribute to increased likelihood of falls. It may take longer for the older adult to integrate information from the vestibular, visual, and somesthetic systems, resulting in less efficient control of posture under changing body positions (Teasdale et al., 1991). Fortunately, one compensatory strategy can be very effective in this crucial area. Older persons can be given training in judging the position of the lower body limbs to make better use of feedback in adjusting their posture (Hu & Woollacott, 1994a; Hu & Woollacott, 1994b; Meeuwsen, Sawicki, & Stelmach, 1993).

Psychological Consequences of Aging of the Vestibular System

Postural balance is an essential element of moving about effectively in the physical environment. Aging of the vestibular system brings with it the potential for the individual to feel insecure in moving around, particularly under conditions that are less than ideal, such as sloping, steep, or uneven surfaces. Dizziness and vertigo can reduce this sense of security and compromise the individual's sense of freedom of movement. Fear of falling due to other changes in mobility can increase the individual's anxiety and perhaps exacerbate any true deficits in vestibular functioning. Conversely, individuals who through identity assimilation ignore signs of dizziness and vertigo may place themselves in real danger as they may not be able to avoid a fall when and if they do lose their balance.

There are social consequences of aging of the vestibular system as well. The older adult who experiences dizziness and vertigo may fear appearing disoriented in front of other people, perhaps concerned about giving the impression of being intoxicated or mentally confused. A desire to avoid such embarrassment may lead the individual to avoid going out, and in the process create unnecessary limitations on opportunities for social interactions.

Nevertheless, it remains the case that vestibular dysfunction is not an inevitable consequence of the aging of the vestibular system and that there is a range of functioning across individuals. Furthermore, compensation is possible if the individual is able to adapt other sensory systems to make up for vestibular losses (Lord, Clark, & Webster, 1991). Such compensation seems to be more likely to occur if the indivdiual is able to react in a calm manner to the experience of dizziness or vertigo. Rather than becoming alarmed, on the one hand, or overly incautious, on the other, the individual would benefit from the problem-focused strategy of seeking other cues, such as those provided by the somesthetic system. During episodes of disequilibrium, the individual can avoid falling by paying special attention to stance and bodily orientation, or taking advantage of external aids, such as handrails. By successfully conquering an episode of dizziness or vertigo, the individual may feel a greater sense of bodily competence in the future and therefore avoid unnecessary social isolation or restriction of activities.

TASTE AND SMELL

The experience of eating is the primary area of functioning that is generally thought of when considering the role of taste in daily life. The taste receptors are the sensory organs that are maximally sensitive to the chemical composition of foods as transmitted through direct contact of food with the tongue. The sensory structures in the nose responsible for smell are important too, however, interacting in a complex way with taste sensation to contribute further to individual's enjoyment of food. Eating is often a social activity as well, and the role of individual age-related changes in taste and smell must be thought of in terms of changes in social patterns regarding meals and meal preparation. Taste and smell also have important functions in areas of life other than eating. In particular, the sensation of smell is important in protecting the individual from environmental dangers that can only be detected as odors.

Age Effects on Taste Sensitivity

The nutritional status of elderly individuals is a matter of great concern to health-care practitioners. Adequate amounts of food and water intake are particularly important for older individuals to maintain proper bodily stores of fluids, proteins, carbohydrates, fats, vitamins, and minerals. Although nutritional concerns are present for every age group, they are particularly critical for the elderly, who are experiencing changes in health status and bodily functioning that can create imbalances in various systems. Furthermore, older individuals experience a number of changes in social and economic circumstances that may alter their previous eating habits in deleterious ways. Finally, nutritional deficiencies may create psychological symptoms mimicking Alzheimer's disease and other forms of dementia, and so result in unnecessary suffering and deprivation. Changes in taste may compound these problems if they take away from the enjoyment of food, causing the individual to lose the motivation to eat a balanced diet or one that is sufficient to meet the daily nutritional intake needs.

Practical concern over the effects of aging on taste has stimulated a fairly large body of research on taste receptor numbers and sensitivity across the adult years. Because they are continuously replenished from their surrounding epithelial cells, the actual number of taste buds in the tongue shows no appreciable decline over the adult years (Engen, 1982). Nevertheless, the detection thresholds for all four primary tastes are signficantly higher for many adults over the age of 60 years (Grzegorczyk, Jones, & Mistretta, 1979; Moore, Nielsen, & Mistretta, 1983), particularly for bitter tastes (Murphy & Gilmore, 1989). However, there are wide individual variations in taste thresholds, particularly for adults in the older age ranges. Although the average threshold of persons over the age of 60 years is higher than among younger adults, there are still a number of older individuals who have no apparent loss of taste sensitivity. Furthermore, there is also considerable redundancy among taste receptors, so that the loss of one area of taste reception may be compensated by the increased activity of other receptors (Bartoshuk, 1989).

The overall discrepancy between anatomical and perceptual data on taste perception might be accounted for by a variety of factors. One possibility is that factors other than the integrity of the receptor structures accoung for taste detection and recognition, and these factors are impaired by aging. A history of smoking, the presence of dentures, intake of certain medications, and exposure to pollutants in the environment may accentuate age effects in the cross-sectional studies reported in the literature (Chauhan, 1989; Stevens, 1989; Zallen, Hooks, & O'Brien, 1990).

Whatever the extent or basis of age reductions in taste sensitivity as reported in the cross-sectional literature, it is likely that many older individuals do lose their appreciation for the flavor of food. Data on food identification task performance across age groups of adults indicate a cross-sectional decrease in the recognition of a large number of familiar food substances, including most types of fruit, vegetables, meats, and coffee (Cain, Reid, & Stevens, 1990; Schiffman, 1977; Stevens, Cain, Demarque, & Ruthruff, 1991). Contributing further to age effects on food appreciation could be distortion of food taste resulting from changes in salivary secretions and dental diseases more prevalent in the aged (Grzegorczyk et al., 1979).

Psychological Consequences of the Aging of Gustation

The effect of reduced taste sensitivity to food in the older adult would be to reduce the intrinsic motivation for eating; that is, the pleasure inherent to the eating experience. In addition, reduced sensitivity to particular tastes may lead the older adult to alter the balance of food intake, eating only those foods whose flavor can be appreciated. Overseasoning with sugar or salt, or preparing stronger drinks containing caffeine or alcohol could make the older adult more vulnerable to certain diseases or exacerbate chronic conditions sensitive to these substances. There is also a loss of a major contributor to the quality of life with diminished food enjoyment. The individual may be less likely to spend time cooking, going out to eat, or taking pleasure in the food that is prepared by family members.

On the positive side, there are tremendous variations in taste sensitivity, particularly as influenced by health and smoking habits. Some individuals may never experience reduced awareness of taste. Furthermore, although it is difficult to judge from cross-sectional studies, the loss of taste sensitivity over adulthood seems to occur in a gradual enough manner so that individuals may be able to adapt to a slow crossing of the threshold to make changes in their food appreciation. Individuals who derive particular enjoyment out of eating may take additional care in meal preparation so as to minimize any age-related disturbances in their flavor-sensing ability. Flavor additives have been found to be successful in helping older adults to derive more benefit from food (Schiffman & Warwick, 1989). It may even boost the older individual's sense of competence to be able to meet the challenge of preparing healthy, economical food that brings pleasure to oneself and one's family or friends.

Age Effects on Olfaction

The sensitivity of olfactory receptors plays many important roles in everyday life and the individual's adaptation, not the least of which is the role of smell in the enjoyment of food. Fumes from foods and liquids may serve as warnings that the substances are potentially harmful, such as the smell of spoiled cheese. The inability to smell natural gas fumes can be fatal. Smoke from an accidental fire can often be smelled before it can be seen, giving the individual valuable extra time for escape or to put out the fire. Smell also has an esthetic role in everyday life, contributing to the enjoyment of perfume, flowers, and scented agents such as soap or air fresheners. It is also the case that failure to detect certain bodily odors in oneself can lead to social embarrassment. Adults who do not notice their own unpleasant odors may find themselves left out of social and possibly business situations. There is large practical value, then, in monitoring the olfactory abilities of the aged. Persons who care for the elderly are concerned about loss of ability to detect odors, for reasons of safety, nutrition, and hygiene. These issues have prompted researchers to examine cross-sectional effects of aging on olfactory receptors and smell sensitivity.

As is true for taste receptors, the olfactory receptors are constantly replenishing themselves by the generation of new cells from their surrounding surfaces. Despite the regeneration of these receptors, there are reports of decreased olfactory cell populations and abnormalities in progressively older age groups, beginning as early as 30 years (Naessen, 1971). It is possible that aging affects the regeneration process or that a lifetime of damage to the olfactory surface creates a situation in which more olfactory receptors degenerate than can be replaced.

Most cross-sectional comparisons of adults of different ages yield a pattern of diminished odor sensitivity among older adults (Cain & Stevens, 1989; Murphy, 1983; Stevens & Cain, 1987). However, there is wide variation among the over-60 population based in large part on health status (Doty, Shaman, Applebaum, Giberson, Sikosorski, & Rosenberg, 1984), and it appears that a variety of diseases can interfere with smell thresholds (Doty, 1989; Weiffenbach & Bartoshuk, 1992). Different odors appear to show different age-related patterns of sensitivity (Wysocki & Gilbert, 1989).

Contributing to age effects in actual olfactory sensitivity may be cognitive difficulties in properly identifying or labeling odors (Corwin, 1992; Schemper, Voss, & Cain, 1981) or alterations in the way that odors are classified (Russell, Cummings, Profitt, Wysocki, Gilbert, & Cotman, 1993). Moreover, some of the differences in odor detection among older samples could be due to differences in experiences accumulated over the course of a lifetime such as the amount of practice individuals have in detecting and labelling odors. Finally, memory for verbal labels of odors may be diminished in older adults, influencing the older individual's ability to perform well on tasks of odor recognition (Larsson & Bäckman, 1993). These findings suggest that higher order cognitive processes may be primarily responsible for what appear to be age effects on odor sensitivity.

Psychological Consequences of Aging on Odor Sensitivity

Keeping in mind the lack of general age trends in odor sensitivity, and the role of cognitive factors, there are important consequences to consider in the life of an aging individual who does suffer loss in this sensory capacity. One important well-recognized consequence is reflected in age differences in the ability to detect the odor of natural gas (Chalke, Dewhurst, & Ward, 1958). Elderly persons who suffer from this particular loss would be more likely to suffer a real danger to their lives should there be gas leakage in their homes. Another potential outcome of reduced odor discrimination is failure to attend to bodily odors that other people might find offensive. Conversely, the individual may overdo the application of perfume, and this can have almost an equally noxious quality. Similarly, the accumulation of foul odors around the home could discourage visitors. Both types of changes could reduce the individual's quantity and quality of social interaction. Apart from these effects on the individual's social relationships, loss of odor sensitivity can detract from the enjoyment of natural and artifical odorants.

Counteracting these negative psychological effects of odor loss is the likelihood that the exercising of odor discrimination skills contributes to their maintenance (Engen, 1982). Whether this effect is due to preservation of the olfactory structures or to the collection over the years of more fine-tuned cognitive abilities relevant to smell is not known. The result, though, may be that the adult's social and esthetic environment is not significantly altered. Another compensating factor is that in the real world, odors are present in suprathreshold amounts, well above the concentrations used to determine threshold abilities in the laboratory. Odor identification and detection also takes place in situations with many other sensory cues present. Older adults who suffer from loss of olfactory sensitivity may learn to use these additional cues as coping strategies to offset whatever age-related reductions they have experienced.

REFERENCES

Anderson, R. G., & Meyerhoff, W. L. (1982). Otologic manifestations of aging. *Otolaryngologic Clinics of North America, 15*, 353–370.

Arlinger, S. (1991). Audiometric profile in presbycusis. *Acta Otolaryngolica (Suppl. No. 476)*, 85–90.

Babin, R. W., & Harker, L. A. (1982). The vestibular system in the elderly. *Otolaryngolic Clinics of North America, 15,* 387–393.

Balazs, E. A., & Denlinger, J. L. (1982). Aging changes in the vitreous. In R. Sekuler, D. Kline, & K. Dismukes (Eds.), *Aging and human visual function.* New York: Alan R. Liss.

Balazsi, A. G., Rootman, J., Drance, S. M., Chulze, M., & Douglas, G. R. (1984). The effect of age on the nerve fiber population of the human optic nerve. *American Journal of Opthalmology, 97,* 760–766.

Bartoshuk, L. M. (1989). Taste. Robust across the age span? *Annals of the New York Academy of Science, 561,* 65–75.

Bergman, M. (1971). Hearing and aging. *Audiology, 10,* 164–171.

Bergman, M. (1983). Central disorders of hearing in the elderly. In R. Hinchcliffe (Eds.), *Hearing and balance in the elderly.* Edinburgh, England: Churchill Livingstone.

Bergman, M., Blumenfeld, V. G., Cascardo, D., Dash, B., Levitt, H., & Margulies, M. K. (1976). Age-related decrement in hearing for speech: Sampling and longitudinal studies. *Journal of Gerontology, 31,* 533–538.

Bergstrom, B. (1973). Morphology of the vestibular nerve: II. The number of myelinated vestibular nerve fibers in man at various ages. *Acta Otolaryngolica, 76,* 173–179.

Bess, F. H., Lichtenstein, M. J., Logan, S. A., & Burger, M. C. (1989). Hearing impairment as a determinant of function in the elderly. *Journal of the American Geriatrics Society, 37,* 123–128.

Bolton, C. F., Winkelmann, R. K., & Dyck, P. J. (1966). A quantitative study of Meissner's corpuscles in man. *Neurology, 16,* 1–9.

Branch, L. G., Horowitz, A., & Carr, C. (1989). The implications for everyday life of incident self-reported visual decline among people over age 65 living in the community. *Gerontologist, 29,* 359–365.

Brenner, M. H., Curbow, B., Javitt, J. C., Legro, M. W., & Sommer, A. (1993). Vision change and quality of life in the elderly: Response to cataract surgery and treatment of other chronic ocular conditions. *Archives of Ophthalmology, 3,* 680–685.

Bruner, A., & Norris, T. (1971). Age related changes in caloric nystagmus. *Acta Otolaryngolica (Supplement), 282.*

Cain, W. S., Reid, F., & Stevens, J. C. (1990). Missing ingredients: Aging and the discrimination of flavor. *Journal of Nutrition in the Elderly, 9,* 3–15.

Cain, W. S., & Stevens, J. C. (1989). Uniformity of olfactory loss in aging. *Annals of the New York Academy of Science, 561,* 29–38.

Carter, J. H. (1982a). The effects of aging on selected visual functions: Color vision, glare sensitivity, field of vision, and accommodation. In R. Sekuler, D. Kline, & K. Dismukes (Eds.), *Aging and human visual function.* New York: Alan R. Liss.

Carter, J. H. (1982b). Predicting visual responses to increasing age. *Journal of the American Optometric Association, 53,* 31–36.

Cauna, N. (1965). The effects of aging on the receptor organs of the human dermis. In W. Montagna (Ed.), *Advances in biology of skin* (Vol. 6, Aging, pp. 63–96). New York: Alan R. Liss.

Chalke, H. D., Dewhurst, J. R., & Ward, C. W. (1958). Loss of sense of smell in old people. *Public Health, 72,* 223–230.

Chauhan, J. (1989). Relationships between sour and salt taste perception and selected subject attributes. *Journal of the American Dietitic Association, 89,* 652–658.

Christian, E., Dluhy, N., & O'Neill, R. (1989). Sounds of silence: Coping with hearing loss and loneliness. *Journal of Gerontological Nursing, 15,* 4–9.

Clark, W. C., & Meehl, L. (1971). Thermal pain: A sensory decision theory analysis of the effect of age and sex on d^1, various response criteria, and 50 percent pain threshold. *Journal of Abnormal Psychology, 78,* 202–212.

Corso, J. F. (1981). *Aging, sensory systems, and perception.* New York: Praeger.

Corwin, J. (1992). Assessing olfaction: Cognitive and measurement issues. In M. J. Serby & K. L. Chobor (Eds.), *Science of olfaction* (pp. 335–354). Berlin: Springer-Verlag.

Cotlier, E. (1981). The lens. In R. A. Moses (Eds.), *Adler's physiology of the eye.* St. Louis: C.V. Mosby.

Cranford, J. L., & Stream, R. W. (1991). Discrimination of short duration tones by elderly subjects. *Journal of Gerontology: Psychological Sciences, 46,* P37–P40.

Devaney, K. O., & Johnson, H. A. (1980). Neuron loss in the aging visual cortex in man. *Journal of Gerontology, 35,* 836–841.

Doty, R. L. (1989). Influence of age and age-related diseases on olfactory function. *Annals of the New York Academy of Science, 561,* 76–86.

Doty, R. L., Shaman, P., Applebaum, S. L., Giberson, R., Sikosorski, L., & Rosenberg, L. (1984). Smell identification ability: Changes with age. *Science, 226,* 1441–1443.

Edelhauser, H. E., VanHorn, D. L., & Records, R. E. (1979). Cornea and sclera. In R. E. Records (Eds.), *Physiology of the human eye and visual system* New York: Harper & Row.

Elliott, D., Whitaker, D., & MacVeigh, D. (1990). Neural contribution to spatiotemporal contrast sensitivity decline in healthy ageing eyes. *Vision Research, 30,* 541–547.

Engen, T. (1982). *The perception of odors.* New York: Academic Press.

Etholm, B., & Belal, A., Jr. (1974). Senile changes in the middle ear joints. *Annals of Otology, Rhinology, and Laryngology, 83,* 49–54.

Felson, D. T., Anderson, J. J., Hannan, M. T., Milton, R. C., Wilson, P. W., & Davis D. P. (1989). Impaired vision and hip fracture: The Framingham Study. *Journal of the American Geriatrics Society, 37,* 495–500.

Fisch, L. (1978). Special senses: The aging auditory system. In J. C. Brocklehurst (Eds.), *Textbook of geriatric medicine and gerontology* (p. 283). New York: Churchill Livingstone.

Fisher, R. F. (1969). Elastic constants of human lens capsule. *Journal of Physiology, 201,* 1–19.

Fozard, J. L., Wolf, E., Bell, B., McFarland, R. A., & Podolsky, S. (Ed.). (1977). *Visual perception and communicaton*. New York: Van Nostrand Reinhold.

Gatehouse, S. (1990). Determinants of self-reported disability in older subjects. *Ear and Hearing, 11 (Suppl.)*.

Grzegorczyk, P. B., Jones, S. W., & Mistretta, C. M. (1979). Age-related differences in salt taste acuity. *Journal of Gerontology, 34,* 834–840.

Hakkinen, L. (1984). Vision in the elderly and its use in the social environment. *Scandanavian Journal of Social Medicine, 35,* 5–60.

Hansen, C. C., & Reske-Nielson, E. (1965). Pathological studies in presbycusis. *Archives of Otolaryngology, 82,* 115–132.

Heller, K. S., & Wilber, L. A. (1990). Hearing loss, aging, and speech perception in reverberation and noise. *Journal of Speech and Hearing Research, 33,* 149–155.

Henderson, G., Tomlinson, B., & Gibson, P. H. (1980). Cell counts in human cerebral cortex in normal adults throughout life using an image analysing computer. *Journal of the Neurological Sciences, 46,* 113–136.

Hensel, H. (1981). *Thermoreception and temperature regulation*. New York: Academic Press.

Hofstetter, H. W., & Bertsch, J. D. (1976). Does stereopsis change with age? *American Journal of Optometry and Physiological Optics, 53,* 644–667.

Howell, T. H. (1949). Senile deterioration of the central nervous system: Clinical study. *British Medical Journal, 1,* 56–58.

Hu, M.-H., & Woollacott, M. H. (1994a). Multisensory training of standing balance in older adults: I. Postural stability and one-leg stance balance. *Journal of Gerontology: Medical Sciences, 49,* M52–61.

Hu, M.-H., & Woollacott, M. H. (1994b). Multisensory training of standing balance in older adutls. II. Kinetic and electromyographic postural responses. *Journal of Gerontology: Medical Sciences, 49,* M62–71.

Humes, L. E., & Christopherson, L. (1991). Speech identification difficulties of hearing-impaired elderly persons: The contributions of auditory processing deficits. *Journal of Speech and Hearing Research, 34,* 686–693.

Jerger, J., & Hayes, D. (1977). Diagnostic speech audiometry. *Archives of Otolaryngology, 103,* 216–222.

Kalayam, B., Alexopoulos, G. S., Merrell, H. B., & Young, R. C. (1991). Patterns of hearing loss and psychiatric morbidity in elderly patients attending a hearing clinic. *International Journal of Geriatric Psychiatry, 6,* 131–136.

Karlsen, E., Hassanein, R., & Goetzinger, C. (1981). The effects of age, sex, hearing loss and water temperature on caloric nystagmus. *Laryngoscope, 91,* 620–627.

Kenshalo, D. R. (1977). Age changes in touch, vibration, temperature, kinesthesis, and pain sensitivity. In J. E. Birren & K. W. Schaie (Eds.), *Handbook of the psychology of aging* New York: Van Nostrand Reinhold.

Kenshalo, D. R. (1979). Changes in the vestibular and somesthetic systems as a function of age. In J. M. Ordy & K. Brizzee (Eds.), *Aging: Vol. 10. Sensory systems and communication in the elderly* (pp. 269–282). New York: Raven Press.

Kline, D. W., & Schieber, F. J. (1982). Visual persistence and termporal resolution. In R. Sekuler, D. Kline, & K. Dismukes (Eds.), *Aging and human visual function.* New York: Alan R. Liss.

Kosnik, W., Winslow, L., Kline, D., Rasinski, K., & Sekuler, R. (1988). Visual changes in daily life throughout adulthood. *Journal of Gerontology: Psychological Sciences, 43,* P63–70.

Kuwabara, T. (1977). Age-related changes of the eye. In S. S. Han & D. H. Coons (Eds.), *Special senses in aging.* Ann Arbor, MI: Institute of Gerontology, University of Michigan.

Laidlaw, R. W., & Hamilton, M. A. (1937). A study of thresholds in apperception of passive movement among normal control subjects. *Bulletin of the Neurological Institute, 6,* 268–273.

Landahl, H. D., & Birren, J. E. (1959). Effects of age on the discrimination of lifted weights. *Journal of Gerontology, 14,* 48–55.

Larsson, M., & Bäckman, L. (1993). Semantic activation and episodic odor recognition in young and older adults. *Psychology and Aging, 8,* 582–588.

Lebo, C. P., & Reddell, R. C. (1972). The presbycusis component in occupational hearing loss. *Laryngoscope, 82,* 1399–1409.

Lindenberger, U., & Baltes, P. B. (1994). Sensory functioning and intelligence in old age: A strong connection. *Psychology and Aging, 9,* 339–355.

Lindenman, H. E., & Platenburg-Gits, F. A. (1991). Communicative skills of the very old in old people's homes. *Acta Otolaryngolica (Suppl. 476),* 232–238.

Loewenfeld, I. E. (1979). Pupillary changes related to age. In H. S. Thompson (Eds.), *Topics in neuro-opthalmology.* Baltimore: Williams & Wilkins.

Lord, S. R., Clark, R. D., & Webster, I. W. (1991). Postural stability and associated physiological factors in a population of aged persons. *Journal of Gerontology: Medical Sciences, 46,* M69–76.

Lutman, M. E. (1991). Hearing disability in the elderly. *Acta Otolaryngolica (Suppl. 476),* 239–248.

Manchester, D., Woollacott, M., Zederbauer-Hylton, N., & Marin, O. (1989). Visual, vestibular and somatosensory contributions to balance control in the older adult. *Journal of Gerontology: Medical Sciences, 44,* M118–127.

Mancil, G. L., & Owsley, C. (1988). "Vision through my aging eyes" revisited. *Journal of the American Optometric Association, 59,* 288–294.

Marmor, M. F. (1977). The eye and vision in the elderly. *Geriatrics, 32,* 63–67.

Marmor, M. F. (1980). Clinical physiology of the retina. In G. A. Reyman, D. R. Sanders, & M. F. Goldberg (Eds.), *Principles and practice of opthalmology* (pp. 823–856). Philadelphia: Saunders.

Marmor, M. F. (1982). Aging of the retina. In R. Sekuler, D. Kline, & K. Dismukes (Eds.), *Aging and human visual function.* New York: Alan R. Liss.

Marshall, L. (1991). Decision criteria for pure-tone detection used by two age groups of normal-hearing and hearing-impaired listeners. *Journal of Gerontology: Psychological Sciences, 46,* P67–70.

McCroskey, R. L., & Kasten, R. N. (1982). Temporal factors and the aging auditory system. *Ear and Hearing, 3,* 124–127.

McMurdo, M. E., & Gaskell, A. (1991). Dark adaptation and falls in the elderly. *Gerontology, 37,* 221–224.

Meeuwsen, H. J., Sawicki, T. M., & Stelmach, G. E. (1993). Improved foot position sense as a result of repetitions in older adults. *Journal of Gerontology: Psychological Sciences, 48,* P137–141.

Moore, L. M., Nielsen, C. R., & Mistretta, C. M. (1983). Sucrose taste thresholds: Age-related differences. *Journal of Gerontology, 37,* 64–69.

Morgan, M. W. (1988). VIsion through my aging eyes. *Journal of the American Optometric Association, 59,* 278–280.

Moses, R. A. (1981). Accommodation. In R. A. Moses (Eds.), *Adler's physiology of the eye.* St. Louis: C.V. Mosby.

Murphy, C. (1983). Age-related effects on the threshold, psychophysiological function, and pleasantness of menthol. *Journal of Gerontology, 38,* 217–222.

Murphy, C., & Gilmore, M. M. (1989). Quality-specific effects of aging on the human taste system. *Perception and Psychophysics, 45,* 121–8.

Naessen, R. (1971). An inquiry on the morphological characteristics of possible changes with age in the olfactory region of man. *Acta Otolaryngolica, 71,* 49–62.

National Highway and Traffic Safety Administration (1989). *Older drivers: The age factor in traffic safety (Report No. DOT HS 807 442).* Washington DC: U.S. Department of Transportation.

Neils, J., Newman, C. W., Hill, M., & Weiler, E. (1991). The effects of rate, sequencing, and memory on auditory processing in the elderly. *Journal of Gerontology: Psychological Sciences, 46,* P71–75.

Norris, M. L., & Cunningham, D. R. (1981). Social impact of hearing loss in the aged. *Journal of Gerontology, 36,* 727–729.

Ordy, J. M., Brizzee, K. R., & Johnson, H. A. (1982). Cellular alterations in visual pathways and the limbic system: Implications for vision and short-term memory. In R. Sekuler, D. Kline, & K. Dismukes (Eds.), *Aging and human visual function.* New York: Alan R. Liss.

Owsley, C., Ball, K., Sloane, M. E., Roenker, D. L., & Bruni, J. R. (1991). Visual/cognitive correlates of vehicle accidents in older drivers. *Psychology and Aging, 6,* 403–415.

Panek, P. E., Barrett, G. V., Sterns, H. L., & Alexander, R. A. (1977). A review of age changes in perceptual information ability with regard to driving. *Experimental Aging Research, 3,* 387–449.

Paterson, C. A. (1979). Crystalline lens. In R. E. Records (Eds.), *Physiology of the human eye and visual system.* New York: Harper & Row.

Pitts, D. G. (1982). The effects of aging on selected visual functions: Dark adaptation, vusal acuity stereopsis, and brightness contrast. In R. Sekuler, D. Kline, & K. Dismukes (Eds.), *Aging and human visual function.* New York: Alan R. Liss.

Plomp, R., & Mimpen, A. M. (1979). Speech reception threshold for sentences as a function of age and noise level. *Journal of the Acoustical Society of America, 66,* 1333–1342.

Powers, J. K., & Powers, E. A. (1978). Hearing problems of elderly persons: Social consequences and prevalence. *American Speech and Hearing Association, 20,* 79–83.

Punch, J., & McConnell, F. (1969). The speech discrimination function of elderly adults. *Journal of Auditory Research, 9,* 159–166.

Revoile, S. G., Pickett, J. M., & Kozma-Spytek, L. (1991). Spectral cues to perception of /d,n,l/ by normal- and impaired-hearing listeners. *Journal of the Acoustical Society of America, 90,* 787–798.

Richards, O. W. (1977). Effects of luminance and contrast on visual acuity ages 16 to 90 years. *American Journal of Optometry and Physiological Optics, 54,* 178–184.

Rosenhall, U. (1973). Degenerative patterns in the aging human vestibular sensory epithelia. *Acta Otolaryngolica, 76,* 208–220.

Ross, M. D., Johnsson, L. G., Peacor, D., & Allard, L. T. (1976). Observations on normal and degenerating human otoconia. *Annals of Otology, Rhinology, and Laryngology, 85,* 310–326.

Rudberg, M. A., Furner, S. E., Dunn, J. E., & Cassel, C. K. (1993). The relationship of visual and hearing impairments to disability: An analysis using the longitudinal study of aging. *Journal of Gerontology: Medical Sciences, 48,* M261–265.

Russell, M. J., Cummings, B. J., Profitt, B. F., Wysocki, C. J., Gilbert, A. N., & Cotman, C. W. (1993). Life span changes in the verbal categorization of odors. *Journal of Gerontology: Psychological Sciences, 48,* P49–53.

Scheie, H. G., & Albert, D. M. (1977). *Textbook of opthalmology* (9th ed.). Philadelphia: W. B. Saunders.

Schemper, T., Voss, S., & Cain, W. S. (1981). Odor identification in young and elderly persons: Sensory and cognitive limitations. *Journal of Gerontology, 36,* 446–452.

Schiffman, S. (1977). Food recognition by the elderly. *Journal of Gerontology, 32,* 586–592.

Schiffman, S. S., & Warwick, Z. S. (1989). Use of flavor-amplified foods to improve nutritional status in elderly patients. *Annals of the New York Academy of Sciences, 561,* 267–276.

Schow, R. L., Christensen, J. M., Hutchinson, J. M., & Nerbonne, M. A. (1978). *Communication disorders of the aged.* Baltimore: University Park Press.

Sekuler, R., & Owsley, C. (1982). The spatial vision of older humans. In R. Sekuler, D. Kline, & K. Dismukes (Eds.), *Aging and human visual function.* New York: Alan R. Liss.

Skinner, H. B., Barrack, R. L., & Cook, S. D. (1984). Age-related decline in proprioception. *Clinics in Orthopedics and Related Research, 184,* 208–211.

Slawinski, E. B., Hartel, D. M., & Kline, D. W. (1993). Self-reported hearing problems in daily life throughout adulthood. *Psychology and Aging, 8,* 552–562.

Stelmach, G. E., & Sirica, A. (1986). Age and proprioception. *Age, 9,* 99–103.

Stevens, J. C. (1989). Food quality reports from noninstitutionalized aged. *Annals of the New York Academy of Science, 561,* 87–93.

Stevens, J. C. (1992). Aging and spatial acuity of touch. *Journal of Gerontology, 47,* 35–40.

Stevens, J. C., & Cain, W. S. (1987). Old-age deficits in the sense of smell as gauged by thresholds, magnitude matching, and odor identification. *Psychology and Aging, 2,* 36–42.

Stevens, J. C., Cain, W. S., Demarque, A., & Ruthruff, A. M. (1991). On the discrimination of missing ingredients: Aging and salt flavor. *Appetite, 16,* 129–40.

Teasdale, N., Stelmach, G. E., & Breunig, A. (1991). Postural sway characteristics of the elderly under normal and altered visual and support surface conditions. *Journal of Gerontology: Biological Sciences, 46,* B238–244.

Thornbury, J. M., & Mistretta, C. M. (1981). Tactile sensitivity as a function of age. *Journal of Gerontology, 36,* 34–39.

Van-Rooij, J. C., & Plomp, R. (1990). Auditive and cognitive factors in speech perception by elderly listeners: II. Multivariate analyses. *Journal of the Acoustical Society of America, 88,* 2611–2624.

Van-Rooij, J. C., & Plomp, R. (1992). How much do working memory deficits contribute to age differences in discourse memory? Special Issue: Cognitive gerontology. *Journal of the Acoustical Society of America, 91,* 1028–1033.

Weale, R. A. (1963). *The aging eye.* London: H.K. Lewis.

Weale, R. A. (1975). Senile changes in visual acuity. *Transactions of the Opthalmological Societies of the United Kingdom, 95,* 36–38.

Weale, R. A. (1982). Senile ocular changes, cell death, and vision. In R. Sekuler, D. Kline, & K. Dismukes (Eds.), *Aging and human visual function.* New York: Alan R. Liss.

Weale, R. A. (1987). Senescent vision: Is it all the fault of the lens? *Eye, 1,* 217–221.

Weiffenbach, J. M., & Bartoshuk, L. M. (1992). Taste and smell. *Clinics in Geriatric Medicine, 8,* 543–55.

Werner, J. S., Peterzell, D. H., & Scheetz, A. J. (1990). Light, vision, and aging. *Optometry and Vision Science, 67,* 214–229.

Wolf, E. (1960). Glare and age. *Archives of Opthalmology, 64,* 502–514.

Wolf, E., & Gardiner, J. S. (1965). Studies on the scatter of light in the dioptric media of the eye as a basis of visual glare. *Archives of Opthalmology, 74,* 338–345.

Wysocki, C. J., & Gilbert, A. N. (1989). The National Geographic smell survey: Effects of age are heterogenous. *Annals of the New York Academy of Sciences, 561,* 12–28.

Young, R. W. (1976). Visual cells and the concept of renewal. *Investigative Ophthalmology, 15,* 700–725.

Zallen, E. M., Hooks, L. B., & O'Brien, K. (1990). Salt taste preferences and perceptions of elderly and young adults. *Journal of the American Dietary Association, 90,* 947–950.

8

Cognitive Processes

The mental processes involved in attention and memory have served as a major focus of gerontological research over the past five decades. Documentation of the effects of aging on speed of processing and ability to learn and remember new material was a topic of great concern to early researchers who were interested in finding out the nature and extent of deficits in laboratory tests of human performance. Apart from the basic information provided by this research on the aging process, such investigations have also led to suggestions of ways to maintain and improve the functioning of older individuals in their daily lives. As these investigations have moved into the 1990s, attention has shifted increasingly toward the correspondence between behavior and brain functioning, and toward the interaction of these changes with personality and other noncognitive influences on performance. Along with these shifts has been movement toward innovative measurement procedures that allow for inferences to be drawn regarding the mechanisms responsible for age differences in performance as well as more realistic assessments of age effects as they appear in the everyday life of the individual.

ATTENTIONAL AND CONTROL PROCESSES

The control processes involved in the analysis and preparation of responses are the focus of extensive research in the psychology of aging. As is so often the case in research on the psychology of aging, there are numerous practical and theoretical implications of this work. Practically speaking, it is of great social significance to determine how aging affects the ability of the individual to make decisions based on perceptual judgments and to act on these decisions reliably and efficiently. Whether workers can continue to perform their jobs in the later years of adulthood is a question that often hinges on such determinations, particularly in occupational areas that depend heavily on psychomotor skills. For example, gerontologists have been called into to consult with the federal government on developing standards for the performance of aging airline pilots. Insurance companies need to know if they must take special precautions in providing policies for older drivers. Work with heavy machinery often requires the ability to make rapid perceptual judgments and to adjust tools and equipment in quickly shifting cirumstances. The ubiquitous presence of computers in all areas of daily life places demands on nonmanual workers and most people in society to learn to process new information from multiple sources.

From a theoretical standpoint, as was noted in Chapter 6, there is also tremendous interest in central processes of attention and control. Measures of these functions provide a "window" into the brain, allowing researchers to make inferences about the underlying neural mechanisms that cause observed patterns of age effects in various measures of performance. Some of the earliest research in gerontology concerned reaction time measures, and although the measures and theoretical models today are obviously far more advanced, the underlying questions remain of vital importance.

Information Processing

Models thought to be responsible for the analysis and synthesis of information provide the basic framework for examining the effect of aging on attentional and control processes. These models represent theories of how the brain processes the vast quantitites of information it receives from all of the senses and how it uses this information to prepare a response. Testing procedures used to assess these functions with regard to aging typically involve preparing a set of stimuli organized in such a way that the individual's response provides an indication of how the information was organized and interpreted within the brain. The types of measures used in this research are, typically, the accuracy of an individual's response and the amount of time it took the individual to prepare the response.

Consider the following example of an information-processing procedure. The individual is presented with a set of pictures of common objects, letters, or words that are called "targets." In the past, these stimuli would be presented on cards or on a projection screen. In current aging laboratories, these stimuli are presented on the screen of a personal computer. The task of the respondent is to push a button or a key on the computer to indicate when a particular stimulus is found or recognized in a new stimulus array. For example, the letter "A" may be shown on the screen for a brief interval. Subsequent experimental trials may require that the subject indicate every time the "A" is presented within sets of four letters at a time shown on the screen. The stimuli in the array can be varied in ways that alter the cognitive demands placed on the subject. The experimenter infers that the time taken to respond by the subject is an indication of the amount of central processing needed to detect the letter's presence. In some conditions, the "A" may always be the second in a series of four letters; in other conditions, the "A" may appear in random locations within a set of letters. Apart from the amount of time needed to respond is the question of accuracy, or how often the respondent makes the correct response.

Researchers who investigate age differences in information processing attempt to find out which experimental conditions yield similar performance between older and younger adults, and to determine which manipulations have a differential effect on older compared to younger respondents. In the case of letter recognition, it is perhaps the case that older adults take considerably longer than their younger counterparts when attempting to identify letters that are in a consistent position on every trial compared to letters that vary randomly in position from trial to trial. If older adults are differentially affected by a change in stimulus conditions, this might indicate that their information processing is deficient in the necessary cognitive operations.

Reaction Time

Most studies on information processing in later adulthood take the form of the above-described "reaction time" study, in which the speed and accuracy of motor (manual) responses are the critical dependent variables of interest. The demands in these reaction time studies are more than idle abstractions; they have counterparts in the everyday life of the individual where stimulation from the environment demands a quick and accurate response. Sometimes these demands are relatively inconsequential, such as picking the correct button to push on the car radio. In other cases, more crucial outcomes rest on the quality of the individual's response, such as stopping on the brake to avoid hitting a pedestrian. The nature of the response also varies from simple to complex. Pushing the "off" button on the radio or hitting the brake pedal is a "yes-or-no" type of response task. More complex actions are involved in adjusting the swing of a tennis racquet to meet the oncoming ball or following a series of steps in using an automated teller machine. The range of responses involved in tasks that involve speed and accuracy is considerable, involving variation in dependence on speed, and demands for skill and judgment.

General findings. It is a well-established laboratory finding that, with increasing age in adulthood, individuals become slower and less accurate in their responses to laboratory tasks (Cerella, 1990; Fozard & Thomas, 1975; Salthouse, 1985). These results are documented in both cross-sectional and longitudinal investigations (Fozard, Vercruyssen, Reynolds, Hancock, & Quilter, 1994). Consistent with reports from the laboratory, social depictions of the elderly, particularly in the media, reinforce the notion of older adults as slow and inefficient when a rapid response is demanded of them. Although the slowing of reaction time is not a finding that engenders great controversy in the gerontological literature, there are a number of explanations that are worth considering. Before moving to these explanations, it is helpful to take a few moments to examine the basis for this general conclusion to discover whether there are mitigating factors involved in the presumed slowness of older people compared to their younger counterparts.

Individual differences. It is often claimed that variability increases with age, and with respect to reaction time, that claim appears to have particular meaning. There are large individual variations among older adults in response time, larger than those that exist for younger adults (Morse, 1993). One important variable that affects reaction time is fitness status. People who are in better physical condition in terms of their cardiovascular functioning have been found not to experience the same degree of change in reaction time as those whose physical fitness is poor (Chodzko-Zajko, 1991; Chodzko-Zajko, Schuler, Solomon, Heinl, & Ellis, 1992; Clarkson-Smith & Hartley, 1989; Milligan, Powell, Harley, & Furchtgott, 1984; Spirduso, 1980). Furthermore, aerobic exercise training aimed at increasing the individual's physical fitness has been found to increase the reaction-time performance of older adults (Dustman et al., 1990; Dustman, et al., 1984; Hawkins, Kramer, & Capaldi, 1992).

Age differences in reaction time also seem to depend on the nature of the required response. Although the idea that reduced muscular efficiency contributes to age losses in reaction time was dismissed some years ago as failing to account adequately for the effects of aging, there is some evidence that by requiring vocal rather than motor responses, age differences in reaction time can be reduced if not eliminated (Cerella & Fozard, 1984). This finding is consistent with what is known about the effects of aging on muscle fiber strength and number, and would suggest that aging does not reduce the quality of information processing at the cognitive level. However, it is unlikely that muscle losses could account entirely for the observed effects of aging on most reaction time tasks as measured in the laboratory.

Other interpretations of the effects of aging on reaction time involve possible differences between age groups in the motivation to perform in laboratory situations. It is possible that older adults are bored or disinterested in the artificial tasks that are prepared for them. Older adults who do not ordinarily spend time in academic settings may feel that the tasks being requested of them are too abstract and disconnected from everyday life to be worth the effort. Consequently, their performance does not accurately represent their abilities. The problem may be exacerbated in more recent reaction-time studies in which personal computers are used for stimulus presentation and the recording of responses. For current cohorts of older adults, particularly those who have not had the opportunity to use computers in business or in a home setting, such situations may be both intimidating and confusing. Although computers allow for optimal control of experimental procedures, they may leave something to be desired from the perspective of the typical older adult. Lacking computer experience, the older adult may have more difficulty performing tasks that require use of the computer, particularly when speed is required (Czaja & Sharit, 1993). If the researcher is aware of this possible confound, it is possible to overcome some of the older adult's skepticism regarding computers. Converting the stimulus situations to games such as those found in the video arcade may help to maintain the interest and motivation of the older research participant (Salthouse & Somberg, 1982).

At the opposite extreme of undermotivation and disinterest are the possible contributing effects of anxiety to reaction time performance in the older adult. Apart from finding the laboratory environment to be somewhat intimidating, the older individual may feel apprehensive about having his or her abilities put to the test in the presence of an experimenter who may be 20 or 30 years younger in age. When told to respond "as quickly as you can," the older adult may feel emotional pressure that a younger subject does not. Fears of appearing infirmed and "senile" may lead to intense overarousal, interfering considerably with the individual's ability to respond quickly and accurately (Coyne, Whitbourne, & Glenwick, 1978). Outside the laboratory, it has been found that even experienced miniature golf players, for example, perform more poorly when they are competing compared to when they are practicing. Older golfers experience dysfunctional levels of overarousal under conditions involving high stress; the performance of younger players improves or is not affected by anxiety (Molander & Bäckman, 1994).

Yet another interfering factor might be the reluctance of the older person to respond, a phenomenon referred to in the gerontological literature as cautiousness. It has long been suspected that older adults are more cautious about responding in laboratory tests of sensory abilities, reaction time, and memory. The cautiousness factor is a potential source of artificially inflated age differences in psychological functioning. It may be manifested in higher sensory thresholds, and apparently poorer memory performance. In terms of reaction time, cautiousness may be reflected by a pattern of responding in which the individual focuses on accuracy at the expense of speed. Although not consistently investigated in the gerontological literature, the problem of cautiousness has been cited by researchers dating back to some of the earliest laboratory investigations (Welford, 1958/1973), continuing through classic analyses of the effects of aging on speeded performance (Botwinick, 1978), and into contemporary investigations (Strayer & Kramer, 1994). There are as yet no definitive explanations of this phenomenon, but several possibilities may be speculated upon.

One explanation is that older people are more cautious in laboratory tasks but not in the real world. Returning to the discussion of nonperformance factors that may interfere with the production of speeded responses, it may be that older subjects feel anxious and intimated by the laboratory atmosphere. The experience of anxiety interferes with the older person's ability to focus on the task, and performance decrements follow as a result. Another possibility is that within the laboratory setting, older people feel as if their every move is being scrutinized (which it is) to look for the effects of aging. Knowing that the study is about the aging process might heighten their self-consciousness about being old and appearing mentally infirmed. To avoid making mistakes, then, the older person becomes more conservative and waits only until certain before responding. It is also possible that the cautiousness in the laboratory reflects response tendencies that have proven valuable in the older person's everyday life. To be more conservative or cautious often means that one avoids accidents while walking or driving, and that one is correct in various tasks such as filling out one's income tax forms or bank statements. It is also the case that cautiousness sometimes leads to problems of a different nature, but these are not generally as serious as actions that reflect a risky or poorly considered decision. Whether older people become more conservative (rigid) with age as a personality trait is also a matter of some debate (Schaie & Willis, 1991) but an alternative is that cautious people live longer than those who engage in high-risk behaviors. Therefore, the people who are still alive in their 70s and 80s may be a selective group within the population who have survived precisely because of their cautiousness.

A final consideration in evaluating the speeded performance of older persons pertains to the applicability of laboratory situations to the real world. Older people may in fact slow significantly when performance is measured by milliseconds, which is the measurement unit used in the laboratory. Depending on the nature of the experiment, significant differences between the response times of older and younger adults may be about 100 milliseconds. In the actual situations in which older people function, however, differences of this magnitude are unlikely to have serious consequences (Schaie, 1988). In support of this possibility, self-reported cognitive difficulties were found not to be related to laboratory reaction time performance in one recent study (Kane, Hasher, Stoltzfus, Zacks, & Connelly, 1994). Furthermore, older adults with expertise in a given area may find ways to compensate for response slowing through experience and training in areas ranging from handwriting to physical speed (Charness, 1989; Dixon, Kurzman, & Friesen, 1993; Spirduso & MacRae, 1990). For example, older typists may compensate for a slower speed of pressing the keys by earlier preparation for the response (Bosman, 1993). A lifetime of practice in arithmetic may also help the older adult compensate for slower encoding and production of numbers in mathematical problems (Geary, Frensch, & Wiley, 1993).

Returning from the real world to the laboratory, evidence that motivational and other experiential factors may play a role in influencing the laboratory task of older adults comes from training studies in which their performance is enhanced by skill enhancement and practice (Ball, Beard, Roenker, Miller, & Griggs, 1988; Baron & Mattilla, 1989; Dustman, Emmerson, Steinhaus, Shearer, & Dustman, 1992; Fisk & Rogers, 1991; Larish, Kramer, DeAntonna, & Strayer, 1993). It is not clear from such research whether the effects of training can be attributed to factors other than improved performance itself. However, it seems likely that the greater familiarity with the testing materials and situation involved in the training experiences generalizes beyond mere effects on reaction time.

Attention

Cognitive psychologists interested in the aging process have looked extensively for sources of increased slowness with age, and within the past decade, have attempted to link psychological models of performance declines with hypothetical causes in the aging of the nervous system. The study of attentional processes has generated a considerable amount of research, and according to some gerontologists, has the potential for linking cognitive, psychologically based models of the mind with findings from the field of neuroscience. Such a possibility is intriguing, and suggests that studies of aging can be of interest not only in their own right, but also for opening the "window" to the mind a little further.

Two underlying models have stimulated many of the research efforts in this area. The generalized resource model postulates that there is a reduction in the energy available for attentional processes due to reductions in central nervous system capacity. Age differences, according to this view, become more pronounced as the task becomes more complex and more demands are placed on the limited attentional resources of the older adult (Salthouse, 1985). The interference model proposes that older adults are more vulnerable to the interfering effects of competing stimuli. Furthermore, the deficient inhibitory processing may reflect an age-related decline in control processes that guide attentional search and screen irrelevant stimuli (Hasher & Zacks, 1988). Research demonstrating age effects on particular tasks has been used to investigate both of these models.

Selective attention tasks. Attention often involves the narrowing of focus down to one particular item or type of item. In everyday life, people constantly use selective attention, such as when turning out the sound of people talking in the room to hear what is being said on television. In visual terms, selective attention involves looking for one particular stimulus out of an array and responding when that stimulus is present. For example, you may be looking for a videotape of a particular movie to rent, and must scan an array of perhaps several hundred covers on the store rack before you find the one you want. In a visual search task such as that which is used in a laboratory study, the respondent is asked to perform a similar task, determining whether one or more members of a prespecified set of targets are present in the display. Just as it is easier to find that videotape when someone tells you that all the "New Releases" labels are "over there," it is easier to find a target in a visual search task when there is a cue regarding its possible location. In a cuing task, the respondent's attention is selectively allocated to information that is relevant to the search. You direct your attention to the New Releases section rather than the section containing Favorite Classics because it would be a waste of time to look anywhere other than the section with contemporary tapes.

The selective attention task in the laboratory can be made more difficult by adding to the number of distractors (items which must be chosen from). Clearly, it is more difficult to focus one's attention when there are 25 items to scan compared to 5. Returning to the videotape example, if the store has 40 new releases, it will take longer to find the right tape than if the store limits its new releases to 10. Of course, if the tapes are arranged in alphabetical order, the selection process becomes even more efficient. An example of a selective attention task used in an experiment by Madden, Connelly, and Pierce (1994) helps illustrate how this procedure works. Respondents were asked to push one of two response keys according to which one of two target letters (S and Y) was shown on a computer screen. The target letter was positioned at one of four sites around the screen. In a cued trial, a black diamond was presented near one of the four target positions, approximately 150 ms before the display of letters flashed on the screen. The experimenter varied the position of the cue, so that in some trials it was in the middle and in other trials it was at various distances away from where the target would be presented. Whenever the respondents saw an "S" or a "Y" in any of the positions, they were told to push a corresponding button on the keyboard (<alt> or <ctrl>). To add complexity to the task, distractors were added in another condition. Asterisks were displayed on the computer screen in positions not occupied by the target letter. The presence of these distractors increased the degree of selective attention required (returning to the example, it is as if random videotapes were thrown into the display of New Releases). Reaction time was measured based on correct responses, with separate analyses conducted for errors.

In this particular study, overall age differences in reaction time were observed, as expected. When given a miscue, however, younger and older respondents were equally able to shift their attention to the correct target location unless there were distractors (the asterisks) present. With the presence of distractors, it took the older people disproportionately longer than the young adults to locate the target when they had been prompted by an incorrect cue. By varying the cue's location and the number of distractors, then, the experimenters were able to show a differential effect on reaction time for the old compared to the young adults. Were the difference in reaction times between old and young the same regardless of condition, the researchers would not be able to make conclusions about age effects on specific processes. In this case, Madden and his colleagues were interested in examining visual search under conditions where the cue provided correct information, leading the respondent to focus attention on the cued part of the visual display. Performance on this task, requiring focused attention, was compared to performance on tasks where the attention of the respondent had to be broadened to include the noncued locations containing the target. The shift between the focused and the more gradient-like form of attention was found to be more difficult (take longer) for the older adults in the sample.

In general, the results of selective attention studies are in agreement that older adults are able to locate a visual target in a display, particularly when given a cue regarding the target's location (Hartley, 1993). The findings are also consistent with those of other researchers in showing greater difficulties for older adults as the number of distractors increases (Fisk & Rogers, 1991). In practical terms, these findings mean that older adults are more likely to be disadvantaged when there are stimuli in the environment competing for the individual's attention and the situation possesses uncertainty regarding where targets of interest may appear. A number of questions follow from this type of finding. What are the practical implications? Does this mean that older adults will have more difficulty when they must search a crowded grocery store shelf? Will they have more difficulty driving through a crowded city street, where there are multiple demands for their attention? What about the theoretical implications? It might appear that older adults are more readily distracted by the need to shift their attentional focus, suggesting they are more vulnerable to interference from competing stimuli. Perhaps the difficulty in attentional shift relates to an inability to move from one form of cognitive processing to another as the situational demands change. Another possibility is that older adults are less able to activate their attention to search the display for the target stimulus (Allen, Weber, & Madden, 1994).

Tasks involving interference. According to the interference hypothesis, increasing age brings with it a diminished ability to screen out irrelevant details, a greater tendency to make erroneous interpretations of presented stimuli, and heightened sensitivity to thoughts unrelated to the task at hand (Hasher & Zacks, 1988). The interference hypothesis would help to explain findings on selective attention, in that the intrusion of task irrelevant information could reduce the older adult's ability to focus attention onto the target during search.

Other evidence from a number of experimental paradigms supports the interference hypothesis (Kramer, Humphrey, Larish, Logan, & Strayer, 1994). A classic paradigm designed to test the individual's ability to inhibit irrelevant information is the Stroop color-word task (Stroop, 1935). The critical task in this procedure involves instructing the subject to read "color" words (such as red, green, blue) printed in ink that is different from the name of the color word. For example, the word "red" might be printed in green ink. In comparison trials, the word and its color are congruent. Accurate performance in the incongruent condition (green ink used to print "red") requires that the subject name the ink color (green) and disregard the meaning of the word (red). In terms of interference, processing the word meaning is irrelevant information that interferes with the correct response, and therefore the word itself must be inhibited. Older adults typically are slowed disproportionately when naming incongruent words compared to congruent words (Cohn, Dustman, & Bradford, 1984; Comalli, Wapner, & Werner, 1962; Hartley, 1993; Houx, Jolles, & Vreeling, 1993), suggesting that they are more vulnerable to the interference effects involved in this task.

The proposal that there is a diminution with age in the ability to inhibit the processing of distractor information has also received support from research using the negative priming paradigm in which stimuli that are distractors on one trial (and must be ignored) become targets on the next trial (Tipper, 1985). For example, pairs of letters might be presented in which one is red and one is green. The subject is told on the priming trial to identify letters in one of the colors (e.g. a green "A") and to ignore letters in the other color (e.g. a red "B").

On the critical trial, which would follow the prime trial, the "B" would appear as the target in green. The subject would be "negatively" primed because the previous trial had presented the letter "B" in the color that was supposed to be ignored. Typically, young adults take longer to respond when the target letter appears in a color that was supposed to be ignored on the negative priming trials. The fact that they demonstrate the negative priming effect indicates that they had inhibited processing the distractor item ("B") when it was the color red. Had they not inhibited their processing of the distractor item, then they would not take longer to respond to it when it was colored green (the target color). Evidence on the negative priming effect in older adults is mixed. In some studies, the elderly do not show this effect, suggesting that they failed to inhibit the processing of information from the distractor items (Hasher, Stoltzfus, Zacks, & Rypma, 1991; Kane et al., 1994; McDowd & Oseas-Kreger, 1991; Stoltzfus, Hasher, Zacks, Ulivi, & Goldstein, 1993; Tipper, 1991). However, the negative priming effect is observed in other studies involving older adults, suggesting that there are some inhibitory mechanisms that are unaffected by the aging process (Kramer et al. 1994; Sullivan & Faust, 1993; Tipper, Brehaut, & Driver, 1990). In particular, it has been suggested that age-related alterations in the frontal area of the cortex, which is involved in planning and integrating cognitive activities, may be responsible for the reduction with age in inhibitory functions (Hartley, 1993; Kramer et al., 1994). Such changes may also account for an inability to suppress interfering thoughts that produce, for example, verbose and "off-target" speech patterns in older adults (Arbuckle & Gold, 1993; Gold & Arbuckle, 1995).

Divided attention tasks. The divided attention task requires the respondent to perform two tasks at the same time. People experience divided attention situations many times in their daily routines. Watching television and trying to complete a course assignment at the same time is one example, as is talking on the phone and washing the dishes. The need to divide one's attention is less of a problem when the tasks require little effort than when each task is complex. It is not that difficult to do the dishes while on the telephone (at least with a cordless phone) but it can be nearly impossible for ordinary students to solve calculus problems while watching, or even listening, to the television.

It is not clear whether tasks involving divided attention demand that the individual literally "divides" attention between multiple tasks or whether the individual's attention simultaneously shifts between the two tasks while they are being performed. Nevertheless, it is still of interest to discover whether older adults are disproportionately affected by the requirement to complete two tasks at once. One set of divided attention tasks involves the procedure known as dichotic listening, in which the subject is presented with auditory information through headphones sending different messages to the two ears. The stimuli consist of pairs of digits, words, or letters—one sent to the left ear and one to the right. The subject is told to repeat the digits heard in one ear and then the other. Summarizing a large number of studies using this procedure, Hartley (1992) concluded that dichotic listening tasks show a clear and consistent age effect. Findings for other dual-attention tasks, however, are not as straightforward. When the tasks involve auditory detection, visual search, memory, motor skills, semantic processing, and problem-solving, the observed age effects vary widely in their magnitude. No clear interpretation regarding possible causes emerges to account for variations in age effects in dual-task studies. Although age differences appear to exist in tasks requiring the dividing of attention, no single underlying cause can be identified.

An attempt to provide clear explanations of the poorer performance of older adults on divided attention tasks is the widely cited study of Somberg and Salthouse (1982). In this experiment, respondents observed two overlapping rectangular matrices consisting of four items each. Different item types were placed in the two matrices, and each matrix contained a target that represented a small addition to one of the elements within the matrix. An important step was taken in this study to control for age differences in performance on either of the separate tasks by lengthening the exposure time for each matrix separately so that each subject was able to achieve almost perfect performance. Furthermore, the "cost" of the divided attention task was mapped under three separate conditions with differing emphasis given to one or the other matrix. Rather than just a 50–50 split of attention, performance was measured under conditions involving a 70–30 split and a 30–70 split. With these controls in place, no age differences were observed in performance on the divided attention task at any of the emphasis positions. Thus, at least in this study, divided attention effects disappeared when single-task attentional performance was equalized between age groups. Using this paradigm in subsequent studies with more complex tasks, however, Salthouse and others have found that the costs of the divided attention task were greater for older than for younger adults. Even when the researchers control for the performance of each of the two tasks alone, older adults suffered disproportionate slowing of reaction time when the two tasks are combined.

In interpreting these findings on divided attention, Hartley (1992) has suggested that aging affects the component processes involved in divided attention tasks rather than the process of dividing attention between the two tasks. In other words, older and younger adults are equally capable of allocating attention to two tasks. However, older adults suffer deficits in the performance of each task individually, and these deficits are what cause them to perform more poorly when they must complete two tasks at once.

Age differences on a divided attention task can be minimized, however, if the experiment involves extensive practice in fulfilling the dual task demands. As observed by Rogers and her colleagues in a study described in more detail to follow (Rogers, Bertus, & Gilbert, 1994), researchers who have provided large numbers of practice trials (ranging from about 500 to 11,000+) have observed an absence of age-related differences in dual task performance. Conversely, those studies in which age differences were reported in divided attention involved far fewer trials (ranging from 50 to less than 300). It is possible, then, that older adults can learn to perform divided attention tasks as long as they are given ample opportunities to master the task requirements.

Automatic process development. Information processing becomes much more efficient and accurate with practice, as the individual learns where and when to expect a stimulus to appear. The development of automatic processes involves the learning, over time, of how to respond to expectable stimuli in the environment (Hasher & Zacks, 1979; Schneider & Shiffrin, 1977). For example, after learning how to play a musical instrument, the performer gives virtually no attention to where the fingers must go in order to play the desired notes. A well-trained athlete does not give any thought to the question of how to hold the ball, bat, or golf club. Automatic tasks are also highly predictable. The letter "Q" on the keyboard is always in the same place, so the skilled typist's fifth finger of the left hand can go to it automatically without needing to look at the keyboard. After an automatic process has developed through repetition and practice, the individual is free to devote attention to other components of a task that place a heavier burden on cognitive resources. When placement of the fingers on the notes of the musical instrument becomes an automatic process, the musician is able to concentrate on other aspects of playing, such as rhythm, tone, and dynamics. Similarly, the development of automaticity in other areas allows individuals to devote their attention to the performance of more complex aspects of a task that involve judgment, analysis, and synthesis.

In everyday life, older adults may be seen as likely to have developed a wide range of automatic tasks. Within selected areas of expertise, the added years of experience that older adults have might give them an edge over younger novices who have only recently begun to tackle a given skill. The 75-year-old golfer who has spent more than 50 years practicing his putting should have many basic elements of the task more than sufficiently mastered.

Research on age differences in automatic process development involves manipulating the characteristics of new tasks to see if older adults are as adept as young adults at achieving a high level of proficiency through repeated practice. The types of tasks involve visual search with "mapping" conditions that vary in the extent to which they facilitate automatic process development. A microcomputer is used for presentation of the stimulus and recording of responses. In the consistent mapping (CM) condition, subjects are told to respond by pushing a particular key on the keyboard whenever they see a target letter that is drawn from one set of letters and to push another key when the target is absent. Another, nonoverlapping, set of letters form the distractors. Each trial consists of presentation on the computer screen of one of the target letters, followed by presentation of another display which either contains the target letter among a set of distractors or does not contain the target letter. For example, the screen may show the target letter "S," and then show the letter "S" among the letters "R, J, M, L, Q, Z." Over trials, the subject "learns" which letters constitute the target set and which constitute the distractor set, and the search at each new trial becomes automatic. In the varied mapping (VM) condition, by constrast, the target and distractor letters are drawn from the same pool of letters. Now the task is more difficult, because a particular item may serve as a target on one trial, but a distractor on another trial. The letter "Q" might be a target in Trial 52, but as a distractor on Trial 53.

The search paradigm can be modified further by requiring that the search be based on memory (memory search) or on visual scanning of the display (visual search). In the memory search condition, the target letter is presented at the center of the screen, and is then shown again at the center of the screen, surrounded by a set of "placeholders" (squares the size of letters). The subject must remember whether the letter shown on the test screen was presented as the target or not. In the visual search condition, the target letter is presented at the center of the screen, but in the subsequent test screen, the subject must look for the target among a set of distractors.

A number of investigators have used the search paradigm to determine whether older adults are similar to younger subjects in the development of automatic search processes. It appears that automatic search processes can develop in the older person, but only if certain conditions are met (Rogers et al., 1994). First, older adults need more practice in the CM condition before recognition of the target letters becomes automatic. Second, the attainment of automatic processing is more likely to occur when the task involves the memory search component (Fisk & Rogers, 1991; Salthouse & Somberg, 1982). If the task involves primarily visual search, older adults do not develop automatic processing; that is, their search processes do not become fast and accurate (Fisk, Hertzog, Lee, Rogers, & Anderson-Garlach, 1994; Fisk, McGee, & Giambra, 1988; Fisk & Rogers, 1991; Rogers & Fisk, 1991).

One possible cause of an age-related deficit in automatic process development is the failure of older adults to develop an automatic response to a stimulus that attracts attention. In such a situation, attention is not needed to process the stimulus, but once the stimulus is presented, attention turns toward it. An example of such a situation occurs when someone's name is called and the individual's attention is immediately drawn toward the speaker. This type of response is called an automatic attention response—in other words, a stimulus that is specific and well-trained can automatically capture one's attention. The development of an automatic attention response was investigated by Rogers, Bertus, and Gilbert (1994) in a dual-task experiment. Conditions involving CM and VM were presented to young adult and elderly subjects in divided attention situations so that, for example, subjects had to complete a visual and memory search at the same time. Consistent with previous research in the CM condition, older adults did not achieve automaticity by the end of the practice trials. The design of the study allowed the investigators to go one step further and suggest a possible cause of the age deficit in automaticity. Based on performance in the dual-task condition, it appeared that the older adults had difficulty developing an automatic attention response. In other words, they scanned each display in looking for the target rather than responding only when the target appeared. The counterpart of this situation in everyday life would be as if while walking through a busy street, one looked at every person to see if that person is an acquaintance rather than waiting for a familiar face to appear among the crowd. Automaticity is not achieved in the search process because the older adult examines each new stimulus situation as it is presented rather than using a set of decision rules or consistent way of responding.

Implications

There is still much to be learned about attentional processes in older adults. Researchers have yet to determine the precise nature and extent of attentional deficits, much less their origins. All that can be stated is that older adults are somewhat slower at laboratory tasks, particularly those that demand the inhibiting of irrelevant information. Such a deficit may contribute to the difficulty that older adults have in laboratory tasks involving the learning of an automatic attention response. In practical terms, it is difficult to know how severely these age differences affect everyday performance in tasks that place demand on the individual's attentional capacities. Even if these effects are minor on attentional tasks per se, it is possible that age effects on attentional capacities play a role in affecting the individual's ability to learn and remember. As we look next at age effects on memory, the findings on attentional processing should be kept in mind. Explanations involving interference, limited resources, and possible associations with neuroscience will again arise, as will consideration of individual differences and the role of experience.

MEMORY

The ability to remember the names of people and places, dates, events, facts, and the skills and knowledge acquired over a lifetime of work, family, and recreational activities is basic to the individual's intellectual and social functioning. Personal identity, as well, is dependent on having a sense of the self over time, a process related to the ability to remember one's experiences over the past minutes, days, hours, and years of life. Partly for these reasons, and partly due to the inconvenience created, it becomes frustrating when one's memory lapses or fails. Given that individuals rely so heavily on memory in virtually all interactions with the environment, it is important to understand the effects of aging on this fundamental psychological process.

The conceptualization of memory by experimental psychologists forms the basis for studies of the effects of aging on memory. As theories about the nature of memory have changed over the past few decades, so have descriptions of the effects of aging. Cognitive aging researchers examine their findings from a new perspective when these theories are revised. With the move toward a cognitive neuroscience perspective in the memory field, researchers who study aging are increasingly arriving at explanations of aging phenomena that are compatible with knowledge and theories regarding the effects of aging on the nervous system. This shift has meant that purely descriptive approaches, in which the magnitude of age effects are reported on various types of tasks, have been replaced by theory-driven research. As is true regarding the study of aging and attention, the cognitive neuroscience perspective in memory research has the potential to unlock some of the secrets to the question of how aging affects mind and brain.

Current approaches to studying memory in the aged have also incorporated an emphasis on understanding how memory loss is subjectively experienced by the individual. Studies on "metamemory," or knowledge about memory processes, give researchers an understanding of how people perceive the changes in their cognitive abilities. Ultimately, these metamemory studies have the potential to link cognitive changes associated with the aging process to individual differences in identity, personality, and lifestyle.

Models of Memory Functioning in Later Adulthood

Virtually every cross-sectional study comparing younger and older adults on measures of memory reveals significant age differences. Although the extent of age differences may vary somewhat, and in some cases be almost eliminated under certain experimental conditions, the general age effect on laboratory memory tasks is fairly well established. Corresponding to findings of laboratory studies are the subjective experiences of many older adults, who are likely to believe that their memory is undergoing deterioration as they age.

Researchers working in the area of memory aging attempt to explain the observed patterns of age differences according to theoretical information-processing models. The debate over models of memory functioning in later life has taken on various forms in the relatively short but productive history of research in this area. Currently, alternative models may be seen as contrasting a "hardware" vs. "software" explanation of aging memory loss. In the "hardware" explanation, age differences are linked to declines in cognitive resources beyond the individual's control. "Software" models look for age effects on memory strategies that may lie within the realm of personal control and modification. At present, the data cannot rule out either explanation, and all that can be said is that each or both may hold validity.

Processing resource hypothesis. Consistent with the view that aging brings with it a slowing of information processing and a deficiency in attentional resources is the hypothesis that memory deficits in later life are the result of deleterious effects of aging on the central nervous system that limit cognitive resources (Hartley, 1993). Presumably, these aging effects target the individual's "working memory," which is the component of memory involved in holding information while that information is being processed. Working memory is used when you are trying to remember a telephone number left in a message on an answering machine while you search for a pad and pencil to write it down. Information in working memory is either processed further and entered into long-term memory or is disposed of when it is no longer needed. Rehearsal, or repeating the information over and over again, is what keeps the information "alive." To transfer information to long-term memory requires that the individual encode it in such a way that it can be retrieved later.

A reduction with age of speed or capacity of working memory would, according to the processing resource hypothesis of memory aging, severely limit the individual's ability to engage in cognitive operations needed to keep information available in working memory (Salthouse, 1985; 1996; Salthouse & Coon,

1993). These reductions, furthermore, would limit the quality of encoding that the individual engages in to transfer the information to long-term storage. Retrieval from long-term memory would similarly be affected, due to its necessary relationship to encoding as well as any other possible independent effects of aging on retrieval processes themselves.

The processing resource hypothesis is based on the premise that the limitation placed by the aging process on the individual's memory is inevitable and irreversible. To the extent that declines in processing capacity and speed are based on neurological changes, the individual's memory will be reduced. Although the individual may engage in activities that maintain the integrity of the nervous system (as discussed in Chapter 6), the fate of one's memory is inextricably linked to the fate of one's brain, according to this hypothesis.

Production deficiency hypothesis. The underlying assumption of the production deficiency hypothesis is based on a very different characterization of the aging memory system. According to this model, memory is deficient in the aged because they are not aware of the strategies they could use that could potentially benefit their encoding and retrieval of information. By being taught to use certain memory strategies, it follows that older people can improve their performance on tasks so that age differences are greatly reduced if not eliminated. A variant of this model is that there is a trade-off in any given memory task between speed (or availability of cognitive resources) and availability of semantic knowledge or experience with memory strategies. The more a task is dependent on speed, the greater will be the age deficit in memory, and the more the task relies upon strategy, the smaller the age differences between older and younger adults (Salthouse, 1993). In some ways, this hypothesis can be likened to the situation involving an aged but experienced tennis player. When competing with a young person, the older player may lack some of the strength and skill demanded by the game. However, the older person can outplay the younger by taking advantage of years of experience in placing the ball in inconvenient spots that even the opponent's speed does not help to reach in time.

The implications of the production deficiency hypothesis are appealing to problem-focused copers who are worried about their own memory loss as they grow older. If poor memory can be compensated by knowing the right strategies to use, then it is possible to overcome the deleterious effects of aging by figuring out what those strategies are and then applying them. Perhaps because of its greater optimism than the processing hypothesis, the production deficiency hypothesis has achieved popularity among cognitive gerontologists.

Empirical Findings

As indicated above, there is a large and comprehensive literature in the field of gerontology consisting of cross-sectional comparisons of young and older adults. Prior to the early 1970s, most memory researchers administered materials that contained nonsense syllables or simple word tasks, basing their designs on paradigms commonly used by researchers in the field of experimental psychology. For example, a "paired-associate" task would be given in which subjects were presented with a list of word pairs, followed by presentation of one set of words alone. The subject's task was to remember the word that each had originally been paired with. This simple paradigm allowed the researcher to manipulate a number of conditions theoretically expected to influence the performance of subjects. One type of experimental condition involved recall, requiring that the subject generate the words that had originally been shown. In the other experimental condition, the subject had only to recognize the word from a choice of similar words. Other manipulations involved the type of words (familiar vs. nonsense), length of the word list, rate of presentation, and availability of cues. Recall of a single word list was another experimental paradigm, involving presentation of one set of words followed by the requirement to recall or recognize the words. Experimental manipulations included the provision of cues, potential organization of the words into clusters or categories, length of the list, and variations in types of words presented.

With the development of information processing models of memory in the early 1970s, memory aging researchers began to adapt their methods and interpretations so that they could provide data on possible mechanisms responsible for memory decline. A generally accepted model for memory that influenced memory aging researchers involved a proposed set of stages based on length of time that an item was in memory (sensory memory, short-term memory, and long-term memory). The processes of interest were those of encoding, storage, and retrieval. The comparison of recall with recognition performance, for example, was used to help shed light on whether encoding or retrieval processes were relatively more affected by the aging process. Since recognition does not involve retrieval, higher performance of older adults on recognition tasks would imply that the retrieval process was not affected by aging. In other studies, researchers arranged the task to guarantee that the material was encoded into long-term memory. If this manipulation wiped out age differences in performance, it could be inferred that age effects on the encoding process were primarily responsible for age differences on other memory tasks. Other manipulations on single-word tasks involved the nature of the words and whether there was an inherent organization possible with them, and whether the provision of retrieval cues improved the performance of the older group (Smith, 1980).

Increasingly, in the 1970s and particularly into the 1990s, memory aging researchers have moved to experiments involving prose materials and situations that would approximate the memory performance of the elderly outside the laboratory. Research designs have also become oriented toward alternative models of memory aging that pertain to deficits in processing or production of strategies. A great deal of interest in recent research has been aroused by the concept of "metamemory," the individual's knowledge about memory and memory strategies. These shifts in focus have been accompanied by increasing efforts from the cognitive neuroscience perspective to link evidence on memory with knowledge about the aging brain.

Working memory. The efficiency of cognitive processing within working memory influences the quality of the information that ultimately is processed into long-term memory. If information is lost while it is in working memory, less information will be consolidated into long-term memory. Speed also plays a role, as the slower the rate of cognitive operations, the more likely it is that information will deteriorate before it can be fully processed. There is a solid body of evidence available suggesting that older adults require more time to complete the cognitive operations in tests of working memory, and are also less accurate in their recall of even short lists of digits (Verhaeghen, Marcoen, & Goossens, 1993). With this documented age effect on working memory, it is reasonable to conclude that older adults are less able to keep new memories alive so that they are lost before the information they contain is either used or stored more permanently.

Episodic memory. Each time you attempt to remember an event that you directly experienced or were told about, you are relying on episodic memory. Most laboratory tests of memory involve episodic memory, as they require the individual to remember information that is presented within the time and setting of the experiment. For example, you are familiar with tens of thousands of words, and all possible numbers. In a laboratory test of memory, you are not asked to remember every word or number you have ever encountered, but only those words and numbers that are presented during the time of the experiment. In this sense, the "episode" is the event within the laboratory. Other tests of episodic memory involve the ability to recall information from events personally experienced, such as what happened on the night of one's senior prom in high school or the contents of one's meal the night before.

As is true for working memory, older adults are found in study after study to perform more poorly on tests of episodic memory (Denney & Larsen, 1994; Verhaeghen & Marcoen, 1993). In one particularly impressive report, results from 122 cross-sectional studies on episodic memory involving almost 12,000 subjects were re-analyzed, leading to estimates of significant age differences on virtually every measure investigated (Verhaeghen et al., 1993). The estimate of the magnitude of age effects was substantial, with age reportedly accounting for 83% of the variance in performance (Verhaeghen & Marcoen, 1993).

It is important to note that the observation of significant age differences in episodic memory applies to not only to abstract or meaningless materials, but also to memory for prose passages, text, stories, and sentences (Drevenstedt & Bellezza, 1993; Giambra & Arenberg, 1993; Hartley, 1993; Hartley, Stojack, Mushaney, Kiku Annon, & Lee, 1994; Tomer, Larrabee, & Crook, 1994; Verhaeghen et al., 1993; Zabrucky & Moore, 1994). Furthermore, the age effect is not limited to cross-sectional studies, but applies also to data derived from longitudinal investigations (Zelinski, Gilewski, & Schaie, 1993).

Another feature of episodic memory is, perhaps paradoxically, memory for the future. In this area of memory functioning, known as prospective memory, the task is like a mental "to do" list. Remembering to feed the cat, take out the garbage, stop by the store for milk, and take an umbrella when leaving home on a cloudy morning, are all examples of prospective memory. Like memory for past events, prospective memory shows patterns of age differences in adulthood, although these are typically less severe than declines in retrospective memory (Mantyla, 1994; Maylor, 1993).

Age deficits in episodic memory are not limited to verbal materials. The elderly are also relatively disadvantaged at spatial memory, or the ability to remember places and locations (Arbuckle, Cooney, Milne, & Melchior, 1994; Uttl & Graf, 1993). Their memory for visual "scenes" also is poorer compared to young adults (Hess, Flannagan, & Tate, 1993). These findings have led researchers to postulate that older adults are less able than young adults to incorporate contextual information into their memories for places and events (Cherry & Park, 1993). As indicated by lower recall of "flashbulb" memories, older adults have difficulty remembering the details surrounding a unique and salient event (Cohen, Conway, & Maylor, 1994). There is also a decrease in the ability to remember the source of information, or the recall of "who" said "what" in a conversation (Schacter, Osowiecki, Kaszniak, Kihlstrom, & Valdiserri, 1994). Again, information regarding context seems to be less accessible to older adults.

Loss of the ability to make connections or associations between pieces of information to be learned or between an event and its context may play an important role in the general memory deficits shown by older adults in laboratory tasks (Light, 1992). It has been suggested that a loss of associational capacity is related to an age-related decrement in frontal-lobe processing

(Spencer & Raz, 1994). However, older adults are able to take advantage of the structure of material that fits into a logical organization. When material is organized in a schematic way, older adults are better able to remember scenes, events, and simple noun-verb phrases (Hess, et al., 1993; Hess & Slaughter, 1990; Hess & Tate, 1992).

In contrast to the well-established decrements in episodic memory, age seems to spare the functions involved in semantic memory, one's repository of gained factual knowledge over a lifetime through education and experience. Older adults show no decrements in the ability to remember word meanings or general information regarding such areas as history, geography, and other specific facts. The organizational structure and factual content of information is maintained intact in the healthy individual, and the elderly are able to remember knowledge that is useful in many everyday activities. For this reason, you would be well-advised to find an older person on your next "Trivial Pursuit" team. Unfortunately, what may become impaired is the access the older individual has to retrieve stored lexical information, particularly in terms of speed (Bowles, 1994). Nevertheless, the material itself seems to be well maintained in memory storage (Light, 1992). The ability to use language, which depends in part on semantic memory, is regarded as one of the more stable cognitive functions in normal aging (Wingfield, Wayland, & Stine, 1992).

Metamemory. The original application of the concept of metamemory to understanding memory in the aged was based on the production deficiency hypothesis that perhaps older persons have poor memories because they do not know how to marshal their resources effectively when they are given a memory task. Based on this hypothesis, researchers began developing ways to test metamemory in the laboratory. One approach to measuring metamemory involves asking older people to predict their own performance on a memory task. Knowledge about memory strategies, and how hard it may be to remember new information is another component of metamemory. Self-monitoring of one's memory processes during memory testing comprises another important component. Increasingly, researchers have also focused on social-cognitive aspects of metamemory, including older people's feelings of confidence about their memory, also known as memory self-efficacy. Self-reported memory complaints also provide useful information regarding the older person's perceived memory functioning.

Based on the finding of lower memory performance among the elderly, it might be expected that older adults would scale downward their predictions about how well they will do on a particular task when asked for a pre-performance estimate. In fact, older adults report that their memory processing is not as efficient as do younger adults (Hultsch, Hertzog, & Dixon, 1987; Loewen, Shaw, & Craik, 1990). However, when it comes to making specific predictions about their performance on a given task, they often overestimate their abilities. For example, in one study, researchers investigated memory for the details present on common objects; specifically, a penny and a telephone dial (try doing this yourself and see how well you can predict your performance). In comparing young and older adults on this task, Foos (1989) found that older adults were more often incorrect than their younger counterparts. In part, the age difference was due to a somewhat overconfident tendency on the part of older adults, who assumed their memory was accurate and as a result, made incautious responses. Unrealistic predictions about performance in the elderly also appear on standard laboratory tasks, such as recall of words in a list (Dobbs & Rule, 1987). These instances seem to provide good examples of identity assimilation—the older person is unwilling to acknowledge the possible crossing of an aging threshold.

Another related process also appears to show age differences. When asked to modify their predictions about future performance based on feedback from previous performance, older adults are less able to take into account specific features of the task (Bieman-Copland & Charness, 1994). Personality or social-cognitive processes may also affect the nature of the individual's memory predictions (Cavanaugh & Murphy, 1986; Dixon & Hultsch, 1983). Individuals who are depressed and have low self-esteem may be more likely to underestimate their abilities (Scogin, 1985) and, conversely, those who view themselves in a more favorable light may be more lenient in evaluating their memories (Rabbitt & Abson, 1990). Along these lines, the particular component of metamemory that involves self-efficacy judgments seems to play an important role in affecting both memory self-perceptions and memory performance (Cavanaugh, 1989; Hertzog, Dixon, Schulenberg, & Hultsch, 1987; Hertzog, Dixon & Hultsch, 1990; Ryan & See, 1993). Indeed, for some older adults self-assessed memory may be affected more by their "implicit theory" of how aging affects memory than by their actual memory performance or memory changes over time (McDonald-Miszczak, Hertzog, & Hultsch, 1995). These findings suggest, again, the role of identity assimilation and accommodation in relation to memory aging as well as interactions with coping.

Locus of control may be another important contributor to memory performance (Dixon & Hultsch, 1983). In one study, higher performance on memory tasks was associated with the belief that the quality of one's memory is determined by internal, stable, and global causes (Lachman, Steinberg, & Trotter, 1987). In other words, all other things being equal, people who believe that they are in control of their memory abilities may be more likely to perform well on laboratory tests of memory.

Evaluation of Memory Research

From the literature documenting age effects in various measures of working memory and episodic memory, it appears clear that there are well-established losses suffered by older individuals. At least some of this deficit can be accounted for by diminished speed of cognitive processes and diminished effectiveness of encoding and perhaps retrieval as well. However, tempering this conclusion are findings regarding the everyday experience of older adults. The tendency to acknowledge memory problems seems to vary by the individual's approach to memory tasks which, in turn, may vary by identity-related personality variables such as locus of control, self-efficacy, and mood. Sensory problems and health are other mitigating factors (Cutler & Grams, 1988), as is activity level. Maintenance of an active lifestyle was found in one investigation to explain approximately one-half the variance in memory scores (Hultsch, Hammer, & Small, 1993). High levels of fluid intelligence (see Chapter 9) are also predictive of good memory performance (Zelinski et al., 1993), a finding consistent with the proposal that the ability to form novel associations is considered an important aspect of memory functioning (Light, 1992).

Another factor to consider in evaluating the findings of memory research is the extent to which the results of laboratory studies are generalizable to everyday life. As was true for reaction time studies, it is possible that the scores of older adults are significantly poorer than the scores of young adults, but in the real world these differences are not of obvious importance. In one investigation, less than a quarter of people over the age of 85 felt that they suffered from memory loss (Cutler & Grams, 1988). Although elderly persons are perhaps quick to acknowledge that memory loss is a threshold phenomenon of old age, they do not feel that their lives are personally affected by this loss. Furthermore, elderly persons are more forgiving than younger adults in judging the seriousness of memory problems experienced by an older individual (Erber, 1989; Erber, Szuchman, & Rothberg, 1990). Even those older persons who acknowledge that they have suffered memory loss may not feel particularly disadvantaged in performing their everyday tasks (Sunderland, Watts, Baddeley, & Harris, 1986). They may be able to find problem-focused coping strategies to compensate for memory problems through their greater knowledge base (Salthouse & Coon, 1993).

Memory Training Studies

Some of the strongest support for the production deficiency hypothesis of memory functioning comes from results of research in which older adults are given training specifically intended to focus on deficient memory strategies. If aging effects on memory can be reversed through these methods, it seems logical to conclude that the "hardware" remains intact, and only the "software" needs to be updated. Memory training studies have had encouraging results. Even mere practice or familiarity with testing materials can lead to enhanced memory performance. As observed by Lachman and colleagues (1992), "The fact that a minimum of practice, in the absense of any instruction, led to significant improvement suggests that decrements in memory performance are due, in part, to disuse" (p. P298).

A number of investigators have now established that procedures in which older adults are taught to form images or associations, organize, and mnemonic techniques (such as the "method of loci") can result in improved memory performance (Anschutz, Camp, Markley, & Kramer, 1985; Kleigl, Smith, & Baltes, 1989; Scogin, 1985; Yesavage, Rose, & Bower, 1983; Zarit, Cole, & Guider, 1981). The benefits of training appear to persist over time. Follow-up studies conducted 3 or more years following the completion of training have shown that older adults showed enhanced performance compared to controls (Neely & Backman, 1993).

However, the benefits of training have not been universally demonstrated. In one investigation, respondents were trained in using the method of loci as a way to remember grocery lists. Three years later, the respondents remembered the method of loci technique, but did not use it to enhance their recall of new grocery list items (Anschutz, Camp, Markley, & Kramer, 1987). Similarly, in another investigation, older individuals reported low rates of using the mnemonic techniques that they had been taught in training sessions (Scogin & Bienias, 1988). Even more discouraging is evidence that although training can produce gains in memory performance, the level of improvement in the performance of older adults does not measure up to that seen in younger adults, even with very extensive practice (Baltes & Kliegl, 1992). Consequently, memory researchers do not advocate the use of formal training in mnemonics to help older adults improve their memory functioning (Park, Smith, & Cavanaugh, 1990). Instead, based on evidence that self-guided practice can enhance cognitive performance at least as much as can training in specific strategies (Kotler-Cope & Camp, 1990; Willis, 1990), it seems more effective to help older individuals devise their own memory enhancement strategies. Self-generated strategies are more likely to reflect the individual's own idiosyncratic approaches to improving memory and can also enhance the older adult's feelings of efficacy and mastery (Cavanaugh & Green, 1990).

It has also been found that for memory training to be effective in enhancing the memory abilities of older adults, the training must be fairly specific to the task (Neely & Backman, 1995). Furthermore, it is not enough to teach older individuals new memory techniques. They must also be given some incentive to use these methods on a daily basis so that memory gains can be maintained over time. Feedback regarding the positive effects of training might provide this incentive. A third factor that may be related to memory enhancement through training is the individual's willingness to explore and try out new techniques. In one fascinating study, researchers observed a greater likelihood of using imagery as a memory enhancement tool among individuals high in the personality trait of openness to experience (Gratzinger, Sheikh, Friedman, & Yesavage, 1990). This finding suggests that specific memory techniques may be adopted more readily if they are consistent with the individual's learning or cognitive style. Those who are willing to explore the use of imagery may benefit from this type of training, while individuals who are more conservative or traditional in their approach might benefit more from straight didactic or rote techniques. In addition to the interaction of memory with identity, then, may be the interaction of cognitive functioning with a broader personality disposition or style.

More evidence for links between cognition and personality comes from research examining memory enhancement strategies in older adults. In research by Lachman and co-workers, the most improvement in memory performance was shown when older adults were given the opportunity to develop their own memory strategies along with "cognitive restructuring" of their beliefs about the effects of aging on memory (Lachman et al., 1992). Although memory performance was equivalent across training conditions, those who were exposed to cognitive restructuring were able to see themselves as having the potential for improvement. Memory control beliefs are in many ways comparable to the processes of coping and identity. Those people who believe that their memory is destined to decline as they grow older can be seen as using accommodation and emotion-focused coping; conversely, those who maintain that they can control the functioning of their memory through effort may be seen as using problem-focused coping. To the extent that problem-focused copers deny the existence of age effects on memory, they may be seen as using identity assimilation. Such individuals may run the risk of suffering frustration and disappointment should they encounter memory deficits that cannot be compensated or ignored. However, in general, the belief in controllability of one's memory appears to have advantages, promoting the "use it or lose it" strategy effective in so many areas of functioning in later adulthood.

REFERENCES

Allen, P. A., Weber, T. A., & Madden, D. J. (1994). Adult age differences in attention: Filtering or selection? *Journal of Gerontology: Psychological Sciences, 49*, P213–222.

Anschutz, L., Camp, C. J., Markley, R. P., & Kramer, J. J. (1985). Maintenance and generalization of mnemonics for grocery shopping by older adults. *Experimental Aging Research, 11,* 157–160.

Anschutz, L., Camp, C. J., Markley, R. P., & Kramer, J. J. (1987). Remembering mnemonics: A three-year follow-up on the effects of mnemonics training in elderly adults. *Experimental Aging Research, 13,* 141–143.

Arbuckle, T. Y., Cooney, R., Milne, J., & Melchior, A. (1994). Memory for spatial layouts in relation to age and schema typicality. *Psychology and Aging, 9,* 467–480.

Arbuckle, T. Y., & Gold, D. P. (1993). Aging, inhibition, and verbosity. *Journal of Gerontology: Psychological Sciences, 48,* P225–232.

Ball, K., Beard, B., Roenker, D., Miller, R., & Griggs, D. (1988). Age and visual search: Expanding the useful field of view. *Journal of the Optical Society of America, 5,* 2210–2219.

Baltes, P. B., & Kliegl, R. (1992). Further testing of limits of cognitive plasticity: Negative age differences in a mnemonic skill are robust. *Developmental Psychology, 28,* 121–125.

Baron, A., & Mattilla, W. (1989). Response slowing of older adults: Effects of time-limit contingencies on single and dual-task performances. *Psychology and Aging, 4,* 66–72.

Bieman-Copland, S., & Charness, N. (1994). Memory knowledge and memory monitoring in adulthood. *Psychology and Aging, 9,* 287–302.

Bosman, E. A. (1993). Age-related differences in the motoric aspects of transcription typing skill. *Psychology and Aging, 8,* 87–102.

Botwinick, J. (1978). *Aging and behavior.* New York: Springer.

Bowles, N. L. (1994). Age and rate of activation in semantic memory. *Psychology and Aging, 9,* 414–429.

Cavanaugh, J. C. (1989). The importance of awareness in memory aging. In L. W. Poon, D. C. Rubin, & B. A. Wilson (Eds.), *Everyday cognition in adulthood and late life* (pp. 416–436). Cambridge: Cambridge University Press.

Cavanaugh, J. C., & Green, E. E. (1990). I believe, therefore I can: Self-efficacy beliefs in memory aging. In E. A. Lovelace (Ed.), *Aging and cognition: Mental processes, self-awareness and interventions* (pp. 189–230). Amsterdam: North Holland.

Cavanaugh, J. C. & Murphy, N. Z. (1986). Personality and metamemory correlates of memory performance in younger and older adults. *Educational Gerontology, 12,* 385–394.

Cerella, J. (1990). Aging and information-processing rate. In J. E. Birren & K. W. Schaie (Eds.), *Handbook of the psychology of aging* (pp. 201–221). San Diego: Academic Press.

Cerella, J., & Fozard, J. L. (1984). Lexical access and age. *Developmental Psychology, 20,* 235–243.

Charness, N. (1989). Age and expertise: Responding to Talland's challenge. In L. W. Poon, D. C. Rubin, & B. A. Wilson (Eds.), *Everyday cognition in adulthood and late life* (pp. 437–456). Cambridge, England: Cambridge University Press.

Cherry, K. E., & Park, D. C. (1993). Individual difference and contextual variables influence spatial memory in younger and older adults. *Psychology and Aging, 8,* 517–526.

Chodzko-Zajko, W. J. (1991). Physical fitness, cognitive performance, and aging. *Medicine and Science in Sports and Exercise, 23,* 868–872.

Chodzko-Zajko, W. J., Schuler, P., Solomon, J., Heinl, B., & Ellis, N. R. (1992). The influence of physical fitness on automatic and effortful memory changes in aging. *International Journal of Aging and Human Development, 35,* 265–285.

Clarkson-Smith, L., & Hartley, A. A. (1989). Relationships between physical exercise and cognitive abilities in older adults. *Psychology and Aging, 4,* 183–189.

Cohen, G., Conway, M. A., & Maylor, E. A. (1994). Flashbulb memories in older adults. *Psychology and Aging, 9,* 454–463.

Cohn, N. B., Dustman, R. E., & Bradford, D. C. (1984). Age-related decrements in Stroop color test performance. *Journal of Clinical Psychology, 40,* 1244–1250.

Comalli, P. E., Jr., Wapner, S., & Werner, H. (1962). Interference effects of Stroop color-word test in childhood, adulthood and aging. *Journal of Genetic Psychology, 100,* 47–53.

Coyne, A. C., Whitbourne, S. K., & Glenwick, D. S. (1978). Adult age differences in reflection-impulsivity. *Journal of Gerontology, 33,* 402–407.

Cutler, S., & Grams, A. E. (1988). Correlates of self-reported everyday memory problems. *Journal of Gerontology: Social Sciences, 43,* S82–90.

Czaja, S. J., & Sharit, J. (1993). Age differences in the performance of computer-based work. *Psychology and Aging, 8,* 59–67.

Denney, N. W., & Larsen, J. E. (1994). Aging and episodic memory: Are elderly adults less likely to make connections between target and contextual information? *Journal of Gerontology: Psychological Sciences, 49,* P270–275.

Dixon, R. A. (1989). Questionnaire research on metamemory and aging: Issues of structure and function. In L. W. Poon, D. C. Rubin, & B. A. Wilson (Ed.), *Everyday cognition in adulthood and late life* (pp. 394–415). Cambridge: Cambridge University Press.

Dixon, R. A., & Hultsch, D. F. (1983). Structure and development of metamemory in adulthood. *Journal of Gerontology, 38,* 682–689.

Dixon, R. A., Kurzman, D., & Friesen, I. C. (1993). Handwriting performance in younger and older adults: Age, familiarity, and practice effects. *Psychology and Aging, 8,* 360–370.

Dobbs, A. R., & Rule, B. G. (1987). Prospective memory and self-reports of memory abilities in older adults. Special Issue: Aging and cognition. *Canadian Journal of Psychology, 41,* 209–222.

Drevenstedt, J., & Bellezza, F. S. (1993). Memory for self-generated narration in the elderly. *Psychology and Aging, 8,* 187–196.

Dustman, R., Emmerson, R., Ruhling, R., Shearer, D., Steinhaus, L., Johnson, S., Bonekat, H., & Shigeoka, J. (1990). Age and fitness effects on EEG, ERPs, visual sensitivity, and cognition. *Neurobiology of Aging, 11,* 193–200.

Dustman, R. E., Emmerson, R. Y., Steinhaus, L. A., Shearer, D. E., & Dustman, T. J. (1992). The effects of videogame playing on neuropsychological performance of elderly individuals. *Journal of Gerontology: Psychological Sciences, 47,* P168–171.

Dustman, R. E., Ruhling, R. O., Russell, E. M., Shearer, D. E., Bonekat, H. W., Shigeoka, J. W., Wood, J. S., & Bradford, D. C. (1984). Aerobic exercise training and improved neurophysiological function of the older individual. *Neurobiology of Aging, 5,* 35–42.

Erber, J. T. (1989). Young and older adults' appraisal of memory failures in young and older adult target persons. *Journal of Gerontology: Psychological Sciences, 44,* P170–175.

Erber, J. T., Szuchman, L. T., & Rothberg, S. T. (1990). Age, gender, and individual differences in memory failure appraisal. *Psychology and Aging, 5,* 600–603.

Fisk, A. D., Hertzog, C., Lee, M. D., Rogers, W. A., & Anderson-Garlach, M. (1994). Long-term retention of skilled visual search: Do young adults retain more than old adults? *Psychology and Aging, 9,* 206–215.

Fisk, A. D., McGee, N. D., & Giambra, L. M. (1988). The influence of age on consistent and varied semantic category search performance. *Psychology and Aging, 3,* 323–333.

Fisk, A. D., & Rogers, W. (1991). Toward an understanding of age-related memory and visual search effects. *Journal of Experimental Psychology: General, 120,* 131–149.

Foos, P. W. (1989). Age differences in memory for two common objects. *Journals of Gerontology, 44,* 178.

Fozard, J. L., & Thomas, J. C. (1975). Psychology of aging: Basic findings and some psychiatric applications. In J. G. Howells (Eds.), *Modern perspectives in the psychiatry of old age* (pp. 107–169). New York: Brunner/Mazel.

Fozard, J. L., Vercruyssen, M., Reynolds, S. L., Hancock, P. A., & Quilter, R. E. (1994). Age differences and changes in reaction time: The Baltimore Longitudinal Study of Aging. *Journal of Gerontology: Psychological Sciences, 49,* P179–189.

Geary, D. C., Frensch, P. A., & Wiley, J. G. (1993). Simple and complex mental subtraction: Strategy choice and speed-of-processing differences in younger and older adults. *Psychology and Aging, 8,* 242–256.

Giambra, L. M., & Arenberg, D. (1993). Adult age differences in forgetting sentences. *Psychology and Aging, 8,* 451–462.

Gold, D. P., & Arbuckle, T. Y. (1995). A longitudinal study of off-target verbosity. *Journal of Gerontology: Psychological Sciences, 50B,* P307-315.

Gratzinger, P., Sheikh, J. L., Friedman, L., & Yesavage, J. A. (1990). Cognitive interventions to improve face-name recall: The role of personality trait differences. *Developmental Psychology, 26,* 889–893.

Hartley, A. A. (1992). Attention. In F. I. M. Craik & T. A. Salthouse (Eds.), *The handbook of aging and cognition* (pp. 3–50). Hillsdale, NJ: Erlbaum.

Hartley, A. A. (1993). Evidence for the selective preservation of spatial selective attention in old age. *Psychology and Aging, 8,* 371–379.

Hartley, J. T., Stojack, C. C., Mushaney, T. J., Kiku Annon, T. A., & Lee, D. W. (1994). Reading speed and prose memory in older and younger adults. *Psychology and Aging, 9,* 216–223.

Hasher, L., Stoltzfus, E. R., Zacks, R. T., & Rypma, B. (1991). Age and inhibition. *Journal of Experimental Psychology: Learning, Memory, and Cognition, 17,* 163–169.

Hasher, L., & Zacks, R. T. (1979). Automatic and effortful processes in memory. *Journal of Experimental Psychology: General, 108,* 356–388.

Hasher, L., & Zacks, R. T. (1988). Working memory, comprehension, and aging: A review and a new view. In G. H. Bower (Eds.), *The psychology of learning and motivation* (pp. 193–225). New York: Academic Press.

Hawkins, H. L., Kramer, A. F., & Capaldi, D. (1992). Aging, exercise, and attention. *Psychology and Aging, 7,* 643–653.

Hertzog, C., Dixon, R. A., & Hultsch, D. F. (1990). Relationships between metamemory, memory predictions, and memory task performance. *Psychology and Aging, 5,* 215–227.

Hertzog, C., Dixon, R. A., Schulenberg, J. E., & Hultsch, D. F. (1987). On the differentiation of memory beliefs from memory knowledge: The factor structure of the Metamemory in Adulthood scale. *Experimental Aging Research, 13*(1–2), 101–107.

Hess, T. M., Flannagan, D. A., & Tate, C. S. (1993). Aging and memory for schematically vs. taxonomically organized verbal materials. *Journal of Gerontology: Psychological Sciences, 48,* P37–44.

Hess, T. M., & Slaughter, S. J. (1990). Schematic knowledge influences on memory for scene information in young and older adults. *Developmental Psychology, 26,* 855–865.

Hess, T. M., & Tate, C. S. (1992). Direct and indirect assessments of memory for script-based narratives in young and older adults. *Cognitive Development, 7,* 467–484.

Houx, P., Jolles, J., & Vreeling, F. (1993). Stroop interference: Aging effects associated with Stroop color-word test. *Experimental Aging Research, 19,* 209–224.

Hultsch, D. F., Hammer, M., & Small, B. J. (1993). Age differences in cognitive performance in later life; Relationships to self-reported health and activity life style. *Journal of Gerontology: Psychological Sciences, 48,* P1–11.

Hultsch, D. F., Hertzog, C., & Dixon, R. A. (1987). Age differences in metamemory: Resolving the inconsistencies. Special Issue: Aging and cognition. *Canadian Journal of Psychology, 41,* 193–208.

Kane, M. J., Hasher, L., Stoltzfus, E. R., Zacks, R. T., & Connelly, S. L. (1994). Inhibitory attentional mechanisms and aging. *Psychology and Aging, 9,* 103–112.

Kleigl, R., Smith, J., & Baltes, P. B. (1989). Testing-the-limits and the study of adult age differences in cognitive plasticity of a mnemonic skill. *Developmental Psychology, 25,* 247–256.

Kotler-Cope, S., & Camp, C. (1990). Memory interventions in aging populations. In E. A. Lovelace (Eds.), *Aging and cognition: Mental processes, self-awareness and interventions* (pp. 231–261). Amsterdam: North Holland.

Kramer, A. F., Humphrey, D. G., Larish, J. F., Logan, G. D., & Strayer, D. L. (1994). Aging and inhibition: Beyond a unitary view of inhibitory processing in attention. *Psychology and Aging, 9,* 491–512.

Lachman, M. E., Steinberg, E. S., & Trotter, S. D. (1987). Effects of control beliefs and attributions on memory self-assessments and performance. *Psychology and Aging, 2,* 266–271.

Lachman, M. E., Weaver, S. L., Bandura, M., Elliott, E., & Lewkowicz, C. J. (1992). Improving memory and control beliefs through cognitive restructuring and self-generated strategies. *Journal of Gerontology: Psychological Sciences, 47,* P293–299.

Larish, J., Kramer, A., DeAntonna, J., & Strayer, D. (1993). Aging and dual-task training. In *Proceedings of the Human Factors Society* (pp. 162–166). Santa Monica, CA:

Light, L. L. (1992). The organization of memory in old age. In F. I. M. Craik & T. A. Salthouse (Eds.), *The handbook of aging and cognition* (pp. 111–165). Hillsdale, NJ: Erlbaum.

Loewen, E. R., Shaw, R. J., & Craik, F. I. (1990). Age differences in components of metamemory. *Experimental Aging Research, 16,* 43–48.

Madden, D. J., Connelly, S. L., & Pierce, T. W. (1994). Adult age differences in shifting focused attention. *Psychology and Aging, 9,* 528–538.

Mantyla, T. (1994). Remembering to remember: Adult age differences in prospective memory. *Journal of Gerontology: Psychological Sciences, 49,* P276–282.

Maylor, E. A. (1993). Aging and memory for frequency of occurrence of novel, visual stimuli: Direct and indirect measures. *Psychology and Aging, 8,* 400–410.

McDonald-Miszczak, L., Hertzog, C., & Hultsch, D. F. (1995). Stability and accuracy of metamemory in adulthood and aging: A longitudinal analysis. *Psychology and Aging, 10,* 553–564.

McDowd, J. M., & Oseas-Kreger, D. M. (1991). Aging, inhibitory processes, and negative priming. *Journal of Gerontology: Psychological sciences, 46,* P340–345.

Milligan, W. L., Powell, A., Harley, C., & Furchtgott, E. (1984). A comparison of physical health and psychosocial variables as predictors of reaction time and serial learning performance. *Journal of Gerontology, 39,* 704–710.

Molander, B., & Bäckman, L. (1994). Attention and performance in miniature golf across the life span. *Journal of Gerontology: Psychological Sciences, 49,* P35–41.

Morse, C. K. (1993). Does variability increase with age? An archival study of cognitive measures. *Psychology and Aging, 8,* 156–164.

Neely, A. S., & Backman, L. (1993). Long-term maintenance of gains from memory training in older adults: Two three-and-a-half-year follow-up studies. *Journal of Gerontology: Psychological sciences, 48,* P233–237.

Neely, A. S., & Backman, L. (1995). Effects of multifactorial memory training in old age: Generalizability across tasks and individuals. *Journal of Gerontology: Psychological Sciences, 50B,* P134–140.

Park, D. C., Smith, A. D., & Cavanaugh, J. C. (1990). Metamemories of memory researchers. *Memory and Cognition, 18,* 321–327.

Rabbitt, P., & Abson, V. (1990). "Lost and found": Some logical and methodological limitations of self-report questionnaires as tools to study cognitive ageing. *British Journal of Psychology, 81,* 1–16.

Rogers, W. A., Bertus, E. L., & Gilbert, D. K. (1994). Dual-task assessment of age differences in automatic process development. *Psychology and Aging, 9,* 398–413.

Rogers, W. A., & Fisk, A. D. (1991). Are age differences in consistent-mapping visual search due to feature learning or attention training? *Psychology and Aging, 6,* 542–550.

Ryan, E. B., & See, S. K. (1993). Age-based beliefs about memory changes for self and others across adulthood. *Journal of Gerontology: Psychological Sciences, 48,* P199–201.

Salthouse, T. A. (1985). Speed of behavior and its implications for cognition. In J. E. Birren & K. W. Schaie (Eds.), *Handbook of the psychology of aging* (pp. 400–426). New York: Van Nostrand Reinhold.

Salthouse, T. A. (1993). Speed and knowledge as determinants of adult age differences in verbal tasks. *Journal of Gerontology: Psychological sciences, 48,* P29–36.

Salthouse, T. A. (1996). General and specific speed mediation of adult age differences in memory. *Journal of Gerontology: Psychological Sciences, 51A,* P30–42.

Salthouse, T. A., & Coon, V. E. (1993). Influence of task-specific processing speed on age differences in memory. *Journal of Gerontology: Psychological sciences, 48,* P245–255.

Salthouse, T. A., & Somberg, G. L. (1982). Skilled performance: Effects of adult age and experience on elementary processes. *Journal of Experimental Psychology: General, 111,* 176–207.

Schacter, D. L., Osowiecki, D., Kaszniak, A. W., Kihlstrom, J. F., & Valdiserri, M. (1994). Source memory: Extending the boundaries of age-related deficits. *Psychology and Aging, 9,* 81–89.

Schaie, K. W. (1988). Ageism in psychological research. *American Psychologist, 43,* 179–184.

Schaie, K. W., & Willis, S. L. (1991). Adult personality and psychomotor performance: Cross-sectional and longitudinal analyses. *Journal of Gerontology: Psychological Sciences, 46,* P275–284.

Schneider, W., & Shiffrin, R. M. (1977). Controlled and automatic human information processing: I. Detection, search, and attention. *Psychological Review, 84,* 1–66.

Scogin, F. (1985). Memory complaints and memory performance: The relationship reexamined. Special Issue: Aging and mental health. *Journal of Applied Gerontology, 4,* 79–89.

Scogin, F., & Bienias, J. L. (1988). A three-year follow-up of older adult participants in a memory-skills training program. *Psychology and Aging, 3,* 334–337.

Smith, A. (1980). Age differences in encoding, storage, and retrieval. In L. W. Poon, L. S. Cermak, D. Arenberg, & L. W. Thompson (Eds.), *New directions in memory and aging* (pp. 23–45). Hillsdale, NJ: Lawrence Erlbaum.

Somberg, B. L., & Salthouse, T. A. (1982). Divided attention abilities in young and old adults. *Journal of Experimental Psychology: Human Perception and Performance, 8,* 651–663.

Spencer, W. D., & Raz, N. (1994). Memory for facts, source, and context: Can frontal lobe dysfunction explain age-related differences? *Psychology and Aging, 9,* 149–159.

Spirduso, W. W. (1980). Physical fitness, aging, and psychomotor speed. *Journal of Gerontology, 35,* 850–865.

Spirduso, W. W., & MacRae, P. G. (1990). Motor performance and aging. In J. E. Birren & K. W. Schaie (Eds.), *Handbook of the psychology of aging* (pp. 184–200). San Diego, CA: Academic Press.

Stoltzfus, E., Hasher, L., Zacks, E., Ulivi, M., & Goldstein, D. (1993). Investigations of inhibition and interference in younger and older adults. *Journal of Gerontology: Psychological Sciences, 48,* P179–188.

Strayer, D. L., & Kramer, A. F. (1994). Aging and skill acquisition: Learning-performance distinctions. *Psychology and Aging, 9,* 589–605.

Stroop, J. R. (1935). Studies of interference in serial verbal reactions. *Journal of Experimental Psychology, 18,* 643–622.

Sullivan, M. P., & Faust, M. E. (1993). Evidence for identity inhibition during selective attention in old adults. *Psychology and Aging, 8,* 589–598.

Sunderland, A., Watts, K., Baddeley, A. D., & Harris, J. E. (1986). Subjective memory assessment and test performance in elderly adults. *Journal of Gerontology, 41,* 376–384.

Tipper, S. (1985). The negative priming effect: Inhibitory priming by ignored objects. *The Quarterly Journal of Experimental Psychology, 37,* 571–590.

Tipper, S. (1991). Less attentional selectivity as a result of declining inhibition in older adults. *Bulletin of the Psychonomic Society, 29,* 45–47.

Tipper, S., Brehaut, J., & Driver, J. (1990). Selective attention and priming: Inhibitory and facilitatory effects of ignored primes. *Journal of Experimental Psychology: Human Perception and Performance, 16*, 492–504.

Tomer, A., Larrabee, G. J., & Crook, T. H. (1994). Structure of everyday memory in adults with age-associated memory impairment. *Psychology and Aging, 9*, 606–615.

Uttl, B., & Graf, P. (1993). Episodic spatial memory in adulthood. *Psychology and Aging, 8*, 257–273.

Verhaeghen, P., & Marcoen, A. (1993). More or less the same? A memorability analysis on episodic memory taks in young and older adults. *Journal of Gerontology: Psychological Sciences, 48*, P172–178.

Verhaeghen, P., Marcoen, A., & Goossens, L. (1993). Facts and fiction about memory aging: A quantitative integration of research findings. *Journal of Gerontology: Psychological Sciences, 48*, P157–171.

Welford, A. T. (1958/1973). *Aging and human skill*. Westport, CT: Greenwood Press.

Willis, S. L. (1990). Current issues in cognitive training research. In E. A. Lovelace (Eds.), *Aging and cognition: Mental processes, self-awareness and interventions* (pp. 263–280). Amsterdam: North Holland.

Wingfield, A., Wayland, S. C., & Stine, E. A. L. (1992). Adult age differences in the use of prosody for syntactic parsing and recall of spoken sentences. *Journal of Gerontology: Psychological Sciences, 47*, P350–356.

Yesavage, J. A., Rose, T. L., & Bower, G. H. (1983). Interactive imagery and affective judgments improve face–name learning in the elderly. *Journal of Gerontology, 38*, 197–203.

Zabrucky, K., & Moore, D. (1994). Contributions of working memory and evaluation and regulation of understanding to adults' recall of texts. *Journal of Gerontology: Psychological Sciences, 49*, P201–212.

Zarit, S. H., Cole, K. D., & Guider, R. L. (1981). Memory training strategies and subjective complaints of memory in the aged. *The Gerontologist, 21*, 158–164.

Zelinski, E. M., Gilewski, M., & Schaie, K. W. (1993). Individual differences in cross-sectional and 3-year longitudinal memory performance across the adult life span. *Psychology and Aging, 8*, 176–186.

9

Intelligence

Questions regarding the nature of intelligence have emerged within recent years with renewed debates raging over the role of heredity and the presence of racially based differences in intelligence test scores (Hernnstein & Murray, 1994). Psychologists have struggled for decades with the issue of "nature vs. nurture," and the problems involved in defining and measuring intelligence. Less in the forefront, but a prominent concern within the fields of education and industry, is the question of what happens to intelligence in the middle and later years of adulthood. The existence of age effects in intellectual functioning has practical ramifications for the training and employment of older workers. From a theoretical point of view, changes in the nature of intelligence in adulthood and old age provide insight into the components of measured intelligence. Evidence on the aging of intelligence is also used to compare the relative contributions of the environment and the aging process to psychological development.

From the standpoint of the individual's awareness of aging, the actual scores one might receive on a test of intelligence perhaps may be seen as below threshold level, playing a relatively small role in influencing one's sense of identity over time. It is more likely that, like the star athlete (McGue, Hirsch, & Lykken, 1993), individuals develop a view of their own intelligence quite early in life, in response to school experiences or feedback from others regarding how "smart" they are. Their identity in this regard may change in adulthood as much in response to actual changes in measured intelligence as to exposure to social attitudes that intelligence shows inevitable declines in later life. The older individual may come to believe that his or her abilities are starting to erode because this is what is "supposed" to happen to older people. Based upon the multiple threshold model, these beliefs may be of particular relevance for those older adults who have always valued their intellectual functioning either because of its importance to a job or to leisure pursuits. Since there is little clarity on what it means to be "intelligent," the older person's identity with regard to intelligence may be based as much on stereotypes of aging and intelligence as on actual feedback from experiences requiring the exercise of one's intellectual "muscle."

It is in the area of intelligence that the sequential research designs described in Chapter 2 have had their widest application. The goal of sequential research on intelligence is to untangle the relative contributions of environmental and maturational factors to adult intelligence, a challenging and important problem in lifespan developmental psychology. As a result of this research, we now know more about the course of intellectual development over the adult years, as well as the factors that affect individual differences in performance on intelligence tests throughout the later years of life.

To some extent, the implications of research on intelligence show overlap with research on memory and other cognitive functions in later adulthood. The major difference between these two sets of findings lies in the means through which conclusions are reached about mental abilities in adulthood. Cognitive studies are based for the most part on principles of experimental design, in which the intent is to describe how performance is affected by the manipulation of specified independent variables. Researchers who study cognitive processes are rarely interested in individual differences in performance except insofar as these relate to age, gender, education, or some other categorical variable. By contrast, the majority of studies on adult intelligence involve attempts to establish patterns of age effects in a large number of abilities. These tests provide a broader and more comprehensive characterization of the individual's abilities than it is possible to obtain with standardized testing procedures.

Despite these differences in approaches, it is possible to draw parallels between the kinds of abilities tested by tests of intelligence and the cognitive skills studied in experimental situations. As views of intelligence begin to incorporate more concepts related to cognitive functioning as measured in the laboratory, these connections will become more direct. Furthermore, challenges within the psychological community to traditional views of intelligence make it more likely that studies of intellectual functioning in adults will gain in relevance to the daily concerns and activities of older persons. The inclusion of concepts such as "practical" intelligence into theories of intelligence (Sternberg, 1985) may allow psychologists to tap more readily into the skill domains of older cohorts of adults.

FLUID AND CRYSTALLIZED INTELLIGENCE

As it is commonly understood, the term "intelligence" refers to the individual's mental abilities. Most psychological tests are based on this definition, which has its origins in the work of British psychologist Charles Spearman who set about in the early 1900s on the ambitious task of formulating a comprehensive theory of intelligence (Spearman, 1904; Spearman, 1927). Spearman proposed a "general factor" of intelligence, which he referred to as "g," otherwise understood as the ability to infer and apply relationships on the basis of experience. Individuals with high levels of "g," according to Spearman, should be able to receive high scores on various tests of specific mental abilities. Despite criticisms of the "g" construct, it has served as a focus for researchers in the area of aging and intelligence who have found it useful to organize their work around the proposal made by psychologists Raymond Cattell and John Horn that there are two forms of the quality "g": fluid and crystallized intelligence. According to this view (Horn & Cattell, 1966), there are two dimensions of mental abilities that are separate and distinct from each other. The metaphors "fluid" and "crystallized" are intended to convey their function and origins.

"Fluid" intelligence refers to the individual's innate or inherited ability, reflecting the quality of biopsychological factors such as the functioning of the central nervous system and the sensory structures. Individuals who have high levels of fluid intelligence should receive high scores on tests of inductive reasoning, which are based not on particular learned skills or areas of expertise, but on the ability to form novel associations and relationships between concepts. To count as a "fluid" test, the associations should be ones that do not depend on prior experience, even though the items may contain familiar elements. For example, a test of fluid intelligence may involve presenting the following series of letters: NOPQ EDFL ABCD HIJK UVWX, and asking the respondent to choose the set that does not belong with the others (EDFL). The elements in this set are highly familiar to any English language speaker, so that discovering the answer relies on seeing the relationship of letters to each other rather than on vocabulary or comprehension. Because fluid intelligence is seen as a "pure" reflection of neuropsychological functioning, it is theorized to be independent of experience or educational training. Theoretically, a person with an 8th grade education can have fluid intelligence scores that are just as high as (or possibly higher than) a nuclear scientist.

By contrast, the concept of "crystallized intelligence" is highly linked to the individual's educational status and attainments. Crystallized intelligence is the learned ability to infer relationships, make judgments, analyze problems, and use problem-solving strategies. It is the type of intelligence that increases when the individual is given particular instruction or experiences that enhance knowledge of a given subject area. Measures of this ability tap the individual's vocabulary skills, knowledge of particular facts and figures, and mathematical expertise.

One way to remember the distinction between crystallized and fluid intelligence is to think about what happens when an individual is forced to adapt to a new culture, as occurs when travelling. Fluid intelligence involves the ability to figure out ways to solve problems created when planning transportation, lodgings, and eating arrangements in an unfamiliar setting. Crystallized intelligence reflects the individual's background knowledge of the country and fluency with the country's language. Fluid intelligence may also be thought of as an amorphous, free-floating pool of moveable elements that can be channeled in different directions. The specific areas into which fluid intelligence becomes channeled and rigidified are the various knowledge areas represented by crystallized intelligence. As you can readily see, crystallized intelligence is theorized to increase across the adult years as the individual gains in particular experiences and knowledge through exposure to new situations and ideas (another good reason to find older adult "Trivial Pursuits" partners!).

Although, fluid and crystallized intelligence are theorized to be orthogonal or independent, the two sets of abilities for practical purposes become somewhat interdependent. For an individual to acquire the skills and knowledge specific to one's culture and educational system, a person must possess the "fluid" ability to learn new information; that is, to form concepts, see relationships, and analyze problems. If one has an ability to follow the logic of a mathematical equation, it is much easier to acquire knowledge of advanced computer programming than if one lacks this fluid ability. Conversely, having had some training in mathematics gives the individual the crystallized ability that makes it easier to learn new programming methods. Fluid and crystallized abilities also interact with the quality of the individual's environment in terms of the amount of intellectual stimulation it provides and, for children, the quality of health and nutrition. Those who are exposed to optimal levels of input from the environment will be most likely to develop to their maximum levels of potential in both components of intelligence.

Age Differences in Fluid and Crystallized Intelligence

The fluid–crystallized theory predicts a specific pattern of age effects in the two components of intelligence (Horn, 1982). Early in development, both abilities are hypothesized to increase at a rapid rate. The increase of fluid intelligence reflects the growth and maturation of the nervous system; growth in crystallized intelligence responds to the intensive schooling that occurs in childhood and adolescence. The peak of fluid intelligence is hypothesized to be reached in late adolescence. After this point, however, fluid intelligence is theorized to decline reflecting deleterious changes due to the death of neurons in the central nervous system and the loss of sensory efficiency.

In contrast to the downward trajectory hypothesized to occur for fluid intelligence, crystallized intelligence is predicted to increase continually throughout adulthood, reflecting the experiences of adults in their jobs, social interactions, exposure to the media, and whatever formal educational programs in which they become involved. Any declines in crystallized intelligence are theorized to occur well into the years of old age, and perhaps not at all for older people who maintain involvement in stimulating activities and whose health remains good.

Support for the possibility of growth in crystallized intelligence throughout adulthood comes from suggestions by proponents of the neurological "plasticity" model. According to this model, neurons within the aging nervous system can grow and elaborate in response to continued exposure to new experiences throughout adulthood. This growth through plasticity may constitute the physiological substrate for gains in crystallized intelligence throughout adulthood. Similarly, evidence from studies of semantic memory and language abilities in the elderly support the predicted age trends in crystallized intelligence.

It would also be consistent with the literature on cognitive functioning in old age to postulate a decline in fluid intelligence. This component of intelligence may be regarded as based in the processes that involve analysis and synthesis of information by the central processing structures in the cerebral cortex. The decreases in the processing capacity of these structures, as evidenced by studies of reaction time, decision processes, and effortful memory operations support the proposed decline in fluid abilities.

Empirical Evidence on Aging and Intelligence

Early studies on the aging of intelligence were based on simple cross-sectional and longitudinal designs in which the effects of age were confounded with the effects of cohort and time of measurement. Typically, cross-sectional studies showed precipitous declines after the early adult years and into old age; by contrast, longitudinal investigations produced results indicating either no age-related losses or increases in intelligence scores. This discrepancy was seen as due to a combination of cohort differences in health and educational level that confounded age effects in cross-sectional studies and selective survival and practice effects that accounted for the lack of age-related changes seen in longitudinal studies. The contradictory results have also been interpreted in terms of the fluid–crystallized distinction (Horn, 1970). When scores on verbal (crystallized) and nonverbal (fluid) performance measures are combined, the pattern of age effects will reflect the predominant ability being tested. Declines will appear when the test reflects fluid abilities and stability or increases will be found when the test is based on verbal or crystallized skills.

EARLY DEBATE ON THE "MYTH" OF INTELLECTUAL AGING

Debate in the literature regarding the effects of aging on intelligence continued throughout the 1970s, with the rallying point being the "myth of intellectual decline." This proposition emerged from the early results of studies that Schaie and his associates had begun in 1956, from which data were becoming available using the newly developed sequential methods on test performance throughout adulthood. The instrument used in this research was the Primary Mental Abilities Test, a standardized set of scales that assesses performance on a set of crystallized and fluid abilities. With evidence showing that cohort effects artificially lowered estimates of intelligence test performance in groups of older adults, Schaie and Baltes proclaimed in both the popular press and scientific literature that they had disproved the commonly held belief that intelligence shows an inevitable progressive decline in old age (Baltes & Schaie, 1974; Schaie, 1974). Such a bold contention did not go unchallenged. In a thorough and highly critical reinterpretation of the Seattle data, Horn and Donaldson (1976) rejected the claims made by Baltes and Schaie, and argued that the Seattle findings provided continued support for the fluid–crystallized theory, a theory that proposes decline. This debate continued for another round of rebuttals and counterrebuttals (Baltes & Schaie, 1976; Horn & Donaldson, 1977; Schaie & Baltes, 1977) until it became clear that a compromise position could not be achieved.

Later writing by Schaie and Baltes after the bitter debate had mellowed, and based on further data collection, represented acceptance, to a certain degree, of conclusions regarding the fact that longitudinal studies are biased by practice effects (Lindenberger & Baltes, 1994; Schaie, 1979a). As stated in the opening to their analysis of the 1984 test data, Schaie and his colleague Sherry Willis described the general pattern of a peak in intellectual abilities in the 30s and into the 40s, a plateau that is maintained through the 50s or early 60s, and a decline beginning in the 70s that becomes more precipitous into the late 70s. Acknowledging, then, that intellectual decline is not "a myth," they moved even closer to the Horn and Donaldson position by organizing their findings in terms of the fluid–crystallized distinction (Schaie & Willis, 1993). However, the search has continued for finding variables that could explain individual differences in these abilities throughout later adulthood, and identifying measures that would serve as useful markers for the primary mental abilities. In addition to laying out more complete patterns of intellectual ability performance over the span of the adult years, subsequent papers based on the 1984 testing explored a number of hypotheses regarding variations in intelligence test performance by age, lifestyle, personality, and other components of cognitive functioning. To understand these findings, it is necessary to go into more depth regarding Schaie's data set, the Seattle Longitudinal Study.

THE SEATTLE LONGITUDINAL STUDY (SLS): SUMMARY OF FINDINGS

The original sample for the SLS studied by Schaie consisted of 500 adults, 50 from each of 10 5–year age intervals, all of whom were living in the Seattle, Washington area. This sample was followed up seven years later and, at the same time, a new sample of adults from the same age groups was added. The same procedure was carried out in the years 1970, 1977, 1984, and 1991. With each new testing, it became possible to investigate increasingly sophisticated questions regarding the contributions of age, cohort, time of testing, practice effects, and selective survival. In addition to data on the average performance of individuals within different age periods, the study's simple but ingenious design made it possible to examine the role of individual differences in personality, health, and lifestyle as they affected intelligence test performance.

By the time of the most recent retest in 1991, the total number of adults tested ranged upwards of 5,000, spanning the adult years with both cross-sectional and longitudinal data. The original PMA measures were expanded considerably to include multiple indicators of the primary mental abilities, as well as personality, health, and life-style measures intended to provide evidence on the correlates of intellectual development in adulthood (Schaie, 1994). More publications will continue to emerge from this retest; for the present, the summary of main findings is based on analyses of the 1984 retest data.

Having conceded that some type of intellectual decline in later adulthood is not a "myth," Schaie and his associates have provided extensive clarification of the issues originally raised in what now appears to have been an overly simplistic set of arguments. A decline in measured intelligence among most abilities is now accepted among the SLS researchers as a reliable phenomenon that begins in the early 60s and advances to the point until by the late 60s, there are clear decrements on all measured abilities, including those in the crystallized domain. One measure, word fluency, is estimated to show signs of decay as early beginning as early as the mid-50s.

However, there are many qualifications to these overall age trends—a case where the exceptions may be as important as the rule. The decline in measured intelligence is considered to be "modest" until the 80s, and even then, fewer than half the individuals tested show reliable decay compared to their own benchmark of performance in the early 70s. Similar findings have been reported on the Baltimore Longitudinal Study of Aging sample, in which cross-sectional and short-term (7-year) follow-up analyses yielded evidence of considerable stability of crystallized intelligence into the late 70s and early 80s, at which point the measured decline was not substantial (Giambra, Arenberg, Zonderman, Kawas, & Costa, 1995). Schaie and others (Field, Schaie, & Leino, 1988) also emphasize the role of variability in intellectual functioning: "as on other abilities, individual differences . . . in the occurrence of decline therein are substantial, overlap between successive age groups is great, and age is not a good predictor of a given individual's likelihood to decline" (Schaie, 1989, p. 452).

Cross-sectionally, verbal intelligence test scores remain the steadiest over adulthood, compared to measures of fluid intelligence, with the most precipitous cross-sectional drop-off for perceptual speed (Schaie & Willis, 1993). Finally, and related to the extensive analyses of the 1984 data, much of the observed decrement in intelligence test scores can be attributed to loss of response speed, a phenomenon that has been amply documented in research on reaction time. When response speed is partialled out of intelligence test scores, even the longitudinal declines in fluid intelligence test scores are substantially reduced (Schaie, 1994) although not completely (Schaie, 1989).

The importance of perceptual speed as a contributor to the apparent decline of intelligence test scores cannot be overemphasized and relates back to the whole question of "g" as an indicator of a person's true abilities. Interestingly, the aging data on intellectual performance have not been incorporated into the controversy surrounding The Bell Curve (Herrnstein & Murray, 1994), which focused mainly on racial differences in IQ. Yet, the information about the "aging" of "g" would certainly seem to be relevant to the question of what intelligence tests actually measure. Having identified perceptual speed as a main component of intellectual test decline over the adult years, researchers within the cognitive aging field now regard tests such as the PMA as measures of the "mechanics" of intelligence—the processes needed to make quick decisions having low to moderate difficulty (Hertzog & Schaie, 1988). Furthermore, there are large variations in the extent to which age declines in perceptual speed exist (Schaie, 1989). It may be that some older adults think more slowly, but not necessarily less intelligently.

Training Studies

Begining in the early 1970s, Baltes embarked on a program of research intended to demonstrate the "plasticity" of the aging intellect. His original and perhaps somewhat modest efforts to demonstrate that older adults can be trained to improve their performance on intelligence tests such as the PMA became the foundation for what is currently a major research program designed to investigate the elusive quality of wisdom in later life. Throughout his career, Baltes has argued against the notion of aging as inevitable decay, and has provided models and data that convincingly support his arguments. Before looking into this fascinating area of research, it is worthwhile to pause and examine the impact of training studies for understanding the effects of aging on psychometric intelligence.

Early studies of the effects of training on measured intelligence by Baltes and his co-workers, demonstrated that, given training and practice, older adults could improve their scores on tests of fluid intelligence that were supposedly insensitive to education and experience. These studies tended not to have young control groups, as their original intention was to demonstrate simply that training could produce gains on these indicators. Later studies carried out by Willis have gained in sophistication and have also addressed various criticisms of the original studies. For example, critics argued that if fluid test performance could be improved through training, then perhaps the test was not a fluid intelligence test after all. Subsequent research involving complex factor analytic models have confirmed that training results in increases in mean levels of performance while maintaining the structural invariance of the tests (Schaie, Willis, Hertzog, & Schulenberg, 1987). Another criticism pertains to the generalizability and durability of training effects. As is true for memory training studies, if the only gains shown are specific to the particular test or if they are not enduring, then the findings do not seriously challenge the notion of inevitable decline. Again, countering this charge are the findings of 7-year retests of respondents in the SLS who were part of training studies. These individuals maintained their advantage over respondents who received no training even after this lengthy interval had elapsed (Schaie, 1994). Other findings by Baltes support the notion that training effects can transfer from one specific task to a set of new test items (Baltes, 1989).

Furthermore, supporting the idea that intellectual decline is not inevitable in old age, other researchers have demonstrated that older adults themselves may have the resources to improve their performance on these tests. In one training study, respondents improved simply by being given the chance to practice with the materials and instructed to find their own training strategies (Blackburn, Papalia-Finlay, Foye, & Serlin, 1988). Learning to handle the stress associated with having one's intellectual performance measured has also been shown to improve fluid ability scores, lending credence to the argument that the performance of older adults is underestimated in novel, and often anxiety-provoking test situations. Furthermore, some elders need practice simply to overcome the lack of practice-the "use it or lose it" principle in action once again (Hayslip, Maloy, & Kohl, 1995). The initial level of the individual's ability is another factor to consider, and for some individuals, success in training may be measured by the prevention of subsequent decline rather than further improvement in test performance (Willis & Schaie, 1986).

In moving from training studies to broader conceptualizations of intelligence in later life, Baltes has suggested several principles that highlight and extend Schaie's admonitions regarding variability in late-life abilities. The first, that of plasticity, implies that the performance of older adults can be modified—a point amply demonstrated in the early training studies. Secondly, Baltes has developed the notion that older adults have "reserve capacity" that usually is untested and hence unproven (Baltes & Lindenberger, 1988; Staudinger, Marsiske, & Baltes, 1995). The concept of reserve capacity is very similar to what individuals experience when they are forced to exert themselves on an occasion in a way that they did not think would be possible, such as running to catch a bus or having to lift a heavy package. Within this framework, older adults are seen as able to perform at higher levels than their test scores ordinarily indicate. This view is very much like that of the production deficiency hypothesis of memory and aging—if older adults are given the opportunity (through instruction or motivational enhancement), they will be able to maximize their test scores even on tests thought to be inevitably affected by the aging process.

Finally, Baltes has introduced the principle of "selective optimization with compensation" (Marsiske, Lang, Baltes, & Baltes, 1995). According to this principle, older adults are able to maximize their performance on the types of tasks or tests that are of most central importance to them. Given limited resources, older individuals may choose to allocate their cognitive abilities in ways that allow them to perform at their best on these specific tasks, letting other less needed abilities fall by the wayside. An important implication of this principle is that training gains can be shown if the pointer is turned to the abilities that have been allowed to atrophy through disuse (Baltes, Kliegl, & Dittmann-Kohli, 1988).

However, not all abilities can be compensated through training. In a variant of the reserve capacity principle, Baltes has advocated a method called "testing the limits" to determine how much the performance of older adults can be increased through training. In studies on memory, Baltes and colleague Kliegl have trained both older and younger adults using the "method of loci" in which subjects are taught to register words in memory by associating them with places that they can visualize (see Chapter 8). This is a highly effective memory training technique, and older adults were shown to improve their performance substantially after learning the procedure. However, this performance gain did not amount to that shown by young adults exposed to similar training. As they observed, "Despite sizable developmental reserve capacity in old age, there is a robust, if not irreversible, negative age difference in some basic components of the mind relevant for the use of the method of loci in achieving superior levels of memory performance" (Baltes & Kliegl, 1992, p. 124). Furthermore, not all elderly individuals may have "reserve capacity" (Baltes, Dittman-Kohli, & Kliegl, 1986), an observation consistent with findings of long-term training effects in the SLS.

Everyday Intelligence and Problem-Solving

As is evident from research involving standardized intelligence test measures, cognitive aging researchers have become increasingly disillusioned with the narrow range of abilities that these tests tap and disenchanted with their dependence on speed. Along with the development of new theories of intelligence are investigations of how adults define and use intelligence in their everyday lives. Not surprisingly, perhaps, what the average adult regards as "intelligent" is not the same as what the average intelligence test measures (Berg, 1990; Berg & Sternberg, 1992; Lachman, Baltes, Nesselroade, & Willis, 1982).

An interest in how older adults perform in their daily lives has also led researchers in cognitive aging to investigate the performance of older adults on "real life" problem solving measures. Perhaps, and again not surprisingly, when older adults in one study were asked to find solutions to problems involving home management and interpersonal conflict, they outperformed younger persons. Furthermore, adding to the criticism of the relevance of psychometric intelligence test performance to everyday life, performance on these everyday problems was not correlated with fluid or crystallized scores (Cornelius & Caspi, 1986). A similar study designed to measure practical problem solving failed to replicate the superiority of older problem-solvers (Denney & Pearce, 1989). Interestingly, however, although the Denney study involved problems defined by older adults as relevant to their lives, the ages of the raters were not given. It is possible that the raters in this study were operating according to different assumptions about the effectiveness of problem-solving strategies. It remains possible that older adults show superiority on some but not all everyday problems, perhaps reflecting the multidimensional nature of problems in real life as well as in the laboratory (Marsiske & Willis, 1995).

Another perspective on the issue of problem-solving abilities in the elderly comes from research on problems varying in their degree of emotional salience. Working on the assumption that adolescents might be disadvantaged in solving difficult interpersonal problems that require objectivity and distancing, Blanchard-Fields and her colleagues (Blanchard-Fields, 1986) compared the problem-solving behavior of adolescents, young adults, and middle-aged adults on problems varying in emotional content. Adolescents found it more difficult to reason abstractly about problems with a high degree of emotional relevance than did the two adult groups, who were able to separate their cognitive reasoning processes from affective components of the problems. Subsequent research expanded on this finding to an older adult population, supporting the idea that greater experience improves an older individual's ability to reason objectively in emotionally salient situations (Blanchard-Fields, Jahnke, & Camp, 1995)

The Elusive Quality of Wisdom

Building on the notion that there is a difference between the "pragmatics" of intelligence as demonstrated in crystallized abilities and the "mechanics" of intelligence as demonstrated in speed-sensitive fluid intelligence tasks, Baltes has continued to pursue the notion that older adults have higher level conceptual abilities not tapped by conventional measures of intelligence. These findings expand greatly upon the observed superiority of older adults on certain "real-life" problem-solving tasks by showing that with increasing age, some individuals become better able to provide insight into life's many dilemmas, particularly those that are psychosocial or interpersonal in nature.

The definition of wisdom arrived at by the Baltes group is that it is "a form of expert knowledge in the domain, fundamental pragmatics of life" (Staudinger, Smith, & Baltes, 1993, p. 272). Within this domain are insights into the essence of the human condition and the nature of life, including the fact that life is finite, that behavior is influenced by cultural conditioning, and that there are variations from person to person in many characteristics, life experiences, and beliefs. Individuals who are wise have a unique understanding of nothing less than the meaning of life (Baltes, Staudinger, Maercker, & Smith, 1995). More specifically, the components of wisdom can be divided into five criteria: (1) rich factual knowledge; (2) rich procedural knowledge; (3) life-span contextualism; (4) value relativism; and (5) recognition and management of uncertainty. Using these criteria, older individuals tend more likely to be found among the wise (Staudinger et al., 1993), but an even more pronounced superiority of age is found when older individuals nominated as "wise" or having expertise in helping individuals solve real-life concerns (clinical psychologists) are compared to younger and older adults with no special claim to wisdom (Baltes et al., 1995).

How do individuals become wise? According to these researchers, the development of wisdom is fostered through a set of favorable life influences including increased experience with life (age), openness to new experiences, interest in the welfare of younger generations (generativity), exposure to good mentorship by others, training, and "well-structured experience with the human condition" (Baltes & Staudinger, 1993, p. 77). Age alone, then, is not sufficient to produce wisdom, as the individual must be able to take advantage of what can be learned from experiences rather than simply surviving for a long number of years (although survival may reflect wisdom to a certain extent).

Relationship to Personality and Lifestyle

As the problem-solving and wisdom research areas illustrate, older individuals may enhance their ability to solve real-life problems requiring maturity and judgment by taking advantage of their greater perspective and life experiences. This notion is supported by several lines of research converging in their emphasis on the role of personality and lifestyle variables in maintaining intellectual functioning in old age.

Rigidity–flexibility is one important personality variable shown to be differentially related to patterns of intellectual aging (Schaie, Dutta, & Willis, 1991). Three dimensions of rigidity–flexibility identified in the SLS studies are psychomotor speed, motor cognitive flexibility, and attitudinal flexibility. Extensive cross-sectional and longitudinal analyses of these factors (Schaie & Willis, 1991) yielded data indicating the adaptive value in complex settings of a flexible response style and the ability to perform quickly. Interestingly, large cohort effects appear in both performance and attitudinal measures of flexibility, indicating greater flexibility on the part of younger cohorts. As noted in Chapter 2, these data help to shed light on the erroneous notion that individuals become more rigid as they age. Rather, individuals seem to be remarkably stable in the extent to which they maintain flexibility, and it may be this quality that helps predict how cognitively able they will remain through old age.

Earlier findings from the SLS provide further evidence for the role of personality as reflected in lifestyle. Schaie (1979b) had reported, on the basis of the first three tests on the SLS data sets, effects on intelligence test scores of a factor he called "Life Complexity." This factor represented the amount of stimulation the individual received from the environment, and it took into account satisfaction with life status, social status, amount of noise in the environment, intactness of the family, the amount of interaction with the environment, exposure to cultural influences, and employment status (for females). People with higher scores on this multifaceted index were found to show maintenance or even an increase in intelligence test scores over the period of the study. By contrast, individuals whose lives were the least "complex" showed the greatest decline. Reflecting on these findings in a later paper, Schaie (1983) described a possible mechanism linking lifestyle and intellectual functioning as involving the varied opportunities that a favorable environment provides for environmental stimulation—the use-it-or-lose-it principle as applied to the maintenance of high levels of intellectual performance.

There is also some evidence that personality may influence the types of experiences individuals seek out early in life, experiences that will then alter the course of their subsequent development either to foster or interfere with subsequent intellectual development. In an archival study of the relationship between personality and intellectual functioning among men in their mid-60s (Gold et al., 1995), a pattern was identified in the relationship between neuroticism and life achievements such that individuals who are more neurotic when young behave in an excessively emotional way in a variety of situations, especially interpersonal ones. Their lack of "emotional ease" reduces their sense of being able to master their desired life goals and can also interfere with their actual advancement within their occupations. In general, the intellectually brighter men in the sample were able to establish a lifestyle that would support their abilities as they grew older, providing stimulation and experiences that maintained their functioning. However, neuroticism, which was negatively related to intellectual performance, can compromise this advantage. Interestingly, and in keeping with the wisdom research, lifestyle variables played a role in verbal intelligence, indicating their relationship to the more pragmatic or experiential aspects of intelligence.

Relating the findings of these studies on personality and intelligence to identity and aging, it might be argued that a certain degree of assimilation may be helpful as individuals think about their intellectual abilities. To become demoralized by social representations of the elderly as "slow" or less able to think efficiently might be to submit to an early and unnecessary defeat. However, findings of one of the SLS studies calls this strategy into question and suggest the advantages of maintaining a more realistic appraisal of one's abilities (Schaie, Willis, & O'Hanlon, 1994). In the 1984 retest, respondents were asked to compare their current performance with their scores in the testing seven years earlier. By comparing these self-assessments with actual performance changes, it was possible to categorize the respondents into three groups: the "Optimists" (those who overestimated positive changes), "Pessimists" (who overestimated negative changes), and "Realists" (those whose ratings were accurate). You might be able to see a connection between the optimists and people who overuse identity assimilation and, likewise, the pessimists and those who overuse identity accommodation. In fact, the data collection strategy seems to have provided an ideal basis for such a categorization, as both objective and subjective data were available for comparison purposes. The findings revealed that it was the pessimists who actually declined the least or even gained, however, compared to the optimists, who declined the most. Thus, identity accommodation seemed to have an oddly protective effect on actual ability. However, the findings may also be seen as support for the defensive strategies used by the optimists. Their overuse of identity assimilation made it possible for them to protect themselves against knowledge of intellectual declines, if not against the declines themselves.

Intellectual Control and its Relation to Performance

This discussion of identity and intellectual aging provides a backdrop for understanding the emerging field of intellectual control and aging. The belief in one's ability to control the destiny of one's mind with age is an important component of intellectual performance, similar in many ways to the constructs of metamemory and memory self-efficacy. In an early investigation of the link between intellectual self-efficacy or control and performance on tests of intelligence, Lachman and her co-workers provided evidence for a moderately strong positive relationship (Lachman et al., 1982). Of course, the existence of a significant correlation does not indicate directionality. Continued efforts within this research enterprise have attempted to determine whether feeling good about one's intelligence helps to predict good performance, or whether those who perform well feel good about their abilities.

In a finding reminiscent of the "optimists" vs. "pessimists" distinction, the initial indications from Lachman's studies involving lagged designs *failed* to provide support for the interpretation that people who feel that they can control their performance on intelligence tests do in fact perform better than people who feel they cannot control their intellectual aging (Lachman, 1983). Instead, those who perform better feel a stronger sense of personal control precisely because their performance is holding up as they age. This finding ran counter to the expectations of the researcher, whose writings on the area of personal control and aging have contributed heavily to the positive view of aging as "a state of mind." Even as studies over a longer (5-year) time interval and with an expanded battery of measures were conducted, the beneficial effect of positive control beliefs on performance could not be demonstrated (Lachman & Leff, 1989). Similar findings were obtained from a short-term (2-year) longitudinal study conducted at Penn State (Grover & Hertzog, 1991).

Taking advantage of the training methodology to go beyond the correlational and longitudinal designs, a group of well-known intervention researchers investigated the outcome on self-efficacy beliefs of cognitive training in intellectual tasks (Dittmann-Kohli, Lachman, Kliegl, & Baltes, 1991). Various training methods were compared, and it was only in the ability training group that respondents showed an increase in intellectual self-efficacy as well as test performance. The impact was very specific, however, to intellectual self-efficacy rather than global self-efficacy. Nevertheless, the point was made that changes in self-efficacy can follow interventions aimed at improving cognitive skills, and that furthermore, such positive changes in self-confidence should have a favorable positive spiraling effect on the acquisition of subsequent abilities.

REFERENCES

Baltes, P. B. (1989). Cognitive training research on fluid intelligence in old age: What can older adults achieve by themselves? *Psychology and Aging, 4,* 217–221.

Baltes, P. B., Dittman-Kohli, F., & Kliegl, R. (1986). Reserve capacity of the elderly in aging-sensitive tests of fluid intelligence: replication and extension. *Psychology and Aging, 1,* 172–177.

Baltes, P. B., & Kliegl, R. (1992). Further testing of limits of cognitive plasticity: Negative age differences in a mnemonic skill are robust. *Developmental Psychology, 28,* 121–125.

Baltes, P. B., Kliegl, R., & Dittmann-Kohli, F. (1988). On the locus of training gains in research on the plasticity of fluid intelligence in old age. *Journal of Educational Psychology, 80*(3), 392–400.

Baltes, P. B., & Lindenberger, U. (1988). On the range of cognitive plasticity in old age as a function of experience: Fifteen years of intervention research. *Behavior Therapy, 19*(3), 283–300.

Baltes, P. B., & Schaie, K. W. (1974, March). Aging and IQ: The myth of the twilight years. *Psychology Today,* pp. 35–38, 40.

Baltes, P. B., & Schaie, K. W. (1976). On the plasticity of intelligence in adulthood and old age: Where Horn and Donaldson fail. *American Psychologist, 31,* 720–725.

Baltes, P. B., & Staudinger, U. M. (1993). The search for a psychology of wisdom. *Current Directions in Psychological Science, 2,* 75–80.

Baltes, P. B., Staudinger, U. M., Maercker, A., & Smith, J. (1995). People nominated as wise: A comparative study of wisdom-related knowledge. *Psychology and Aging, 10,* 155–166.

Berg, C. A. (1990). What is intellectual efficacy over the life course? Using adults' concepts to address the question. In J. A. Rodin, C. Schooler, & K. W. Schaie (Ed.), *Self-directedness and efficacy: Causes and effects throughout the life course* (pp. 155–181). Hillsdale NJ: Erlbaum.

Berg, C. A., & Sternberg, R. J. (1992). Adults' conceptions of intelligence across the adult life span. *Psychology and Aging, 7,* 221–231.

Blackburn, J. A., Papalia-Finlay, D., Foye, B. F., & Serlin, R. C. (1988). Modifiability of figural relations performance among elderly adults. *Journal of Gerontology: Psychological Sciences, 43,* P87–89.

Blanchard-Fields, F. (1986). Reasoning on social dilemmas varying in emotional saliency: An adult developmental perspective. *Psychology and Aging, 1,* 325–333.

Blanchard-Fields, F., Jahnke, H. C., & Camp, C. (1995). Age differences in problem-solving style: The role of emotional salience. *Psychology and Aging, 10,* 173–180.

Cornelius, S. W., & Caspi, A. (1986). Self-perceptions of intellectual control and aging. *Educational Gerontology, 12,* 345–357.

Denney, N. W., & Pearce, K. A. (1989). A developmental study of practical problem-solving in adults. *Psychology and Aging, 4,* 438–442.

Dittmann-Kohli, F., Lachman, M. E., Kliegl, R., & Baltes, P. B. (1991). Effects of cognitive training and testing on intellectual efficacy beliefs in elderly adults. *Journals of Gerontology, 46*(4), 162.

Field, D., Schaie, K. W., & Leino, E. V. (1988). Continuity in intellectual functioning: The role of self-reported health. *Psychology and Aging, 3,* 385–392.

Giambra, L. M., Arenberg, D., Zonderman, A. B., Kawas, C., & Costa, P. T., Jr. (1995). Adult life span changes in immediate visual memory and verbal intelligence. *Psychology and Aging, 10,* 123–139.

Gold, D. P., Andres, D., Etezadi, J., Arbuckle, T., Schwartzman, A., & Chaikelson, J. (1995). Structural equation model of intellectual change and continuity and predictors of intelligence in older men. *Psychology and Aging, 10,* 294–303.

Grover, D. R., & Hertzog, C. (1991). Relationships between intellectual control beliefs and psychometric intelligence in adulthood. *Journal of Gerontology: Psychological Sciences, 46,* P109–115.

Hayslip, B., Jr., Maloy, R. M., & Kohl, R. (1995). Long-term efficacy of fluid ability interventions with older adults. *Journal of Gerontology: Psychological Sciences, 50B,* P141–149.

Hernnstein, R. J., & Murray, C. (1994). *The bell curve.* New York: Free Press.

Hertzog, C., & Schaie, K. W. (1988). Stability and change in adult intelligence: 2. Simultaneous analysis of longitudinal means. *Psychology and Aging, 3,* 122–130.

Horn, J. L. (1970). Organization of data on life-span development of human abilities. In L. R. Goulet & P. B. Baltes (Ed.), *Life-span developmental psychology: Theory and research* (Vol. 1, pp. 211–256). New York: Academic Press.

Horn, J. L. (1982). The theory of fluid and crystallized intelligence in relation to concepts of cognitive psychology and aging in adulthood. In F. I. M. Craik & S. Trehub (Ed.), *Aging and cognitive processes* (pp. 237–278). New York: Plenum.

Horn, J. L., & Cattell, R. B. (1966). Refinement and test of the theory of fluid and crystallized intelligence. *Journal of Educational Psychology, 57,* 253–270.

Horn, J. L., & Donaldson, G. (1976). On the myth of intellectual decline in adulthood. *American Psychologist, 31,* 701–719.

Horn, J. L., & Donaldson, G. (1977). Faith is not enough: A resonse to the Baltes-Schaie claim that intelligence does not wane. *American Psychologist, 32,* 369–373.

Lachman, M. (1983). Perceptions of intellectual aging: Antecedent or consequence of intellectual functioning? *Developmental Psychology, 19,* 482–498.

Lachman, M. E., Baltes, P. B., Nesselroade, J. R., & Willis, S. L. (1982). Examination of personality-ability relationships in the elderly: The role of the contextual (interface) assessment mode. *Journal of Research in Personality, 16,* 485–501.

Lachman, M. E., & Leff, R. (1989). Perceived control and intellectual functioning in the elderly: A 5-year longitudinal study. *Developmental Psychology, 25*(5), 722–728.

Lindenberger, U., & Baltes, P. B. (1994). Aging and intelligence. In R. J. Sternberg (Ed.), *Encyclopedia of human intelligence* (Vol. 1, pp. 52–66). New York: Macmillan.

Marsiske, M., Lang, F. R., Baltes, P. B., & Baltes, M. M. (1995). Selective optimization with compensation: Life-span perspectives on successful human development. In R. A. Dixon & L. Backman (Eds.), *Compensating for psychological deficits and declines: Managing losses and promoting gains* (pp. 35–79). Mahwah, NJ: Erlbaum.

Marsiske, M., & Willis, S. L. (1995). Dimensionality of everyday problem solving in older adults. *Psychology and Aging, 10,* 269–283.

McGue, M., Hirsch, B., & Lykken, D. T. (1993). Age and the self-perception of ability: A twin study analysis. *Psychology and Aging, 8,* 72–80.

Schaie, K. W. (1974). Translations in gerontology—from lab to life. *American Psychologist, 29,* 802–807.

Schaie, K. W. (1979a). The primary mental abilities in adulthood: An exploration of the development of psychometric intelligence. In P. B. Baltes & J. O. G. Brim (Ed.), *Life-span development and behavior* (Vol. 2, pp. 67–115). New York: Academic Press.

Schaie, K. W. (1979b). The primary mental abilities in adulthood: An exploration of the development of psychometric intelligence. In P. B. Baltes & J. O. G. Brim (Ed.), *Life-span development and behavior* (Vol. 2, pp. 67–115). New York: Academic Press.

Schaie, K. W. (1983). The Seattle Longitudinal Study: A 21-year exploration of psychometric intelligence in adulthood. In K. W. Schaie (Ed.), *Longitudinal studies of adult psychological development* (pp. 64–135). New York: Guilford.

Schaie, K. W. (1989). Perceptual speed in adulthood: Cross-sectional and longitudinal analyses. *Psychology and Aging, 4,* 443–453.

Schaie, K. W. (1994). The course of adult intellectual development. *American Psychologist, 49,* 304–313.

Schaie, K. W., & Baltes, P. B. (1977). Some faith helps to see the forest: A final comment on the Horn–Donaldson myth of the Baltes–Schaie position on adult intelligence. *American Psychologist, 32,* 1118–1120.

Schaie, K. W., Dutta, R., & Willis, S. L. (1991). Relationship between rigidity–flexibility and cognitive abilities in adulthood. *Psychology and Aging, 6,* 371–383.

Schaie, K. W., & Willis, S. L. (1991). Adult personality and psychomotor performance: Cross-sectional and longitudinal analyses. *Journal of Gerontology: Psychological Sciences, 46,* P275–284.

Schaie, K. W., & Willis, S. L. (1993). Age difference patterns of psychometric intelligence in adulthood: Generalizability within and across domains. *Psychology and Aging, 8,* 44–55.

Schaie, K. W., Willis, S. L., Hertzog, C., & Schulenberg, J. E. (1987). Effects of cognitive training on primary mental ability structure. *Psychology and Aging, 2,* 233–242.

Schaie, K. W., Willis, S. L., & O'Hanlon, A. M. (1994). Perceived intellectual performance change over seven years. *Journal of Gerontology: Psychological Sciences, 49,* P108–118.

Spearman, C. (1904). "General intelligence": Objectively determined and measured. *American Journal of Psychology, 15,* 201–292.

Spearman, C. (1927). *The abilities of man.* New York: Macmillan.

Staudinger, U. M., Marsiske, M., & Baltes, P. B. (1995). Resilience and reserve capacity in later adulthood: Potentials and limits of development across the life span. In D. Cicchetti & D. J. Cohen (Eds.), *Developmental psychopathology* (Vol. 2: Risk, disorder, and adaptation, pp. 801-847). New York: Wiley.

Staudinger, U. M., Smith, J., & Baltes, P. B. (1993). Wisdom-related knowledge in a life review task: Age differences and role of professional specialization. *Psychology and Aging, 7,* 271–281.

Sternberg, R. J. (1985). *A triarchic theory of human intelligence.* New York: Cambridge University Press.

Willis, S. L., & Schaie, K. W. (1986). Training the elderly on the ability factors of spatial orientation and inductive reasoning. *Psychology and Aging, 1,* 239–247.

10

Identity and Personality

In Chapter 1, a theoretical model of identity was briefly described that forms the underlying foundation for this book. In this chapter a fuller description of this model is presented, addressing its assumptions and ramifications, and later in the chapter, theories and research on personality with relevance to aging and issues of identity will be elaborated on.

The model of identity development presented in this chapter originated in the work of Erikson, who defined identity in psychosocial terms as a product of individual and experiential factors. From Piaget's theory the processes of assimilation and accommodation are added, which serve as the basis for the individual's interactions with the environment through the schema of identity. The idea of a dialectical process of development, derived from Piaget's theory by Riegel and others (Berzonsky, 1990; Riegel, 1976) is a fundamental aspect of this model, accounting for movement back and forth from equilibrium to disequilibrium across the years of adulthood. The model is also informed by other theories that address the concept of congruence between self and experiences as inherent to personality growth and adjustment. Sociological perspectives are also incorporated into this model as providing an understanding of how individuals define themselves in relation to their major social roles, cultural background, and age-related stereotypes and expectations.

From these diverse sources the following definition of adult identity was constructed: Adult identity is the integration of the individual's physical characteristics, abilities, motives, goals, attitudes, values, and social roles as attributed to the self and as conceived of as consistent over time. Identity forms a basis for the individual's interpretation of experiences and is in turn further modified by experiences. These experiences include ones that reflect on one's physical and

278

intellectual competencies, and also events and social interactions that have relevance to the self's regard by others.

IDENTITY PROCESSES

The two basic identity processes that determine how knowledge about the self is formulated and reformulated by experiences are identity assimilation and identity accommodation. These two processes, conceived here in terms of identity, are taken directly from Piaget's description of assimilation and accommodation in the cognitive or intellectual domain. Their meanings are the same as they are in Piaget's theory in terms of the way they interact with experience. What differs in the present identity model is the content on which these processes are assumed to operate. Where Piaget describes a system of cognitive schemas, the present model describes a system of schemas about the self organized into the totality of identity.

Identity assimilation refers to the process through which the individual imposes his or her existing framework of self-knowledge of identity onto experiences. As seen in earlier chapters, assimilation can involve seeing the self as "youthful," or as possessing characteristics that have become altered over time, denying the fact that the aging process has led to alterations in appearance and competence. This process provides reassurance to the individual, making the environment a place that can be understood in terms that are familiar and comfortable. By contrast, when experiences cannot easily be assimilated into the individual's existing framework of the self, the process of accommodation is triggered so that the information from these experiences becomes incorporated into identity. As was described in the multiple threshold model, identity accommodation may be seen as stimulated by the entry into consciousness of an altered physical or cognitive function.

Up until now, identity assimilation and accommodation have been described in fairly generic terms, specifying the content to which they apply rather than the details of what each process involves. At this point in the discussion, it will be helpful to the reader to see particular instances of these identity processes through the description of categories of assimilation and accommodation. These instances come from an indepth interview study of 94 adults ranging from 24 to 61 years, published in *The Me I Know: A Study of Adult Identity* (Whitbourne, 1986) (which will be referred to here as "the interview study"). Currently, scale development is in process to convert these category descriptions to assimilation–accommodation scores on the "Identity and Experiences Scale." Further data from this instrument should serve to refine and validate the specific forms of assimilation and accommodation.

The Subjective Content of Identity

Chapter 1 outlined six content domains of identity that form the basis for organizing and interpreting experiences relevant to the self. As determined by the interviews, although adults may not be aware of these subdivisions within identity, they have a subjective sense of the self based on the implicit assumption of being "loving, competent, and good"—a positive ego-enhancing bias that allows individuals to maintain their self-esteem in the face of potentially threatening or challenging information about the self that may come in one of any number of identity domains. The "loving" component of this positive triad is that one is loved by family and other significant people. The "competent" component, has already been examined in depth with regard to physical and cognitive functioning, and pertains to the view of oneself as healthy, strong, and able in these domains. The "good" component of this triad refers to the view of the self as morally and ethically upstanding. Individuals prefer to see themselves as honest, as adhering to society's major values, and as possessing integrity.

This set of attributions will be referred to as the "positive triad," borrowing from the "cognitive triad" of Beck's (Beck, Rush, Shaw, & Emery, 1975) theory of depression. In Beck's theory, depressed individuals are seen as ascribing to the cognitive triad of negative views about the self, the world, and the future. The positive triad with regard to identity may be thought of as the set of organizing principles used by normal, nondepressed individuals as their implicit positive bias for viewing themselves in relation to their experiences.

Identity Assimilation

The protection of the positive triad of self-attributions is handled by identity assimilation, whose function is to provide the individual with basically positive feedback about the self, even if this means that the information is in some ways inaccurate. The various forms that identity assimilation can take all involve some degree of distortion and denial of factors that are inconsistent with this identity.

Self-justification. In self-justification, the individual relies on simple assertions of his or her lovingness, competence, and goodness. Self-justification is regarded as a form of assimilation because it involves a process of imposing one's identity onto experiences without simultaneously looking for any weaknesses in the "fit" between the two. The individual defensively asserts that "I'm right about myself and what I'm doing is right, and that's that!"

There is a proactive quality to this form of identity assimilation in that the individual appears to have a need to take experiences and transform them actively into a form that will be compatible with a positive identity. This form of assimilation may be seen as a kind of "chip on the shoulder" of identity—"this is how I feel about myself, I dare you to prove me wrong." A good example from the interview study of self-justification involved a mother who stated that she was "the pillar of this house—"without me things just don't go right"—an assertion that may be correct, but just as likely reflects her need to see herself as central to the family's well-being. Without other data, it is hard to judge the accuracy of her appraisal, but other examples of self-justification allow some inferences to be made. Another example was of a man who asserted that he had to give up cherished outdoor adventure activities because his family is now "number one" to him. This compelling testimony was contradicted by his statement elsewhere in the interview that "okay, . . . I still go hiking, I still go canoeing." These discrepancies, even by the respondent's own admission, make it possible to infer some distortions in the original statement about what a great family man he was. Another example of a mother, although not discredited elsewhere in the interview, conveys this sense of justification. When asked how important to her was the work of a homemaker, she replied that it is "very important. Everything I do is very important. Everything I have is very important."

In terms of other areas of functioning, self-justification may apply to physical functioning when an older adult refuses to acknowledge weaknesses of the cardiovascular system that may lead to disaster when a highly physically stressful activity is attempted. Or the individual may refuse to buy or use bifocals or hearing aids when needed. Similarly, an older person who could benefit from exercise or dietary restrictions insists that he or she does not need to resort to these activities. As revealed in numerous studies of aging and well-being, the consistent findings of high levels of life satisfaction in the elderly, despite many areas of loss, suggests that self-justification may be operating in many older people who survive to the later years of adulthood.

Examples of self-justification items on the Identity and Experiences Scale further illustrate the nature of this category of identity assimilation. These items include: "I try not to think of things that make me feel bad about myself"; "I prefer to think about my strengths rather than my weaknesses" (and reliability item "My weaknesses are less important to me than my strengths"); and "When I think of myself, I like to focus on the positive"; These items convey the style of an individual who likes to project a positive image and believe in that image as well.

Identity projection. There is a well-known psychodynamic form of defense mechanism known as "projection" which comes close to identity projection as a form of identity assimilation. In projection, the individual attributes to others undesirable motives that lurk within the individual's own unconscious. In identity projection, the individual describes in an extremely negative way the beliefs or practices of "other people" in order to appear, by comparison, as having a favorable identity with regard to the characteristic in question—a "saint," as it were. In part, this form of identity assimilation involves self-justification, as the individual is emerging from the comparison as someone who is loving, competent, and good. The projection component is the implication that perhaps the negative qualities that the respondent points to in others are ones that he or she in fact possesses. The individual "doth protest too much."

Examples from the interview study of identity projection again involved a leap of faith at times in making inferences from comparisons individuals made between themselves and others whom they disparaged. A homemaker might compare herself to other homemakers whom she criticizes for watching too much TV—although she admits to becoming bored, she claims she would never waste her time this way. A worker might berate his superiors or others who succeeded in the company because they were willing to "play the game" and he or she was not. Or others may be seen as morally inferior, dishonest, and disloyal. The self, by contrast, is of the highest and most upstanding moral character.

In terms of the aging process, identity projection may be seen in the way that individuals compare themselves favorably to others, whom they see as suffering ill effects. The successful use of downward social comparisons noted by life satisfaction researchers (Heidrich & Ryff, 1993) is a good example of the successful use of identity projection. The danger, however, may be that the individual fails to identify with his or her age group and is perceived by them to be conceited and arrogant. Younger individuals may regard such a person as seriously out of touch with reality, complaining about "old people," when to all appearances, he or she fits very comfortably into this category.

Examples of identity projection items from the Identity and Experiences Scale reflect this quality of seeing the self as better than others or of seeing others as having problems rather oneself: "When something bad happens to me, I assume it's not my fault"; "If someone is unfriendly to me, I assume it is not due to anything bad about me"; "People who criticize me are usually wrong." It is difficult to measure this form of assimilation, however, from an instrument based entirely on self-report.

Defensive rigidity. The third form of identity assimilation is the unwillingness or inability to consider the possibility of a flaw in one's identity as loving, competent, and good. The "rigidity" of this form of assimilation refers to a lack of consideration of alternatives to one's present view of the self and it is "defensive" because it is assumed that the rigidity protects the individual from negative self-disconfirming information. When this form of identity assimilation is used, it is assumed that area of identity it protects is based on a precarious and unstable foundation. The risks entailed in questioning or challenging this weak identity are seen as too great. As a result, the individual maintains a particular position or view of the self but does not stop to wonder about it or doubt whether it is actually the one that is best or right under all circumstances.

One excellent example from the interview study was the response of an individual addressing the issue of values:

> These values tell me how I must live and how I must perform at various times . . . but I have never really thought about me personally and what they are doing for me personally . . . if someone told you a rule do not step on the grass, I don't think about whether I'm upset or indifferent or whatever because I can't walk on the grass. The rule is don't do this, and . . . I think values have their own reasons so I don't really question how I feel about it . . . it would cease to be a value somewhat if I was trying to change it.

This statement implies that one's own personal values, like rules, are not to be questioned once they have been established.

Defensive rigidity also can be seen when individuals state that they have "always" felt this way in the past and will "always" continue to feel the same way in the future. They may feel that their particular identity choices represent a "way of life" that is "natural" or "instinctive." These terms cast a reflexive quality onto identity—that the individual is fulfilling a predetermined destiny and that little introspection about the desirability of this identity is either required or even healthy.

Another related tendency that falls into the category of defensive rigidity is a resistance to social changes that might reflect negatively on an identity adopted by the individual before those social changes took place; the ideals and beliefs of the "young." Oddly enough, such individuals may pride themselves on their flexibility and regard themselves as able to keep up with "today's" values. However, when asked specific questions pertaining to their own beliefs and values, they indicate a preference for their long-held beliefs and feel challenged by the thought that the world might be changing.

Ultimately, defensive rigidity in terms of identity may come to take the form of personality rigidity as studied by, for example, Schaie and his co-workers

(Schaie, Dutta, & Willis, 1991; Schaie & Willis, 1991). The individual who is high on attitudinal rigidity may also be the one who prefers not to challenge or question the contents of an identity formed early in life and maintained thereafter at an increasingly precarious risk to the self. The danger associated with defensive rigidity is that the individual's self-views become increasingly removed from experiences in adulthood that, by definition, require at least occasional self-examination. Am I walking as fast as I used to? Do I hear as well? Is it time to reconsider my success as a parent? What will I do after I retire? These and many other questions invariably should be addressed at some point between the 20s and the 70s. Furthermore, as discrepancies over time between the self-of-the-past and the self-of-the-present become more and more glaring (especially to others), the individual must exert increasingly firm control over all potentially self-threatening information that is fed back from experiences. The longer one goes without examining or scrutinizing the self, the more difficult it is to initiate the process of putting oneself to the test. As this happens, the individual restricts the range of new experiences further, and the process becomes self-perpetuating.

Items on the Identity and Experiences Scale that are intended to measure defensive rigidity try to capture this general quality of staying away from self-invalidating information. These items are: "Not very interested in advice from others"; "Have very few doubts or questions about myself"; and "Generally try to avoid change in how I see myself."

Lack of insight. Individuals may avoid threats to their identity created by discrepancies with experiences by simply ignoring the problem altogether. This more benign form of rigidity protects the individual from negative feedback about the self through indifference, feigned innocence, or a disingenuous lack of concern for questions or problems related to the self. This "lack of insight" type of assimilation was identified in the interview study through instances in which respondents stated that they had never thought about these questions, or when they were not able to give an answer. The question may have been one that "I never ask myself." Avoidance of a question may indicate an unwillingness to confront the pain of answering the question in a negative way as this would cast aspersions on the individual's positive sense of self.

Lack of insight may appear not just in avoidance of certain questions, but in the unwillingness or inability to recognize possible unhappiness or discrepancies in one's own self-report of experiences. In the case of aging, for example, the individual may enumerate a number of so-called "aches and pains," but not see these as contradictory with an overall positive global self-assessment of health. Many studies on subjective health in the elderly document this type of apparent contradiction. In the case of lack of insight, as compared to defensive rigidity, it is not that the individual is actively working to build a protective wall around the self, but that assimilation takes a more passive form.

Examples of lack of insight on the Identity and Experiences Scale reflect this type of passive avoidance of potentially charged issues: "Spend little time wondering 'why' I do things"; "Don't spend much effort reflecting on 'who' I am"; "Don't think very deeply about my goals because I know what they are."

Identity Accommodation

The process of identity accommodation involves attempts to arrive at a realistic appraisal of the self in relation to experiences. Even if the individual's appraisal arrived at through accommodation is inaccurate, it is nevertheless the case that the effort involved in the process may be regarded as eventually promoting greater congruence. Ultimately, identity accommodation is the process that will result in changes made to identity. Even though the positive triad of the self as "loving, competent, and good" may be maintained in the long run, the immediate process may involve serious introspection or a differentiation within particular identity domains.

Favorable changes in identity. Although there seems to be a certain fear or reluctance attached to admitting to weaknesses within the self, individuals who engage in identity accommodation may come out on the other side with more a favorable view of the self than they initially had at the outset. In part, this sense of positive change may come about as a contrast effect in comparison to the dysphoria that may have accompanied the need for change in the first place—a sense that things have to "get worse before they get better."

It is possible that a favorable change in identity may be reported through an assimilative process of rationalization or distortion. In other words, the individual takes a negative experience and reframes it to be more positive than it actually was. Nevertheless, statements made in the interview study seemed to provide a rationale for including this form of accommodation as a valid category of change in identity in response to self-experience incongruity, particularly when statements attesting to change are specific and lack a self-serving quality. These statements may also possess a certain degree of candor or humor that give them a sense of being grounded in reality, as in the following observation from a man in the interview study reflecting on how his view of himself was affected by his work:

If I have a good day at work I come home and I feel good that I got something accomplished and I start looking for the next thing to accomplish. If I had a rotten day at work, I'm a grouchy son of a bitch.

Overall, this individual felt that his identity as a worker reflected favorably on himself, but his willingness to admit to problems at work, including those he may have helped to create, adds credence to his claim.

Looking at the aging process, views of the self as having grown psychologically or having been able to adapt to age-related changes may be seen as instances of favorable identity change. Although there is evidence that gains are more readily integrated into identity than losses of physical functioning (McGue, Hirsch, & Lykken, 1993), it is nevertheless the case that individuals may achieve optimal adaptation through a lifetime of assimilative strategies that protect the self along with the judicious use of accommodation when circumstances warrant. As stated by Ryff in observing the views of older adults regarding the future (Ryff, 1991) "these older individuals have reined in their personal ideals relative to the two younger age groups. Thus, there appears to be a later life gain wherein the ideal self better fits the real self, warts and all, with whom one has become an accustomed traveler" (p. 293).

The identity accommodation dimension of the Identity and Experiences Scale contains these items to indicate favorable changes in identity: "Have benefited as much from my failures as my successes"; "Am largely a product of my experiences"; and "Feel the bad things I've experienced were worth the pain." As stated earlier, it may be the case that these items tap into identity assimilation, particularly the second item, but the inclusion of terms such as "failure" and "bad things" decreases the chances that individuals who cannot acknowledge their own limitations will agree with these items.

Self-doubts. A less positive bias may be inherent in the identity accommodation strategy of self-doubts involving the recognition of limitations or questions about the self. It is assumed that self-doubts are generated when individuals perceive a discrepancy between their experiences and the positive triad of their identities. This discrepancy may be assumed to trigger a questioning of the self and whether one's own personal shortcomings were the cause.

The period of questioning and self-doubts may go through a multistage process. In the first stage, the individual attempts to determine whether a disparity between the self and experience actually exists. As stated in the interview study by one respondent, "it gives me a reference point I can . . . look at in what I have accomplished and I can say 'is this what was expected of me?'; and, conversely, 'what have I accomplished. . .?'" If the individual concludes that a discrepancy between identity and experiences does exist, then the next step is to look for its source. At this point, there may be a period in which self-doubts are actively raised and the question addressed of whether the positive triad needs to be altered or scaled down in some way. In the interview study, a woman who saw herself as the protective "older sister" described such a process in beginning to question her role in the family: "Maybe I'm overprotective. Maybe on occasions they feel that I'm being over-curious or doing, asking questions that really aren't, shouldn't be in my department." Such a statement might very easily come from the mother of teenagers, who starts to see that her children require more autonomy (Tolman & Whitbourne, in press). Although it is not possible to know how close to reality are the self-perceptions of these respondents, it remains the case that they at least acknowledge that they are having questions or doubts about their roles and accomplishments.

At its most intense, self-doubting can be an extremely painful process involving active confrontation between the individual's identity as positive and experiences that prove this identity to be false. These cases can reach catastrophic levels and, indeed, some of the greatest tragedies in literature involve the sudden lifting of a curtain in which the protagonist sees the "warts" that have led to personal downfall or the death of loved ones. In terms of the aging process, the most difficult period of self-doubting or questioning may occur as a threshold is being crossed and the individual had no preparation or warning about its occurrence. The experience of a myocardial infarction, as frightening as it is for one's sense of mortality, may constitute such an "identity shock" as it triggers sudden recognition of the vulnerability of the body and the serious possibility of death. Indeed such moments may bring out an "epiphany" (Kiecolt, 1994) or turning point, after which life and identity are never the same.

Not all individuals may enter into such an in-depth period of questioning, however, and self-doubts may remain at a more chronic and perhaps more subtle level for long periods of time. Indeed, those individuals who rely heavily on the process of identity accommodation are precisely those who are likely to maintain a high level of self-doubting. Corresponding to this potential variability, the items on the Identity and Experiences Scale are designed to be responsive to variations in the level of doubts or questions: "Have many doubts and questions about myself"; "At times seriously question 'who' I am"; "Often wonder whether others like me or not"; "Need people to tell me they like me." Presumably, those individuals who maintain a more chronic sense of doubting have come to rely on the opinions and regard of others to bolster their own weak sense of self.

Looking at alternatives. If the individual is able to work through the intense period of disequilibrium triggered by self-doubts and questions, what remains on the other side is a new and altered equilibrium between identity and experiences. The process of examining alternatives, in which self-doubts and questions become translated into an active period of identity choices, is likely to facilitate this development.

The case of one interview study respondent provided an interesting parallel to the way that the aging process might trigger a period of examining alternatives to one's youthful identity. This respondent, who broke his leg while auto racing, had "about six or eight weeks to think and do nothing except lay around." During this time, he decided that working on cars was not the ideal occupation for him. He quit his job and went to school so that he would be able to pursue a more rewarding occupation. Similarly, individuals who are forced through physical or cognitive changes in later adulthood to alter their lifestyles may find that when old patterns are broken they can be replaced with more intrinsically satisfying activities, or at least ones that involve different sets of skills and interests. The ability to adapt to changing abilities and competencies may in and of itself provide the individual with a sense of personal efficacy and become a source of well-being (Brandtstadter & Rothermund, 1994), perhaps as one begins to identify with the "survivor" mentality of having made it through the many precipitous paths along the way to advanced old age.

On the Identity and Experiences Scale, items that measure this form of identity accommodation are "Have thought about other lifestyles that may be better for me"; "Feel that it's hard to decide on which course I want to take in life"; and "Often wonder about how my life could be different than it is." Although these items may not capture the sense of immediacy or urgency involved in serious periods of identity exploration, they tap into the notion that individuals who demonstrate this form of accommodation are not locked into or wedded to their present set of identity commitments. Again, these items may tap the more chronic or persistent use of identity accommodation than that implied in evaluation of the response to change.

Responsivity to external influences. Although not identified in the interview study, the form of identity accommodation involving the individual's responsiveness to forces outside the self seems relevant to the overaccommodative type of individual who lacks a clear sense of direction. Such an individual may be considered to be high on the quality of "self-monitoring" (Snyder, 1974), looking outward to provide sources of inner guidance. It may be assumed that individuals who maintain a high level of self-monitoring are chronically high on the accommodation dimension, even though they never enter a discrete period of crisis.

With regard to the aging process, individuals who are highly responsive to external influences may be assumed to be the most affected by aging expectations and stereotypes. They would be the ones to conclude that you are "over the hill" when you have reached a certain age, by virtue of having reached that age and not necessarily due to any particular age-related event. The opinion and approbation of others may motivate them to the point of feeling that they must comply with the needs of others rather than satisfying their own desires or living up to their own beliefs.

Items tapping this dimension on the Identity and Experiences Scale are : "Behave according to what I think others want from me"; "Find it very easy to change in response to new experiences"; "Very influenced by what others think"; "Depend heavily on others for advice and feedback." Although some people who are high on assimilation might actually view themselves as easily changeable, a quality that is currently high on social desirability (Schaie & Willis, 1991), it is the constellation of defining one's identity in terms of others' constructions of the self that characterizes those who overaccommodate in this regard.

Identity Assimilation and Accommodation in Relation to Specific Events

Up to this point, the definition and measurement of identity processes have been framed in fairly generic terms. As measured by the Identity and Experiences Scale, the identity processes describe one's general style rather than the way that individuals respond to particular instances in which identity issues form the focus of attention and concern. A "Specific" form of the Identity and Experiences Scale was developed to measure assimilation and accommodation processes with regard to particular, isolatable events in which one's identity was called into question. These items may be answered with regard to two types of events: (1) a particular "threshold" event in which a physical or cognitive ability has become of major concern; and (2) a general life event that was "difficult or challenging to your sense of 'who' you are."

Examples of assimilation items rated for these events are as follows: "I don't pay much attention to it" (lack of insight); "It seems to be a problem for other people but not for me" (identity projection); "It doesn't reflect anything bad about me" (self-justification); "It doesn't change the way I think about myself" (defensive rigidity). The forms of accommodation on this scale are "It is having a major effect on me" (self-doubts); "I realize how much I have changed" (favorable identity change); "Other people's views about this have influenced me" (responsivity to external influences); and "I see myself very differently as a result of this" (looking at alternatives). Although these scales are shorter than the general forms of the Identity and Experiences Scale (14 items compared to 35), they are actually more reliable. By assessing identity responses with regard to specific experiences, it is possible to compare the value of looking at identity processes as general stylistic features of personality compared to reactions to particular identity-relevant age changes and events.

Preliminary pilot data based on samples of approximately 200 adults from 26 to 85 years old (Whitbourne, Hussey, & Primus, 1995) provide support for the constructs of identity assimilation and accommodation and their proposed relation to physical changes. Adults over 60 years of age reporting a large number of "threshold" experiences received higher scores on the accommodation scale, particularly the "specific" form with regard to aging. Furthermore, this research is moving in the direction of identifying the "identity styles" described at a theoretical level in an earlier analysis of relationships among personality, health, and well-being (Whitbourne, 1987). Individuals may be categorized using a median split technique into assimilative, accommodative, and balanced, and then compared on relevant measures of interest such as objective and physical health, coping, and well-being.

Having examined the identity model in depth, it is now instructive to turn to general theories of personality, looking for connections to identity and to the research on adult personality development. As mentioned earlier, the identity model is based on a tradition primarily influenced by Erikson and Piaget, but it has close ties to social-cognitive, cognitive-behavioral, humanistic, and other psychodynamic views of personality. Less relevant, but of importance in terms of the overall literature, are trait models of personality that emphasize enduring dispositions and stability over time. Nevertheless, this journey through the psychological literature on development in later adulthood would be incomplete without this body of work. Where relevant, connections to identity will be made here in the text, with the recognition that all personality theories must ultimately address certain fundamental issues pertaining to the self's relation to experiences.

THEORIES AND RESEARCH ON PERSONALITY IN ADULTHOOD

The term "personality" has a variety of everyday and theoretical meanings. When used in the context of ordinary speech, it is usually intended to refer to some unobservable quality possessed by the individual that at some level accounts for the individual's behavior. Although the definition offered by academic psychology takes on more formal characteristics, there is still the same sense conveyed that personality is an unobservable entity that underlies much of human behavior. Also implied is the assumption that there are individual differences in personality that account for the individual differences in behavior. Much of personality research is devoted to measuring and explaining the individual variations in behavior that cause each of us to behave differently in life's situations.

As is the case for intelligence, there is no consensually agreed upon definition of personality, as well as doubt about whether such an "unobservable" entity even exists. Because of the diversity of views regarding personality, those of us who teach personality psychology are as likely to organize the course by "theories" as we are by concepts. Each theoretical perspective has a rich background involving philosophical viewpoints, empirical research, and clinical applications to psychotherapy. Each attempts to answer questions regarding the "whys" of behavior, or underlying motivational elements of personality, the structure of personality, and the reasons for individual differences. In addition, many of the personality theories deal at great length with the question of how personality develops in childhood, with exceptional emphasis on the first year or two of life. For the most part, an understanding of the normal "adult" personality is not a specific focus, and attempts to extrapolate to old age are even rarer. Nevertheless, contemporary personality researchers in the field of gerontology, borrowing pages from the playbooks of the great theorists, are making these connections themselves. We can see in the writings of the 1990s the influences from the 1890s and up, with various researchers exploring such classic concepts as values, ego defenses, traits, and motives. Newer theories involving concepts such as controllability and self-efficacy are being rapidly incorporated into the gerontological literature with researchers specifically testing propositions of these theories as they are applied to the phenomena examined in this book.

Psychodynamic, Trait, and Humanistic Perspectives

A long-held tradition within the personality theory has its roots in the Freudian view of adulthood as a time of quiescence between the formative years of adolescence to early adulthood and the onset of decline in old age. Freud virtually signed the death sentence of the study of personality in later adulthood with his observation that the mental processes past the age of 50 lack the "elasticity on which the treatment depends" (Freud, 1906/1942). Although arriving at this position from an entirely different starting point, trait theorists such as Eysenck (1967) and Cattell (1982) regarded personality structure as invariant from a very early age onward, reflecting the influence of genetic and constitutional factors on enduring personal dispositions. More recently, the five-factor model of personality proposed by Costa and McCrae (McCrae & Costa, 1990) and Cloninger's (Cloninger, Svrakic, & Przybeck, 1994) general theory of "temperament and character" have updated the trait position with substantial amounts of supporting evidence to indicate consistency of underlying personality dimensions well into the later years of adulthood.

Since the time of Freud's work, some psychoanalysts have broken from the Freudian model and proposed that middle adulthood is a time when personality ripens and matures to newer and healthier forms than could be attained in the earlier years. Jung (1968) believed that fully mature development is not likely to occur before the middle years of adulthood (40s-50s) when the individual's psyche becomes fully individuated. More recent psychodynamic models incorporated the idea that the individual's ego defenses continue to evolve into higher levels of maturity throughout the middle years (Vaillant, 1977) and into old age, with evidence that older adults use more mature defenses as ways of coping with negative life events (Labouvie-Vief, Hakim-Larson, & Hobart, 1987). Along similar lines, a renewed interest in the topic of emotions in later adulthood (Magai, in press; Magai & Hunziker, 1994) has emerged, with investigations indicating a greater salience of emotions in the lives of older adults (Carstensen, Gottman, & Levenson, 1995; Carstensen & Turk-Charles, 1994). Furthermore, with increasing age and particularly level of ego development, individuals appear better able to regulate and control their emotional experiences (Labouvie-Vief, Hakim-Larson, DeVoe, & Schoeberlein, 1989). Applications of psychoanalytic methods to the treatment of middle-aged and older adults provide further evidence of the possibility of significant personality change well into the later years (Leszcz, 1990; Nemiroff & Colarusso, 1985; Sadavoy & Leszcz, 1987). Increasingly, theorists from the "object relations" tradition are incorporating principles of psychodynamic therapy into understandings of long-standing patterns of attachments that individuals carry from their earliest relationships in infancy through their adult romantic attachments. Researchers have also adapted the concept of infant attachment style to the ways that individuals relate as adults to significant figures in their lives, such as a romantic partner (Bartholomew, 1993; Davis, Kirkpatrick, Levy, & O'Hearn, 1994; Hatfield & Rapson, 1994; Sharabany, 1994).

A sequential study on psychosocial development from the college years to middle adulthood provided further support for Erikson's theory, at least for the stages most pertinent to the young adult years (identity and intimacy) (Whitbourne, Zuschlag, Elliot, & Waterman, 1992). Over two successive cohorts of college students, longitudinal increases in favorable resolutions of these psychosocial crisis stages were observed, much as in keeping with Erikson's predictions. Furthermore, the influence of social and historical factors was evident among cohorts of college students, young adults, and middle-aged adults. The data were consistent with the interpretation that during the "me" generation of the 1980s, individuals across all three age groups showed a dip in the quality of ego integrity, representing a turning away from concern for social responsibility. Interestingly, this finding paralleled the conclusions based on the SLS among a much larger sample across a greater variety of ages. Given the "psychosocial" nature of Erikson's theory, such observations are consistent with predictions and indicate the inroads that social climate can make into individual personality development.

Humanistic models of personality are also of considerable relevance to an understanding of development in the later adult years. These theories propose that middle adulthood brings with it the opportunity for continued growth. According to Maslow (1962), the state of self-actualization, in which one's potential is fully being realized, cannot develop until a person is past the period of youth. Maslow's biographical and empirical analyses have received some support in the adult development literature, with growth reported in scales measuring self-actualization in midlife women (Hyman, 1988). Rogers (1961) similarly described the fully functioning individual as one who has achieved congruence between the self and experiences, a process that is constantly evolving and changing. Although these theorists were not developmental in the traditional sense, their observations on the "mature" or "healthy" personality point to the expected movement in midlife toward an optimum of individual functioning. And if you have been following the logic of the identity model, you can clearly see the influence of the concept of congruence in the theory of Rogers on the notion of equilibrium between identity and experiences.

Cognitive-Behavioral and Social-Cognitive Perspectives

The cognitive perspective has become increasingly emphasized within the literature on adult personality, particularly because of its relatively direct applicability to empirical testing as well as its fit with the view that aging is in some ways "a state of mind." This literature also reflects a virtual cognitive revolution in personality psychology which stands in interesting contrast to the equally prevalent dispositional approach. Increasingly, theorists are proposing ways that individuals can influence their own life outcomes through changing the ways they view themselves and the world. The work of Beck, described earlier, was a foundation to these new formulations that have now expanded well beyond the realm of cognitive models of depression.

Cognitive-behavioral perspective. Beck's approach falls within the tradition of the cognitive personality theory of George Kelly, which was based on the notion that personality is made up of a set of personal constructs, or ways of viewing the world and the self. Psychological disorder, Kelly proposed, occurs when these constructs fail to organize the individual's world. Anxiety, for example, is the consequence of feeling that one's ideas about the world are being threatened or challenged by experiences (Kelly, 1955). The cognitive-behavioral theories share Kelly's emphasis on the importance of thought processes in influencing people's emotions and behavior.

According to Beck, a pervasive feature of many psychological disorders is the existence of automatic thoughts—ideas about the self so deeply entrenched that the individual is not even aware that they lead to feelings of unhappiness and discouragement. Automatic thoughts appear to arise spontaneously and are difficult to ignore. They are theorized to be the product of dysfunctional attitudes, a set of personal rules or values people hold that interfere with adequate adjustment. The process leading to automatic thoughts begins with a dysfunctional attitude. Next, the person encounters an experience to which this dysfunctional attitude applies (being alone, asking a question, failing). The individual is then likely to interpret this experience in an excessively negative way, having been primed by the dysfunctional attitude to regard it as a negative reflection on the self. Depression-prone individuals make many other errors of logic in their thinking, which contribute to the frequency of their negative automatic thoughts. These processes may be seen as precisely the opposite of the way that nondepressed individuals interpret experiences which, consistent with the identity model, generally involve positive self-attributions.

Another variant of the cognitive approach focuses on the ways that individuals acquire "expectancies" for reinforcement that become part of their framework for interpreting the world. According to the social cognitive approach represented by Julian Rotter (1966) and others, individuals differ in their expectancies for control, and whether control is seen as arising from within the person (internal locus of control) or from within the environment (external locus of control). External locus of control can further be subdivided into whether control is seen as originating from powerful others or from chance forces such as fate or luck (Levenson, 1974). There is a huge body of research on locus of control within the fields of personality and social psychology; personality aging researchers have also found it to be a fruitful concept for understanding how individuals interpret their own aging, as described briefly in Chapter 1. Although the results of the relationship between age and locus of control are murky, at best, the concept has had tremendous heuristic value in illustrating how individuals differ in their beliefs about whether they can alter or modify the course of their own aging.

The construct of self-efficacy also falls within the social-cognitive tradition. This characteristic (described in Chapter 9 in terms of memory self-efficacy) was developed by Albert Bandura, whose focus, similar to those of other cognitive theorists, was on the ways individuals can serve as "agents" to influence their environments. Self-efficacy, as the perception of one's own competence in various life situations, is seen as having a transactional relationship with events in one's life. According to Bandura (1977, 1982, 1991), people will try harder to succeed in difficult tasks if they are confident that they can complete these tasks. Furthermore, if they do succeed at these tasks, their sense of self-efficacy is bolstered and they will attempt even more difficult tasks in the future. The concept of self-efficacy has been applied to a variety of psychological phenomena (Bandura, 1992) including an understanding of motivation, self-esteem, addictions, and interpersonal relations. People who lack self-efficacy in a given situation can be trained to increase their confidence in their abilities to succeed and thus enhance their feelings of self-worth. The concept of self-efficacy has been incorporated into the identity model with the proposition that the individual's perceptions of his or her own competence is a content domain of identity. Furthermore, as part of identity, self-perceptions of competence influence and are influenced by competence-related experiences.

Falling within the cognitive tradition is another model (briefly referred to in Chapter 1) that has proved highly testable within the framework of research on aging and the self. According to the "possible self" (or "selves") model (Markus & Nurius, 1986), individuals are guided in their actions by the elements of the self that represent what the individual could become, would like to become, and is afraid of becoming. Possible selves can include the hoped-for and dreaded self, both of which are internally defined within the context of the self as a whole. Possible selves are theorized to serve as psychological resources that can both motivate the individual toward future behavior and serve as a defense of the self in the present. The individual is motivated to strive to achieve a hoped-for possible self and will attempt to avoid a dreaded or feared possible self. To the extent that the individual is successful in this process, positive feelings of life satisfaction are theorized to emerge. When the individual is unable to realize a hoped-for possible self or is unable to avoid the dreaded possible self, negative self-evaluations and affect will follow. However, here the defensive function of the possible self construct comes into play. Assuming that most psychologically healthy adults attempt to preserve a positive self-concept, the realization that one is approaching a state of unfulfillment will lead the individual to revise the possible self so that it is more consistent with current experiences.

The possible selves construct is assessed through a questionnaire measure that asks respondents to describe their hoped-for and feared or dreaded possible selves, and to evaluate their capability of, respectively, achieving or avoiding these states. Applications of the possible selves construct to middle-aged and older adults has revealed that the possible selves are accessible to conscious awareness, can be objectively rated into content-based categories, and relate in predicted ways to life satisfaction and self-reports of behavior (Cross & Markus, 1991). As reviewed in Chapter 1, there is a growing body of literature on the possible selves construct, and it has proven to have value in identifying the ways individuals anticipate their own aging processes.

One limitation in the possible selves model is lack of an explicit set of proposals for how the selves are organized, as they tend to be enumerated in a fairly linear rather than hierarchical fashion. However, parallels with the identity model can be seen. The process of identity assimilation, viewed in terms of possible selves, can be regarded as the defensive function of maintaining consistency of the self over time and maintaining positive life satisfaction even in the face of failure to realize desired possible selves or avoid dreaded ones. The process of identity accommodation can be seen as comparable to revisions of possible selves when the realization of positive goals is in jeopardy. Providing context for the possible selves would be the individual's identity as it has evolved through psychosocial development in adolescence and adulthood. Ideas about expected events throughout the lifespan, and revision in age-specific goals would also be seen as proceeding within the context of the lifespan construct. An ordering of possible selves in terms of importance would be an important step in altering the methodology of the possible selves model to conform to the propositions of the identity model with its emphasis on a hierarchical or integrated structure.

Combining many of the elements of psychosocial and cognitive theories is a framework called the "lifespan construct" model (Whitbourne, 1985), proposed as a mechanism for linking identity development in adulthood with the processes involved in adapting to life experiences. This construct is theorized to be a translation of the content of adult identity into a subjective model of age-appropriate and expectable events and themes. Briefly, the lifespan construct model proposes that adults plan and evaluate their life events in terms of an underlying set of assumptions, expectations, and ideas about what their lives could be. For example, if an individual's identity is largely defined in terms of involvement in the family, then family-related events would be expected to form the basis of the lifespan construct. To the extent that these themes are age linked, it is hypothesized that these age-related expectations reflect the prevailing society's age norms and structure. Themes related to gender-based expectations would also be reflected in the lifespan construct, as these expectations often pertain to the ages at which it is considered normative for women and men to have experienced certain events.

Derived from the lifespan construct model are the concepts of the "scenario" and the "life story." The scenario is the individual's projection of the future events based on personal and social norms regarding age and gender as these are reflected in the individual's sense of identity. For example, a 51-year-old woman may include in her scenario the expectation that by the age of 60 years, she will have become a grandmother. Events in the past are hypothesized to be woven into a "life story," the individual's autobiography that is continually constructed and re-constructed throughout life. Although the life story is theorized to change in a way that is responsive to actual life events, it is theorized to evolve in a way that enhances and maintains the individual's identity.

Essential to the model is the assumption that the lifespan construct underlies many general and specific evaluations that individuals make of their life experiences, but that this evaluation is rarely conducted at the conscious level of awareness. The individual's sense of satisfaction or dissatisfaction with her life would, it is theorized, reflect the extent to which the life story enhances the lifespan construct and the scenario includes future possibilities that appear achievable. To maintain a positive sense of identity, it is proposed that individuals use the processes of identity assimilation and accommodation. In the context of this model, these are defined as involving, on the one hand, denial of life events inconsistent with a person's inferred lifespan construct (assimilation), and on the other hand, as a willingness to report these life events, particularly those with a highly negative content (accommodation). A person may use identity assimilation to re-interpret an event into the life story in a way that does not detract from the individual's sense of identity in that domain. Returning to the previous example, if at age 72 years, the woman has not become a grandmother due to the divorce of her daughter before she had her own children, her life story may resolve this discrepancy through assimilation by attributing the change in her own family's circumstances to the demise of "family values" in contemporary society.

By contrast, identity accommodation involves incorporating the reality of an event that was inconsistent with the scenario in a way that causes the individual to change the lifespan construct. In the example of the 72-year-old woman, identity accommodation would be said to occur if she blamed herself for failing to raise her daughter "right."

In keeping with the assumption that the lifespan construct operates below the level of conscious awareness, the measure designed to assess the lifespan construct of an individual involves a projective type of format. This measure, the "life drawing," is a free-hand drawing of an individual's personal time line of life events, with the only reference point being a horizontal line at the bottom of the page marked "age and/or year." Respondents are instructed to write or draw in a timeline fashion their life events (past, present, and future) along this time line. In the original research using this measure on men and women ranging from their early 20s to the 60s, (Whitbourne & Dannefer, 1985-1986), age differences were established on measures derived from the life drawing on the dimensions of temporal dominance. The life drawings were also used to assess the processes of identity assimilation and accommodation. The processes of identity assimilation and accommodation were investigated in a group of hospitalized psychiatric patients ranging in age from the 20s to 60s (Whitbourne & Sherry, 1991). By comparing the life drawings with hospital records, which provided objective documentation of the respondents' life histories, it was possible to determine whether respondents were using identity assimilation, in which they denied the reality of their hospitalizations, or identity accommodation, in which they integrated into their lifespan constructs the reality of their disorders. The life drawing, then, has proven to be a useful measure in these preliminary investigations of theoretically derived concepts based on the lifespan construct.

In subsequent research on a sample of 86 community-dwelling older women, it was possible to test predictions that dimensions of the lifespan construct would be related to adaptation in later adulthood (Whitbourne & Powers, 1994). For this purpose, new measures were derived from the life drawing and a larger sample of older adults used than in previous studies. Further, the similarity of cohort- and gender-based age expectations in an age- and gender-homogenous group made it possible to control for contextual variables that might impact the lifespan construct. Thus, all women in the sample would have been exposed to the cultural norms of the 1920s and 1930s, when they were in their teenage and early adult years, a time when their lifespan constructs would be emerging. Cohort or period influences, such as the changing expectations regarding women's roles in society, should be similar for all respondents. With these influences minimized, the relationships could be explored among temporal and content-related measures derived from the life drawing, well-being, a sense of control over one's personal destiny, and affective dimensions of time perspective. Based on Erikson's theory, it was expected that a positive sense of adaptation would be related to a life drawing with the individual as the protagonist and an orientation toward past life events. It was also predicted that a belief that one has controlled her own destiny should relate to a positive sense of well-being. The findings indicated that the individuals willing and able to provide complete data had a positive bias in their orientations to their life drawings. Qualitative impressions from the life drawings added weight to this interpretation, with at least 15 women spontaneously providing "advice" on how they managed to cope with their lives by focusing on the positive, maintaining "faith," and using denial when dealing with stress. Other similar statements reflected the importance of hard work and persistence, and the ability to enjoy life, one day at a time. These observations, interestingly, reflect the moderating effects of "self-complexity." According to this view, the more ways in which an individual can define herself as competent, the more likely it is that she can buffer herself against failure or loss in any of those domains.

In terms of the theoretical concepts of identity assimilation and accommodation, it would appear that the women who maintained a positive view of their lives by focusing on these coping methods tended to use assimilation more than accommodation. Although it is not possible to determine with certainty the nature of the actual life events to which these women referred, the fact that they professed the value of maintaining a positive attitude despite losses would suggest an outward adherence to the mechanism of identity assimilation in producing their life stories. Also apparent in these statements was a major theme in the life drawings concerning the role of family. As observed in the quantitative findings, family events figured prominently in the life drawings and a focus on family was modestly related to positive affect statements. In inspecting the life drawings, this importance of family was evident in the number of family members who were drawn in conjunction with particular events (usually as stick figures) or whose entry and exit into the woman's life provided a demarcation point in her own lifespan construct. One of the most striking of these instances was a drawing that was almost exclusively composed of stick figures. There appeared to be several generations represented in this drawing, all of whom were centered around a church. For these women, their place in the progression of generations appeared to be a central feature of their lifespan constructs.

The findings of this study suggest that older women who construct their life stories around themes of an external orientation, involvement in the lives of family, and an unwillingness to remain lodged in the past are able to attain a positive approach to their lives. Interestingly, these findings correspond to those of other researchers who have emphasized the role of the "other" in successful aging (Ryff, 1989). They counter the established wisdom regarding Erikson's theory and the importance of an inner orientation to achieving acceptance with one's past, present, and future.

IDENTITY: RETROSPECTIVES AND PROSPECTIVES

In this book, I have reviewed a broad scope of studies on aging, beginning with the aging of the body and moving on to the aging of the "soul." The field of psychological gerontology is growing at such a tremendous rate that I am afraid there is much that I could not cover in depth in a book of this scope. I hope that I have communicated to the reader a sense of excitement about the many important areas of new discoveries in aging; some of these have the potential to alter radically our tried and true conceptions about the aging process.

I think it is important to recognize, however, that there remain limitations in our knowledge that seem to be inherent in the nature of the beast. The lens of gerontological researchers, for example, is certainly clouded by the selective nature of the samples we study. The elders available for our scrutiny are, after all, the ones who have survived death in youth, middle age and beyond due to illness, high-risk behavior, or exposure to accidents, disasters, and war. To make generalizations from the available populations to the "aging process" and, even further, to "successful" aging, runs the risk of becoming tautological. The nonsuccessful agers are no longer represented in the population. Thus, the observation that successful elders have managed to learn to titrate their emotional experiences (Carstensen, 1993) or coping mechanisms (McCrae, 1989) may say less about the aging process than about the nature of people who are survivors and have been for their entire lives.

Furthermore, it is important to maintain a clear sense of what is meant by "positive" adaptation, "successful" aging, or "favorable" adjustment. In this book, as in much of the literature on psychological aspects of the aging process, there is an implicit assumption that the best we can hope for in old age is to "adapt" or, in the sense of the identity model, to "accommodate" to the trials and tribulations of aging. Within this research, elders who cope well are seen as reactive rather than proactive—able to match wits with the vagaries of the aging process and not lose ground until the very end. However, we must also keep in mind the possibility that aging can bring with it emotional satisfaction from the pursuit of new goals and challenges (Rapkin & Fischer, 1992). The terms "assimilation" and "accommodation" do not give credit to this creative element of the self, in which experiences are sought because they elaborate one's identity rather than being adapted to in a passive manner. Future research should address the creative capacities of the elderly, and the unique perspective offered by their lifetime of experiences in both seeking and adjusting to change.

Finally, I hope that I have managed to interest the reader who approaches the aging process from a psychological vantage point in the processes of biological aging. Too often, psychologists ignore or give short shrift to the fact that the aging mind is part of an aging body. Intuitively, most people (including the "aging" gerontological researcher) are aware of the importance of physical functioning to one's sense of well-being. Yet, there remains a tendency to downplay the many specific and concrete ways in which aging changes the body's ability to operate in important life situations. By providing my readers with greater knowledge about these changes in the body, I hope to spark future researchers to explore more comprehensively these mind–body interactions.

As I bring this volume to a close, I find that the words of the pioneering developmental psychologist G. Stanley Hall (1922) seem most appropriate: "It is hoped that the data here garnered and the views propounded may help to a better and more correct understanding of the nature and functions of old age, and also be a psychologist's contribution to the long-desired but long-delayed science of gerontology" (pp. v–vi.). Even though the study of gerontology is well off the ground, there is still much to be learned about the psychology of aging!

REFERENCES

Bandura, A. (1977). Self-efficacy: Toward a unifying theory of behavioral change. *Psychological Review, 84,* 191–215.

Bandura, A. (1982). Self-efficacy mechanism in human agency. *American Psychologist, 37,* 122–147.

Bandura, A. (1991). Human agency: The rhetoric and the reality. *American Psychologist, 46,* 157–162.

Bandura, A. (1992). On rectifying the comparative anatomy of perceived control: Comments on "Cognates of personal control." *Applied and Preventive Psychology, 1*(2), 121–126.

Bartholomew, K. (1993). From childhood to adult relationships: Attachment theory and research. In S. Duck (Ed.), *Learning about relationships* (pp. 30–62). Newbury Park, CA: Sage.

Beck, A. T., Rush, A. J., Shaw, B. F., & Emery, G. (1975). *Cognitive therapy of depression.* New York: Guilford.

Berzonsky, M. D. (1990). Self-construction over the life span: A process perspective on identity formation. *Advances in Personal Construct Psychology, 1,* 155–186.

Brandtstadter, J., & Rothermund, K. (1994). Self-percepts of control in middle and later adulthood: Buffering losses by rescaling goals. *Psychology and Aging, 9,* 265–273.

Carstensen, L. L. (1993). Motivation for social contact across the life span: A theory of socioemotional selectivity. In J. Jacobs (Ed.), *Nebraska Symposium on Motivation* (Vol. 40, pp. 209–254). Lincoln: University of Nebraska Press.

Carstensen, L. L., Gottman, J. M., & Levenson, R. W. (1995). Emotional behavior in long-term marriage. *Psychology and Aging, 10,* 140–149.

Carstensen, L. L., & Turk-Charles, S. (1994). The salience of emotion across the adult life span. *Psychology and Aging, 9,* 259–264.

Cattell, R. B. (1982). *The inheritance of personality and ability*. New York: Academic Press.

Cloninger, C. R., Svrakic, D. M., & Przybeck, T. R. (1994). A psychobiological model of temperament and character. *Archives of General Psychiatry, 50,* 975–990.

Cross, S., & Markus, H. (1991). Possible selves across the lifespan. *Human Development, 34,* 230–255.

Davis, K. D., Kirkpatrick, L. A., Levy, M. B., & O'Hearn, R. E. (1994). Stalking the elusive love style: Attachment styles, love styles, and relationship development. In R. Erber & R. Gilmore (Ed.), *Theoretical frameworks for personal relationships* (pp. 179–210). Hillsdale, NJ: Erlbaum.

Erikson, E. H. (1963). *Childhood and society.* (2nd ed.). New York: Norton.

Eysenck, H. J. (1967). *The biological basis of personality*. Springfield, IL: Charles C. Thomas.

Freud, S. (1906/1942). On psychotherapy. In E. Jones (Ed.), *Collected papers* (Vol. I). London: Hogarth Press.

Hall, G. S. (1922). *Senescence: The last half of life*. New York: D. Appleton.

Hatfield, E., & Rapson, R. (1994). Love and attachment processes. In M. Lewis & J. M. Haviland (Ed.), *Handbook of emotions* (pp. 595–604). New York: Guilford Press.

Heidrich, S. M., & Ryff, C. D. (1993). The role of social comparison processes in the psychological adaptation of elderly adults. *Journal of Gerontology: Psychological Sciences, 48,* 127–136.

Hyman, R. B. (1988). Four stages of adulthood: An exploratory study of growth patterns of inner-direction and time-competence in women. *Journal of Research in Personality, 22*(1), 117–127.

Jung, C. G. (1968). *Analytical psychology: Its theory and practice*. New York: Vintage Books.

Kelly, G. A. (1955). *The psychology of personal constructs*. New York: Norton.

Kiecolt, K. J. (1994). Stress and the decision to change oneself: A theoretical model. *Social Psychology Quarterly, 57,* 49–63.

Labouvie-Vief, G., Hakim-Larson, J., DeVoe, M., & Schoeberlein, S. (1989). Emotions and self-regulation: A life-span view. *Human Development, 32,* 279–299.

Labouvie-Vief, G., Hakim-Larson, J., & Hobart, C. J. (1987). Age, ego level, and the life-span development of coping and defense processes. *Psychology and Aging, 2,* 286–293.

Leszcz, M. (1990). Towards an integrated model of group psychotherapy with the elderly. *International Journal of Group Psychotherapy, 40,* 379–399.

Levenson, H. (1974). Activism and powerful others: Distinctions within the concept of internal-external control. *Journal of Personality Assessment, 38,* 377–383.

Magai, C. (in press). *Handbook of aging and the emotions*. San Diego, CA: Academic Press.

Magai, C., & Hunziker, J. (1994). Tolstoy and the riddle of developmental transformation: A lifespan analysis of the role of emotions in personality development. In

M. Lewis & J. Haveland (Ed.), *Handbook of emotions* (pp. 247–259). New York: Guilford.

Markus, H., & Nurius, P. (1986). Possible selves. *American Psychologist, 41,* 954–969.

Maslow, A. (1962). *Toward a psychology of being.* Princeton, NJ: Van Nostrand Reinhold.

McCrae, R. R. (1989). Age differences and changes in the use of coping mechanisms. *Journal of Gerontology: Psychological Sciences, 44,* P161–169.

McCrae, R. R., & Costa, P. T., Jr. (1990). *Personality in adulthood.* New York: Guilford.

McGue, M., Hirsch, B., & Lykken, D. T. (1993). Age and the self-perception of ability: A twin study analysis. *Psychology and Aging, 8,* 72–80.

Nemiroff, R. A., & Colarusso, C. A. (1985). *The race against time: Psychotherapy and psychoanalysis in the half of life.* New York: Plenum.

Rapkin, B. D., & Fischer, K. (1992). Framing the construct of life satisfaction in terms of older adults' personal goals. *Psychology and Aging, 7,* 138–149.

Riegel, K. F. (1976). The dialectics of human development. *American Psychologist, 31,* 689–700.

Rogers, C. R. (1961). *On becoming a person.* Boston: Houghton Mifflin.

Rotter, J. B. (1966). Generalized expectancies for internal versus external control of reinforcement. *Psychological Monographs, 80* (1, Whole No. 609).

Ryff, C. D. (1989). In the eye of the beholder: Views of psychological well-being among middle-aged and older adults. *Psychology and Aging, 4,* 195–210.

Ryff, C. D. (1991). Possible selves in adulthood and old age: A tale of shifting horizons. *Psychology and Aging, 6,* 286–295.

Sadavoy, J., & Leszcz, M. (1987). *Treating the elderly with psychotherapy: The scope for change in later life.* Madison, CT: International Universities Press.

Schaie, K. W., Dutta, R., & Willis, S. L. (1991). Relationship between rigidity–flexibility and cognitive abilities in adulthood. *Psychology and Aging, 6,* 371–383.

Schaie, K. W., & Willis, S. L. (1991). Adult personality and psychomotor performance: Cross-sectional and longitudinal analyses. *Journal of Gerontology: Psychological Sciences, 46,* P275–284.

Sharabany, R. (1994). Continuities in the development of intimate friendships: Object relations, interpersonal, and attachment perspectives. In R. Erber & R. Gilmore (Ed.), *Theoretical frameworks for personal relationships* (pp. 157–178). Hillsdale, NJ: Erlbaum.

Snyder, M. (1974). Self-monitoring of expressive behavior. *Journal of Personality and Social Psychology, 30,* 526–537.

Tolman, A., & Whitbourne, S. K. (in press). Remothering the self: The impact of adolescent children on women's sense of identity.

Vaillant, G. E. (1977). *Adaptation to life.* Boston: Little, Brown.

Whitbourne, S. K. (1985). The psychological construction of the life span. In J. E. Birren & K. W. Schaie (Ed.), *Handbook of the psychology of aging* (pp. 594–618). New York: Van Nostrand Reinhold.

Whitbourne, S. K. (1986). *The me I know: A study of adult identity*. New York: Springer-Verlag.

Whitbourne, S. K. (1987). Personality development in adulthood and old age: Relationships among identity style, health, and well-being. In K. W. Schaie, (Ed.), *Annual Review of Gerontology and Geriatrics* (Vol. 7, pp. 189–216). New York: Springer.

Whitbourne, S. K., & Dannefer, W. D. (1985–1986). The life drawing as a measure of time perspective in adulthood. *International Journal of Aging and Human Development, 22,* 147–155.

Whitbourne, S. K., Hussey, A., & Primus, L. (1995, November). *Coping with physical changes in later adulthood: Relation to identity*. Paper presented at the 48th Annual Meeting of the Gerontological Society, Los Angeles, CA.

Whitbourne, S. K., & Powers, C. B. (1994). Older women's constructs of their lives: A quantitative and qualitative exploration. *International Journal of Aging and Human Development, 38,* 298–306.

Whitbourne, S. K., & Sherry, M. S. (1991). Subjective perceptions of the life span in chronic mental patients. *International Journal of Aging and Human Development, 33,* 65–73.

Whitbourne, S. K., Zuschlag, M. K., Elliot, L. B., & Waterman, A. S. (1992). Psychosocial development in adulthood: A 22-year sequential study. *Journal of Personality and Social Psychology, 63,* 260–271.

Index

SP *Springer Publishing Company*

DELAYING THE ONSET OF LATE-LIFE DYSFUNCTION

Robert N. Butler, MD, and
Jacob A. Brody, MD, Editors

This volume presents the most current medical strategies for postponing the onset of chronic illnesses and other functional losses associated with aging. Expert authors point out that while many preventive measures are available today, they are not yet fully implemented and more research is still needed. This volume highlights important areas for further research, such as Alzheimer's disease, immune dysfunction, and brain and neuronal aging. For geriatricians, geriatric researchers and academics, as well as other aging and health professionals.

Contents:

1994   200pp   0-8261-8880-X   hardcover

536 Broadway, New York, NY 10012-3955 • (212) 431-4370 • Fax (212) 941-7842

Springer Publishing Company

THE AGING CARDIOVASCULAR SYSTEM
Physiology and Pathology

Vladimir V. Frolkis, MD, **Vladislav V. Bezrukov**, MD, and **Oleg K. Kulchitsky**, MD

This important volume is based on original research in the former Soviet Union, which was previously unavailable in the U.S. It presents the latest findings on cardiovascular aging by respected medical scholars of the Health Ministry of the Ukraine. They provide extensive data on age-related cardiovascular disease that is of interest to geriatric and medical researchers, as well as other health professionals, worldwide. Also appropriate for students and professors of geriatrics and the biology of aging.

> The Aging Cardiovascular System
> Physiology and Pathology
>
> Vladimir V. Frolkis, MD
> Vladislav V. Bezrukov, MD
> Oleg K. Kulchitsky, MD
>
> 🛚
> SPRINGER PUBLISHING COMPANY

Contents:
- Hemodynamic Centre — Central Neural Regulation
- Direct Relationships in the System of Neurohumoral Regulation
- Local Mechanisms of Regulation
- Feedback Relationships with the Neurohumoral Regulation System
- Atherosclerosis
- Arterial Hypertension
- Coronary Insufficiency
- Cardiac Failure
- Individual, Populational and Species-Specific Peculiarities of Cardiovascular System Aging

1996 256pp 0-8261-9050-2 hardcover

536 Broadway, New York, NY 10012-3955 • (212) 431-4370 • Fax (212) 941-7842

Springer Publishing Company

BEHAVIOR AND PERSONALITY
Psychological Behaviorism

Arthur W. Staats, PhD

In this capstone work, Arthur Staats synthesizes more than four decades of research, theory, and study to offer a unified theory called Psychological Behaviorism. Drawing upon the study of abnormal behavior, psychological measurement, personality, and child development, he provides an overarching theoretical framework that accounts for all aspects of human behavior. He also develops a theory of personality to show how his unifying theory is derived from these various approaches. This book is useful for professionals, researchers, and students interested in a unified approach to psychology, behavior therapy, abnormal behavior, psychological measurement and personality.

Contents:
- Behaviorizing Psychology and Psychologizing Behaviorism: A New Unified Approach
- The Basic Learning / Behavior Therapy
- The Human Learning Theory
- The Child Development and Social Interaction Theories
- The Psychological Behaviorism Theory of Personality
- The Content of Personality: Behaviorizing Psychological Testing
- The PB Theory of Abnormal Behavior
- Psychological Behavior Therapy
- A Theory of Theories, Heuristic, with a Plan and Program

Springer Series: Behavior Therapy and Behavioral Medicine
1996   420pp   0-8261-9311-0   hard $54.95 (outside US $59.80)

536 Broadway, New York, NY 10012-3955 • (212) 431-4370 • Fax (212) 941-7842